Lecture Notes of the Institute for Computer Sciences, Social Informatics and Telecommunications Engineering 62

Vinu V. Das   Ezendu Ariwa
Syarifah Bahiyah Rahayu (Eds.)

Signal Processing and Information Technology

First International Joint Conference
SPIT 2011 and IPC 2011
Amsterdam, The Netherlands, December 1-2, 2011
Revised Selected Papers

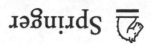 Springer

Volume Editors

Vinu V. Das
Institute of Doctors Engineering and Scientists
1191 GT Amsterdam, The Netherlands
E-mail: prof.vinuvdas@gmail.com

Ezendu Ariwa
London Metropolitan University
London N7 8DB, UK
E-mail: e.ariwa@londonmet.ac.uk

Syarifah Bahiyah Rahayu
Universiti Kebangsaan Malaysia UKM
Faculty of Information Science and Technology
43600 Bangi, Selangor, Malaysia
E-mail: sbrahayu@gmail.com

ISSN 1867-8211   ISSN 1867-822X
ISBN 978-3-642-32572-4   ISBN 978-3-642-32573-1 (eBook)
DOI 10.1007/978-3-642-32573-1
Springer Heidelberg Dordrecht London New York

Library of Congress Control Number: 2012944031

CR Subject Classification (1998): H.4, C.2, I.2, H.3, D.2, I.4, H.5, K.6.5

Typesetting: Camera-ready by author, data conversion by Scientific Publishing Services, Chennai, India

Printed on acid-free paper

Springer is part of Springer Science+Business Media (www.springer.com)

Preface

Welcome to the proceedings of the Joint International Conference on Advances in Signal Processing and Information Technology – SPIT 2011—and the International Conference on Recent Trends in Information Processing and Computing - IPC2011. The primary goal of the conference is to promote research and developmental activities in computer science, information technology, computational engineering, image and signal processing, and communication. Another goal is to promote scientific information interchange between researchers, developers, engineers, students, and practitioners working in Egypt and abroad. The conference is held every year to make it an ideal platform for people to share views and experiences.

Following tradition, the program contained keynote addresses by Ezendu Ariwa (London Metropolitan University, UK) "Trends in Cloud Computing" and Yogesh Chaba on the subject "Micro Waves for Industrial Scientific and Medical Applications (ISM)." The conference received 298 submissions overall. Only 50 papers were accepted and registered for the proceedings.

Efforts were made to remove errors and to improve the quality of the proceedings. The conference organizer and I are very confident that you will find the papers included in the proceedings very useful. We believe that technology will continue to infuse education, thus enriching the educational experience of both students and teachers.

Organizing a conference like this one is not possible without the assistance and continuous support of many people and institutions. Particularly, I would like to express my gratitude to the organizers of sessions on dedicated topics that took place during the conference.

I also thank Dr. Pessent, Prof. P.M. Thankachan, and Dr. Janahanlala Stephen for the constant support and guidance. I would like to express my gratitude to the Springer LNICST editorial team for producing such a wonderful quality proceedings book.

October 2011   Vinu V. Das

Organization

Honorary Chairs

Mohiy Hadhoud   Menoufia University, Egypt
Waiel Fathi Abd EL-Wahed   Menoufia University, Shiben El-Kom, Egypt

Technical Chairs

Ali Fahmy   Cairo University, Cairo, Egypt
Mohamed Fahmy Tolba   Ain Shams University, Cairo, Egypt
Ali ElMeligy   Menoufia University, Egypt

Technical Co-chairs

Fatma Omara   Cairo University, Cairo, Egypt
Abd elBadeeh M. Salem   Ain Shams University, Cairo, Egypt
Hatem Mohamed Sayed
  Ahmed   Menoufia University, Egypt
Mohamed Amin   Menoufia University, Egypt
Mostafa Abd Elhaleem   Menoufia University, Egypt
Osama Abd El-Raoof   Menoufia University, Egypt
Hamdy Mossa   Menoufia University, Egypt
Fathi ElSaid   Menoufia University, Egypt
Walid Fakhry   Cairo University, Cairo, Egypt
Hadj Hamma Tadjine   Volkswagen AG, Wolfsburg, Germany
Mingli Song   Hong Kong Polytechnical University,
     Hong Kong
Tianhao Zhang   University of Pennsylvania, USA
Huiqiong Wang   City University, Hong Kong
Harjanto Prabowo   Bina Nusantara University, Indonesia
Gerardus Polla   Bina Nusantara University, Indonesia

Organizing Chairs

Passent M. El-Kafrawy   Menoufia University, Shiben EL-Kom, Egypt
Janahanlal Stephen   Ilahia College of Engineering and Technology,
     India

General Chair

Vinu V. Das   The IDES, The Netherlands

Finance Chair

P.M. Thankachan   Mar Ivnios College, Trivandrum, India

Publicity Chairs

Amlan Chakrabarti   University of Culcutta, India
Prafulla Kumar Behera   Utkal University, India

Publication Chairs

Vijayakumar   NSS College of Engineering, India
T.S.B. Sudarshan   BITS Pilani, India
K.P. Soman   Amritha University, India
N. Jaisankar   VIT University, India

Poster Chair

Ashadi Salim   Bina Nusantara University, Indonesia

National Advisory Committee Chair

Togar Alam Napitupulu   Bina Nusantara University, Indonesia

Program Committee Chairs

Raymond Kosala   Bina Nusantara University, Indonesia
Richard Kumaradjaja   Bina Nusantara University, Indonesia

International Advisory Committee

Marc van Dongen   University College Cork, Ireland
Hooman Mohseni   Northwestern University, USA
Suresh Subramoniam   Prince Sultan University, Saudi Arabia
A. Louise Perkins   University of Sothern Mississippi, USA
Sumanth Yenduri   The University of Southern Mississippi, USA
Hamid Bagheri   Sharif University of Technology, Iran
Mehran Garmehi   Bojnord University, Iran
Kabekode V. Bhat   The Pennsylvania State University, USA
Gordon Reynolds   Dublin Institute of Technology, Ireland
Shashi Phoha   The Pennsylvania State University, USA
Chilukuri K. Mohan   Syracuse University, USA
Debopam Acharya   Georgia Southern University, USA
David Hall   Louisiana Tech University, USA
Cecilia Chan   University of Hong Kong, Hong Kong

Kristian J. Hammond   Northwestern University, USA
Long Que   Louisiana Tech University, USA
Peter Vadasz   Northern Arizona University, USA

Review Committee

Haryono Soeparno   Bina Nusantara University, Indonesia
Suryadi Liawatimena   Bina Nusantara University, Indonesia
Diaz Santika   LIPI, Indonesia
Anto Satriyo Nugroho   BPPT, Indonesia
Dwi Handoko   BPPT, Indonesia
M. Mustafa Sarinanto   BPPT, Indonesia
Tatang Akhmad Taufik   BPPT, Indonesia
Bernadetta Kwintiana   Universität Stuttgart, Germany
Rahmat Widyanto   UI, Indonesia
Son Kuswadi   ITS, Indonesia
Rila Mandala   ITB, Indonesia
Pekik Argo Dahono   ITS, Indonesia
Eko Tjipto Rahardjo   UI, Indonesia
Arnold Ph. Djiwatampu   IEEE Indonesia
Dadang Gunawan   UI, Indonesia
Wahidin Wahab   UI, Indonesia
Henri Uranus   UPH, Indonesia
Gunawan Wibisono   UI, Indonesia

Program Committee

Shu-Ching Chen   Florida International University, USA
Stefan Wagner   Technische Universität München, Germany
Juha Puustjärvi   Helsinki University of Technology, Finland
Selwyn Piramuthu   University of Florida, USA
Werner Retschitzegger   University of Linz, Austria
Habibollah Haro   Universiti Teknologi Malaysia
Derek Molloy   Dublin City University, Ireland
Anirban Mukhopadhyay   University of Kalyani, India
Malabika Basu   Dublin Institute of Technology, Ireland
Tahseen Al-Doori   American University in Dubai
V.K. Bhat   SMVD University, India
Ranjit Abraham   Armia Systems, India
Naomie Salim   Universiti Teknologi Malaysia
Abdullah Ibrahim   Universiti Malaysia Pahang
Charles McCorkell   Dublin City University, Ireland
Neeraj Nehra   SMVD University, India
Muhammad Nubli   Universiti Malaysia Pahang
Zhenyu Y. Angz   Florida International University, USA
Keivan Navi   Shahid Beheshti University, Tehran, Iran

Table of Contents

Full Paper

Short Paper

Poster Paper

FingRF: A Generalized Fingerprints Research Framework

Ali Ismail Awad[1] and Kensuke Baba[2]

[1] Graduate School of Information Science and Electrical Engineering,
Kyushu University, Japan
[2] Research and Development Division, Kyushu University Library, Japan
{awad,baba}@soc.ait.kyushu-u.ac.jp

Abstract. Biometrics is an emerging technology for consistent automatic identification and authentication applications. Fingerprint is the dominant trait between different biometrics like iris, retina, and face. Many fingerprint-based algorithms have been individually developed to investigate, build, or enhance different AFIS components such as fingerprint acquisition, pre-processing, features extraction, and matching. The common shortage of these contributions is the missing of complete platform to ensemble all system components to study the impact of developing one component on the others. This paper introduces FingRF as ongoing fingerprint research framework that links all fingerprint system components with some other supporting tools for performance evaluation. FingRF aims to provide a facility for conducting fingerprint research in a reliable environment. Moreover, it can be extended to include both off-line and on-line operational modes. The prototype version of FingRF is targeted to work as a stable research environment, and hence, it may be extended further for other biometrics technologies.

Keywords: Biometrics, Fingerprints, Performance Evaluation, Matlab®.

1 Introduction

Personal identification and authentication have become a crucial need for wide variety of applications such as Electronic Commerce, Remote Banking, and Accessing Heath Care Archives in an electronically connected era. Biometrics uses physiological characteristics such as fingerprint and iris, or behavioral characteristics like voice and gait to determine person identity. It is an emerging technology for accepting or denying the claimed identity. Biometrics overcomes many problems of using traditional techniques such as ID-cards, passwords, or a combination of both for better security. Fingerprint is defined as the ridges and furrows patterns drawn on the tip of the human finger. Due to the full understanding of biological properties, characteristics, and formation of human fingerprint, it has been used extensively for civilian and forensic identification purposes for centuries [1]. It is considered as one of the dominant traits between different biometrics, and it is widely used for personal identification according to

V.V. Das, E. Ariwa, and S.B. Rahayu (Eds.): SPIT 2011, LNICST 62, pp. 1–6, 2012.

its easier accessibility, uniqueness, reliability, and lowcost. Automatic Fingerprint Identification System (AFIS) has six common components or phases, as shown in Fig. 1, these phases are expressed as: acquisition, pre-processing, features extraction, classification, storage in database, and fingerprint matching. Through the last decades, many algorithms have been developed for each system component explained in Fig.1. Different fingerprint sensor technologies are used for capturing small or coarse details of fingerprint images such as capacitive sensors, solid-state-sensors, and thermal sensors [2]. Fingerprint enhancement is the most important step in the pre-processing phase, and it is varying from using spatial domain filtering [3], frequency domain filtering [4], Gabor filters [5], to using wavelet coefficients [6]. Fingerprint classification is the problem of assigning fingerprint image into labeled classes to reduce the total search time inside the large database. Fingerprint classification is still a hot research area, therefore, many classification approaches found in the literature. They can be classified into rule-based [7], Neural Networks [8, 9], Gabor filter [10], and frequency domain [11]. Finally many standard databases are available for research purposes such as NIST-4 [12] and FVC2004 [13].

However, the conducted researches in AFIS have increased the reliability, accuracy, and have overcame many problems to enhance the AFIS system performance, a complete and ensemble research framework was totally missing. Therefore, there was no suitable environment for measuring the overall system performance. Wherefore, some conducted researches have been evaluated individually. As an example, the classification algorithm proposed in [14] is used to classify fingerprints database into five sub-sets to speed up the total matching time. The classification method was consuming (4.8 seconds) for Adaboost learning phase, and (1.6 seconds) for real time classification process. Although, the algorithm achieved high classification accuracy, but the classification time is considered very high comparing to the acquisition time (0.04 to 0.26 seconds) [15], and enhancement time (0.1 seconds). Therefore, an ensemble research framework becomes indispensable requirement for measuring the overall system performance with different algorithms.This paper presents FingRF as ongoing research framework for broadly investigating the overall AFIS system performance in different phases with different algorithms. The contributions of this work are three-folds: Firstly, the conceptual design and the implementations of each module in the AFIS, shown in Fig.1. Secondly, FingRF is going to provide a useful set of tools for performance evaluation and data visualization to accurately measure different algorithms performance on both individual and broad scales. Thirdly, the proposed framework will be used not only for fingerprint, but also it can be extended further to include other biometrics traits. The reminder part of this paper is organized as follows: Section 2 explains the conceptual design of the proposed framework from software engineering point of view. Section 3 explains some system implementations, and it also shows some output results from the implemented prototype version. Finally, conclusions and future work are reported in Section 4.

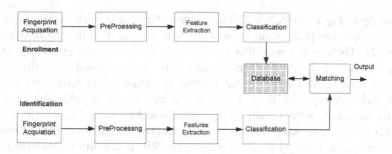

Fig. 1. Common AFIS system components from acquisition to matching

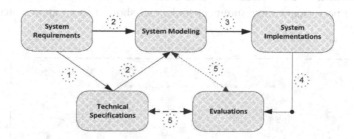

Fig. 2. Conceptual system design from software engineering point of view

2 Conceptual System Design

From software engineering point of view, the conceptual framework design follows five sequential phases including system requirements, technical specification, modeling and design, system implementations, and system evaluations. Fig. 2 shows a block diagram of the conceptual system design phases. A system requirement is a very early stage in the system design. By working on that stage, we have extrapolated that the prototype version of the FingRF should achieve the following requirements:

1. Can be extended for adding different biometrics systems like face
2. Includes common tools for the system performance evaluation
3. Represents all phases of AFIS from acquisition to matching
4. Possibility to add/remove algorithms in the same structure
5. Platform independent as Windows, Linux, and MAC
6. Works on off -line/on-line operational modes.

The above requirements have been translated into technical specifications, and they have also been reflected on the system modeling phase. In order to achieve the above requirements, we have divided every system component into small individual modules which can be easy modified, updated, or replaced without impacting the system architecture. Fig. 3 shows the overall architecture of the proposed framework. Fingerprint acquisition depends on using an Application Programming Interface (API) for reading fingerprint images from different sensors and exports them into the main application via PC connection. The evaluation tool of this stage measures the quality of the captured images, the capturing speed, and reports any capturing failure.

According to Fig.1, AFIS has different types of errors in each system phase. For example, in capturing phase many errors may be generated from the sensor or the user behavior [2]. There are some other parameters to measure the efficiency and the accuracy of the whole AFIS. These parameters are explained as [16]: Genuine Acceptance Rate (GAR) which is the number of samples that have been correctly accepted, False Acceptance Rate (FAR) as the number of samples that have been incorrectly accepted and it should be rejected, False Rejection Rate (FRR) which is the number of falsely rejected samples but it should be accepted, and Equal Error Rate (ERR) is the system point where FAR is equal to FRR. It is worth mentioning that the above parameters are highly related, and they can be tuned to achieve the targeted system performance. Data visualization is a set of tools that automatically reads the output of the performance measurement tools, and show it in an appreciated formats and graphs.

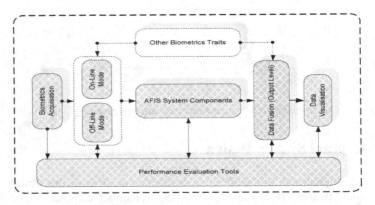

Fig. 3. A global structure of the ongoing FingRF research framework

3   Implementations and Results

The implementation process is going through each module shown in Fig. 3. It is worth mentioning that the other biometric system in the grey block may be included in the future extension of the framework.Singular points (core and delta) are one the most important global characteristics of a fingerprint. Core point is defined as thetopmost point of the innermost curving ridge, and the delta point is the center of triangular regions where three different direction flows meet. Singular points detection is an essential concept of fingerprint recognition and classification. Singular point detection process is sensitive to different conditionssuch as noise, sensor type, and also fingerprints status like dryness and wetness levels. Driven from the former definitions, complex filters [17] is a proposed method to extract regions with high orientation changes using first order complex filter.Complex filter with Gaussian window has been applied on the complex directional image to extract the symmetry singular points from fingerprint images.The main steps of the complex filter implementations are: orientation field estimation, complex filter construction and the convolution between both complex filter and directional image. In order to speed up the total consumed time, convolution process has been performed in frequency domain with great investment of the separable Gaussian window. Some implementations of the complex filter have been expressed in [18]. Fig. 4 shows sample results of the prototype implementation of the singular point detection module. Fig. 4 points out seven different graphs including: main widow, input image, spatial domain representation of the complex filter, shifted frequency domain representation, absolute filter response, the localized singular point, and the otal consumed time.

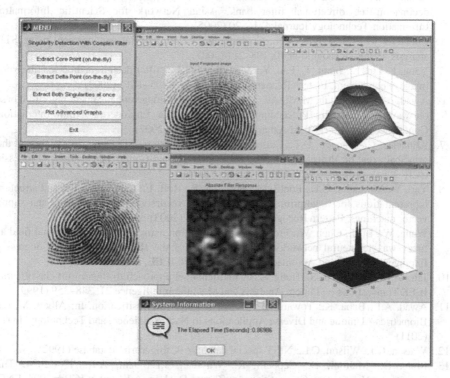

Fig. 4. Screenshots from running singular points detection module

4 Conclusions and Future Work

In order to fairly evaluate and compare different methods or algorithms in the fingerprint research area, we need to conduct the evaluation process in a unique environment. This paper introduced the design of FingRF as ongoing fingerprint research framework for creating a unique environment for the purpose of testing and evaluation of different research algorithms in AFIS. The contributions of this work are three-folds: firstly, the design of overall architecture of the framework, and the conceptual design of each individual component; secondly, in details implementations of the prototype version of framework and producing acceptable results; thirdly, the possibility to extend the FingRF to include different biometrics traits. Moreover, FingRF can be further developed to use Parallel Processing and Graphical Processing Unit (GPU) facilities that are available in the commodity personal computers to increase the research framework reliability and efficiency.

References

1. Yager, N., Amin, A.: Fingerprint classification: a review. Pattern Analysis & Applications 7, 77–93 (2004)
2. Maltoni, D., Maio, D., Jain, A.K., Prabhakar, S.: Handbook of fingerprint recognition. Springer (2009)
3. Khan, M.A.U., Khan, M.K., Khan, M.A.: Fingerprint image enhancement using decimation-free directional filter bank. Asian Network for Scientific Information, Information Technology Journal 4, 16–20 (2005)
4. Chikkerur, S., Cartwright, A.N., Govindaraju, V.: Fingerprint enhancement using STFT analysis. Pattern Recognition 40, 198–211 (2007)
5. Yang, J., Liu, L., Jiang, T., Fan, Y.: A modified Gabor filter design method for fingerprint image enhancement. Pattern Recognition Letters 24, 1805–1817 (2003)
6. Awad, A.I., Abd Allah, M.M., Ali, M.M.: Fingerprint image enhancement algorithm based on wavelet filters. In: Proceedings of the Al Azhar Engineering Ninth International Conference, pp. 100–113. Al Azhar University, Cairo (2007)
7. Klimanee, C., Nguyen, D.T.: Classification of fingerprints using singular points and their principal axes. In: Proceedings of the IEEE International Conference on Image Processing (ICIP 2004), pp. 849–852. IEEE, Singapore (2004)
8. Yao, Y., Marcialis, G.L., Pontil, M., Frasconi, P., Roli, F.: Combining flat and structured representations for fingerprint classification with recursive neural networks and support vector machines. Pattern Recognition 36, 397–406 (2003)
9. Wang, W., Li, J., Chen, W.: Fingerprint classification using improved directional field and fuzzy wavelet neural networks. In: Proceedings of the IEEE Sixth World Congress on Intelligent Control and Automation, pp. 9961–9964. IEEE, Dalian (2006)
10. Jain, A.K., Prabhakar, S., Hong, L.: A multichannel approach to fingerprint classification. IEEE Transactions on Pattern Analysis and Machine Intelligence 21, 348–359 (1999)
11. Awad, A.I., Baba, K.: Toward an efficient fingerprint classification. In: Albert, M. (ed.) Biometrics - Unique and Diverse Applications in Nature, Science, and Technology. InTech (2011)
12. Watson, C.I., Wilson, C.L.: NIST special database 4, fingerprint database (1992)
13. Maio, D., Maltoni, D., Cappelli, R., Wayman, J.L., Jain, A.K.: FVC2004: Third Fingerprint Verification Competition. In: Zhang, D., Jain, A.K. (eds.) ICBA 2004. LNCS, vol. 3072, pp. 1–7. Springer, Heidelberg (2004)
14. Liu, M.: Fingerprint classification based on Adaboost learning from singularity features. Pattern Recognition 43, 1062–1070 (2010)
15. SecuGen: Biometric Solution, http://www.secugen.com/products/sensor_usb.html
16. Jain, A.K., Bolle, R., Pankanti, S.: Biometrics personal identification in networked society. Springer (2005)
17. Nilsson, K., Bigun, J.: Localization of corresponding points in fingerprints by complex filtering. Pattern Recognition Letters 24, 2135–2144 (2003)
18. Awad, A.I., Baba, K.: Fingerprint Singularity Detection: A Comparative Study. In: Mohamad Zain, J., Wan Mohd, W.M.B., El-Qawasmeh, E. (eds.) ICSECS 2011, Part I. CCIS, vol. 179, pp. 122–132. Springer, Heidelberg (2011)

Wireless Mesh Network in Integrated Web Base Monitoring Systems for Production Line Automation

Che Zalina Zulkifli, Raed M.T. Abdulla, Widad Ismail,
and Mohammad Ghulam Rahman

Auto-ID Lab, School of Electrical and Electronic Engineering, Universiti Sains Malaysia
(USM), Engineering Campus, 14300 Nibong Tebal, Pulau Pinang, Malaysia

Abstract. Industrial automation plays an important role in the manufacturing plant. In this paper a system is being proposed that integrate real time Managerial Control and Data Acquisition System (MCDAS) with 2.45GHz active RFID (radio frequency identification) adopts through wireless mesh network, the ZigBee technology to render the automation system more reliable. MCDAS aims to improve managerial skills by enhancing awareness of emerging technology and related concepts to improve the industrial manager's aspects for more effective monitoring, better communications and corporate integration. In this paper general structure of the technology used and process framework, the web-based monitoring system for industrial automation in selected company are presented in detail.

Keywords: RFID, Mesh Network, Web base monitoring system.

1 Introduction

Internet base monitoring and control system has been introduced in recent years in numerous applications. This technology contributes a lot of beneficial for many areas, not only in the industry, but also in the field of military, education and hospitality. Now a day's famous research work on the Internet based process control has resulted in small-scale demonstrations like Sun Microsystems and Cyberonix, Foxboro, and Valmet. Most of them were developed in Java. Additionally, the OPC (Open Process Control) Foundation is working on supporting XML within Visual Studio so that the Internet based process control using XML is widely used. Intuitive Technology Corporation has provided web@aGlance for feeding real-time data to a Java graphics console [1]. The International Federation of Control (IFAC) has held the first workshop on Internet Based Control Education in Spain in 2002 [1]. The SCADA system funded by the European Council targets Internet based protocols enabling the monitoring and optimization of the process via the web [1]. The objectives of establishing Internet-based process control systems is to enhance rather than replace computer based process control systems by adding an extra Internet-level in the hierarchy [2]. Even though SCADA system is the solution of controlling and managing in wide range of industries, the proposed project holds the promise of replacing the existing controlling system. In fact, the proposed system has the advantages where RFID module is embedded in it and

V.V. Das, E. Ariwa, and S.B. Rahayu (Eds.): SPIT 2011, LNICST 62, pp. 7–15, 2012.
© Institute for Computer Sciences, Social Informatics and Telecommunications Engineering 2012

it is designed specifically for manufacturing sector. Using technology is not enough without developing managerial, communication and technical abilities. In MCDAS we designed the system that works best to help industrial sector to meet responsibilities.

Implementation of Wireless Mesh Network for monitoring of production output achievement can revolutionize industrial processing and help industries meet the demands of increasing competitiveness. Intelligent ZigBee technology with 2.4GHz Active RFID as wireless network and web-base monitoring in industrial environments enables real-time data sharing throughout a facility and this will increases industrial safety, efficiency, and productivity. This automated monitoring technology offers reliable, autonomous, and improved process control enhancing safety, ameliorating product quality, increasing yield, and reducing costs [3]. In industrial automation, users have realized the benefits of adopting wireless technologies in eliminating the need for cables in hard to reach areas within the plant, increasing data availability and quality and monitoring and controlling that otherwise were inaccessible [4]. Direct interfacing of sensors to the industrial communications network improves the system performance, because process data and diagnostics can be simultaneously available to many systems and also shared on the Web [5]. ZigBee mesh networks consist of low-cost, battery-powered sensor modules and embedded networking intelligence. Furthermore, ZigBee is also a growing technology that will gain more advantage in industrial automation. Hence, in our proposed system ZigBee is integrated with MCDAS to achieve real time automation monitoring and control in industrial manufacturing environment. From our study, integrated Wireless Sensor Network (WSN) with MCDAS is a new level of data acquisition and communication in manufacturing plant that permits finely-tuned remote monitoring. This paper is structured as follows: Section 2 review the related work, section 3 describes characteristics of MCDAS and its application in automated production monitoring. Section 4 gives an overview of system components and highlights the system architecture of the proposed system. Section 5 discusses system design and process flow framework. Finally section 6 gives conclusion.

2   Related Work

Recently, the use of WSN in industrial automation has gained attention. In industrial environments, the coverage area of WSN as well as the reliability of the data may suffer from noise, co-channel interferences, and other interferers. For example, the signal strength may be severely affected by the reflections from the walls (multi-path propagation), interferences from other devices using ISM bands and by the noise generated from the equipments or heavy machinery. In these circumstances, data integrity and availability of operation-critical data on the fly is very crucial. Every part of these issues set a special prominence on automation design and the fact that WSN are technically challenging systems, requiring expertise from several different disciplines. Additionally, requirements for industrial applications are often stricter than in other domains, since the failure may lead to loss of production or even loss of lives [6]. Johan Potgieter et al., [7] proposed Computer Integrated manufacturing (CIM) and Modular Mechatronics for the development of an internet controlled manufacturing environment, which utilizes wireless network technology. The CIM control strategy was developed as a PC-based technology using the modular mechatronics design methodology. According to Hu et al., [8] Internet controlled machines require a high degree of autonomy and local intelligence to deal with the restricted bandwidth and arbitrary transmission delays of the internet, to be successful in real world applications. In order to allow the proposed system to be widely deployed to meet the maximum reliability and flexibility, we explore active RFID in integrated wireless mesh network and MCDAS for communication and monitoring in industrial application. The study shows that both of the hardware and software technology used to develop the complete MCDAS is a new competitive and valuable platform in industrial automation.

3   MCDAS Usability

In this part we explore the capabilities and benefits of MCDAS software system compared to traditional monitoring system in industrial environment applied for 9 line electronic goods production industry, in Seberang Perai Penang, Malaysia as shown in Figure 6. In ordinary monitoring system, it is difficult for the management group to monitor in real time the performance of output due to the information about the output status is just on the paper. In MCDAS the real time information on production output achievement for individual production line not only appear on display counter, moreover the management group can monitor from the LAN (local area network) or where ever have internet coverage. Automated monitoring system able to update the production line activities, not only the number of product has been produced but also can detect the error occurrence during manufacturing. In the same time, data collection is very important and is an expensive business; it should always be remembered that data collection and manipulation is a cost of quality. Therefore MCDAS here has been designed and developed the strategic data collection to increase online revenue by timely, complete and accurate. In this paper, we suggest that it is useful to consider four categories of data source; which is data input from the counter system to the RFID tag by USART communication, data renew from the active RFID tag to the reader, data generated by other users or other subsystem, as for example from planning system and maintenance system and data generated by local use of a remote data source, as for example data from email system, data import and export with the other format.

4   System Components and Architecture

Our proposed system is divided into three main portions. First stage of this system consists of integration of collecting data. In second stage, output from first stage will be transmitted by active RFID tag to RFID reader using Zigbee wireless technology. In this part, it is necessary for the RFID reader to communicate to the real time database server. The last stage is web based monitoring part, where the end user can access the system to view the outputs produced from each line through internet access. By integrating the sensor, counter system, and active RFID to support ZigBee mesh network, the web based monitoring system i.e., MCDAS will be developed, which would be enable to update the details of production line activities.

Figure 1 shows the block diagram for development of proposed system. The hardware elements consist of sensors, counters and active RFID tags. As the input to counter system, a photo sensor is integrated with the counter. At the end of each line, the photo sensor detects the products appear in front of it. The system will send the product count from the sensor to the counter. Each counter system needs to be paired with their individual RFID tags. Universal Asynchronous Receiver/Transmitter (USART) is used as Serial Communication Interface (SCI) to enable communication from counter system to RFID tag. In this development stage we explore the capabilities by embedded RFID tag to the counter system. The circuit is designed to enable RFID tag receive the power from MCU (microcontroller unit). One of the fundamentals obstacles in the RFID system is the power consumption. Clearly with the circuit enhanced capabilities the problem of power in the RFID tag can be eliminate. This RFID tag will update the data to the reader accordingly when the data from counter is renewed. The RFID reader will receive the data from the active RFID tag through Zigbee network. Whilst, the software elements consist of three subsystems: planning subsystem, maintenance subsystem and administrator subsystem.

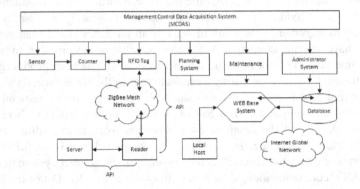

Fig. 1. Development of Hardware and Software System

RFID tags transmit production output data to the reader is through wireless mesh (ZigBee) network. The RFID readers, through wired infrastructure network are connected to the backend database server, which manages the user requirements. The end user can access MCDAS system to view the results produced from the production line accordingly. This accessibility is controlled by management group directly from the administrator subsystem. When designing the architecture for web base monitoring and control system, it is interesting to bring modularity into the design by using layers as entities that can perform different tasks. So each layer can perform its own jobs and communicate closely with others to make the whole system work seamlessly. Each layer acts independently. We divide MCDAS in different layers according to several stages of permitted users. As an example when the user is classified as an administrator, they can go in to the administration scopes such as, can manage the staff data, edit line production information etc. If the user is classified as normal user, they only can view the output achievement. For the production control (PC) group, they have permission to manage the output planning system. What makes this proposed automated monitoring system different is that it will track the accumulated quantity production output of good products versus faulty products by each model run by individual line instead of tracking individual product or location. Furthermore, this system is complete with a wireless mesh network and a web-based monitoring system.

5   System Design

Figure 2 shows the main flow chart of the whole system.

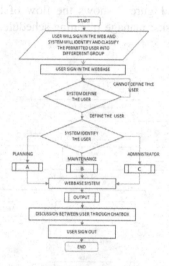

Fig. 2. Flow Chart Main System

The system begins with the user signing in to web base GUI (graphical user interface). The system will define the Permitted user. If the user is not in the user list database, message 'failed' will appear. Moreover, these systems can differentiate the groups by individual tasks. For example, if the user is from the administration group, then he can access the subsystems like user list system, planning system and maintenance system. While, if the user is from the line leader group, then he can only access the maintenance system that manage the production line's information. As mentioned earlier, main system has three sub systems: planning subsystem, maintenance subsystem and administrator subsystem. The details about subsystems are described below:

5.1   Planning Sub System

Planning sub system is designed for Production Control (PC) to input the schedule and output target for all production lines according to management requirement.

In strategic plan, the planner needs to identify the target output for each model running through individual production line. Production scheduling addresses what model to produce, where to produce and how much to produce within the context of manufacturing plants. Thus through production scheduling, manufacturing are able to monitor the line production output achievement to meet the target. In the complete production planning software, system enables forecasting and planning of manufacturing resource requirements and machine capacity utilization. Nevertheless, in our system we designed for planning manufacturing and used to prioritize and schedule accordingly to feed the data to the database to update the real time production output monitoring system. This production scheduling sub system enables planer to update the tracking of manufacturing output across multiple areas of production line and model. Scheduling is based on order priority. Priorities for production are assigned for each line on each shift. Figure 3 shows the flow of the planning system. This subsystem has three main tasks: manage planning schedule, control working calendar and deal with model running.

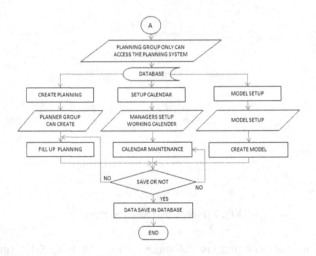

Fig. 3. Flow Chart Planning Sub System

5.2   Maintenance Sub System

Maintenance subsystem is designed for line leader or line supervisor to manage production line information, create new line, edit and delete details of line such as product models, line rename etc. and control production lines specifications – within the context of production plants. Thus through production maintenance subsystem user are able to manage the production lines information. Figure 4 shows the process flow for maintenance subsystem.

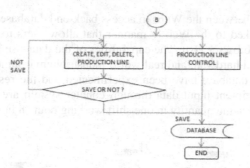

Fig. 4. Flow Chart Maintenance Sub System

5.3   End User GUI

Real time effective monitoring can lead to management efficiencies and reduce costs associated with public reporting on internal control because difficulties are identified and addressed in a proactive manner. By implementing, the management can perform the continuous monitoring, analysis, and appropriate follow-up on, line performance reports that might identify problem of a control failure. Figure 5 depicts the end-user GUI. Line or shift supervisor can review and control target achievement and line performance as a normal part of processing. Top management can perform individual line performance assessment regarding the line achievement they set in the factory.

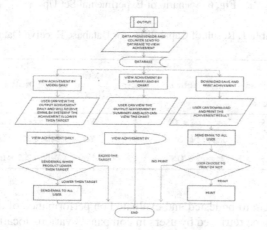

Fig. 5. Flow Chart WEB-GUI

5.4   Database Web Server

The database stores all the information about the production outputs and their interaction with the system. The databases designed can be linked to the Web in a manner that allows user to access data through a web GUI. These databases applying Web-to-database connecting technologies called JDBC (Java Database Connectivity) as a linking method between the Webs to access back-end databases [9]. The corporate databases can be linked to the Web in manner that allow users to access to corporate data through a web browser [10]. The capabilities of the database have been tested by integrating to the real hardware and real world industrial environment. The build mesh network link to the database have been experimented and the result obtain depict in table 1. In the experiment input data through counter system are continuous send to each RFID tag in the same quantity in one shift working hour (8 hours).

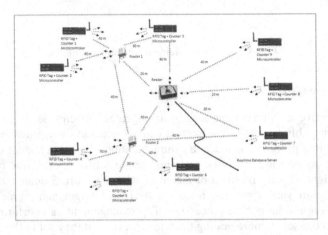

Fig. 6. Scenario of Experimental Set Up

Table 1. Result of Capabilities for Database Receive Data

Distance to reader	No of embedded hardware	Router selection	Reader	Mesh Network	Database Performance
5m ~ 100m	9	Router 1&2 is 'ON'	1	Yes	Real time from all counter
5m ~ 100m	9	Router 1 is 'ON'	1	Yes	Delay 0.002sec from counter 1 and 2
5m ~ 100m	9	Router 2 is 'ON'	1	Yes	Delay 0.002sec from counter 4, 5 and 6

The overall system to be tested and evaluated on performance of data transfer using the build network to be retrieved by users in company's various locations.

6   Conclusion

In this paper an overview of comparatively new technology and architecture for web-based system and active RFID integrated in wireless mesh network in industrial applications has been presented. The state of the art has been summarized by describing the framework of "real industrial environment" case study. It is likely that web-based architecture and wireless mesh network platform play an important role in the future of computer and communication technology specifically in industrial environment. The result shows that, the MCDAS architecture and capabilities is designed to best suite these applications. Specifically, wireless mesh network can be exploited to reduce cost and time constraints to gain optimum profit. The intent is to show ways on how industrial manufacturers can use wireless technologies to improve their monitoring systems.

References

1. Yang, S.H., Yang, L.: Guidance on design of Internet-based Process Control Systems. Acta Automatica Sinica 31(1), 56–63 (2005)
2. Yang, S.H., Chen, X., Edwards, D.W., Alty, J.L.: Development of an Internet-base Process Control System, pp. 601–606. Elsevier Science, London (2002)
3. Khor, J.H., Ismail, W., Younis, M.I., Sulaiman, M.K., Rahman, M.G.: Security Problems in an RFID System. Journal of Wireless Personal Communication 59(1), 17–26 (2011)
4. Fouda, H.: A Review of Wireless Network for Remote Monitoring and Control Applications. Control Microsystems White Paper, 1–8 (2006)
5. Flammini, A., Ferrari, P., Marioli, D., Sisinni, E., Taroni, A.: Wired and Wireless Sensor Networks for Industrial Applications. Microelectronics Journal 40, 1322–1336 (2009)
6. Low, K.S., Win, W.N.N., Meng, J.E.: Wireless Sensor Network for Industrial Environments. In: IEEE International Conference on Computational Modelling, Technologies and Internet Commerce, Hamburg, Germany, pp. 271–276 (2005)
7. Johan, P., Glen, B., Xu, W.L., Olaf, D., Sylvester, T.: Wireless Network Control for Internet Manufacturing. In: Proceeding Australian Conference on Robotics and Automation, Auckland, pp. 202–205 (2002)
8. Hu, H., Min, Y., Xie, X., Wang, F., Yuan, J.: Distributed Cooperative Dynamic Spectrum Management Schemes for Industrial Wireless Sensor Networks. In: IEEE 2nd International Conference on Future Generation Communication and Networking, Sanya, China, pp. 143–151 (2008)
9. Gaifang, N.: The Development of Logging Large-scale Management Information System. In: International Conference on Challenges in Environment Science and Computer Engineering, Xinxiang, China, pp. 425–428 (2010)
10. Hopfner, H., Schad, J.: MyMIDP: An JDBC Driver for Accessing MySQL from Mobile Devices. In: 1st International Conference on Advances in Databases, Knowledge and Data Applications, Germany, pp. 74–80 (2009)

An Arabic-Based Tutorial System
for Children with Special Needs

Moutaz Saleh[1], Jihad Mohamad Aljaam[1], Ali Jaoua[1], Abdulmotaleb Elsaddik[2]

[1] Department of Computer Science & Engineering, Qatar University, Doha, Qatar
{moutaz.saleh,jaam,jaoua}@qu.edu.qa
[2] School of information Technology and Engineering, University of Ottawa, Canada
elsaddik@mcrlab.uottawa.ca

Abstract. In spite of the current advance of the use of computers in education in the Arab world, complete suites of solutions for students with special needs are very scarce. This paper presents an assistive system managing learning content for children with intellectual challenges. The system provides educational multimedia contents, inspired from the local environment, in different subjects such as math and science to target specific learning goals. The system tracks the individual student progress against the student individualized learning plan assigned by the teachers and according to their abilities. Upon completion of learning a particular task, the system will test the learner to order a set of sub-tasks in its logical sequence necessary to successfully accomplish the main task. The system also facilitates deploying intelligent tutoring algorithms to automatically correct mistakes after a number of trials working adaptively with the learner to successfully learn how to complete the task.

Keywords: Intellectual Disability, Computerized Learning, Educational Multimedia Contents, Personalized Learning.

1 Introduction

Since more than two decades, the use of computer as an assistive teaching tool shows a significant improvement in learning process especially for school children [1, 2]. Besides, with the continuous development of computer software and applications, it becomes attractive to use computers in teaching children with intellectual disabilities. This can be clearly seen through the possibility of teaching students according to their level of abilities and speed of interaction, providing a continuous feedback, and motivating them with interactive educational multimedia contents [3]. Indeed, lots of research studies [4, 5, 6] show the great benefit of using computer to effectively enhance the teaching process for such kind of children who require special and continuous training in order to facilitate their learning process [7]. In the State of Qatar, it is estimated to have more than 3% of children with some intellectual challenges. This percentage is higher in the MEAN region. The educational needs for such children should not be ignored considering the importance of building their skills and merging them into the society. Recently, in 2010, the population statistics in

V.V. Das, E. Ariwa, and S.B. Rahayu (Eds.): SPIT 2011, LNICST 62, pp. 16–20, 2012.
© Institute for Computer Sciences, Social Informatics and Telecommunications Engineering 2012

Qatar show that 1290 are suffering of speaking difficulties, 883 are suffering of hearing difficulties, 1284 are suffering of vision difficulties, and 1255 are suffering of memory difficulties. In the Arab world, despite the increasing attention given to the children with special needs, employing the computer in the educational process of such children is still limited due to the following reasons: First, there are little computer software that supports both Arabic language and culture. Second, most of the computer teaching tools are only relying on the rigid power point presentation. Third, software development companies do not effectively participate in providing high quality educational multimedia contents. Finally, if some software applications are available, ordinary people don't afford to buy it for their children. The state of Qatar shows a great concern towards improving the learning process for the children with special needs. They established recently the Shafallah center [8] as the leading center in Qatar provides such children with several services to educate them, build their personal skills, and eventually merge them in the community for better living. The center is now serving more than 450 children distributed into different teaching classes according to their intellectual abilities. The classes are made up of 7 to 8 children with 2 to 3 teachers who facilitate the learning process and monitor the children. Each child has one educational plan, called the personalized plan, which is matched to the teaching objectives that this child has to fulfill within a certain period of time usually set to one year. During this period, the child's progress will be monitored, evaluated, and the plan will be updated accordingly until the teaching plan objectives are achieved. The teachers are using power point presentations to deliver the lessons. Students assessment is currently done manually.

2   Proposed System

The importance of the system that we propose is to reduce the administrative and teaching overhead of the Shafallah center through automating the management procedures and involving the children's parents in the learning process.

2.1   System Architecture

The system supports and monitors the learning process through providing several interactive educational multimedia contents consisting of text, images, and short clips. These multimedia elements are linked to the objectives of teaching personalized plan. The system can provide dynamicity in offering its educational multimedia contents when considering children's level of abilities and speed of interaction. The system records the children progress to allows issuing reports. To accommodate the children difficulties in using the computer, the system provides each child with a PC tablet equipped with touch screen. The system can be used in two ways:

- *Group activities*: the system uses a smart board to view multimedia contents, i.e. lessons, puzzles, quizzes, etc. The children can interact with these contents.
- *Individual activities*: each child has his own tablet. The teacher controls the class by sending different multimedia contents to the children's tablets according to

their level of abilities and personalized teaching plan. The children are able to practice the contents at home as the teacher will daily transfer a copy of these contents to the children's tablets. A web-based application is being developed.

2.2   The Users of the System

The system has four types which are: *administrator*, *teacher*, *parent*, and *student*.

A. *Administrator*: it is the responsibility of the administrator to manage all users' accounts including adding deleting, and updating. He/she uploads the multimedia contents and the plans. He/She links these contents with their corresponding objectives. System settings like sending parents periodic SMS/Email for feedback on their children progress are also handled by the administrator.

B. *Teacher*: the learning process in the class is managed by the teacher who can control the educational multimedia contents to be viewed on the smart board as well as the students PC tablets. The teacher also transfers the daily covered contents of each student to his/her tablet for home revision with the parents.

C. *Parent*: the system effectively contributes in increasing the level of interaction between the parents and their children through: First, sending periodic short SMS and Emails about the children progress. Second, ability of accessing the system website to post feedbacks about their children personalized plan. Third, having the class materials installed on the children PC tablet gives the parent the opportunity to follow up with their children's daily classes. Finally, parents can review their children's daily lessons and contact teachers for any inquiries.

D. *Student*: this is the main user of the system who can smoothly interact with the contents available on both class smart board and PC tablet. Upon completion of a lesson, the system provides the student with several puzzles and games to evaluate his/her understanding of that lesson. This process is done with multiple trials, and intelligent algorithms are built to indicate student's mistakes. The system tracks all student results, record it in database and eventually reports the student performance.

2.3   The System Features

1. Provides several interactive multimedia contents (video, audio, image, text) inspired from the Qatari environment to achieve student learning objectives.
2. Provides principles of effective teaching by stimulating students through several multimedia educational games that encourage them for practicing required skills.
3. Supports individual learning style as it treats each student independently according to his/her personalized study plan and then monitor the performance individually.
4. Involves parents in the teaching process through the automatic delivery of SMS/Email and remote website access to track the students' performance and give feedback on their personalized plan.

5. Accelerates the teaching process by having the parents follow up with the students' daily classes installed on their PC tablet.
6. Reduces the administrative overhead on the teachers and save their time and effort in preparing assistive teaching tools.

3   Educational Content

The system provides a large number of contents to meet the objectives of the learning process for the children. These contents are designed and customized based on the international educational system FACE adopted by the center which cover different scopes including math, science, reading, writing, religion, and social life. The contents are divided according to both learning objectives and stages. This can facilitate the role of the teacher in matching personalized plan objectives with its associated contents. Each student is characterized independently based on his/her intellectual challenge. Then, a personalized study plan is prepared with long-term objectives to be achieved within a specific period of time. These objectives are, in turn, divided into short-term objectives to be served with well-designed multimedia contents that suit the student's abilities. The contents are designed with a focus on:

1. Inspired from the local Qatari environment such as dress, food, shops, currency.
2. Suites students' intellectual, vision, and hearing capabilities such as sounds/color clarity, and levels' difficulties.
3. Includes different types of knowledge such as social and functional knowledge.
4. Easily interacts with student to achieve the learning objectives of a the study plan.
5. Motivates students through using excitements contents apart from rigid teaching.
6. Varies in teaching styles i.e. match objects, drag and drop, and puzzles.
7. Features the ability to repeatedly updates, improves, and personalizes contents.
8. Organized and sequenced logically i.e. from basic to advanced.

4   Evaluation and Assessment

The evaluation and assessment process for children with special needs takes different aspects compared to those for normal children due to the limited capabilities of the first group. Here, we consider two main types: individual assessment and curriculum-based assessment. In individual assessment, children performance is monitored individually and differently according to their disability. This can help us in determining children weaknesses points and how it is related to their disabilities to eventually lead us towards designing their most effective educational contents. In the curriculum-based assessment the children performance is continuously evaluated against a predefined group study plan objectives and then the collected results are used to make comparisons and update existing teaching methods whenever necessary. Regardless of the assessment method adopted, the system will record children results in a specific database and generate reports accordingly. This can assist the teacher in choosing the next educational contents to be delivered for the children. Moreover, the system adopts a feedback mechanism to periodically improve the teaching process as follows: Teaching Objectives → Educational Contents → Teaching Methods → Evaluation → Assessment → Improvement → Teaching Objectives. A practical teaching improvement is also achieved with the use of this system especially when we compare the traditional teaching method in [9], directly from teacher to student, with the newly adopted interactive method that fully includes both teacher and parents.

5   Conclusions

We proposed an assistive system that manages the learning content for children with intellectual challenges. The system provides educational multimedia content, inspired from the local environment, to target specific learning goals suitable for this group of children. The system tracks the individual student progress against his individualized learning plan assigned by the specialized teacher and automatically generates reports that will assist the teacher in updating the student's study plan.

Acknowledgments. This publication was made possible by a grant from the Qatar National Research Fund under its award NPRP 09-052-5-003. Its contents are solely the responsibility of the authors and do not necessarily represent the official views of the Qatar National Research Fund.

References

1. Bangert-Drowns, R.L., Kulik, J.A., Kulik, C.-L.C.: Effectiveness of Computer-Based Education in Secondary Schools. Journal of Computer-Based Instruction 12(3), 59–68 (1985)
2. Kulik, C.-L.C., Kulik, J.A., Shwalb, B.J.: Effectiveness of computer based adult education. Journal of Educational Computing Research 2, 235–252 (1986)
3. Kirk, S., Gallagher, J., Coleman, M., Anastasiow, N.: Educating Exceptional Children, 12th edn. Houghton Mifflin, Boston (2009)
4. Schery, T.K., O'Connor, L.C.: The Effectiveness of School Based Computer Language Intervention with Severally Handicapped Children. Language, Speech, and Hearing Services in Schools 23, 43–47 (1992)
5. Aveyard, R.L.: A Visual Attention Study for developing Learning Cues for Individual with Mental Retardation. Psychological and Cultural Studies, Lincoln, Nebrasca (2001)
6. Hawsawi, A.: Teachers Perceptions of Computers Technology Competencies Working with Students with Mild Cognitive Delay. Doctoral Dissertation, University of Idaho, USA (2002)
7. American Association on Intellectual and Developmental Disabilities, http://aaidd.org
8. Shafallah Center for Children with Special Needs, in Doha, Qatar, http://www.shafallah.org.qa
9. Adam, T., Tatnall, A.: Using ICT to Improve the Education of Students with Learning Disabilities. In: Kendall, M., Samways, B. (eds.) Learning to Live in the Knowledge Society. IFIP, vol. 281, pp. 63–70. Springer, Boston (2008)

Multi-Criteria Business Intelligence Approach

Torky Sultan[1], Ayman E. Khedr[1], and Mohamed M.R. Ali[2]

[1] Faculty of Computers and Information, Helwan University, Helwan, Egypt
tsultan@consultant.com, aymankhedr@gmail.com,
aymankhedr@helwan.edu.eg
[2] Central Lab of Agriculture Expert Systems (CLAES), ARC, Giza, Egypt
mreda@claes.sci.eg, m_reda25@yahoo.com

Abstract. Multi Criteria Business Intelligence approach (MCBI) aims to enhancement Business Intelligence Applications (BIA) by applying Multi-Criteria Decision Making (MCDM). MCBI approach contributes to improve Business Intelligence Decision Support System (BIDSS) for BIA. Also MCBI approach presents a standard method to evaluate and select business decisions. The recommended business decision is the suitable and optimal choice to implement. The proposed model for MCBI approach that consists of five major components. The first component is business objectives, problem definition and main goals. The second component is a business heterogeneous data treatment which gathering from different resources and related with different areas. The third component is a unified business intelligence databases. The fourth component is a business intelligence processing. The fifth component is a evaluating the business decisions to select the suitable and optimal solution.

Keywords: Multi–Criteria Business Intelligence (MCBI), Business Intelligence Applications (BIA), Multi–Criteria Decision making (MCDM), Business Intelligence Decision Support System (BIDSS), Decision Support System (DSS), Data Warehouse (DW), Spider Data Warehouse (SDW), Analytic Hierarchy Process (AHP).

1 Introduction

This study presents MCBI approach to make better decision to enhancement BIA model by applying MCDM its impact on quality and evaluation processes for business decision in Business Intelligence Decision Support System (BIDSS). MCBI approach have many criteria and alternatives that effect on business decision making processes and business DSS and we could defined MCBI as "a set of models, descriptions and analysis methodologies that systematically exploit the available data to retrieve information, knowledge and advice useful in supporting complex decision-making processes according to many criteria and alternatives. Where MCBI approach produce from the integration between BIA, MCDM methods. This paper is divided into seven sections. Section 2 presents surveys and literature reviews for previous work in BIA and MCDM. Problem statement and definitions are presented in section 3. Section 4 presents research plan and methodology. The integration between BIA and MCDM presents MCBI Model in section 5 by using AHP method. Section 6

V.V. Das, E. Ariwa, and S.B. Rahayu (Eds.): SPIT 2011, LNICST 62, pp. 21–28, 2012.

presents the deployment and implementing for MCBI model: deployment and implementing for MCBI model: BOVIS case study. Finally, conclusion and future work are presented in section 7.

2   Survey and Previous Work

In this section we discuss the previous work that related to BIA and MCDM methods. As well as, we are explore methodologies, methods and applying techniques that allows to making integration between BIA and MCDM. BIA defines as "a set of mathematical models and analysis methodologies that systematically exploit the available data to retrieve information and knowledge useful in supporting complex decision-making processes [3]. MCDM could be define as well as a set of methods to help the decision makers to describe, evaluate, rank and select alternatives according to several criteria"[2,11]. DSS define as " a computer program application that analyzes business data and presents it so that users can make business decisions more easily [1,3]. BIA needs to make many analysis and mining processes by using Multi-dimensional Data Warehouse (MDW), On-Line Analytical Processing (OLAP), mining processes such as classification , clustering , association, statistical mining and regression to make prediction to increasing the effectiveness and efficiency of decision making processes for BIA [3]. Business DW and data marts collecting data from different resources to store in databases to extracting, transforming and loading these data by using ETL tools [3]. Figure 1. Illustrates the main components of a BIA.

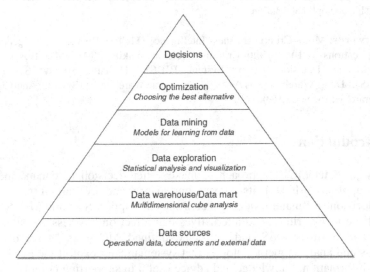

Fig. 1. The main components of BIA, Source: Vercellis, 2009

MCDM can define as "making the right decision, at the right time, for the right property" [2, 3, 11]. Analytic Hierarchy Process (AHP) is one method of MCDM methods to find the best alternative according to their needs by using preference table technique [2, 11]. Figure 2 illustrates the structure of the AHP method.

3   Problem Statement and Definition

The central research question will be "How can we better make standard decision to enhancement BIA model by applying MCDM its impact on quality and evaluation processes for business decision in BIDSS?" This study wish to find answers for some questions as the following:

- What are the main factors that might effect on processes of a new integrated model?
- How to covers the problems of heterogeneous and incompleteness of data?
- What is the new architecture of synthesis model for MCBI approach?
- How to make development for cattle wealth by using MCBI approach.

4   Research Plan and Methodology

MCBI model have both qualitative and quantitative approaches. In the qualitative part of the study, purposive sampling is used to search on literatures which enhancement the decision of new BI model. In the quantitative part of the study, the use of survey questionnaires and quantitative analysis of the data will further enhance the significance of the research findings. Data is collected by many of questionnaires and in-depth interviews from BOVIS project database, documentations and stakeholders [8]. MCBI system aims to produce recommended decisions to make investment and development for the productions of cattle and buffalo wealth to satisfy the sufficient requirement from red meat in new Egypt.

5   The Proposed Model for MCBI Integrated Approach

The proposed model for MCBI approach is integration between BIA and MCDM methods to enhancement BIDSS for BIA by using AHP method.

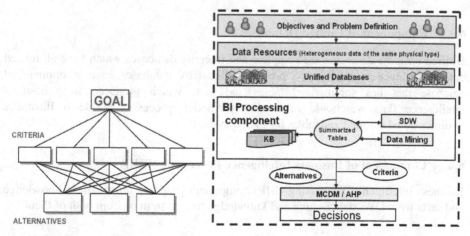

Fig. 2. AHP flow method, Source: Vincke, 1992   **Fig. 3.** Components of MCBI model

This integration model finds a standard methodology to evaluating and selecting an optimal business decision through the five components of MCBI model which as shown in figure 3. The technology that used to implement MBCI approach based on the client/server technique through internet communication technology. The software technology that used is web2 and Structured Query Language (SQL) databases infrastructure to implement MCBI model. Business intelligence decision making processes depend on the amount of information and knowledge which extracting from analytical processing from a huge amount of business data by mining classification and visualization methods to make better business decisions.

6   Deployment and Implementing for MCBI Model

A case study in the area of cattle production has been adapted to prove the concept of applying MCBI in national development as the following sub-sections.

6.1   Component of Business Objectives, Problem Definition and Main Goals

The main goal in this case study are producing a recommended solutions to development the cattle investment in Egypt according to fund, cattle heads, regions … etc, to satisfy the sufficient requirements from red meat by using MCBI approach.

6.2   Component of Heterogeneous Data Treatment

Data are not complete and need to other gathering data from different related areas by interviews, surveys, statistics and reports. Business data collect from different resources but have the same physical data type in different formats for the content. The gathering data it should be unified and complete integrity. Data are specific and have relative connection between business areas such as time, region, cattle… etc [9].

6.3   Component of Unified Databases

Unified business databases are complete and integrity databases which have all related data with business intelligence processes [9]. BIA databases have a summarized database that has summarized tables and facts which produced from business intelligence data warehouse or mining prediction processes. Table 6 Illustrates N-dimensional summarized tables for MCBI system.

6.4   Component of Business Intelligence Processing (PIB)

Business intelligence processing (BIP) component prepares information, knowledge and facts from DW, data mining and knowledge base system or from both of them.

6.4.1 Data Warehouse

Business DW is multi-dimensions DW which based on the technique of galaxy DW to produce a SDW. The dimensions of SDW are related areas with BIA to extracting facts to development cattle investment projects. This development will be satisfied a requirements of food security in Egypt as shown in figure 5. The SDW which express of these dimensions in cattle wealth investment projects as the following: (1)Cattle {(pc, fc , buff, mc) , (male, female) , …}. (2) Time (year, moth, day, hour, sec). (3)Region {(.......), Land (…..)}. (4) Water {…}. (5)Plant {…}.(6) Population of Egypt {…} . (7) Industrials {…}. (8) Transport and communications {physical () , other media(...)}. (9)Effective science {political (….), Economic (...), social (…), Management (…), Education (...)}.(10) Energy{}. Figure 4. Illustrates Spider DW for MCBI model of Investment Cattle production Projects.

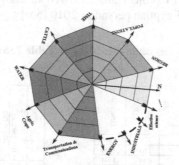

Fig. 4. SDW for Cattle investment Projects by using MCBI approach

6.4.2 Data Mining

The outputs of BIP collect in summarized tables which have criteria, alternatives and facts that produced from SDW and predicting results of mining processes [9,10].

We apply Bayesian statistical classification to perform probabilistic predictions to make optimal decision. Where X are active investment project, belongs to class C, have hypothesis H, and probability for hypothesis holds observed data sample X are P(H|X). Where

$$P(H|X)=\frac{P(X|H)P(H)}{P(X)} \quad P(C_i|X)=\frac{P(X|C_i)P(C_i)}{P(X)} \tag{1}$$

The current investment projects not suitable and not sufficient to satisfy the expected results such as local productions from requirements of a red meats and business developments for cattle wealth. Table1 expresses the cattle experts' vision for the new development and investment cattle projects in new Egypt [6,7,8,9,10].

Where P_i are the type of project based on the number of cattle heads, where $1 \le i \le 8$ according to survey of development cattle production project in Egypt and satisfy

$$P_1 \subseteq P_2 \subseteq P_3 \subseteq P_4 \subseteq P_5 \subseteq P_6 \subseteq P_7 \subseteq P_8 , P_m = \bigcup_{i=1}^{m-1} N_{P_i} P_i , \qquad 2 \le m \le 8 \tag{2}$$

Where N_{pi} is project number of project type P_i, the number of cattle heads for project of type P_m are $N_h(p_m)$, where $\forall P_m, N_{h_{min}}(p_m) \le N_h(p_m) < N_{h_{max}}(p_m)$ (3)

The total number of investment cattle projects is p, where $P = \sum\limits_{i=1}^{n} N_{Pi}$, $1 \leq n \leq 8$ (4)

Total numbers of investment cattle projects in Egyptian are $P = \sum\limits_{i=1}^{27} \sum\limits_{j=1}^{8} a_{ij}$ (5)

Where a_{ij} are number of cattle projects of type j in governorates i.

6.4.3 Knowledge Base

Knowledge base (KB) collects from experts as a cases saved in storage files [1, 3]. PIB collects facts in summarized table to evaluating a business decisions according to criteria and alternatives to make investment for related areas. The total numbers of fattening and dairy cattle are 444738 heads from four types of projects P1,P2,p3 and P4 shown in table 2 additional to a new others [4, 5, 6]. The total numbers of registered cattle and buffalos in BOVIS project are 2357418 heads [8].Table 3 illustrate the requirement form red meat/ Egyptian person at 2010 [5,6].

Table 1. The new structure for cattle heads in investment projects

INVESTMENT PROJECTS	Category	Project	Heads density	Head average. No.	No. projects	Heads No.
	SMAL	P1	h<10	4	37500	.15M
		P2	10<=h<25	10	15000	.15M
		P3	25<=h<50	25	6000	.15M
		P4	h>=50	50	6000	.3M
	LARGE	P5	500<=h<1000	500	300	.15M
		P6	h>=1.000	1000	600	.6M
		P7	h>=10.000	10000	150	1.5M
		P8	h>=100.000	100000	45	4.5M
		Total			65595	7.5M

Table 2. Survey for requirements Red meat[s]

year	red meats (Kg./ person	Cattle No. (Million Head)	Buff No. (Million Head)	(Million Head)	Goats No (Million Head)	(1000 head)	Requires Red Meats (1000 tons)	Available Red Meats(1000 tons)	import Red Meats (1000 tons)
2010	10.9	4.326	4.104	2.5	3	143	863	510	353

The Average % or weights for cattle types ratio in cattle projects as Pure cow (PC)=Foreign cow (FC)=10%, Mixture Cow (MC)=43% and buffalo (Buff)= 37% [4].Table 4 and table 5 illustrate cattle heads requirements to obtain the sufficient amount of red meat. The average net red meat/ one cattle (400 Kg x .5) = 200 kg. [4, 5, 6]. Figure 5 Illustrates the requirements of red meat mean with time and Figure 6. Illustrates the investment production for red meat with time.

Table 3. Red meat requirements

Year	E.P. per Million	Red Meats (1000Tons)	75% cattle (1000Tons)	M. Cattle Heads for markets
2010	79.5	866.6	649.9	3.25
....				
2017	90	981	735.8	3.68

Table 4. Red meat requirements studies

Year	Real Red Meats%	Agri Study %	MCBI Study%	Mean%
2010	60	60	60	60
....				
2017	66	77.6	100	81.2

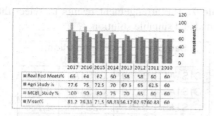

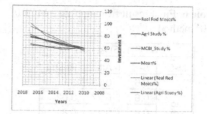

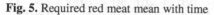

Fig. 5. Required red meat mean with time   **Fig. 6.** Red meat investment with time

6.5 Component of Evaluation and Selecting the Optimal Business Decisions

AHP method evaluates the business decisions to select the optimal solution to implement. MCBI system determine the main criteria, sub-criteria and alternatives by business owner, mining techniques, SDW, expertise, etc. the structure of AHP method of cattle development MCBI system flow shown in figure 7.

Table 5. N-Dim. summarize tables
Source: adapted from Lala, 2009

Summary table type	Dimension of analysis
1-dimensional	Time
2-dimensional	Time and Area
2-dimensional	Time and Customer
2-dimensional	Time and Product
2-dimensional	Product and Area
2-dimensional	Product and Customer
3-dimensional	Time, Product and Area
3-dimensional	Time,Product,Customer
....	....
N-dimensional	Time, Product,...etc.

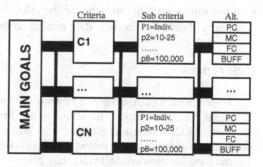

Fig. 7. AHP method for MCBI system

The normalization for main criteria matrix into weights as the following (Cattle = Crops = Water = Region=13.6%; Population = Time = 10.6%; Energy = Industrials = 7.6%; Transport and Communications = Other sciences= 4.6) as the total=100%. The normalization for sub-criteria matrix into weights as the following ($P_1=P_2=P_3= P_5 = 2\%$, P4=4%, P6=8%, P7=20%, P8=60%) as the totally=100%. MCBI system has weight for 10 main criteria, 8 sub- criteria and 4 alternatives to calculate the ranking results which have 320 values (10 x 8 x 4 = 320 decisions). Then make a grouping for criteria which have a same weight to be 4 types and so for sub- criteria to be 5 types and alternative are 4 types. When applying AHP method produced as the following output values / decisions in table 7 to implement where the number of output decision are (4 ×5×4) = 80 results. MCBI system arrangements the output decisions which produced from previous evaluation process to select the implementing solution in table 8. The recommended solution is optimal and suitable choice to satisfying the investment conditions according to business criteria and alternatives. At the case of open fund, large investment and project type, the recommended decision is C1S1A1.

Table 6. Final result from applying MCBI/ AHP method

C1 S(1..5) A(1..4)			
M-C	S-C	Alt.	Result
13.6	0.6	0.43	3.51
	0.6	0.37	3.02
	0.6	0.1	0.81
	0.6	0.1	0.81
	0.2	0.43	1.16

Table 7. The arrangement results to select the optimal and suitable solution

Sample of Sorting solutions CnSnAn from 1 to 80			
C1S1A1	3.509	C1S1A1	3.509
C1S1A2	3.019	C1S1A2	3.019
C1S1A3	0.816	C2S1A1	2.735
C1S1A4	0.816	C2S1A2	2.35
C1S2A1	1.17	C3S1A1	1.961

7   Conclusion and Future Work

- BIDSS for BIA are enhanced by applying MCDM /AHP method to evaluate and select the optimal and suitable choices to implement. MCBI model add a new trend for BIA as a national investment based on the architecture of globalization. MCBI model treats a heterogeneous data of the same physical type format to have unified databases for different development areas. Business data using in analysis, mining classification, statistical prediction and visualization processes mining.
- In the future we hope to increase the effectiveness of MCBI model by using other features of data warehouses, data mining techniques and other MCDM methods.

References

1. Turban, et al.: Decision Support Systems and Intelligent Systems. Prentice Hall (2005)
2. Saaty, T.L.: The Analytic Hierarchy Process. McGraw-Hill, New York (1980)
3. Vercellis, C.: Business intelligence. John Wiley (2009)
4. Statistics of food security projects 2009, Economics Affairs Sector, Ministry of Agriculture and Land Reclamation (MOALR) (July 2010)
5. Sustainable Agriculture development: business plan from 2010 to 2017, MOALR (2010)
6. Reports and statistics about Egyptian population, CAPMAS (2011), http://www.capmas.gov.eg
7. Han, Kamber: Data Mining: Concepts and Techniques. Kaufmann Publishers (2006)
8. Bovis project Online system (2011), http://www.govs.gov.eg/bovis/
9. Peng, Y., et al.: An incident information management framework based on data integration, data mining, and MCDM. DSS Journal 51, 316–327 (2011)
10. El Dahshan, Lala: Data Warehouse based Statistical Mining. ICGST Journal 9 (2009)
11. Vincke, P.: Multi criteria Decision Aid. John Wiley and Sons, New York (1992)

Solving Classification and Curve Fitting Problems Using Grammatical Evolution

Passent M. El-Kafrawy

Department of Mathematics, Faculty of Science, Menoufia University, Egypt
passentmk@gmail.com

Abstract. Grammatical Evolution is related to the idea of genetic programming in that the objective is to find an executable program or function. GE offers a solution by evolving solutions according to a user specified grammar (Backus-Naur Form). In this paper GE is used to construct a classifier for some well known datasets. and curve fitting problems without the need to assume the equation shape.

Keywords: Classification, Curve fitting, Grammatical Evolution, Computational methods, Least Squares error, Backus-Naur Form.

1   Introduction

Grammatical Evolution (GE) is an extension of genetic programming in that it is an algorithm for evolving complete programs in an arbitrary language. Classification is one of the most researched questions in machine learning and data mining. The learning process in classification consists of predicting the value of the outputs from the value of the inputs as a supervised technique [12]. The goal of the classification algorithm is to find relationships between the values of the predictors and the values of the target. Different classification algorithms are employed whereas all of them represent the problem as a model, which can then be applied to different input sets in which the class assignments are unknown. The goal of regression is to find the line or curve that best predicts the values of dependent value of (Y) from the value of independent values of (X). Regression does this by finding the line or curve that minimizes the sum of the squares of the vertical distances of the points from the line or curve. Although regression technique has no understanding of the scientific context of the experiment that brings the data but it is useful in some situations when a smooth curve is required, without the need for a model. In regression techniques, the curve's equation has to be predefined to find the equation's parameters, [3]. Least-Squares is a well-known curve fitting method for a long time. The Least Squares method minimizes the square of the error between the original data and the values predicted by the equation. While this technique may not be the most statistically robust method of fitting a function to a data set, it has the advantage of being relatively simple and of being well understood. The major weakness of the Least Square method is its sensitivity to outliers in the data. For this reason, the data should always be examined for reasonableness before fitting, [5, 11]. The method of least squares assumes that the best-fit curve of a given type is the curve that has the

V.V. Das, E. Ariwa, and S.B. Rahayu (Eds.): SPIT 2011, LNICST 62, pp. 29–33, 2012.

minimal sum of the deviations squared (least square error) from a given set of data [5]. Suppose that the data points are (x_1, y_1), (x_2, y_2) ... (x_n, y_n) where x is the independent variable and y is the dependent variable. The fitting curve f(x) has the deviation (error) d from each data point, $d1 = y1 - f(x1)$, $d2 = y2 - f(x2)$...$dn = yn - f(x_n)$. According to the least squares method, best fitting curve has the property that:

$$|| = \ldots \quad - \sum \quad - \sum \quad \ldots \quad = \text{minimum}$$

The goal of this paper is to use Grammatical Evolution to develop models of equations for curve fitting and classification. In Section 2 we introduced Grammatical Evolution and its methodology. In section 3 we presented solution of some curve fitting problems using Grammatical Evolution. Section 4 presents a solution for classification using GE, and finally in section 5 conclusions and some future work.

2   Grammatical Evolution

By utilizing a Backus Naur Form (B.N.F) grammar the advantages of defining the problem is achieved as well as a separation of genotype and phenotype, [9, 10].In Grammatical Evolution a Backus Naur Form (B.N.F) grammar is used to map the genotype to the phenotype. A separation of genotype and phenotype allows the implementation of various operators (for instance by crossover and mutation). The genotype in Grammatical Evolution is a sequence of bits, [9]. Grammatical Evolution presents a unique way of using grammar in the process of automatic programming, [7]. Variable length binary string genomes are used with each codon presenting an integer value where codons are consecutive groups of 8-bits. The integer values are used in a mapping function to select an appropriate production rule from the B.N.F. definition, the numbers generated always representing one of the rules that can be used at that time, [4, 7, 8]. To solve any problem using GE, a suitable B.N.F. definition must first be developed, [7, 8].

A   Backus Naur Form (B.N.F) Grammar

B.N.F is a notation for expressing the grammar of a language in the form of production rules, [1, 4, 7]. A grammar can be represented by the tuple {N,T,P,S}, where N is the set of non-terminals, T the set of terminals , P is a set of production rules that maps the elements of N to T, and S is a start symbol that is a member of N. In a production rule, when there is a number of productions that can be applied to one particular N, the choice is delimited with the '|' symbol. In GE, the B.N.F. definition is used to describe the output language that is to be produced by the system, i.e. the compilable code produced will consist of elements of the terminal set T. The B.N.F. is a plug in component of the system, it means that GE can produce code in any language there by giving the system a unique flexibility, [7].

B   Grammatical Evolution Methodology

GE is an automatic programming system similar to genetic programming (GP), in that it uses an evolutionary process to automatically generate computer programs. GE uses a population of linear genotypic binary strings, which are transformed into functional phenotypic programs, through a genotype-to-phenotype mapping process. This transformation is governed through the use of a B.N.F. grammar [6]. GE methodology consists of two important parts. The first part is mapping process and the second part is evolution algorithm that is described in the following two subsections. In the GE *mapping process* the genotype maps the start symbol onto terminals by reading codon of 8 bits to generate a corresponding integer from which an appropriate production rule is selected by using the following mapping function, [1, 4, 6, 7, 8, 9]. Rule = (codon integer value) MOD (number of rules for the current non-terminal). The evolutionary algorithm evolves over the population that comprises a simple binary strings. We do not have to employ any special crossover or mutation operators and an unconstrained search is performed on these strings due to the genotype-to-phenotype mapping process that will generate syntactically correct individuals. The Evolutionary Algorithm (EA) adopted in this case is a variable-length genetic algorithm. Individual initialization is achieved by randomly generating variable-length binary strings within a pre-specified range of codons, [7].

3   Curve Fitting and Grammatical Evolution

B.N.F. for curve fitting problem is
<prog> ::= <expr>
<expr> ::= (<expr> <op> <expr>) | <protected-op> | <pre-op>|<digit> | <var>
<op> ::= -| + | *   <protected-op> ::= div(<expr>, <expr>)
<pre-op> ::= sin | cos | log | exp   <var> ::= x
<digit> :: = -1 | -2 | -3 | -4 | -5 | -6 | -7 | -8 | -9 | 0 | 1 | 2 | 3 | 4 | 5 | 6 |7 |8 | 9

Example 1

x	0	0.1	0.2	0.3	0.4	0.5	0.6	0.7	0.8	0.9	1
y	0	0.3	0.4	0.55	0.63	0.71	0.77	0.84	0.89	0.95	1

Figure 1. show the graphical drawing of the curves in every generation and figure 2. show the graphical drawing of the best curve of best function that produced from GE.

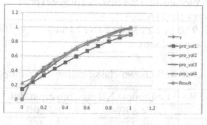
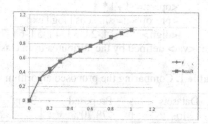

Fig. 1. Graphical drawing of curves in generations

Fig. 2. Graphical drawing of the best curve

Example 2

x	-2	-1.6	-1.2	-0.8	-0.4	0	0.4	0.8	1.2	1.6	2
y	0	0	0	0.05	0.3	0.57	0.3	0.05	0	0	0

Figure 3. is a graphical representation of the curves in every generation and figure 4. presents the best curve of the best function that is produced from GE.

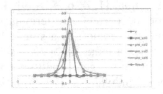   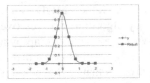

Fig. 3. Graphical drawing of curves in   **Fig. 4.** Graphical drawing of the best curve
generation

4   Classification with GE

The goal of classification is to take an input vector X and assigns it to one of K discrete classes Ck where k=1, 2, 3,..., K, [3, 8]. In our methodology we try to find a mathematical formula that defines a classifier for a problem. Suppose that we need to convert a class name or label to class value. For example, if the problem contains three classes (A, B, and C) we replace them with (1, 2, and 3) to use in the mathematical function. In the next step, we will define each record in the data set by real number, like (2.002) the integer value (2) refers to a class number and the fractional number (002) refers to the record number representing this class. By this method we can convert the class labels to class values.

x1	x2	x3	Class name	Class value
0	2	3	A	1.001
1	1	1	A	1.002
0	3	2	B	2.001
2	4	5	B	2.002

The following B.N.F. grammar is used for extracting the mathematical function.
     <prog> ::= <expr>
     <expr> ::= (<expr><op><expr>) | <protected-op> | <pre-op>|<digit> | <var>
     <op> ::= -| + | *   <protected-op> ::= div(<expr>, <expr>)
     <pre-op> ::= sin | cos | log | exp   <var> ::= x1|x2|x3
     <digit> :: = -1 | -2 | -3 | -4 | -5 | -6 | -7 | -8 | -9 | 0 | 1 | 2 | 3 | 4 | 5 | 6 | 7 | 8 | 9
Note; <var> defined by the attributes from classification problem.

Table 1. Comparing the proposed algorithm with other well known classification algorithms

Datasets	Proposed	Simple BaysNB	Logitboost NB	Bayesian Net
Iris	78.70%	95.53%	94.87%	93.20%
Monk1	100.00%	73.38%	85.33%	73.46%
Monk2	70.60%	56.83%	59.92%	56.78%
Monk3	80.56%	93.45%	91.87%	93.45%
Haberman	72.88%	75.06%	71.48%	71.57%

The results shows that GE achieved higher accuracy in Monk1 and Monk2 and the other algorithms achieved higher in Monk3, Iris, and Haberman because they have a large number of attributes and thus the training process takes time. Also, The data in Monk3 is not filtered, whereas, Monk1 is filtered so that the accuracy reached 100

5   Conclusion and Future Work

In this paper we used Grammatical Evolution (GE) to solve curve fitting problems. Grammatical Evolution successes in solving curve fitting problems. Moreover, this paper proposed a method for the classification problem. We used grammatical evolution (GE) to extract a mathematical formula to define a classifier. This method succeeds in many problems but it takes long time in the training process when the problem contains a large number of attributes. In future work we would try to decrease the training time by using a parallel technique. In future we can benefit from this idea to solve different problems by Grammatical Evolution.

References

1. Cetinkaya, A.: Regular Expression Generation through Grammatical Evolution. In: GECCO 2007, London, England, United Kingdom, July 7-11, pp. 2643–2646 (2007)
2. Elseth, G., Baumgardner, K.: Principles of Modern Genetics. West, St. Paul (1995)
3. Kamal, H.A., Eassa, M.H.: Solving Curve Fitting problems using Genetic Programming. In: IEEE MELECON 2002, Cairo, Egypt, May 7-9, pp. 316–321 (2002)
4. Dempsey, I., O'Neill, M., Brabazon, A.: Foundations in Grammatical Evolution for Dynamic Environments. Springer, Heidelberg (2009)
5. Wolberg, J.: Data Analysis Using the Method of Least Squares. Springer (2006)
6. Nicolau, M., Dempsey, I.: Introducing Grammar Based Extensions for Grammatical Evolution. In: 2006 IEEE Congress on Evolutionary Computation Sheraton Vancouver Wall Centre Hotel, Vancouver, BC, Canada, July 16-21, pp. 648–655 (2006)
7. O'Neill, M., Ryan, C.: Grammatical Evolution. IEEE Transactions on Evolutionary Computation 5(4), 349–358 (2001)
8. O'Neill, M., Ryan, C.: Under the hood of Grammatical Evolution. In: Banzhaf, W., Daida, J., Eiben, A.E., Garzon, M.H., Honavar, V., Jakiela, M., Smith, R.E. (eds.) Proceedings of the Genetic and Evolutionary Computation Conference, Orlando, Florida, USA, July13-17, vol. 2, pp. 1143–1148. Morgan Kaufmann (1999)
9. Harper, R., Blair, A.: Dynamically Defined Functions In Grammatical Evolution. In: 2006 IEEE Congress on Evolutionary Computation Sheraton Vancouver Wall Centre Hotel, Vancouver, BC, Canada, July 16-21, pp. 2638–2645 (2006)
10. Matousek, R.: Grammatical Evolution: STE criterion in Symbolic Regression Task. In: Proceedings of the World Congress on Engineering and Computer Science, WCECS 2009, San Francisco, USA, October 20-22, vol. II (2009)
11. Kolb, W.M.: Curve Fitting for programmable Calculators. IMTEC in Bowie, Md. (1983)
12. Espejo, P.G., Ventura, S., Herrera, F.: A Survey on the Application of Genetic Programming to Classification. IEEE Transactions on Systems, Man, and Cybernetics—Part C: Applications and Reviews 40(2), 121–144 (2010)

Fuzzy Three Time Scale Congestion Controller

Mehdi Mohtashamzadeh and Mohsen Soryani

Computer Engineering Department, Iran University of Science & Technology, Tehran, Iran
Mohtashamzadeh@gmail.com, soryani@iust.ac.ir

Abstract. Although loss rate, length of the queues in the routers and throughput are affected by self similar property of traffic, but classic congestion control algorithms work in short time scales and do not consider self similarity and long range (time) dependency phenomenon of data. To profit these properties, researchers have proposed several methods. Multi time scale congestion control is one of the successful ways to adapt with self similar traffic and predict network status. In this research, a three part structure has been implemented in which second and third parts take advantage of fuzzy engines. Results show throughput improvement in case of using fuzzy three time scale controller instead of a two time scale controller or a classic controller such as New Reno.

Keywords: Self similarity, multi time scale, long range dependency, fuzzy congestion control.

1   Introduction

Most network protocols have been designed according to Poisson probability distribution for network traffic, but researchers found that network traffic imitate Heavy-tail distribution [1-3] and have self similarity property. Erramilli et al. [4] proved that Long Range Dependency (LRD) which is the most important property of self similar traffic, strongly affects network performance. Also author of [5] showed undesirable effect of self similarity on loss rate and queue length. To diminish these effects, researchers have proposed two main solutions, first to overwrite network protocols and other to modify existing control mechanisms to gain from self similarity and LRD property. Multi time scale congestion control [5-7] is a technique which belongs to the second solution. Controllers of this type have multiple sub-controllers inside, in which first part is a classic controller which acts in short time scales (Reno, Tahoe ...) and controllers in other two parts make decisions based on prediction of traffic levels in future and decision of the first part. False predictions may lead to network failure, so controllers of different parts must be precise enough to predict accurate traffic levels in future.

2   Fuzzy Three Time Scale Congestion Controller

Three time scale controller performs congestion control in three stages, short time scales (20-200 ms), mid time scales (3 seconds) and at the longer intervals (12 seconds). The part of algorithm which works in the short time scales is a classic congestion controller

V.V. Das, E. Ariwa, and S.B. Rahayu (Eds.): SPIT 2011, LNICST 62, pp. 34–42, 2012.
© Institute for Computer Sciences, Social Informatics and Telecommunications Engineering 2012

(New Reno). This type of controller increases size of sending window in linear form, after achieving a threshold. Assume the data traffic which is running on the network is burst; it means that sometimes there are a lot of data on the network and mostly often network traffic is very low. Since classic congestion control algorithms perform window size increase in the linear way, most of available bandwidth would be wasted in case there is no burst traffic. Therefore to take advantage of bandwidth, the second and third parts of controller (mid time and long time controllers) should be active and enter more data to the network, by augmenting the increase factor of window. In fact the second and third parts do not change decision which is taken by the first part, but they make mid and long time decisions compatible with decision of the first part. For example if the first part decides to increase the size of window, second and third parts make increasing factor strengthening or weakening, but do not lead to decrease in window size. To have a steady congestion controller, two fuzzy controllers have been used beside a classic short time scale controller. The three time scale controller functions as follows. If second and third parts of the controller sense an increase in bit rate by the first part, increasing factor would be $(\alpha+\beta)$ in which α and β are figured out by the second and third parts of controller, respectively. Considering future status of network is essential to fuzzy controllers. If fuzzy controllers predict low level traffic for future, they can consider α and β large enough to profit bandwidth. Each fuzzy controller presents a predicted traffic level at the end of its time scale. α and β can be acquired by reversing these predicted values. Predicting large traffic level results to small values for α and β and consequently a small increasing factor. Before describing the controller, let's take a look at some essential prerequisites such as specifying traffic levels and selecting time scales.

2.1   Specifying Traffic Level

To specify traffic level at previous time scale, quantity of sent bits should be mapped to one of eight congestion levels (assume there are eight traffic levels). The controller forms a time series and saves quantity of sent bits in that every 200 milliseconds. Then average (μ) and standard deviation (σ) is computed. Each level stands for a range of bit rate. These ranges (which are in [x,y) format in this paper) can be figured out using following equations.

$$x = \begin{cases} -\infty & k=1 \\ \mu-\left(\dfrac{m}{2}-k+1\right)\sigma & 1<k<m \end{cases} \tag{1}$$

$$y = \begin{cases} \mu - \dfrac{(m-2)}{2}\sigma & k=1 \\ x + \sigma & 1 < k < m \\ +\infty & k = m \end{cases} \tag{2}$$

"m" stands for quantity of levels in these equations.

In accordance with the above equations, having eight traffic levels results to have eight ranges of bit rates which are listed below:

(-∞, μ-3α) [μ-3α, μ-2α) [μ-2α, μ-α) .... [μ+2α, μ+3α) [μ+3α, ∞)

2.2   Selection of the Second Time Scale

To design an efficient multi time scale congestion controller, an important issue is to specify time scales. As in Fig. 1 probability Pr{L2|L1=l} will be more concentrated if the large time scale increases. This concentration means having more precise predictability.

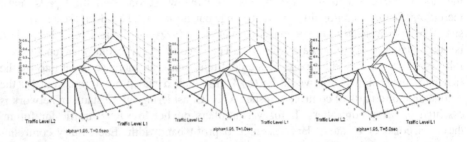

Fig. 1. Probability density used to identify L2 according to recent traffic level L1 [5]

Entropy is a method by which we can discuss about distributions. Entropy is maximum when the probability distribution is not concentrated and otherwise entropy will be low.

For probability density function (Pi) entropy can be calculated as follow,

$$S(P_i) = \sum_i p_i \log 1 / p_i \tag{3}$$

where Pi is the probability density function. So in our case entropy is,

$$S_l = -\sum_{l'} \Pr\{L2 = l' | L1 = l\} \log \Pr\{L2 = l' | L1 = l\} \tag{4}$$

Authors of [5] have shown that increasing the time scale leads to reduction of entropy. Therefore larger time scales would be more adequate. Also it has been mentioned that decrease of entropy is negligible for time scales larger than 3 seconds.

2.3   Selection of the Third Time Scale

Choosing a proper time scale for the third part of controller depends on several issues such as types of first and second parts (short-time and mid-time controllers), second time scale, self similarity of traffic and average time of connections.

Hagivara et.al [8] have shown that in case of having self-similar traffic (e.g. H=0.9) burst property of throughput would be evident in 10-seconds time scales, and for larger time scales traffic will be more smooth. The authors have mentioned that if the self similarity is to some extent low (e.g. H=0.5) burst property would not be apparent enough, so shorter time scales should be chosen.

2.4   Mid Time Fuzzy Controller [9]

To make decisions, controller should be aware of recent traffic level. Traffic level can be attained according to bit rate at last mid time scale, using described intervals in section "2.1". The controller has two input linguistic variables and an output. Input variables refer to traffic level and throughput experienced at the last mid time scale. The controller is of Mamdani type and has 40 rules. Performance of the controller is severely affected by selected rules.

2.5   Long Time Fuzzy Controller

Third part of the design takes advantage of a Mamdani fuzzy controller with three input linguistic variables namely "Recent traffic", "Predicted traffic" and "Effective throughput" which refer to traffic level in the last mid time scale, predicted traffic level by mid time controller and effective throughput in the last long time scale, respectively. This controller has also an output linguistic variable namely "Predicted traffic2" which its membership functions are the same as membership functions of "predicted traffic" input.

Table 1 presents some of the rules used for long time scale controller.

Table 1. Fuzzy rules used in long time scale part of the fuzzy controller

If (Predicted-traffic1 is VL) and (Recent-traffic is VL) and (Effective-throughput is VH) then (Predicted-traffic2 is L)
If (Predicted-traffic1 is VL) and (Recent-traffic is VL) and (Effective-throughput is M) then (Predicted-traffic2 is H)
If (Predicted-traffic1 is VL) and (Recent-traffic is M) and (Effective-throughput is M) then (Predicted-traffic2 is M)
If (Predicted-traffic1 is VL) and (Recent-traffic is M) and (Effective-throughput is H) then (Predicted-traffic2 is H)
If (Predicted-traffic1 is VL) and (Recent-traffic is L) and (Effective-throughput is H) then (Predicted-traffic2 is H)

3   Simulation and Results

3.1   Producing Self-similar Traffic Using ON/OFF Traffic Generators

Simulations have been done using Omnet++ version 3.3 [10]. To have self-similar traffic during simulations, workstations have taken advantage of Pareto distribution in

Omnet++ simulator to generate Heavy-tailed ON/OFF traffic, in which both on and off times conform Pareto distribution. In this research, 30 ON/OFF traffic generators have been used. Fig. 2 presents generated traffic for 1000 seconds of simulation for various values of α (α is shape parameter in Pareto distribution) and bit rate. Network consists of 30 workstations. Each node runs fuzzy three time scale congestion control algorithm to detect congestion and make proper decisions to utilize network resources in case of low traffic. As expected, in accordance with equation $H=(3-\alpha)/2$ having a smaller value of α leads to a greater Hurst parameter (H) and a traffic which is more self-similar, as in Fig. 2 (Down-right).

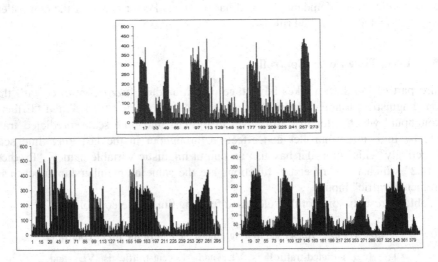

Fig. 2. Generated traffic, simulation time 1000 seconds, α=1.5 and bit rate 22 Mbps (up) Generated traffic, simulation time 1000 seconds, α=1.5 and bit rate 27 Mbps (Down-left) Generated traffic, simulation time 1000 seconds, α=1.05 and bit rate 27 Mbps (Down-right)

3.2   Second Time Scale

Results show that in case of using larger time scales, entropy is lower. For example with T2=1sec (T2 is the second time scale in our design) Entropy is approximately 0.71 and for T2=3sec it is 0.65. According to [5] entropy does not change for time scales larger than 3 seconds (it shows negligible increase). So T2 has been considered to be 3sec.

3.3   Third Time Scale

The third time scale (T3) has been considered to be 10, 12 and 15 seconds in simulations. Table 2, 3 and Table 4 show results of simulations for 1000 seconds. Tian et al. [11] have shown that enlarging time scales leads to more smooth traffics.

Also authors of [8] have shown that in case of a self similar traffic with large value of H (e.g. 0.9) burst property of throughput rate is clear enough in 10 seconds time scales and as time scale increases, clarity of burst property becomes less.

Table 2. Results for 1000 seconds of simulation and T3=10 seconds

L1/L2	1	2	3	4	5	6	7	8	E(L2|L1=...)
1	0.23	0.35	0.3	0.05	0.03	0	0.01	0.03	2.49
2	0	0.22	0.1	0.2	0.1	0.23	0	0.15	4.62
3	0.11	0	0.12	0	0.27	0.28	0.22	0	5.04
4	0.01	0	0.25	0.28	0.3	0.14	0.01	0	4.29
5	0.13	0	0.17	0.26	0.1	0.32	0.02	0	4.24
6	0	0.14	0	0.01	0.11	0.21	0.22	0.31	6.17
7	0	0.08	0	0.11	0.06	0.31	0.14	0.3	6.14
8	0	0	0.09	0	0.22	0.26	0.32	0.11	6.05

Table 3. Results for 1000 seconds of simulation and T3=12 seconds

L1/L2	1	2	3	4	5	6	7	8	E(L2|L1=...)
1	0.33	0.36	0.22	0.05	0.04	0	0	0	2.11
2	0.29	0.29	0.31	0.02	0.07	0	0.02	0	2.37
3	0.11	0.15	0.28	0.27	0.18	0	0	0.01	3.31
4	0.13	0.08	0.08	0.19	0.17	0.12	0.13	0.1	4.57
5	0.02	0	0.22	0.21	0.18	0.27	0.09	0.08	5.31
6	0	0.01	0	0.1	0.24	0.21	0.21	0.23	6.19
7	0	0.02	0.07	0	0.06	0.22	0.24	0.41	6.83
8	0	0.02	0	0.12	0.02	0.31	0.28	0.25	6.44

Table 4. Results for 1000 seconds of simulation and T3=15 seconds

L1/L2	1	2	3	4	5	6	7	8	E(L2|L1=...)
1	0.17	0.08	0	0.24	0.06	0.13	0.11	0.21	4.82
2	0.24	0.12	0	0	0.1	0.43	0.05	0.06	4.39
3	0.34	0.04	0.02	0.03	0.24	0	0	0.33	4.44
4	0.11	0	0.2	0.18	0.23	0.14	0	0.24	5.34
5	0	0.26	0	0.11	0.07	0.05	0.07	0.44	5.62
6	0.31	0.02	0.01	0.18	0.11	0	0.01	0.36	4.6
7	0.21	0.18	0.21	0	0.09	0.02	0.06	0.23	3.76
8	0.22	0.1	0.1	0.2	0	0	0.1	0.28	4.46

So among these time scales 10 seconds would prepare better predictability. As the above tables show, for T3=15 seconds results are non-concentrated and Long Range Dependency (LRD) is not obvious. In contrast, for 10 and 12 seconds, tables' values show LRD property well. Results for T3=12 seconds seem to be better, so T3 has been considered to be 12 seconds in further simulations.

3.4   Number of Traffic Levels

Increasing traffic levels may augment controller performance. For example in case of having eight traffic levels, values μ+3α, μ+4α and μ+5α are all related to traffic level 8, whereas in case of having twelve levels, the above mentioned values are related to levels 10, 11 and 12 respectively. Facing various traffic levels, fuzzy controller would respond in different ways.

Although level increase may cause performance improvement, it has some drawbacks. To have a reliable controller, average and deviation should be computed every 200 milliseconds. Hence at the end of each long time scale, time periods' bounds should be computed because of changes in average and deviation values. So, expanding the number of traffic levels leads to computation overheads.

In this research, 8 levels of traffic have been considered. Fig. 3 presents results of having different number of traffic levels. Simulations have shown that few changes in quantity of levels make it necessary to have a new set of fuzzy rules.

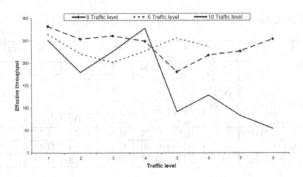

Fig. 3. Fuzzy three time scale controller in case of having 6, 8 and 10 traffic levels

3.5   Comparisons

In this section, performance of the fuzzy three time-scale congestion controller is compared to the performance of a fuzzy two time-scale controller. This comparison is presented in Fig. 4 in which, throughput related to each traffic level is the average of throughput values corresponding to that level during simulation. One can deduce that in most cases fuzzy three time-scale controller performs better than two time-scale controller. Also Fig. 5 presents performance improvement in case of replacing a classic controller with fuzzy two and three time-scale controllers based on different values of shape parameters (α). For example for $\alpha = 1.05$ replacing the classic controller (New Reno in our case) by a three time-scale controller would increase the throughput 15.5% and by a two time-scale controller throughput would be 14% greater.

Fig. 5 demonstrates that using fuzzy three time-scale controller leads to achieve more throughput except for $\alpha = 1.95$. In such a case modifying fuzzy rules may remove this drawback. As mentioned in section "3.2", increasing α would decrease Hurst parameter and self-similarity. Also it is possible to slow down the speed of performance decrease for shape parameters larger than 1.5 by improving rules.

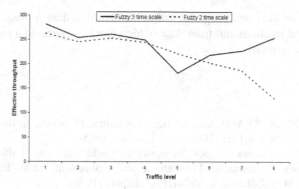

Fig. 4. Comparing performance of fuzzy two and three time-scale controllers

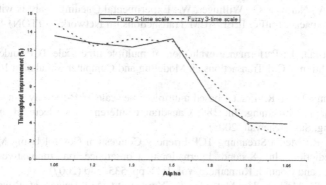

Fig. 5. Percentage of performance improvement in case of replacing New Reno controller by fuzzy two and three time-scale controllers

4   Conclusions

Self similarity causes kind of disorders in performance of classic controllers. To have congestion control algorithms which consider self similarity, researchers have proposed two methods; first to rewrite all protocols to get on with self similarity and second to modify existing protocols and standards. Our implementation has been based on the second solution. In addition to the New Reno controller which acts in short time scales (200-500 milliseconds), two other parts have been used to predict network status in larger time scales (up to 12 seconds). Results have shown that the proposed structure would improve network throughput.

Network traffic has been categorized into 8 levels. The long time scale controller predicts Future traffic level based on prediction of the second part, latest traffic level and throughput of the network. According to the predicted level, an increase factor will be obtained by which amount of bit rate increase (decision of first part) is controlled. For future works, data mining techniques can be used instead of fuzzy logic. Accuracy of a fuzzy engine depends on programmer experience of extracting useful items from data and preparing rules; in contrast, data mining techniques use various statistical methods and train data (which can be related to a real network, not a simulated one) to predict.

References

1. Paxon, V., Floyd, S.: Wide-area traffic: The failure of poison modeling. IEEE/ACM Transactions on Networking (TON) 3(3), 226–244 (1995)
2. Crovella, M., Bestavors, A.: Self similarity in world wide web traffic: Evidence and possible causes. In: International Conference on Measurement and Modeling of Computer Systems (ACM SIGMETRICS). ACM, Philadelphia (1996)
3. Willinger, W., Taqqu, M., Sherman, R., Wilson, D.: Self-similarity through high-variability: statistical analysis of Ethernet LAN traffic at source level. IEEE/ACM Transactions on Networking (TON) 5(1), 71–86 (1997)
4. Erramilli, A., Narayan, O., Willinger, W.: Experimental Queuing analysis with long range dependence packet traffic. IEEE/ACM Transactions on Networking (TON) 4(2), 209–223 (1996)
5. Park, K., Tuan, T.: Performance evaluation of multiple time scale TCP under self similar traffic condition. ACM Transactions on Modeling and Computer Simulation 10(2), 152–177 (2000)
6. Lu, J., Ruan, Q., Ni, R.: Fractal-based multiple time scale TCP-friendly congestion control for multimedia Streaming. In: 18th Canadian Conference on Electrical and Computer Engineering, Saskatchewan (2005)
7. Lu, J., Ni, R.: Media Streaming TCP-Friendly Congestion Control Using Multiple Time Scale Prediction. In: Second International Conference on Innovative Computing, Information and Control, Kumamoto, vol. 1(1), pp. 535–540 (2007)
8. Hagivara, T., Majima, H., Matsuda, T., Yamamoto, M.: Impact of Round Trip self-similarity on TCP performance. In: 10th International Conference on Computer Communications and Networks (2001)
9. Mohtashamzadeh, M., Soryani, M., Fathy, M.: Fuzzy two time-scale congestion control algorithm. In: International Conference on Computational Intelligence, Communication Systems and Networks. IEEE, Indore (2009)
10. Omnetpp V3.3 simulator, http://www.omnetpp.com
11. Tian, X., Wu, H., Ji, C.: A unified framework for understanding network traffic using independent wavelet models. In: Proceedings of IEEE Infocom 2002, New York (2002)

A New Method for Conceptual Classification of Multi-label Texts in Web Mining Based on Ontology

Mahnaz Khani, Hamid Reza Naji[*], and Mohammad Malakooti

Department of Computer Engineering,
Islamic Azad University
Dubai, UAE
mahnaz_khani2000@yahoo.com, hamidnaji@ieee.org,
malakooti@iau.ae

Abstract. This paper presents a new inductive learning method for conceptual classification of multi-label texts in web mining based on ontology through Term Space Reduction (TSR) and through using mutual information measure. Laboratory results show the presented method has high precision in compare to existing methods of SVM, Find Similar, Naïve Bayes Nets, and Decision Trees. It should be noted that break–even point is used in micro–averaging for appropriate classification of data complex entitled "Reuters–21578 Apte Split".

Keywords: Ontology, TSR, Conceptual Classification, Web Mining.

1   Introduction

Primarily, web pages show textual data with no semantic interpretation adaptability. Therefore, processing according to keyword-based methods has been turned into one of major problems of web. Working with websites will turn much more difficult without appropriate semantic knowledge on them i.e. websites. Vivid and clear-cut data semantic display is associated by theories of domain (for example, ontology). Using ontology is considered as one of main methods in semantic web. Recently, ontology has been turned as one of the most important subjects in knowledge, management and e-commerce engineering. It should be noted that ontology is pillar of knowledge which provides official display of specific domains. At this study, an inductive learning method has been presented for conceptual classification of Multi-label texts for web mining based on ontology through using Term Space Reduction (TSR) and also using mutual information (MI).For, Term Space Reduction (TSR) may increase efficacy and performance averagely equal to or less than 5% [1]. Recall and Precision is criterion of evaluation for the proposed method [2]. If a term is classified inside a category, that term is positive towards that category, otherwise, that term is negative towards that category. At this method, micro–averaging is used for evaluation of proposed Recall and Precision method. If some terms are turned positive towards category, based on used ontology, the term which is nearer to C category

---

[*] Corresponding author.

V.V. Das, E. Ariwa, and S.B. Rahayu (Eds.): SPIT 2011, LNICST 62, pp. 43–48, 2012.

semantically is considered positive (correct) while the rest terms towards C category are considered negative (incorrect). Principally, at this stage, significance of ontology will be taken into consideration, causing terms to be classified accurately and precisely in correct categories. The Laboratory results show that the presented method has high precision average than existing methods of SVM, Find Similar, Naïve Bayes, Bayes Nets, and Decision Trees.

2   Presenting a New Method for Conceptual Sectioning of Text for Web Mining Based on Ontology

At this part, a new inductive learning method has been presented for classification of Multi-label text based on Term Space Reduction (TSR) and Mutual Information (MI) measure through using ontology. The difference of new proposed method with method presented by[3] is as follows: Depending on type of classification which may increase efficacy and performance averagely less than or equal to five percent, in this method, we use ontology and Term Space Reduction (TSR) [1]. Similar to method [3], we use mutual information (MI) measure for selection of term.The main stages of the method include as follows:

1. The specified Stop Words are removed from set of series of documents [2].such as a, an, the, that.
2. Root of words is specified through the application of Porter algorithm and terms are reduced according to their roots form. [4] (For example, "Compute", "Computing" , "Computer" are reduced to "Compute" and "Walker", "Walking" and "Walks" is reduced to "Walk".
3. The terms which occur less than five times at set of series of test are removed [4][5][6].because, the word which occurs only some terms, it is not reliable statistically.
4. The terms which have been used only in one document are removed [7].
5. MI size of remaining terms is obtained and 300 terms, which their size are more than remaining terms, are used for testing categories in one category [2].

$$MI(t_i, C) = P(t_i, C) \log_2 \frac{P(t_i, c)}{P(t_i)P(c)}. \qquad (1)$$

$$P(t_i, C) = \frac{N_c(t_i)}{N_C} \quad , \quad P(t_i) = \frac{N(t_i)}{N_C} \quad P_C = \frac{N_C}{N}.$$

$N_C(t_i)$ denotes the number of occurrences of term t_i in category C, N_C denotes the number of occurrences of all terms in category C,$N(t_i)$ denotes the number of occurrences of term t_i in the collection, N denotes the number of occurrences of all terms in the collection After specifying 300 terms, which enjoys the highest size of

MI in category, a K × N matrix is considered. K is number of terms and N is the number of documents in each category. This matrix is document descriptor matrix and shows binary [1, 0] weight of terms in documents. If term t_i has existed in di document, the amount one is specified, otherwise, the zero amount is displayed. Then, cosine similarity measurement [3] is used for constructing "S" document similarity matrix.

$$S_{(i,j)} = \frac{A(i)A(j)}{\|A(i)\| \times \|A(j)\|}.$$

(2)

$S_{(i,j)}$: shows similarity degree between document di and document dj and $S(i, j) \in [0,1]$

A(i), A(j) :ith and jth column vectors of the document descriptor matrix A.

We can obtain the term-document relevance matrix R by applying the inner product of the document descriptor matrix A to the document-similarity matrix S, shown as follows:

$$R=A.S$$

(3)

Then, R matrix is multiplied in $\overline{1}$ vector and $\overline{V}_c$ vector is obtained for C category.

$$\overline{V}_c = R.\overline{1}\, \overline{V}_c = R.\overline{1}\,\overline{1} = [1,1,...,1]^T$$

(4)

$\overline{V}_c$ vector is normalized through the application of average weight. At this method, each vector element is divided into total elements of vector, aimed at obtaining its normal. In fact, ith term weight in c category is obtained through the application of $\overline{V}_c$ into W_{C_i} as follows:

$$W_{C_i} = w_{c_i} \times \log_2 \frac{|c|}{cf_i}.$$

(5)

W_{C_i} : denotes the refined weight of the ith term in the refined category descriptor vector $w_c . |c|$: denotes the number of categories. cf_i : denotes the number of category descriptor vectors containing term t_i.

This refinement reduces the weights of the terms that appear in most of the categories and increases the weights of the terms that only appear in a few categories. Assume that the document descriptor vector of a testing document d_{new} is $\overline{d}_{new}$. We can then apply the inner product to calculate the relevance score Score(c, d_{new}) of category c with respect to the testing document d_{new} as follows:

$$Score(c, d_{new}) = \overline{d}_{new}.\overline{w}_c.$$

(6)

In other words, we choose the maximum relevance score L among them. If the relevance score between a category and the testing document divided by L is not less than a predefined threshold value , where $\lambda \in [0,1]$, then the document is classified into that category.

1) Using Ontology: If rank of some terms to C category is turned positive, according to the used ontology, the term, which is nearer to C category semantically, is classified positive as correct (TPi) while the rest terms to C category, as categorized positive, will be considered as incorrect. Principally, significance of ontology is specified at this stage and will cause categorization of terms in correct categories with more precision and accuracy. Because, when ontology is used, the number of categorized positive documents are turned zero incorrectly, causing singularity precision with various threshold limit between zero and one. This procedure is shown in the flowchart of Figure 1.

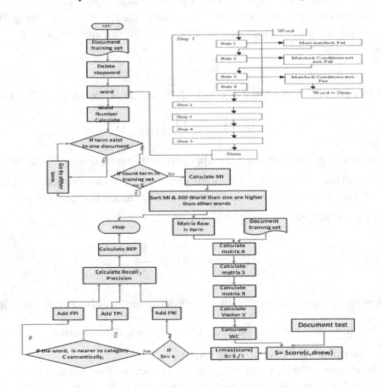

Fig. 1. Flowchart of the new proposed method

3   Implementation and Comparison of Methods

For implementation of proposed method for categorization of Multi-label text, set of 10-category data of "Reuters–21578 &Apte Split" and Delphi 7.0 version and SQL

Server 2005 are used through the application of XP Windows. Table1 shows results of six various algorithms in 10 normal categories appropriately. The presented new proposed method shows better results than other methods, indicating average 94.5 percent for 10 normal categories. After it, SVMs has shown better results, indicating 2.5 percent less than our proposed method and contains average 92 percent for 10 normal categories. The authenticity and accuracy of Decision Tree stands at 3.6 percent less than SVM, indicating average 88.4 percent for 10 normal categories. Bayes Nets has the efficacies for improvement of naïve Bayes as it is expected, but its privileges are rather partial. All advance learning algorithms increase efficacy and performance as much as 15 to 20 percent in comparison with development of searching of Rocchio (Find Similar) type. It should be noted that inductive learning method based on ontology and SVMs show satisfactory and best results in categorization and produce the best results for this set of test series.

Table 1. Breakeven performance for Reuters-21578 Aptè split 10 categories

Method Category	Find similar Rocchio 1971	Naïve Bayes Lewis 1994	Bayes Nets Sahami 1996	Decision trees Chinkering, 1997	Linear SVM Vapnik 1995	Multilabel Method Chang, Chen 2006	The proposed method With ontology
Earn	92. 9 %	95. 9 %	95. 8 %	97. 8 %	98. 0%	97.5%	60%
Acq	64. 7 %	87. 8 %	88. 3 %	89. 7 %	93. 6%	95.1%	100%
Money-fx	46. 7 %	56. 6 %	58. 8 %	66. 2 %	74. 5%	79.2%	100%
Grain	67. 5 %	78. 8 %	81. 4 %	85. 0 %	94. 6%	84.7%	100%
Crude	70. 1 %	79. 5 %	79. 6 %	85. 0 %	88. 9%	84.4%	100%
Trade	65. 1 %	63. 9 %	69. 0 %	72. 5 %	75. 9	85%	100%
Interest	63. 4 %	64. 9 %	71. 3 %	67. 1 %	77. 7%	81%	100%
Ship	49. 2 %	85. 4 %	84. 4 %	74. 2 %	85. 6%	85.4%	93.64%
Wheat	68. 9%	69. 7%	82. 7%	92. 5%	91. 8%	79.8%	93.64%
corn	48. 2 %	65. 3 %	76. 4 %	91. 8 %	90. 3%	78.2%	96.36%
Average	64. 6 %	81. 5 %	85 %	88. 4 %	92. 0%	91.3%	94.5%

In our implementation singularity is observed for all precision points. As the result show for our proposed method based on ontology, the average separation point stood at approx. 94.5 percent through 100 percent of training data in 8categories and 10 percent of training data in two "earn" and "acq" categories. The results show that if 100 percent of data are used in these two categories, the average separation point will be exceeded. It should be noted that threshold limit used in our proposed model is based on (R–cut) [8].Figure 2 Shows ROC curve for grain category and SVM privileges are observed in the length of Recall – Precision space.

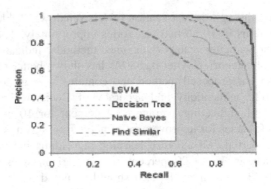

Fig. 2. ROC curve for grain category

4   Conclusion and Future Research

Laboratory results shown in Table1 indicate that the presented method has high average precision than methods of SVM, Find Similar, Naïve Bayes, Bayes Nets and Decision Tree. The issue of paralleling and improvement of performance up to proposed method can be operational. Regards to the capabilities of ontology, effective steps can be carried out on subject of training and synchronization of ontology based on obtained feedbacks, with the aim of producing best results. Also, ontology can be used in Term Space Reduction (TSR) of text with the aim of obtaining better and certain results.

References

1. Yang, Y., Pedersen, J.O.: A Comparative Study on Feature Selection in Text Categorization. In: Proceedings of the 14th International Conference on Machine Learning, Nashville, USA, pp. 412–420 (1997)
2. Sebastiani, F.: Machine Learning in Automated Text Categorization. ACM Computing Survey 34(1), 1–47 (2002)
3. Chang, Y.-C., Chen, S.-M., Liau, C.-J.: A New Inductive Learning Method for Multilabel Text Categorization. In: Ali, M., Dapoigny, R. (eds.) IEA/AIE 2006. LNCS (LNAI), vol. 4031, pp. 1249–1258. Springer, Heidelberg (2006)
4. Sever, H., Gorur, A., Tolun, M.R.: Text Categorization with ILA. In: Yazıcı, A., Şener, C. (eds.) ISCIS 2003. LNCS, vol. 2869, pp. 300–307. Springer, Heidelberg (2003)
5. Baker, L.D., McCallum, A.K.: Distributional clustering of words for text classification. In: SIGIR 1998, 21st ACM Int. Conference on Research and Development in Information Retrieval (Melbourne, AU), pp. 96–103 (1998)
6. Cohen, W.W.: Learning to classify English text with ILP methods. In: De Raedt, L. (ed.) Advances in Inductive Logic Programming, pp. 124–143. IOS Press, Amsterdam (1995)
7. Dumais, S., Platt, J., Heckerman, D.: Inductive Learning Algorithms and Representations for Text Categorization (1995)
8. Yang, Y.: An Evaluation of Statistical Approaches to Text Categorization. Information Retrieval 1 (1999)

Image Super-Resolution Based on Alternative Registration, Blur Identification and Reconstruction

Osama A. Omer

Department of Electrical Engineering, South Valley University, Aswan 81542, Egypt
omer.osama@gmail.com

Abstract. A solution to the problem of obtaining a high-resolution image from several low-resolution images is provided. In general, this problem can be broken up into three sub-problems: registration, blur identification, and reconstruction. Conventional super-resolution approaches solve these sub-problems independently. In this paper, we propose a method to simultaneously solve all the sub-problems. The proposed method minimizes a nonlinear least squares error function. The cost function is alternatively minimized with respect to registration parameters, blurring operators, and high resolution image. The objective and subjective results are shown to demonstrate the effectiveness of the proposed method.

Keywords: Super-resolution, image registration, blurs identification.

1 Introduction

Super-resolution (SR) is an approach to obtain high-resolution (HR) image(s) from a set of low-resolution (LR) images. In its most general form, HR image reconstruction can be broken up into three sub-problems: registration, blur identification, and reconstruction. Image registration is the process to align images to the reference image [1]. Image blur identification is the process to estimate the blurring operators appearing in the observation model. The reconstruction step uses the resulting registered and restored LR images to reconstruct the desired HR image.SR approaches can be categorized based on the cue, by which the SR process is performed, into motion-based approaches and non-motion-based approaches. In previous works, a few approaches have assumed no scene motion, and use other cues such as lighting or varying zoom. Most of the motion-based approaches either pre-register the inputs using standard registration techniques [2,3], or assume that a perfect registration is given a priori before carrying out the super-resolution estimate [4]. However, the steps taken in super-resolution are seldom truly independent, and this is too often ignored in current super-resolution techniques [2,3,4]. Recently, the dependency between registration and reconstruction steps has been taken into consideration [5,6,7]. However, these approaches assumed known or pre-estimated blurring operators which are seldom known in the practical situations.The main idea behind the proposed method is that; due to the dependency of the SR steps, an improvement in the HR image leads to more accurate registration parameters and

V.V. Das, E. Ariwa, and S.B. Rahayu (Eds.): SPIT 2011, LNICST 62, pp. 49–55, 2012.

blurring coefficients. Hence, we introduce an alternative minimization of a nonlinear least squares cost function with respect to the HR image, registration parameters, and blurring coefficients which can greatly improve the performance of SR. Three cases of the proposed approach are examined. First, perform simultaneous registration and reconstruction with known blurring operators. Second, estimate blurring operators assuming the HR image is known. In this case, we use the initially interpolated image as HR image and we simultaneously estimate motion operator. Finally, we perform simultaneous registration, blur identification, and reconstruction.

2   Problem Description

Assume that K LR frames of the same scene in lexicographical order denoted by Y^k ($1 \leq k \leq K$), are observed, and they are generated from the HR frame denoted by X. The observation of K LR frames are modeled by the following degradation process:

$$Y^k = DB^kF^kX + DB^k\Delta F^kX + V^k$$
$$= DB^kF^kX + \mathcal{V}^k \tag{1}$$

Where F^k, B^k and D^k are the motion operator, the blurring operator (due to camera), and the down-sampling operator respectively, X is the unknown HR frame, Y^k is the k-th observed LR frame, V^k is an additive random noise for the k-th frame, and $\mathcal{V}^k$ is the combination of additive noise and motion error.

Throughout this work, we assume that D is known, the additive noise is Gaussian with zero mean, and the blurring operators are shift invariant hence they can be described as moving averaging as $B^kX = \sum_{l=-\rho}^{\rho}\sum_{m=-\rho}^{\rho} b_{l,m,k}S_x^lS_y^mX$ where b_l,m,k ($-\rho \leq l,m \leq \rho$) are the coefficients of the blurring operator and S_x^l and S_y^m are shifting operators by l and m pixels in x and y direction respectively. We will use B^k and $\sum_{l=-\rho}^{\rho}\sum_{m=-\rho}^{\rho} b_{l,m,k}S_x^lS_y^mX$ interchangeably. Therefore the problem is to reconstruct HR image, X, while estimating blurring operators, B^k, and motion operators F^k.

3   Blind Super-Resolution

3.1   The Proposed Cost Function

The SR problem can be viewed as the minimization of a nonlinear least squares error function [1]. The cost function is described by the difference between pixel intensities of the warped, blurred, and down-sampled version of the estimated HR image and observed LR images. The proposed cost function is described as follows:

$$J(X,B,p) = \sum_{k=1}^{K} \left\| DB^kX\left(W_{\uparrow}^k(x;p)\right) - Y^k \right\|_2^2 + \lambda(X,B,p)\|CX\|_2^2 \tag{2}$$

Where x is a MN×2 matrix containing the pixels' coordinates and W is the warping operator. The second term is used to regularize the cost function with thesmoothness constraint of the HR image. C is a general high pass operator, and λ is theregularization factor. Throughout this paper we will use F^kX and $X(W^k(x, p))$ interchangeably. The warping operator is defined as

$$W(x; p) = \begin{pmatrix} 1 + p_1 & p_2 & p_3 \\ p_4 & 1 + p_5 & p_6 \end{pmatrix} \begin{pmatrix} x_1 & \cdots & x_{MN} \\ y_1 & \cdots & y_{MN} \\ 1 & \cdots & 1 \end{pmatrix} \tag{3}$$

Where p1, ..., p6 are the registration parameters. Instead of minimizing Eq. (2) with respect to p, we proposed to minimize

$$J(X, B, p) = \sum_{k=1}^{K} \left\| DB^k X \left(W_\uparrow^k(x; p) \right) - Y^k \left(W^k(x; \Delta p) \right) \right\|_2^2 + \lambda(X, B, p) \|CX\|_2^2$$

$$= \sum_{k=1}^{K} \left\| DB^k X \left(W_\uparrow^k(x; p) \right) - Y^k \left(W^k(x; 0) \right) + \nabla Y^k \frac{\partial W}{\partial p} \Delta p \right\|_2^2$$

$$+ \lambda(X, B, p) \|CX\|_2^2$$

With respect to Δp by getting the derivative with respect to Δp equals zero, we get

$$\Delta p = H^{-1} \sum_{k=1}^{K} \left[\nabla Y^k \frac{\partial W}{\partial p} \right]^T \left[Y^k(W(x; \Delta p)) - DB^k X(W_\uparrow^k(x, p)) \right] \tag{4}$$

Where $H = \sum_{k=1}^{K} \left[\nabla Y^k \frac{\partial W}{\partial p} \right]^T \left[\nabla Y^k \frac{\partial W}{\partial p} \right]$ (5)

The HR image (X) and blurring operator parameters (bi,j, $-\rho \leq i,j \leq \rho$) can be updated by the increment in the inverse direction of the gradient of the cost function with respect to X and bi,j respectively. The gradient of J(X,B, p) with respect to X may be approximated by

$$\nabla_X J(X, B, p) \cong 2 \sum_{k=1}^{k} F^{k^T} B^{k^T} D^T (DB^k F^k X - Y^k) + \lambda(X, B, p) C^T C X, \tag{6}$$

Where we assume that the gradient of the weight $\lambda(X,B,p)$ with respect to X is negligible with respect to that of the L2-norm. The gradient of J(X,B,p) with respect to bl,m,k is given by

$$\nabla_{b_{i,j,k}} J(X, B, p) = 2X^T F^{k^T} S_y^{-j} S_x^{-i} D^T \left(\sum_{l=-\rho}^{\rho} \sum_{m=-\rho}^{\rho} b_{l,m} DS_x^l S_y^m F^k X - Y^k \right) \tag{7}$$

The optimization of J(X,B,p) is performed with respect to p, X and $b_{,}$m,k alternatively. Where, the blurring coefficients are constrained to be bi-symmetric, non-negative, and unit-sum.

3.2   Adaptive Regularization and Step Size

The regularization parameter, $\lambda(X, B, p)$, controls the trade-off between fidelity to the data and smoothness of the solution. The following choice of the regularization parameter [8] can be useful:

$$\lambda(X, B, p) = \tau \left[\sum_{k=1}^{K} \left\| DB^k F^k X - Y^k \right\|_2^2 + \lambda(X, B, p) \|CX\|_2^2 \right] \tag{8}$$

Implying

$$\lambda(X, B, p) = \frac{\sum_{k=1}^{K} \left\| DB^k F^k X - Y^k \right\|_2^2}{\frac{1}{\tau} - \|CX\|_2^2} \tag{9}$$

Where τ is chosen so that λ is non-negative; therefore it can be chosen as [8]

$$\frac{1}{\tau} \geq \|CX\|_2^2 = \|C\|_2^2 \|X\|_2^2 \geq \|X\|_2^2. \tag{10}$$

The step size $\beta_X^{(n)}$ and $\beta_B^{(n)}$ are calculated by minimizing the cost function

$$J\left(X^{(n+1)}, B^{(n)}, p^{(n)}\right) = J\left(X^{(n)} - \beta_X^{(n)} \nabla_X^{(n)} J, B^{(n)}, p^{(n)}\right) \tag{11}$$

and

$$J\left(X^{(n)}, B^{(n+1)}, p^{(n)}\right) = J\left(X^{(n)}, B^{(n)} - \beta_X^{(n)} \nabla_B^{(n)} J, p^{(n)}\right) \tag{12}$$

with respect to $\beta_X^{(n)}$ and $\beta_B^{(n)}$ respectively. Then $\beta_X^{(n)}$ and $\beta_B^{(n)}$ are obtained as $\beta_X^{(n)} = \frac{\zeta^{(n)}}{\eta^{(n)}}$, where

$$\zeta^{(n)} = \sum_{k=1}^{K} X^{(n)} \left(\nabla_X^{(n)} J\right)^T F^{k^T} B^{k^T} D^T (DB^k F^k X^{(n)} - Y^k)$$
$$+ \lambda\left(X^{(n)}, B^{(n)}, p^{(n)}\right) \left(\nabla_X^{(n)} J\right)^T C^T C X^{(n)}$$

$$\eta^{(n)} = \sum_{k=1}^{K} X^{(n)} \left(\nabla_X^{(n)} J\right)^T F^{k^T} B^{k^T} D^T DB^k F^k X^{(n)} + \lambda\left(X^{(n)}, B^{(n)}, p^{(n)}\right) \left(\nabla_X^{(n)} J\right)^T C^T C \nabla_X^{(n)} J$$

and $\beta_B^{(n)} = \vartheta^{(n)} / \gamma^{(n)}$, where

$$\vartheta^{(n)} = \sum_{k=1}^{K} X^{(n)^T} F^{k^T} \sum_{i=-\rho}^{\rho} \sum_{j=-\rho}^{\rho} \nabla_{b_{i,j}}^{(n)} J S_y^{-j} S_x^{-i} D^T (DB^k F^k X^{(n)} - Y^{(n)}),$$

$$\gamma^{(n)} = \sum_{k=1}^{K} X^{(n)^T} F^{k^T} \sum_{i=-\rho}^{\rho} \sum_{j=-\rho}^{\rho} \nabla_{b_{i,j}}^{(n)} J S_y^{-j} S_x^{-i} D^T \left(DB^k F^k \nabla_X^{(n)} J\right).$$

4   Simulation Results

In this section, the simulation results are shown for an example including human face image. For that example we used four low-resolution images to reconstruct one HR image. The simultaneous registration and reconstruction is compared with independent registration and reconstruction algorithm in the three cases.

The regularization term is defined as follows:

$$\|CX\|_2^2 = \sum_{l=-\varepsilon}^{\varepsilon} \sum_{m=-\varepsilon}^{\varepsilon} \alpha^{|l|+|m|} \left\| X - S_x^{-l} S_y^{-m} X \right\|_2^2. \tag{17}$$

The parameters are used as follows: $\alpha = 0.1$ and $\varepsilon = 1$. Since only LR versions of X are available, we used $1/\tau$ as the summation of squared L2-norm of these LR images as $\frac{1}{\tau} = 2 \sum_{k=1}^{K} \left\| Y^k \right\|_2^2$.

In this experiment we estimate the HR image in case of unknown blurring operator. In this case, the blurring operator, the registration parameters and the HR image are estimated simultaneously. Figure 1 shows the PSNR comparison between simultaneous and independent registration and reconstruction steps in case of using estimated blurring operators. From this figure, it can be shown that performing simultaneous registration and reconstruction steps is more efficient than performing independent registration and reconstruction steps.

The visual results shown in Figs. 2 demonstrate the results obtained by the PSNR comparison. From this figure we can see that the reconstructed HR image using simultaneous registration and reconstruction steps is clearer than that obtained by independent registration and reconstruction steps. Figure 3 shows the efficiency of estimated blurring operator compared to the original blurring operator.

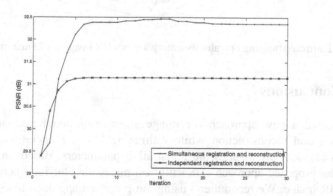

Fig. 1. Using estimated blurring operator for Lenna image sequence

Fig. 2. From left to right and from up to down, (a) Original HR Lenna image; estimated HR image using (b) Bicubic interpolation; (c) Independent registration and reconstruction with known blurring operator; (d) Simultaneous registration and reconstruction with known blurring operator; (e) Independent registration and reconstruction while estimating blurring operator; (f) Blind super-resolution

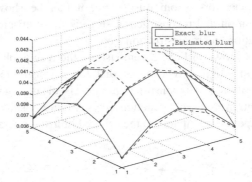

Fig. 3. Estimated blurring operator assuming known HR image for Lenna image sequence

5   Conclusions

We presented a new approach for image super-resolution based on simultaneous registration and reconstruction while estimating blurring operators. The proposed approach alternatively updates the registration parameters. Based on the simulation results, the proposed approach efficiently estimates the blurring operators in case of known HR image. We recommend using the proposed approach to estimate blurring operators while assuming known HR image and then use the estimated blurring operators to reconstruct HR image.

References

1. Baker, S., Matthews, I.: Lucas-Kanade 20 years on: a unifying framework: part 1, tech. report CMU-RI-TR-02-16, Robotics Institute, Carnegie Mellon University (July 2002)
2. Farsiu, S., Robinson, D., Elad, M., Milanfar, P.: Fast and robust multi-frame super-resolution. IEEE Trans. Image Processing 13(10), 1327–1344 (2004)
3. Omer, O.A., Tanaka, T.: Region-based weighted-norm with adaptive regularization for resolution enhancement. Digital Signal Proc. (March 2011), doi:10.1016/j.dsp.2011.02.005
4. He, H., Kondi, L.P.: An image super-resolution algorithm for different error levels per frame. IEEE Trans. on Image Processing 15(3), 592–603 (2006)
5. Tom, B.C., Katsaggelos, A.K.: Reconstruction of a high-resolution image by simultaneous registration, restoration, and interpolation of low-resolution images. In: Proc. Int. Conf. Image Processing (ICIP 1995), vol. 2, pp. 2539–2542 (October 1995)
6. Yang, H., Gao, J., Wu, Z.: Blur identification and image super-resolution reconstruction using an approach similar to variable projection. Sig. Proc. Let. (1), 289–292 (2008)
7. Bai, Y., Hu, J., Luo, Y.: Self-Adaptive Blind Super-Resolution Image Reconstruction. In: 3rd International Congress on Image and Signal Processing (2010)
8. Kang, M.G., Katsaggelos, A.K.: General choice of the regularization functional in regularized image restoration. IEEE Trans. Image Processing 4(5), 594–602 (1995)

Detection of Several Flicker Sources
in a Non-radial Power System

Jalal Khodaparast and Ali Dastfan

Department of Electrical and Robotic Engineering, Shahrood University of Technology,
Shahrood, Iran

Abstract. Detection of flicker sources is the first step to mitigate the effect of flicker in power system. In this paper, in order to reduce the number of measurement devices, instantaneous voltages are estimated by using state estimation methods and then root mean square of the voltages and currents variation are detected and then sign of flicker powers is obtained in selected branches. By comparing the sign of flicker power with direction of fundamental active power, the places of flicker sources are obtained. For validation, the 6-bus non-radial network is simulated and algorithm for flicker sources detection is tested in this paper. The simulations results show that by using the proposed algorithm, all flicker sources in a non-radial network can be detected correctly.

Keywords: Flicker Power, Flicker Sources, Non radial Network, Power Quality.

1   Introduction

In recentyears, by Proliferation of non linear load in power network, power quality became of great importance for both consumers and utilities. One of the most important power quality events is flicker. Detection of flicker source's place is the first step to mitigate flicker in power system. Since now, many different methods for detection of place of flicker sources have been presented. In one of them, the slop of V-I characteristic is used [1]. Another method proposed flicker power [2]. Detection of flicker source in multi side supplied network has been considered in [3], and intelligent identification of flicker source is proposed by using S-transform and neural network in [4]. Generally in these methods only dominate flicker source is considered, while existence of multiple flicker sources in a power system is more realistic than single source.In this paper, by modifying the definition of upstream and downstream, they are generalized to non-radial network.State estimation is used to generate the best estimationof the state variables from limited measurements that are companied with measurement noise [5]. Due to the fact that in practice in a network, measurement of currents is easier than measurement of voltage [5], all bus voltages have been estimated by using state estimation. To detect multiple flicker sources in a non-radial power system, first bus voltages are estimated by using state estimation. Then envelop of voltages and currents are extracted and flicker power is calculated by

V.V. Das, E. Ariwa, and S.B. Rahayu (Eds.): SPIT 2011, LNICST 62, pp. 56–60, 2012.

using Discrete Fourier Transform (DFT).In the next step sign of flickerpower in every lineis specified and by using them,the places of flicker source are detected.

2   Instantaneous State Estimation

For determination of the place of flicker sources in N-bus power network, minimum number of measurements is necessary that cause network become observable. There are N lines that flicker power should be analyzed in them and two possible choices are available. The first one is using power quality meter (PQ meter) in any selected line which is expensive and impractical for a large system. The second choice is using available measurement devices in network which is available in thecontrol center. So in general, N currents and N voltages are needed. In real network, by using current measurements and relationships which exist in network, voltages can becalculated. If line current and some bus voltages are chosen as measurements (z), the main equation of state estimation is given as:

$$z = Hx + \varepsilon \tag{1}$$

If branch model is considered as PI model,Arrays of H are determined as follow:

$$H(k,i) = \frac{2C_{ij}}{\Delta t(1+\alpha)} + \frac{1+\alpha}{\frac{2L_{ij}}{\Delta t} + (1+\alpha)R_{ij}} \tag{2}$$

$$H(k,j) = -\frac{1+\alpha}{\frac{2L_{ij}}{\Delta t} + (1+\alpha)R_{ij}} \tag{3}$$

whereα is a constant between 0 and 1, referred to as the compensating factor. R_{ij}, $L_{ij}$and C_{ij} are resistance, inductance and capacitance of branch K respectively, which is locatedbetween buses i and j, and Δt is sampling time [5]. Instantaneous bus voltages are then calculated as (4). Where R is diagonal matrix and its arrows are the measurements errors.

$$x_{est} = [H^T R^{-1} H]^{-1} H^T R^{-1} z_{meas} \tag{4}$$

3   Envelope Separation

Modulated voltage and current signals are as follow:

$$u_{AM}(t) = (U_c + m_u(t))\cos(2\pi f_c t) \tag{5}$$

$$i_{AM}(t) = (I_c + m_i(t))\cos(2\pi f_c t) \tag{6}$$

where $m_u(t)$ and $m_i(t)$ are low frequency fluctuation generating from flicker source and f_c is fundamental carrier signals (50 Hz/60 Hz). The complete demodulation process which is shown in Fig. 1,is used in this paper [2].

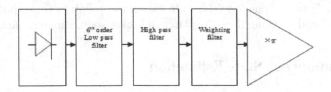

Fig. 1. Method of envelop separation

4   Proposed Method for Detection of Flicker Sources

The main purpose of this paper is the detection of flicker sources in a non-radial power network.In radial network, recognition of upstream and downstream is easy. Upstream is toward utility and downstream is toward load. But in non radial system it is hard to recognize as each feeder is supplied from more than one side. In this case fundamental power flow direction in any line under study should be determined and then upstream is in the opposite direction from fundamental power flow and downstream is in the same direction as fundamental power flow. Due to the presence of some sub-harmonic, DFT has been applied to voltages and currents envelopes to calculate power flicker and then all of flicker sources could bedetected. Measured values of currents and base voltage in form of discrete data, which is created from simulated power system in PSCAD, have been used as input.The proposed method has four parts and MATLAB has been used for simulation for these parts.

4.1   First Part: State Estimation

In an N-bus power system, N measured current and one measured voltage (base voltage), is used as input for state estimation. The complete process of this part is given in section 2.

4.2   Second Part: Envelope Separation

In this part, as it is possible to have more than one sub-harmonic, a demodulation method, as shown in Fig. 1, has been used. Inputs of this stage are measured currents and estimated voltages extracted from first part and outputs of this stage are voltages and currents envelopes.

4.3   Third Part: Flicker Power Calculation Using DFT

In this part, tracked envelopes of voltages and currents extracted in previous stage pass to DFT and then by multiplying DFT of current envelope and DFT of voltage envelope, flicker power is calculated in any sub-harmonic.

$$U = [|U_1| \angle \beta_1, |U_2| \angle \beta_2, \ldots |U_N| \angle \beta_N]$$

(7)

$$I = [|I_1| \angle \alpha_1, |I_2| \angle \alpha_2, \dots |I_N| \angle \alpha_N]$$

(8)

In (7) and (8), U and I are array of complex values showing the DFT of voltage and current envelopes. U_K and I_K' where $K = 1, 2, \dots, N$ are the orders of frequency derived by DFT analysis, are the voltage and current phasors of the sub-harmonics respectively. Therefore flickers power in any sub-harmonic can be expressed as:

$$S_k = U_k . I_k^* = P_k + jQ_k$$
$$P_k = real\{S_k\}$$

(9)

4.4   Fourth Part: Detection of All Flicker Sources in Non-radial Power System

In non-radial power system, upstream and downstream are defined with respect to fundamental power flow direction in any line. Fundamental power flow directions in each line are calculated using by measured currents and estimated voltages. With comparing fundamental power flow direction with power flickers in any sub-harmonic, places of all flicker sources are determined. If flicker power was positive, it implies that flicker source is upstream with respect to fundamental power flow direction and if flicker power was negative, it implies that flicker source is downstream with respect to fundamental power flow direction.

5   Simulation Results

In this section, simulations have been carried out to verify the effectiveness of the proposed algorithm in detecting the multiple flicker sources in non-radial network. The PSCAD software has been used to capture the instantaneous waveforms of the voltages and currents in test cases. Then these results have been used as input for MATLAB simulations to conduct. Arc furnaces are used as flicker loads in simulations. A simulation based on 6-bus test system is used to demonstrate the proposed approach. Fig. 2 shows a 220 KV power network which is supplied by two 11 KV generators [6]. In this study, a network with two flicker sources has been considered. First arc furnace is connected to bus 2 with envelope frequency of 10 Hz and amplitude modulation of 0.1 PU and the second arc furnace is connected to bus 5 with envelope frequency of 5 Hz and amplitude modulation of 0.07PU. Flicker powers (FP) and fundamental active powers are given in Table 1. Sign of flicker power is used to decide whether flicker source is downstream or upstream with respect to point of study. Based on the values of the powers shown in Table 1, direction of fundamental and flicker power flows are shown in Fig. 2. In this figure, long curved arrow represents flicker power of 5 Hz and short curved arrow represents flicker power of 10 Hz, also dashed arrow are presented direction of fundamental power flow. By following the long curved arrow, bus 2 which is the place of arc furnace producing 10 Hz sub-harmonic, is achieved. In the same way by following short limber arrow, bus 5 which is the place of other arc furnace is determined.

Table 1. Simulation Result Of The Second Case

Branch No.	Fundamental power (MWatt)	FP (MWatt) At f_1(10 Hz)	Sign of FP at f_1(10 Hz)	FP (MWatt) At f_2(5 Hz)	Sign of Fp at f_2(5 Hz)
1	92.11	-0.765	negative	+0.031	positive
2	58.82	+0.077	positive	-0.060	negative
3	58.62	+0.076	positive	-0.061	negative
4	58.41	+0.076	positive	-0.061	negative
5	142	+0.212	positive	-0.152	negative
6	62.61	-0.537	negative	+0.057	positive

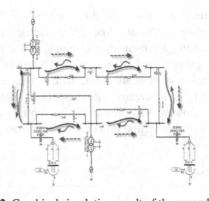

Fig. 2. Graphical simulation result of the second case

References

1. Nassif, B., Nino, E.E., Xu, W.: A V-I Slope-Based Method for Flicker Source Detection. IEEE Transaction on Power Delivery 21, 755–760 (2006)
2. Axelberg, P.G.V., Bollen, M.H.J.: Trace of Flicker Source by Using the Quantity of Flicker Power. IEEE Transaction on Power Delivery 23(1) (January 2008)
3. Dastfan, Mirzayi, M.R.: Identification of Dominate Flicker Source in Multi side Supplied Power Systems. International Review of Electrical Engineering (I.R.E.E.) 3(5) (September-October 2008)
4. Eghtedarpour, N., Farjah, E., Khayatian, A.: Intelligent Identification of Flicker Source in Distribution Systems. IET Generation, Transmission, Distribution 4(9), 1016–1027 (2010)
5. Mazadi, M., Hosseinian, S.H., Rosehart, W.: Instantaneous Voltage Estimation for Assessment and Monitoring of Flicker Indices in Power System. IEEE Transaction on Power Delivery 22(3) (July 2007)
6. Moaddabi, N., Sadeghi, S.H.H.: A Lookup Method for Power System Flicker Source Detection Using Direction of Propagation. In: 13th International Conference on Harmonic and Quality of Power (2008)

A Novel Bats Echolocation System Based Back Propagation Algorithm for Feed Forward Neural Network

G. Kumaravel and C. Kumar

[1] Research Scholar, Sathyabama University, Chennai, Tamilnadu, India
gkumar_aec@yahoo.com
[2] Director-Academic, SKP Engineering College, Tiruvannamalai, Tamilnadu, India
drchkumararima@gmail.com

Abstract. Recently several research works have been done on supervised learning in Feed Forward Neural Networks based on different Swarm intelligence techniques rather than conventional Back Propagation algorithm. This paper discussed about the Bats Echolocation System based Back Propagation algorithm as a learning rule for Feed Forward Network. It was found that it increases the learning rate of the network. The performance of Bats Echolocation system based Back Propagation algorithm was validated by simulation and results were compared with conventional Back Propagation algorithm in terms of convergence speed.

Keywords: Feed Forward Neural Network, Swarm intelligence, Back Propagation algorithm, Bats Echolocation System.

1 Introduction

Swarm intelligence was a kind of computational intelligent technique, which had the ability to solve optimization problems [1], [2]. It was developed from the behavior of ants, bees, flocking of birds and fish schooling, where large group of individuals locate their food by coordinated motion [3], [4]. These techniques were found very useful to find a good solution for the system whose parameters are dynamically changing [5]. Bats Echolocation algorithm was proposed as a kind of Swarm intelligence technique called Bats Echolocation algorithm. It was used to increase the convergence speed of Back Propagation algorithm. Back Propagation algorithm was used to train the Artificial Neural Networks for the desired output [6]-[9]. This paper was organized in the following manner. Feed Forward Network was described with diagram and learning process was discussed. The Back Propagation Algorithm was then briefed and the simulation result of Back Propagation algorithm was discussed. Then, the Bats Echolocation system based BP algorithm was discussed. Finally the simulation result of the Bats Echolocation system based BP algorithm was discussed and compared with conventional Back Propagation algorithm.

V.V. Das, E. Ariwa, and S.B. Rahayu (Eds.): SPIT 2011, LNICST 62, pp. 61–69, 2012.
© Institute for Computer Sciences, Social Informatics and Telecommunications Engineering 2012

2   Feed Forward Network

The Feed Forward Networks generally possessed the input layer and output layer with hidden layers. The computational units in the hidden layer were called as hidden units. Intermediary computations were performed by these units on the input data before directing to output layer [7], [10]. The neurons in the input layer were linked with the hidden layer neurons, the weights on the links were referred as input-hidden layer weights. Similarly the hidden layer neurons were linked with the output layer neurons and the corresponding weights were referred as hidden-output layer weights. The architecture of Multilayer Feed Forward Network shown in Figure 1 with l neurons in the input layer, m neurons in the hidden layer and n neurons in the output layer.

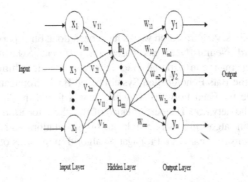

Fig. 1. Architecture of Multilayer Feed forward network

3   Learning Process

A Neural Network was a parallel distributed processor with the capability of storing experimental knowledge and made it available while it was in use [6], [11]. The experimental knowledge was acquired by learning process. Learning process was a kind of process by which network parameters were adapted to the environment through continuous stimulation. In general, learning processes were classified as (i) Supervised learning, (ii) Unsupervised learning [6],[12] and (iii) Reinforced learning [12],[13]. The proposed BP algorithm was a kind of supervised learning. Where the network output was compared with the target which was assigned by an external system. Then the network parameters were adapted (tuned) to reach the target [6], [7], [12].

3.1   Learning with Back Propagation Algorithm

The Back Propagation algorithmwas also called as generalized delta rule. In it, error in the output layer was back propagated to earlier ones in order to update the current input-hidden layer weights and hidden-output layer weights. By updating these weights, the network would learn to reach the target [7]. During learning process, The responses in the input layer was caused by the input , which in turn caused the response in the hidden layer, and then the response of hidden layer causes response in output layer. This response was compared with the target and the error was calculated. Now the algorithm propagated backwards to hidden layer forupdation of weights (updationin weights carried out based on rate of error changes in the output layer) in output layer, by this the error was minimized in the output [7]-[9]. Then the error was calculated in the error in the output and the new values were computed by its weights in the hidden layer. In the algorithm, the error was calculatedin the output the new values of weights were computed in each layer by backward movement to the input until the error was minimized in to a considerable value. Then the next input was selected and the same process was repeated.

3.2   Simulation Results of Back Propagation Algorithm in Feed Forward Network

The simulation results of Back Propagation algorithm were numerically analyzed and shown in table 1. The graphical representation of the simulation results were shown in figure 2.

Table 1. Simulation results of Back Propagation algorithm in Feed Forward Network for number of epochs

Epochs	Input vectors		Input-Hidden layer weights				Hidden-Output layer weights		Error
	I_1	I_2	V_{11}	V_{12}	V_{21}	V_{22}	W_1	W_2	
1	0.4	-0.7	0.1	0.4	-0.2	0.2	0.2	-0.5	0.13264
10	0.4	-0.7	0.0959	0.4266	-0.1927	0.1534	-0.041	-0.7267	0.0911
20	0.4	-0.7	0.1012	0.4584	-0.2021	0.0978	-0.2535	-0.9294	0.0613
30	0.4	-0.7	0.1110	0.4885	-0.2192	0.0452	-0.4184	-1.0904	0.0424
40	0.4	-0.7	01221	0.5153	-0.2387	-0.0019	-0.5485	-1.2192	0.0301
50	0.4	-0.7	0.1332	0.5388	-0.2580	-0.0429	-0.6528	-1.3235	0.0220
60	0.4	-0.7	0.1435	0.5591	-0.2761	-0.0785	-0.7378	-1.4093	0.0165
70	0.4	-0.7	0.1530	0.5768	-0.2927	-0.1094	-0.8083	-1.4808	0.0126
80	0.4	-0.7	0.1615	0.5921	-0.3076	-0.1362	-0.8675	-1.5412	0.0098
90	0.4	-0.7	0.1692	0.6055	-0.3211	-0.1597	-0.9179	-1.5928	0.0078
100	0.4	-0.7	0.1762	0.6174	-0.3333	-0.1804	-0.9614	-1.6375	0.0062
120	0.4	-0.7	0.1881	0.6371	-0.3541	-0.2149	-1.0322	-1.7105	0.0042
140	0.4	-0.7	0.1978	0.6529	-0.3712	-0.2426	-1.0874	-1.7678	0.0029
160	0.4	-0.7	0.2060	0.6658	-0.3854	-0.2651	-1.1316	-1.8137	0.0020
180	0.4	-0.7	0.2128	0.6764	-0.3974	-0.2837	-1.1677	-1.8513	0.0015
200	0.4	-0.7	0.2186	0.6853	-0.4075	-0.2993	-1.1976	-1.8824	0.0011
206	0.4	-0.7	0.2201	0.6877	-0.4102	-0.3035	-1.2055	-1.8908	0.0010

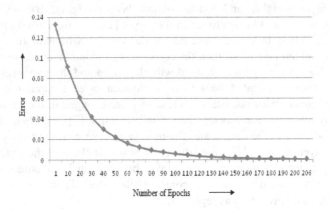

Fig. 2. Error Vs Number of epochs

The Back Propagation algorithm was very simple for implementation and also it had less computational complexity. But it was very slow in convergence [14], [15]. The simulation results, showed that, the target was achieved (expected output 0.1) after 206 epochs. It had 20 epochs to converge 0.02 (approximate) errors in order to reach the target. Particularly this case got worse when we deal the large network with difficult learning task [14]. Theconvergence speed of Back Propagation algorithm was improved by implementing the concept of Bats Echolocation system withinit. The network parameters were used to build the Feed Forward Network and the important parameters which were very essential to invoke the Back Propagation algorithm wre shown in table 2.

Table 2. Network parameters of Feed Forward Network with Back Propagation algorithm

Network parameters	Values
Number of Epochs	206
Number of neurons in input layer	2
Number of neurons in hidden layer	2
Number of neurons in output layer	1
Target	0.1
Input data	0.4,-0.7
Sigmoidal gain (α)	1
Learning rate coefficient (η)	0.6

4   Bats Echolocation System

Several animals in the world had the ability to navigate in the dark and locate the pray using sound waves, like cave swift lets, oil birds, cetaceans and bats. The ultrasonic sound bursts in the form of series of clicks was transmitted by Bats in 5 to 20ms duration at a rate of 10 Hz while searching for pray[16]. Once target of interest was detected, bats entered in to the approach mode. In this mode, the distance between the bats and pray was reduced. So the pulse repetition rates increased by bats up to 200 Hz in order to avoid overlapping of pulses which would create great loss in resolution [16], [18]. To get the information about angular position of pray, the bats used their sonar broadcast and their ears towards different targets. But this was not enough to identify the too close objects in the same direction. So, to increase their angular resolution the bats used sound pressure level difference and time difference of arrival between their ears[16]-[19]. By using this technique the bats were able to identify the too close objects with angular resolution of $\pm 2°$ to $\pm 5°$. This paper proposed the Bats Echolocation System to improve the convergence speed of Back Propagation algorithm.

4.1 Implementation of Bats Echolocation System Based Back Propagation Algorithm in Feed Forward Network

In conventional Back Propagation Algorithm, the error was calculated based on the response in the output layer. But in Bats Echolocation based Back Propagation algorithm, the error was calculated with the response which was achieved by adding and subtracting the bats coefficient with the actual response in the output layer based on the target in order to increase the error convergence rate. This concept was achieved by the bats Echolocation system where ultrasonic sound bursts were initially transmitted by bats to identify the prey and its location judged by the difference in the repetition pulses. This behavior of bats was used in Back Propagation algorithm by adding and subtracting Bats coefficient with response of the output layer in order to got the output response which was closer to the target. This would leads to faster convergence in the Back propagation algorithm. The computational steps involved in the Bats Echolocation system based BP Algorithm, used to train the Feed Forward Network was as follows:

Step 1: The input and output patterns with respect to their maximum values were normalized.
Input pattern were represented as $\{I\}_{I(l*1)}$ and
Output pattern were represented as $\{O\}_{O(n*1)}$.

Step 2: The total number of hidden layer neurons were assumed in between $l < m < 21$.

Step 3: $[V]^0 = $ [input-hidden layer weights]
$[W]0 = $ [hidden-output layer weights] were assumed.
Assume $[\Delta V]0 = [\Delta W]0 = [0]$ (1)
The weights were initialized to small random values,$\lambda = 1$ and threshold values set to be zero.

Step 4: For the training, one set of input and output were selected from the pattern. by using linear activation function,
$\{O\}I(l*1) = \{I\}_{I(l*1)}$

Step 5: The inputs of the hidden layer were computed by

$$\{I\}_{H(m*1)} = [V]^T_{(m*l)} \{O\}_{I(l*1)} \tag{2}$$

Step 6: The hidden layer outputs were evaluated by the sigmoidal function as

$$\{O\}_H = \left\{ \frac{i}{\left(1 + e^{-I_{Hi}}\right)} \right\}_{m*1} \tag{3}$$

Step 7: The input of the output layer were computed from,

$$\{I\}_{O\,(n*1)} = [W]^{T}_{\,(n*m)}\,\{O\}_{H\,(m*1)} \tag{4}$$

Step 8: The output layer outputs are evaluated by sigmoidal function as

$$\{O\}_{OI} = \left\{ \frac{i}{\left(1 + e^{-I_{Oj}}\right)} \right\} \tag{5}$$

Step 9: by adding and subtracting Bats coefficient O_{BC} with $\{O\}_{OI}$

$$\{O\}_{O1} = \{O\}_{OI} + O_{BC}$$
$$\{O\}_{O2} = \{O\}_{OI} - O_{BC} \text{ were computed}$$
If $\{O\}_{O1} - \{O\}_{O2} < 0$, then $\{O\}_{O} - \{O\}_{O1}$
If $\{O\}_{O2} - \{O\}_{O1} < 0$, then $\{O\}_{O} - \{O\}_{O2}$

Step 10: The error for the ith training set was calculated as

$$E^P = \frac{\sqrt{\sum \left(T_j - O_{Oj}\right)^2}}{n} \tag{6}$$

Step 11: $\{d\}$ was calculated as

$$\{d\} = \left\{ (T_k - O_{Ok})O_{Ok}\,(1 - O_{Ok}) \right\}_{n*1} \tag{7}$$

Step 12: $[Y]$ matrix was calculated from

$$[Y]_{(m*n)} = \{O\}_{H\,(m*1)} \langle d \rangle_{1*n} \tag{8}$$

Step 13: change in weights were evaluated from

$$[\Delta W]^{t+1}_{(m*n)} = \alpha\,[\Delta W]^{t}_{(m*n)} + \eta [Y]_{(m*n)} \tag{9}$$

Step 14: $\{e\}$, $\{d\}$ and $\{X\}$ were evaluated by

$$\{e\}_{(m*1)} = [W]_{(m*n)}\{d\}_{(n*1)} \tag{10}$$

$$\{d^*\} = \left\{ \begin{array}{c} \vdots \\ e_i(O_{Hi})(1-O_{Hi}) \\ \vdots \end{array} \right\}_{m*1} \tag{11}$$

$$[X]_{(l*m)} = \{O\}_{I(l*1)} \langle d^* \rangle_{(1*m)} = \{I\}_{I(l*1)} \langle d^* \rangle_{(1*m)} \tag{12}$$

Step 15: change in weightswere obtained by

$$[\Delta V]^{t+1}_{(1*m)} = \alpha [\Delta V]^{t}_{(1*m)} + \eta [X]_{(1*m)} \tag{13}$$

Step 16: The new weights were obtained by

$$[V]t+1 = [V]t + [\Delta V] t+1 \tag{14}$$

$$[W]t+1 = [W]t + [\Delta W] t+1 \tag{15}$$

Step 17: steps 4-16 were repeated till the error was reduced to tolerance value.

4.2 Simulation Results of Bats Echolocation System Based Back Propagation Algorithm in Feed Forward Network

Using the algorithm described above, the simulation results were obtained as shown in table 3. The graphical representations of simulation results were shown in figure 3. The parameters needed for Feed Forward Network with Bats Echolocation system based BP Algorithm were similar to Back propagation algorithm with Bats coefficient is 0.27.

Table 3. Simulation results of Bats Echolocation system based BP Algorithm in Feed Forward Network for number of epochs

Ep oc hs	Input vectors		Input-Hidden layer weights				Hidden-Output layer weights		Error
	I_1	I_2	V_{11}	V_{12}	V_{21}	V_{22}	W_1	W_2	
1	0.4	-0.7	0.1	0.4	-0.2	0.2	0.2	-0.5	0.0089
10	0.4	-0.7	0.0987	0.4038	-0.1977	0.1933	0.1596	-0.5375	0.0070
20	0.4	-0.7	0.0977	0.4077	-0.1959	0.1865	0.1215	-0.5730	0.0055
30	0.4	-0.7	0.0970	0.4112	-0.1948	0.1804	0.0892	-0.6032	0.0043
40	0.4	-0.7	0.0967	0.4143	-0.1941	0.1749	0.0616	-0.6292	0.0034
50	0.4	-0.7	0.0964	0.4171	-0.1938	0.1700	0.0377	-0.6516	0.0027
60	0.4	-0.7	0.0963	0.4196	-0.1936	0.1656	0.0170	-0.6712	0.0022
70	0.4	-0.7	0.0963	0.4219	-0.1935	0.1617	-0.0012	-0.6883	0.0018
80	0.4	-0.7	0.0963	0.4239	-0.1936	0.1581	-0.0171	-0.7034	0.0015
90	0.4	-0.7	0.0964	0.4258	-0.1937	0.1549	-0.0311	-0.7167	0.0012
97	0.4	-0.7	0.0964	0.4269	-0.1938	0.1528	-0.0400	-0.7251	0.0010

The simulation results obtained from the Feed Forward Network with Bats Echolocation system based BP Algorithm showedthat the target was achieved in 97 epochs itself where as Back Propagation algorithm took 206 epochs and also this algorithm took only 10 epochs to converge with 0.015 error to reach the target. The convergence speed of the Bats Echolocation system based BP algorithm was 47.8 percent better than Back Propagation algorithm. The proper selection of the Bats coefficient (it depended on the error rate of the network) would increase the convergence speed of the Bats Echolocation system based BP algorithm.

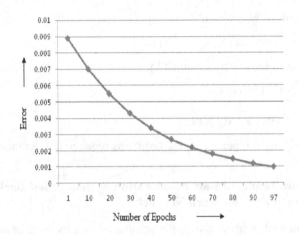

Fig. 3. Error Vs Number of epochs

5   Conclusion

The effectiveness of Bats Echolocation system based Back Propagation algorithm was proved by simulation results over the conventional Back Propagation algorithm for Feed Forward Network. The simulation results revealed that convergence speed of Bats Echolocation system based Back Propagation algorithm was 47.8 times better than conventional Back Propagation algorithm.

References

1. Kennedy, J., Eberhart, R.: Particle Swarm Optimization. In: Proceeding of IEEE International Conference on Neural Network, Perth, Australia, vol. IV, pp. 1942–1948 (November 1995)
2. Bautista, J., Pereira, J.: Ant algorithms for a time and space constrained assembly line balancing problem. European Journal of Operational Research 177(3) (2007)
3. Bonabeau, E., Dorigo, M., Theraulaz, G.: Swarm Intelligence: From Natural to Artificial Systems. Oxford University Press, New York (1999)
4. Bonabeau, E., Theraulaz, G., Deneubourg, J.-L., Aron, S., Camazine, S.: Self-organization in social insects. Trends in Ecology and Evolution 12(5), 188–193 (1997)

5. Blackwell, T., Branke, J.: Multi-swarms, exclusion and anti-convergence in dynamic environments. IEEE Transactions on Evolutionary Computation 10(4), 459–472 (2006)
6. Hush, D., Horne, B.: Progress in supervised Neural Networks. IEEE Signal Processing Magazine, 8–39 (January 1993)
7. HetchtNielsen, R.: Theory of the back propagation neural networks. In: Proceeding of International Joint Conference in Neural Networks, vol. I, pp. 593–611 (June 1989)
8. Fahlman, S.E.: An empirical study of learning speed in back propagation networks. Technical Report, CMU-CS-88-162 (1988)
9. Silva, F.M., Almeida, L.B.: Acceleration techniques for the back propagation algorithm. In: Neural Networks EURASIP Workshop, Sesim (1990)
10. Hornik, K., Stinchcombe, M., White, H.: Multilayer feed forward networks are universal approximators. Neural Networks 2(5), 359–366 (1989)
11. Anderson, J.A., Rosenfeld, E.: Neurocomputing: Foundations of Research Cambridge, p. 9. The MIT Press, MA (1988)
12. Schalkoff, R.J.: Artificial Neural Networks. McGraw-Hill International Editions (1997)
13. Moriarty, D.E., Miikkulainen, R.: Efficient reinforcement learning through symbiotic evolution. Machine Learning, 22–32 (1996)
14. Otair, M.A., Salameh, W.A.: Speeding up Back Propagation Neural Networks. In: Proceedings of the 2005 Informing Science and IT Education Joint Conference (2005)
15. Jin-Wei, W., Jia-Li, Z., Si-Wei, L., Zhen, H.: The Improvement of Back Propagation Neural Network Learning Algorithm. In: Proceedings of ICSP 2000, Department of Computer Science Technology, Northern Jiaotong University Beijing, PR China (2000)
16. Airas, M.: Echolocation in bats. In Spatial sound perception and reproduction (April 2003)
17. Grossetete, A., Moss, C.F.: Target flutter rate discrimination by bats using frequency-modulated sonar sounds: Behavior and signal processing models. Journal of Acoustical Society of America 103(4), 2167–2175 (1997)
18. Kalko, E.K.V., Schnitzler, H.U.: The echolocation and hunting behaviour of daubenton's bat, Myotisemarginatus. Behavioral Ecology and Sociobiology 24, 225–238 (1989)
19. Lawrence, B.D., Simmons, J.A.: Echolocation in bats: the external ear and perception of the vertical positions of targets. Science 218, 481–483 (1982)

An Efficient Spatial Scalable Video Encoder Based on DWT

Saoussen Cheikhrouhou[1], Yousra Ben Jemaa[2], Mohamed Ali Ben Ayed[1], and Nouri Masmoudi[1]

[1] Laboratory of Electronics and Information Technology
Sfax National School of Engineering, BP W 3038, Sfax, Tunisia
[2] Signal and System Unit, ENIT, Tunisia
nouri.masmoudi@enis.rnu.tn

Abstract. Multimedia applications reach a dramatic increase in nowadays life. Therefore, video coding scalability is more and more desirable. Spatial scalability allows the adaptation of the bit-stream to end users as well as varying terminal capabilities. This paper presents a new Discrete Wavelet Transform (DWT) based coding scheme, which offers spatial scalability from one hand and ensures a simple hardware implementation compared to the other predictive scalable compression techniques from the other. Experimental results have shown that our new compression scheme offers also good compression efficiency. Indeed, it achieves up to 61\% of bit-rate saving for Common Intermediate Format (CIF) sequences using lossy compression and up to 57\% using lossless compression compared with the Motion JPEG2000 standard and 64\% compared with a DWT-coder based on Embedded Zero tree Wavelet (EZW) entropy encoder.

Keywords: video conference, temporal redundancy, spatial scalability, discrete wavelet transform dwt, tier1 and tier2 entropy coding.

1 Introduction

Advances in video coding technology are enabling an increasing number of video applications ranging from multimedia messaging, and video conferencing to standard and high-definition TV broadcasting. Furthermore, video content is delivered to a variety of decoding devices with heterogeneous display and computational capabilities [1]. In these heterogeneous environments, flexible adaptation of once-encoded content is desirable. This heterogeneity warranted the development of many scalable video codecs [2]. Our main interest is to study naturally scalable video codecs based mainly on DWT compression since the DWT-based video coding has been a fast-expanding research field in the last years[3] [4]. This paper is organized as follows. Section 2 enumerates some limitations of the existing DWT-based scalable video codecs. In section 3, we present the details of our new DWT-based video codec. The experimental results and analysis of the results are presented in section 4. Finally, concluding remarks and future work are presented in section 5.

V.V. Das, E. Ariwa, and S.B. Rahayu (Eds.): SPIT 2011, LNICST 62, pp. 70–75, 2012.
© Institute for Computer Sciences, Social Informatics and Telecommunications Engineering 2012

2   Limitation of the Existing Scalable Video Compression Schemes

There are multitudes of related research in the field of scalable video coding. The Joint Video Team of the ITU-T VCEG and the ISO/IEC MPEG has recently standardized the Scalable Video Coding extension (SVC) of the H.264/MPEG-4 Advanced Video Coding (AVC) standard (H.264/AVC) which is the latest amendment for this successful specification.SVC enables the transmission and decoding of partial bit streams to provide video services with lower temporal or spatial resolutions or reduced fidelity. SVC is highly efficient but this efficiency is on the expense of the coding/decoding compression complexity scheme since the scalability function in the SVC is added to another compression scheme, the AVC, which is initially very complex [2].

Thus, we have focused our studies on DWT-based video codecs which offer naturally scalable compression schemes.The DWT is used to ensure scalability in the JPEG 2000 image compression standard. Embedded ZeroTree Wavelet "EZW" [5] and Set Partitioning in Hierarchical Trees "SPIHT" [6] are DWT-based entropy coders. In this context, many video compression schemes are proposed in the literature. These methods, however, suffer from a low performance problem since they do not include any motion compensation feedback loop [7].A commonly used alternative in the literature is to extend the 2D DWT-based algorithms to the time component [8].In [9], three dimensional DWT are used with the "SPIHT" coding, extended into the temporal dimension, and used without motion compensation.

We should notice that, many other approaches have combined the three dimensional DWT and motion compensation [10] [11] [12].However, temporal filtering always produces very clear disturbing ghosting artifacts, also called the drift error, especially in the low-pass temporal subband.

It is clear that the challenge now is how to exploit the motion within the spatio-temporal transform.It is interesting to mention that none of the related work cited above is based on a pre existing standardized compression scheme. On the other side, Shih-Ta Hsiang [13], has proposed a new intra-frame dyadic spatial scalable coding framework based on a subband/wavelet coding approach for MPEG-4 AVC/H.264 scalable video coding (SVC). It is the first attempt in the literature to join the subband filter banks with the traditional macroblock and DCT based video coding system.

Although this approach has achieved a bit rate saving of 13.75\%, compared with the standard H.264/MPEG-4 SVC, it is considered to be very complex since it is based originally on a complex compression scheme.As mentioned before, the two most annoying problems are even the drift error due to three dimensional wavelet transform or the high complexity of the compression scheme. Thus, we propose to ameliorate the Motion JPEG2000 which is a relatively simple DWT-based video compression standard. Indeed, it compresses frames independently each other without utilizing any interframe redundancy. Consequently, in this paper, we propose to code not the original frame but the difference between the source (I) frame and the reconstructed (I-1) frame along with the heritage of many features from Motion JPEG2000 compression schemes especially its entropy coder Tier1 and Tier2 [14] [15].

3   Structure of the Proposed DWT-Based Video Codec

This video compression scheme (Fig. 1) aims to offer spatial scalable coding. Its main idea is to eliminate the temporal redundancy by coding only the first frame of the video followed by the residuals resulting from the differential frames. In fact, these residual frames are obtained by subtracting the source image (I) from the reconstructed (I-1) which is generated by the encoder similar to the one in the decoder side by undergoing the inverse quantization and inverse DWT on the close loop path. The DWT will ensure the spatial scalability and thus, adapt the encoded stream to the corresponding terminal display. Indeed, the same transform as that used in Motion JPEG2000 is used to process the first image of the video. For the residual frames, a new transform and a new disposition of the different sub-bands for the multi-resolution analysis are used and are detailed in [16].The wavelet coefficients obtained will be quantized based on a perceptual quantization matrix "DWTune"[17] which differs from the quantization method of the Motion JPEG2000 standard. Finally, the quantized DWT coefficients will be entropy coded similar to the Motion JPEG 2000's entropy coder based on Tier1 and Tier2 [14] [15].The same process will be conducted for the luminance (Y) and the two chrominance components (Cb, Cr) for each frame.

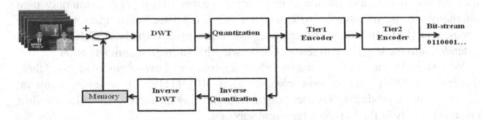

Fig. 1. Structure of the proposed DWT-based video codec

4   Experimental Results and Discussion

4.1   Performances Comparison with the Motion JPEG2000 Standard

During these experiments, the rate controller block for the Motion JPEG2000 standard is disabled in order to ensure more objective comparison and inhibit any other interference.Experimental results show that the proposed approach presents a very clear improvement in terms of PSNR for the sequences akiyo and silent compared to the Motion JPEG2000 standard. Nevertheless, we note that the PSNR of the foreman sequence obtained by the new codec is lower than that obtained by the standard Motion JPEG2000. This proves that our proposed encoder goes along with video conference scenes more than any other content. In fact, Akiyo and Silent sequences present less motion than Foreman sequence.Figures 2, 3 and 4 depict the comparative results for the different video sequences in a lossy mode. Table 1 shows the comparative results for the different video sequences in lossless mode.

Table 1. Bit Rate Comparaison Between Motion Jpeg2000 And The Proposed Codec For The Lossless Compression For The Sequences Foreman.Cif And Akiyo.Cif And News.Cif

Sequence	Bit rate (Kbits/s)	
	Motion JPEG2000	Proposed codec
Akiyo.cif	10479,33	4488,66
News.cif	12038,66	6534,66
Foreman.cif	13626,66	14043,33

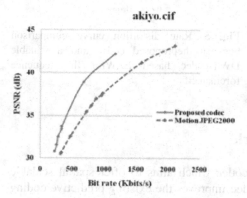

Fig. 2. Rate distortion curve comparison betweenMotion JPEG2000 and the proposed codec for thesequence akiyo.cif

Fig. 3. Rate distortion curve comparison betweenMotion JPEG2000 and the proposed codec for the sequence news.cif

4.2 Performances Comparison with a DWT-Coder Based EZW

On the other hand, our proposed coding scheme is compared with a DWT-codec based on EZW [16]. It is very similar to our new coder with one major difference: it uses the EZW as an entropy coder instead of the Tier1 and Tier2.

As shown by figure 5, the proposed video codec outperforms the EZW-based coder. In fact, more than 50\% reduction in bit rate has been obtained for the same PSNR.

Table 2. Bit rate comparaison between the proposed codec and a scalable dwt-codec based on ezw for the lossless compression for the sequence foreman.cif

Codec	Bit rate (Kbits/s)
EZW-based codec	23203,30
Proposed codec	14043,33

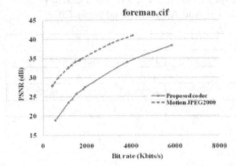
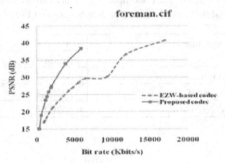

Fig. 4. Rate distortion curve comparison between Motion JPEG2000 and the proposed codec for the sequence foreman.cif

Fig. 5. Rate distortion curve comparison between theproposed codec and a scalable DWT-codec based EZWfor the sequence foreman.cif

5   Conclusion and Future Work

In this paper, a new DWT-based video codec which aims to offer spatial scalable coding is proposed. In fact, this video codec improves the existing predictive coding standards by reducing dramatically the complexity of implementation.The new compression scheme induces a significant improvement for objective quality tests compared to the Motion JPEG2000 standard. Indeed, it achieves up to 61\% of bit-rate saving for Common Intermediate Format (CIF) sequences using lossy compression and up to 57\% using lossless compression compared with the Motion JPEG2000 standard. Furthermore, the proposed video codec outperforms the EZW-based coder by more than 50\% in terms of bit rate reduction.As perspectives, we propose to add an inter-frequency prediction block exploiting the inter-band redundancies. Likewise, better results are promised by implementing an Adaptive Loop Filter (ALF) in order to reduce the gap between the source frame (I) and the reconstructed frame (I-1) from the statistical point of view prior to the determination of the residual frame.

References

1. Man, H., Kossentini, F., Smith, M.J.T.: A family of efficient and channel error resilient wavelet/subband image coders. IEEE Transactions on Circuits and Systems for Video Technology 9(1), 95–108 (1999)
2. Schwarz, H., Marpe, D., Wiegand, T.: Overview of the scalable video coding extension of the h.264/avc standard. IEEE Transactions on Circuits and Systems for Video Technology 17(9), 1103–1120 (2007)
3. Marpe, D., Cycon, H.L.: Very low bit-rate video coding using wavelet-based techniques. IEEE Transactions on Circuits and Systems for Video Technology 9(1), 85–94 (1999)

4. Shen, K., Delp, E.J.: Wavelet based rate scalable video compression. IEEE Transactions on Circuits and Systems for Video Technology 9(1), 109–122 (1999)
5. Shapiro, J.M.: Embedded image coding using zerotrees of wavelets coefficients. IEEE Transactions on Signal Processing 41(12), 3445–3462 (1993)
6. Said, A., Pearlman, W.A.: A new, fast, and efficient image codec based on set partitioning in hierarchical trees. IEEE Transactions on Circuits and Systems for Video Technology 6(3), 243–250 (1996)
7. Choupani, R., Wong, S., Tolun, M.R.: A drift-reduced hierarchical wavelet coding scheme for scalable video transmissions. In: First International Conference on Advances in Multimedia, pp. 68–73 (2009)
8. Karlsson, G., Vetterli, M.: Three-dimensional subband coding of video. In: Internatioanl Conference on Acoustics Speech and Signal Processing, vol. 2, pp. 1100–1103 (April 1988)
9. Kim, B.J., Pearlman, W.A.: An embedded wavelet video coder using three-dimensional set partitioning in hierarchical trees (spiht). In: IEEE Data Compression Conference, pp. 251–260 (March 1997)
10. Asbun, E., Salama, P., Shen, K., Delp, E.J.: Very low bit rate wavelet-based scalable video compression. In: International Conference on Image Processing, vol. 3, pp. 948–952 (1998)
11. Marpe, D., Cycon, H.L.: Very low bit-rate video coding using wavelet-based techniques. IEEE Transactions on Circuits and Systems for Video Technology 9(1), 85–94 (1999)
12. Mehrseresht, N., Taubman, D.: An efficient content-adaptive motion-compensated 3-d dwt with enhanced spatial and temporal scalability. IEEE Transactions on Image Processing 15(6), 1397–1412 (2006)
13. Hsiang, S.: Intra-frame dyadic spatial scalable coding based on a subband/wavelet framework for mpeg-4 avc/h.264 scalable video coding. In: IEEE International Conference on Image Processing, pp. 73–76 (November 2007)
14. Iso/iec, jtc1/sc29 and wg1, jpeg 2000 final committee draft version 1.0 fcd15444-1, jpeg 2000 image coding system (March 2000)
15. Taubman, D., Ordentlich, E., Weinberger, M., Seroussi, G., Ueno, I., Ono, F.: Embedded bloc coding in jpeg 2000. In: IEEE International Conference on Image Processing, vol. 2, pp. 33–36 (September 2000)
16. Cheikhrouhou, S., Ben Jemaa, Y., Samet, A., Ben Ayed, M.A., Masmoudi, N.: Toward an optimal residual frame coding for dwt based video codec. In: IEEE International Conference on Electronics and Systems, pp. 876–879 (December 2009)
17. Ben Ayed, M.A., Samet, A., Loulou, M., Masmoudi, N.: Dwtune: a technique for visual optimization of dwt quantization matrix for continuous still images. In: ISSPIT 2002, marroco (2002)

Establishing Global Ontology
by Matching and Merging

Susan F. Ellakwa[1], Passent M. El-Kafrawy[2],
Mohamed Amin[2], and El Sayed ElAzhary[1]

[1] Central Lab for Agricultural Expert Systems (CLAES), ARC, Giza, Egypt
fisalsusan@yahoo.com, sayed@claes.sci.eg
[2] Mathematics and CS Department, Faculty of Science, Menoufia University, Egypt
passentmk@gmail.com

Abstract. Ontology is used for communication between people and organizations by providing a common terminology over a domain. This work presents a system of establishing global ontology from existing ontologies. Establishing ontology from scratch is hard and expensive. This work establishes ontology by matching and merging existing ontologies. Ontologies can be matched and merged to produce a single integrated ontology. Integrated ontology has consistent and coherent information rather than using multiple ontologies, which may be heterogeneous and inconsistent. Heterogeneity between different ontologies in the same domain is the primary obstacle for interoperation between systems. Heterogeneity leads to the absence of a standard terminology for any given domain that may cause problems when an agent, service, or application uses information from two different ontologies. Integrating ontologies is a very important process to enable applications, agents and services to communicate and understand each other.

Keywords: Artificial Intelligence, Knowledge Representation, Ontology, Matching, Merging.

1 Introduction

The term ontology refers to a wide range of formal representations, including taxonomies, hierarchical terminology vocabularies or detailed logical theories describing a domain [1]. One commonly used definition is based on the original use of the term in philosophy, where ontology is a systematic account of Existence. For artificial intelligence (AI) systems, what "exists" is that what can be represented [2]. "An Ontology is a formal, explicit specification of a shared conceptualization [3]. *Conceptualization* refers to an abstract model of some phenomenon in the world by having identified the relevant concepts of that phenomenon. *Explicit* means that the type of concepts used, and the constraints on their use, are explicitly defined. *Formal* refers to the fact that the ontology should be machine-readable. *Shared* reflects the notion that an ontology captures consensual knowledge, that is, it is not private of some individual, but accepted by a group. This paper presents a system to establish

V.V. Das, E. Ariwa, and S.B. Rahayu (Eds.): SPIT 2011, LNICST 62, pp. 76–83, 2012.
© Institute for Computer Sciences, Social Informatics and Telecommunications Engineering 2012

dynamic global ontology in specific domain from existing ontologies by matching and merging. Global ontology allows users to avoid querying the local ontologies one by one, and to obtain a result from them just by querying a global ontology. Global ontology has standard and shared terminology. It is consistent and coherent. It has no redundancy. There are a large variety of languages for expressing ontologies. Fortunately, most of these languages share the same kinds of entities, often with different names but comparable interpretations. Source ontologies in the proposed system have been expressed in XML language. Ontology language in the proposed system deal with the following kinds of entities: Concepts, properties, and values according to Common KADS Methodology [4]. In this system, we introduce an ontology matching and merging problem and propose a solution technique called Multi-Matching and Merging Algorithm (MMMA) (table 1.a,1.b), which uses a multi search algorithm to find the correspondences between entities in the input ontologies and to merge these ontologies. An important feature of this technique is that it benefits from existing individual match methods and combines their results to provide enhanced ontology matching. This system proposes a new technique in matching; it performs three iterations, each iteration manipulates one type of entities. The first iteration manipulates the concepts, while the second iteration handles the properties, and the third iteration handles the values. In each iteration, the system uses hybrid matchers which are combined in a sequential composition. This multilevel decomposition reduces redundancy alignments and speeds up the system's final alignments. The system uses different kinds of matchers to cover different kinds of alignments to reduce redundant entities of resulted merged ontology. Using variety of matchers solve the string and language matching problem. This system extracts entities in two ontologies which have same string or same meaning. The system uses thresholds to reduce useless alignments and involves user to confirm alignments. This system can merge the ontologies in hierarchy structure. This paper consists of five sections; first section is introduction, second section shows definition for matching and merging, third section introduces related work, fourth section presents the proposed system and fifth section is conclusion and future work.

2   Ontology Matching and Merging

Matching is the process of finding relationships or correspondences between entities of different ontologies. Alignment is a set of correspondences between two or more (in case of multiple matching) ontologies. The alignment is the output of the matching.

The matching process can be seen as a function f which, from a pair of ontologies to match o and o', an input alignment A, a set of parameters p and a set of oracles and resources r, returns an alignment A' between these ontologies: A'=f (o, o', A, p, r)

The proposed system uses the matching techniques; string-based technique [5] (String equality method, Substring method and Prefix/suffix method) and language-based technique [5] (tokenization method, Stopword elimination method and WordNet [6] method) as blocks on which a matching solution is built. Each of these methods is called a matcher. Each matcher gives its similarity. Once the similarity between ontology entities is available, the alignment remains to be computed.

Merging is a first natural use of ontology matching, it consists of obtaining a new ontology o'' from two matched ontologies o and o' so that the matched entities in o and o' are related by the alignment. Merging can be presented as the following operator: Merge (o, o', A') = o''

When the ontologies are expressed in the same language, merging often involves putting the ontologies together and generating bridge or articulation axioms. Merging does not usually require a total alignment: those entities which have no corresponding entity in the other ontology will remain unchanged in the merged ontology. Ontology merging is especially used when it is necessary to carry out reasoning involving several ontologies. It is also used when editing ontologies in order to create ontologies tailored for a particular application.

3   Related Work

Several tools exist for ontology establishment, ranging from fully manual to fully automated. Many of the semi-automated ontology merging and matching tools are listed in this section. PROMPT [7] begins with the linguistic-similarity matches for the initial comparison, but generates a list of suggestions for the user based on linguistic and structural knowledge and then points the user to possible effects of these changes. OntoMorph [8] provides a powerful rule language for specifying mappings, and facilitates ontology merging and the rapid generation of knowledge-base translators. It combines two powerful mechanisms for knowledge-base transformations such as syntactic rewriting and semantic rewriting. Syntactic rewriting is done through pattern-directed rewrite rules for sentence-level transformation based on pattern matching. Semantic rewriting is done through semantic models and logical inference.

4   System for Establishing Global Ontology

This section presents a new semi-automated system for establishing global ontology by merging pre-existing ontologies. This technique consists of two main components: matching process and merging process.

4.1   System Structure

The structure of the two main components, matching process and merging process, are shown in fig.1. Ontology matching tries to identify similarities between heterogeneous ontologies and to automatically create suitable mappings for merging. Matching is an essential aspect of merging and could also be used to initiate merging. Ontology merging is the process that will create a single global coherent ontology by unifying two or more existing ontologies.

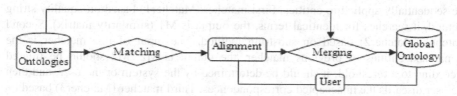

Fig. 1. Framework for establishing global ontology

4.2   System Components

As mentioned before the system is composed of two main components: matching process is shown in fig.2 and merging process is shown in fig.3

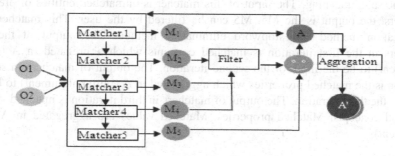

Fig. 2. Matching process

Matching Process: The previous matchers are the building blocks on which the matching solution is built. Once the similarities between ontology entities are available, the alignment can be computed. Matching strategy is built by organizing the combination matchers, aggregating the results of matchers (basic methods) in order to compute the compound similarity between entities, involving users in the system and extracting the alignments from the resulting similarity.

Matcher composition is a global method to combine local methods (or basic matchers) in order to define the matching algorithm. A way of composing matchers in the proposed system uses sequential composition. In sequential composition, combination of matchers is more classically used to improve an alignment. In the proposed system, it consists of five matchers; each matcher extracts additional alignment without redundancy, the input of each matcher depends on the output of the previous matcher. The inputs of the system are two ontologies o1, o2 and initial alignment A. Entities of source ontology are concepts C, properties P and values V. The input of a matcher is the matched entities of the last matcher and the unmatched entities. The matched entities are to be aggregated in final alignment A'. This cycle performs three times; first iteration for extracting matched concepts, second iteration for extracting matched properties of the matched concepts and third iteration for extracting matched values of the matched properties. In each iteration, all matchers are sequentially applied to entities. First matcher (Matcher1) based on equality string method, it searches for identical terms, the output is M1 (similarity matrix). Second matcher (Matcher2) based on substring method. The input of this matcher is the unmatched entities of previous matcher, the output is M2. M2 should be filtered according to a threshold, it should be determined by the system or the user, and then the user discards the unaccepted correspondences. Third matcher (Matcher3) based on prefix method. The input of this matcher is unmatched entities of previous matchers, the output is the M3. M3 should be filtered according to the pre-determined threshold, and then the user discards the unaccepted correspondences. Fourth matcher (Matcher4) is based on suffix method. The input of this matcher is unmatched entities of previous matchers, the output is the M4. M4 should be filtered according to the pre-determined threshold, and then the user discards the unaccepted correspondences. Fifth matcher (Matcher5) based on WordNet method; it searches for terms which have the same meaning. The input of this matcher is unmatched entities of previous matchers, the output is the M5. M5 can be filtered by the user. This matcher uses tokenization method and stopword elimination method. The output of the five matchers in the first iteration is matched concepts which aggregated in A (initial alignment) to be the input of the second iteration. The output of matchers in second iteration is the matched properties which aggregated in A (initial alignment) to be the input of the third iteration. The output of matchers in third iteration is matched values. Matched concepts, Matched properties, Matched values are aggregated in A'(final alignment).

Merging Process: Consists of five operations (fig.3): *Determine unmatched entities, Select concepts, Merge hierarchical classification, Collect properties and Collect values.* The input of this process is the source ontologies o1, o2 besides the output of the matching process A'. The output is the merged ontology o'. *Determine unmatched entities* operation identifies unmatched concepts C' and its properties P' and its values V'. *Select concepts* operation selects a concept from its correspondence. *Merge hierarchical classification* determines concept location in the hierarchy structure. *Collect properties* determines properties of the selected concept from its correspondence. *Collect values* determines values of a property from its correspondence. The output of the system is the merged ontology of two source ontologies o1, o2. The system can merge more than two ontologies by matching and merging two ontologies and the output can be matched and merged with the another ontology, and so on.

In this paper we studied different matching techniques; we presented a novel framework to support matching and merging. We discussed different matchers to ontology matching. To obtain better quality matching results, we extended the multi-matching strategy by introducing a multi-level matching strategy, each matcher introduces new alignment based on its method and the system collects these alignments. This system can manipulate small and large ontologies, it manipulates ontologies in hierarchy structure, and the merged ontology has no redundancy and no inconsistency.

Table 1.a. Matching part of Multi-Matching and Merging Algorithm (MMMA)

/*Matching*/	
/*Matching Concepts*/	Repeat
List of Ontologies [o1, o2]	Mat = Mat + 1
List of concepts (LC1) of o1 [c1, c2… cn]	Repeat
List of concepts (LC2) of o2 [c1, c2… cm]	A3 = [H	Tail]
Number of Matchers = 5	H = [(C1, P1), (C2, P2)]
List of concept alignments is A	Get VI of P1/*VI: list of values of P1 */
A = [ ], L = n, W = m, Mat = 0	Get VJ of P2/*VJ:list of values of P2 */
Repeat	Repeat
Mat = Mat + 1, I = 0	VI = [HVI| T1], VJ = [HVJ	T2]
Repeat	IF match (HVI, HVJ) THEN {A4 =
I = I + 1	[[(C1,P1, HVI), (C2, P2, HVJ)]	
Select concept cI of o1	A4],
J = 0	VI = [T1], VJ = [T2]}
K = 0	Else VJ = [T2]
Repeat	IF VJ = [ ] THEN VI = [T1]
J= J + 1	Until VI = [ ]
Select concept cJ of o2	A3 = [Tail]
IF match (cI, cJ)	Until A3 = [ ]
THEN {A= [(cI, cJ|A],K=1, L = L – 1,	Until Mat = 5
W = W – 1,	A'=append (A, A2, A4)
LC1 = SUBSTRACT (LC1, cI),	**/*Matching Function*/**
LC2 = Subtract (LC2, cJ)}	A, B, C, X, Yare strings
Until J = W OR K = 1	$\sigma1(X,Y) = (2 * |X|) / (|X|+|Y|)$
Until I = L	$\sigma2(X,Y)= |C| / (|X|+|Y|)$ /*C is the longest
Until mat=5	common string for X and Y */
/*Matching Properties*/	T is the threshold of similarity
A1 = A, A2 = [ ], Mat = 0	Function: match(X, Y)
Repeat	{Case Mat=1: /* matcher1 is executed*/
Mat=Mat+1	IF $\sigma1$ (X, Y) = 1
Repeat	THEN match(X, Y) = TRUE
A1 = [H	Tail]	Case Mat=2: /* matcher2 is executed*/
H = (c1, c2)	IF (X⊂Y AND σ 1(X, Y) >= T AND
Get PI of c1	correspondence of X, Y is accepted from
/* PI is the list of properties of c1 from o1*/	user)
Get PJ of c2	THEN match(X, Y) = TRUE
/* PJ is the list of properties of c2 from o2*/	Case Mat =3: /* matcher3 is executed*/
Repeat	IF (X= conc(C, A) AND Y= conc(C, B),
PI = [HPI| T1]	$\sigma2$(X, Y) >= T, AND correspondence of X,
PJ = [HPJ	T2]	Y is accepted from user)
If match (HPI, HPJ)	THEN match(X, Y) = TRUE
T HEN {A2 = [[(c1, HPI), (c2, HPJ)]	Case Mat =4: /* matcher4 is executed*/
A2], PI = [T1], PJ = [T2]}	IF (X= conc(A, C) AND Y= conc (B, C),
Else PJ = [T2]	$\sigma2$(X, Y) >= T, AND correspondence of X,
IF PJ = [ ] THEN PI = [T1]	Y is accepted from user)
Until PI = [ ]	THEN match(X, Y) = TRUE
A1 = [Tail]	Case Mat =5: /* matcher5 is executed*/
Until A1 = [ ]	IF (WordNet(X, Y), correspondence of X, Y
Until mat=5	is accepted from user)
/*Matching Values*/	THEN match(X, Y) = TRUE }
A3 = A2, A4 = [ ], Mat = 0	/* WordNet(X, Y) means that X and Y are
	synonyms */

Table 1.b. Merging part of Multi-Matching and Merging Algorithm (MMMA)

/ * **Merging** */	IF (I > 0 AND Z < > C)
List of concept alignments is A	THEN {LCPV = [(C, LPV) I LCPV]
List of property alignments is A2	LPV = [ ], I = 0}
LC = [ ], LC2= [ ]	X = P1
/* **Select Concepts** */	IF (I > 0 AND X < > P)
Repeat	THEN OldV = V
A = [(C1, C2)ITail], LC = [C1, LC],	IF (I = 0 OR X < > P)
A = [Tail]	THEN {Get Val of P2 from o2,
Until A = [ ]	SUBSTRACT (V, V2, VY),V = VY}
Selected Concepts = LC	IF (I > 0 AND X = P)
/* **Unmatched Concepts** */	THEN {SUBSTRACT (V, V2, VY),
Get concepts C O1 of o1	V = VY}
Get concepts C O2 of o2	IF (I > 0 AND X < > P)
Unmatched concepts of o1 (UCO1) =	THEN {Get Val of P from o1, A6 = Val of
CO1 DIFFERENCE LC	P ∪ OldV, LPV = [(P, A6) I LPV]}
Repeat	I = I + 1, P = P1, A4 = [Tail]
A = [(C1, C2)ITail],	IF A4 = [ ]
LC2 = [C2, LC2],	THEN{Get Val of P from o1, A6 = Val of
A = [Tail]	P ∪ V, LPV = [(P, A6) I LPV]}
Until A = [ ]	C = C1
Matched Concepts of o2 = LC2	Until A4 = [ ]
Unmatched concepts of o2 (UCO2) =	/* **Merge Hierarchical Classification***/
CO2 DIFFERENCE LC2	Two ontologies o1, o2
C' = UCO1 ∪ UCO2	Offspring of o1 is Co1
/* **Collect Properties** */	/* Co1 is a list of concepts */
I = 0, LCP = [ ]	Offspring of o2 is Co2
Repeat	A is the alignment concepts of o1, o2
A2 = [[(C1, P1), (C2, P2)] I Tail]	/* A is a list of matched concepts */
X = C1	Co11 = Co1
IF I > 0 AND X < > C	Repeat
THEN OldP= P/*P set of properties of c2*/	Co1 = [H I Tail]
IF I = 0 OR X < > C	IF match (H, C)
THEN {Get P of C2 from o2,	/*H is a concept in o1,C is a concept in o2
SUBSTRACT (P, P2, PY), P = PY}	*/
IF (I > 0 AND X = C)	THEN {Get Offspring OC of C,
THEN {SUBSTRACT (P, P2, PY),	Link OC with H,
P = PY}	Co11 = [Co11I OC],
IF (I > 0 AND X < > C) THEN {Get Prop	Co2 = Subtract(C, Co2),
of C from o1, A5 = Prop of C ∪OldP}	Co2 = Subtract (OC, Co2)}
I = I + 1, C = C1, A2 = [Tail]	Co1 = [Tail]
IF A2 = [ ]	Until Co1 = [ ] OR Co2 = [ ]
THEN {Get Prop of C from o1,	Repeat
A5 = Prop of C∪P,	Co11 = [H I Tail]
LCP = [(C, A5) I LCP] }	IF match (H, C)
Until A2 = [ ]	/* H, C are two concepts in Co11 of o1*/
/* **Collect Values** */	THEN {Get Offspring OC of C,
LCPV = [ ], LPV = [ ], I = 0	Link OC with H,
Repeat	[Tail] = Subtract(C, [Tail])}
A4 = [[(C1, P1, V1), (C2, P2, V2)] I Tail]	Co11 = [Tail]
Z = C1	Until Co11 = [ ]

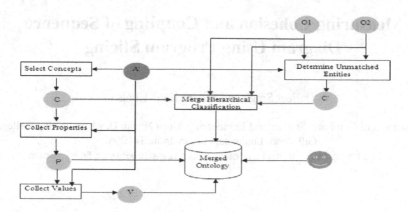

Fig. 3. Merging process

5   Conclusions and Future Work

This paper presents a system to build a global ontology from different ontologies in the same domain. This work presents Multi-Matching and Merging Algorithm (MMMA) for reusing and sharing existing ontologies by matching and merging. We are working on implementation currently now. The system will have graphical user interface to allow browsing to get ontologies to be matched and merged. It allows user to confirm alignments, edits source ontologies, edits merged ontology and gives information about ontologies and their entities.

References

1. Noy, N., Klein, M.: Ontotlogy Evolution: Not the Same as Schema Evolution. Knowledge and Information Systems 6(4), 428–440 (2004); also available as SMI technical report SMI-2002-0926
2. Gruber, T.R.: A Translation Approach to Portable Ontology Specifications. Knowledge Acquisition 5(2), 199–220 (1993)
3. Borst, P., Akkermans, H., Top, J.: Engineering ontologies. International Journal of Human-Computer Studies 46, 365–406 (1997)
4. Wielinga, B.J.: Expertise Model Definition Document. University of Amsterdam (1994)
5. Euzenat, J., Shvaiko, P.: Ontology matching, 333 p. Springer, Heidelberg (2007)
6. Pedersen, T., Patwardhan, S., Patwardhan, S.: WordNet:Similarity – Measuring the Relatedness of Concepts. In: Proc. of 19th National Conf. on AI, San Jose (2004)
7. Noy, N., Musen, M.: PROMPT: Algorithm and Tool for Automated Ontology Merging and Alignment. In: Proc. of 17th National Conference on Artificial Intelligence (AAAI), Austin, Texas, pp. 450–455 (2000)
8. Chalupsky, H.: Ontomorph: A Translation System for Symbolic Knowledge. Principles of Knowledge Representation and Reasoning (2000)

Measuring Cohesion and Coupling of Sequence Diagram Using Program Slicing

Daljeet Singh and Sunint Kaur Khalsa

Department of Computer Science and Engineering, Guru Nanak Dev Engineering College
Gill Road, Ludhiana, Punjab, India 141006
diljitsingh007@gmail.com, sunintkaur@rediffmail.com

Abstract. This paper proposes a technique for the measurement of Cohesion and Coupling of Sequence Diagram using the Program Slicing. The sequence diagram contains the dynamic information of the Object Oriented system. In this work Sequence Dependency Graph (SDG) is generated from the states and scenarios of Sequence diagram. The SDG is then dynamically sliced taking various aspects into consideration. These slices can then be used to measure Cohesion and Coupling. The novelty of this approach is the direct measurement of Cohesion and Coupling of an object oriented system from Sequence diagram.

Keywords: Sequence Diagram, Program Slicing, Cohesion, Coupling.

1 Introduction

The UML Sequence Diagram refers to time dependent sequences of interactions between objects. They show the sequence of the messages. A Sequence Diagram has two dimensions: the vertical dimension represents time, and the horizontal dimension represents various instances. In UML, a message is a request for a service from one UML actor to another. In fig. 1 the Sequence Diagram is showing the various transactions of messages from one object to another object. The figure shows three objects A, B and C which are having flow of messages in various directions. Each message is given a message number for ease of understanding which is discussed in the following sections.

2 Related Work

The slicing of the Sequence diagram has been proposed in [1] and coupling metrics are analyzed in [2]. Pam Green [3] in there paper proposes a report that provides an overview of slice-based software metrics.Philip Samuel [4]presents a new approach and a novel methodology for test case generation based on UML sequence diagrams using Sequence Dependence Graph.

V.V. Das, E. Ariwa, and S.B. Rahayu (Eds.): SPIT 2011, LNICST 62, pp. 84–88, 2012.

3   Recognition of Scenarios and States of Sequence Diagram and Sequence Dependency Graph

A sample Sequence Diagram (SD) is shown in figure 1. It is converted into Sequence Dependency Graph (SDG) using various states and scenarios as shown in table 1.

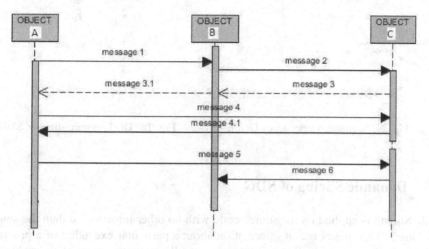

Fig. 1. Sample Sequence Diagram

Table 1. Scenarios with start and end state

Scenario 1	Scenario 2	Scenario 3
Start state x	Start state x	Start state x
S1 : (m1,a,b)	S5 :(m4,a,c)	S7 : (m5,a,c)
S2 : (m2 ,b ,c)	S6 : (m4.1,c,a)	S8 : (m6,c,b)
S3 : (m3 ,c ,b)		
S4 : (m3.1 ,b, a)		
End state x	End state x	End state z

The message requests the service from one UML actor to another. In table 1 different scenario were taken according to the sequence diagram in fig 1. If the starting and ending object of the scenario is A then the Start State and End State is X. If the starting and ending object of the scenario is B then the Start State and End State is Z and if the starting and ending object of the scenario is C then the Start State and End State is Y. The SD is then transformed into SDG by using the scenarios and states.This approach refers the one proposed in [5]. States S1, S2, S3, S4, S5, S6, S7, S8 represents the transition from one object to another as shown in figure 2a.

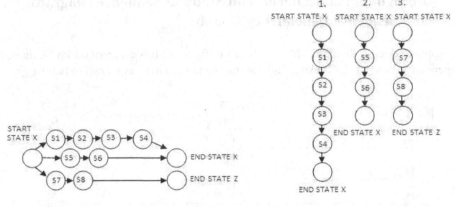

Fig. 2a. Sequence Dependency Graph   **Fig. 2b.** The Dynamic slices of SDG

4   Dynamic Slicing of SDG

Static Slicing is applied on the source code with no other information than the source code itself. This makes use of information about a particular execution of a program. A dynamic slice contains all statements that actually affect the value of a variable at a program point, for a particular execution of the program, rather than all statements that may have affected the value of a variable, at a program point, for any arbitrary execution of the program. Sequence diagrams shows the dynamic function and if we make the slices of the sequence dependencies by taking the criteria as the start and end state of the each scenario then in figure2(b) slice 1 , slice 2 , slice 3 is formulated from the fig 2(a) as the dynamic program slices of SDG. These slices can then be used to calculate cohesion and coupling in the coming sections.

5   Calculating Cohesion Using Slicing

This section details the calculation of Cohesion. There are three slices in figure 3 with their corresponding number of nodes as 4, 2, and 2 respectively. The total number of nodes by combining all the slices is called Module Size which is 8 as shown in fig 2b. The various terms used in the formulas are Size of slice (Common node in every slice), Number of slices (Total number of slices made), Min slice size (Number of nodes in the smallest slice), Max slice size (Number of nodes in the largest slice).

- Tightness is the number of nodes included in every slice compared to the number

$$\text{Tightness (M)} = \frac{|SL\,\text{int}|}{length(M)} = \frac{sizeofslice}{mod ulesize} = \frac{0}{8} = 0$$

- Coverage is a comparison of the length of the slices to the length of the module.

$$\text{Coverage (M)} = \frac{1}{V_\circ}\sum_{i=1}^{v_o}\frac{SL}{length(M)} = \frac{sumofslices}{(no.ofslices)\times(modulesize)} = \frac{8}{3\times8} = 0.33$$

- Min coverage is the ratio of the size of the smallest slice to the module size.

$$\text{Min coverage (M)} = \frac{1}{length(M)}\min i|SLi| = \frac{min\ slicesize}{modulesize} = \frac{2}{8} = 0.25$$

- Max coverage is the ratio of the size of the largest slice to the module size.

$$\text{Max coverage (M)} = \frac{1}{length(M)}\max i|SLi| = \frac{max\ slicesize}{modulesize} = \frac{4}{8} = 0.5$$

- Overlap is the average ratio of the number of the nodes in the intersection of all slices to the size of each slice.

$$\text{Overlap (M)}= \frac{1}{|V_\circ|}\sum_{i=1}^{|v_o|}\frac{|SL\ int|}{|SLi|} = \frac{\sum intersectionsize}{slicesize}\Big/ noofslices = \frac{0}{4}+\frac{0}{2}+\frac{0}{2}\Big/3 = \frac{0}{3}=0$$

6   Calculation of Slice Based Coupling of SDG

This section explains slice-based coupling metrics of the sequence dependency graph as in [6]. Worked examples are shown as under with calculations. The coupling between two functions f and g can be calculated as:

$$\text{Coupling (f, g)} = \frac{FF(f,g)\times length(f)+FF(g,f)\times length(g)}{length(f)\times length(g)}$$

Table 2. Intra Slice Coupling between slice 1 and slice 2

Module (G)	Module Size	Module (F)	Common Nodes	Total	
1	4	2	0	0	Coupling= $\frac{0+0}{6}$ = 0
2	2	1	0	0	

The slice based coupling is of two types: Inter slice Coupling and Intra Slice Coupling. Inter Slice Coupling is the coupling between the slices having different end states e.g. Slice 1 and Slice 3, Slice 2 and Slice 3. Intra Slice Coupling is the coupling between the slices having the same end state e.g. Slice 1 and Slice 2. The Final coupling is shown in table 2, 3 and 4.

Table 3. Inter Slice Coupling between slice 2 and slice 3

Module (G)	Module Size	Module (F)	Common Nodes	Total	
2	2	3	0	0	Coupling= $\frac{0+0}{4}$ = 0
3	2	2	0	0	

Table 4. Inter Slice Coupling between slice 1 and slice 3

Module (G)	Module Size	Module (F)	Common Nodes	Total
1	4	3	0	0
3	2	1	0	0

$$\text{Coupling} = \frac{0+0}{6} = 0$$

7   Conclusion

The method to calculate cohesion and coupling directly from the Sequence Diagram has been proposed in this paper. We are planning to extend this approach to other diagrams of UML to capture static and dynamic aspects of the system.

References

1. Noda, K., Kobayashi, T., Agusa, K.: Sequence Diagram Slicing, Grant-in-Aid or Scientific Research of MEXT Japan (2009)
2. Simon Allier, S., Vaucher, S., Dufour, B., Sahraoui, H.: Deriving Coupling Metrics from Call Graphs. Natural Sciences and Engineering Research Council of Canada (2010)
3. Green, P., Lane, P.C.R., Rainer, A., Scholz, S.: An Introduction to Slice-Based Cohesion and Coupling Metrics, Technical report no. 488 School of Computer Science, University of Hertfordshire (2009)
4. Samuel, P., Mall, R.: A Novel Test Case Design Technique Using Dynamic Slicing of UML Sequence Diagrams. e-Informatics Software Engineering Journal 2(1) (2008)
5. Sharma, M., Mall, R.: Automatic Test Case Generation from UML Models. In: 10th International Conference on Information Technology, pp. 196–201. IEEE Computer Society, Washington (2007)
6. Harman, M., Okuiawon, M., Sivagurunathan, B., Danicic, S.: Slice Based Measurement of Function Coupling. In: 18th International Software Quality Week (QW 1995), San Francisco, CA (1995)
7. Lallchandani, J.T., Mall, R.: Computation of dynamic slices for Object oriented concurrent programs. In: 12th Asia Pacific Software Engineering Conference, pp. 341–350. IEEE Computer Society, Taipei (2005)

DDoS Attack Detection through Flow Analysis and Traffic Modeling

J. Udhayan[1], T. Hamsapriya[2], and N.A. Vasanthi[3]

[1] Dr. NGP Institute of Technology, Kalapatti
[2] Information Technology, PSG College of Technology
[3] Information Technology, Park College of Engineering & Technology
Coimbatore, India
{udhayangodwin,hamsapriya.t,vasanti.au}@gmail.com

Abstract. DDoS attack is the formidable cyber warfare of 20th century. Lot of research has already been taking place to mitigate DDoS attack. However DDoS attack still remains a potential threat. This research work considers the model level solution. Having a proper model of the traffic flow will help the administration unit to closely monitor the unusual behavior of the traffic; it will also help to identify the flash crowd which is the occasional accumulation of legitimate traffic. Hence in this paper, the normal traffic behavior is modeled, with the help of that the abnormal traffic which is evident during the DDoS attack is detected. Then the methodology to do the flow specific detection to segregate attack flow from the normal flow is discussed. Finally the possibility to curb the attack from the various hops is discussed.

Keywords: DDoS, Zombie, Goodput, Throughput, Botnet, Flash Crowd.

1 Introduction

The DDoS attacks over the servers of SCO corporate Website, Estonia service, Blue Frog service, and against several prominent Web sites like Yahoo, eBay, Amazon have caused severe damage to the victim [1]. Apart from this, plenty of victims around the World, from petite commercial sites to government organizations one time or another have faced DDoS attack. The DDoS attack is performed with the intent to deplete the server resources and make it unavailable to the legitimate clients, therefore it involves dumping of chunk data over victim's resources from many compromised computers (zombies) or network of zombies (Botnet)[2]. Attacker performs two things before manipulating a DDoS attack. First the attacker sets up a master component in a networked entity. Once the master component is installed, then the attacker spreads out the agent component which will get itself installed in less or unsecured computers. Once the installation is over the agent component communicates back with the master. Now it is up to the attacker to pass on the command to the zombies through master. The activities that the zombie performs in favor of the attacker are hidden to the owner of that system. Once this has been done the attacker can command a devastating attack over a specific target by passing on the commands through the master component.

V.V. Das, E. Ariwa, and S.B. Rahayu (Eds.): SPIT 2011, LNICST 62, pp. 89–94, 2012.

2   Related Work

Nowadays any DDoS attack is devastating because of its ability to generate mammoth volume of traffic from the millions of zombies [2]. Therefore understanding the rate criterion behind the DDoS attack is essential to model the behavior of the DDoS traffic. Hence various DDoS attack rates are discussed as follows.

2.1   Moderate Rate Attack

Smart DDoS attackers usually masquerades the flood as a normal (legitimate) flow throughout the network to avoid the detection. Moreover the traffic is generated from the millions or billions of zombies, each zombie generates normal or less than normal rate traffic in a way that, it never floods the network bandwidth but when it reaches the victim it overloads it to stalemate condition. This attack cannot be mitigated without eliminating moderate amount of genuine flows, since it always maintains the rate between less than the normal to slightly over normal.

2.2   Other Rate Attack

Constant rate attack [4] usually generates steady traffic with the rate greater than the legitimate traffic. However this attack can be segregated from the normal flow because the rate at which the packets generated was always above the normal rate and it is almost constant. This attack usually floods the network bandwidth, thus gets filtered by various network packet filters. As the result it is rarely used nowadays. Increasing rate attack [4] starts from the lowest possible rate and keep on increasing. This attack aims to cripple the victim server bit slowly than constant rate attack by taking its time. However this mechanism exhibits steady increase in the rate which is unusual and easily detectable.Fluctuating rate attack [4] is hard to predict because it is normally meager rate and lacks continuation therefore it is not a potential threat.

3   Proposed Detection Model

In this section a DDoS defense framework is discussed which focuses on efficient detection and mitigation of various DDoS attacks real-time.

3.1   DDoS Premonition Strategy

Most of the cases backlogs of the traffic are cached in the server for monitoring. Making use of such backlog will always help improving the detection procedure. However a thorough knowledge on the history is necessary to precisely detecting the ongoing attack at its inception stage. For instance, College web server receives enormous hits while the results are published which is called as flash crowd [3]. However if no result is published and if the hits still goes up, then the traffic must be monitored for DDoS attack. This kind of knowledge on the history helps to adjudge the occasional raise in the legitimate traffic. However attackers still may fool the history based detection through imitating the normal behavior of the traffic and staging it on right occasion.Any server will have a processing limit on the incoming requests. Based on the processing need the administration would have chosen the server. Hence through analyzing the server the amount of traffic that environment generates can be admonished [5]. From our analysis any server will works fine and processes requests quickly and without any struggle until it receives 75% requests out of its processing capability. Hence the proposed DDoS premonition procedure works as follows. Consider the ability of server to process 75% requests out of its maximum processing capability without any juggle as Tolerance factor T_f. Now if the traffic arrives less than the Tolerance factor, it is no harm to the server. If the traffic starts to arrive more than the tolerance factor then it has to be monitored for the potential attack. Hence if the incoming packets/second i.e. throughput $T_i^* > T_f$ then the traffic is analyzed for the DDoS attack through triggering the attack confirmation procedure.

3.2   Attack Confirmation Procedure

Let $T_n(t)$ be the normal traffic, i.e. the total number of flows arriving at Target server in α time interval, Say the time interval $\alpha = \alpha_1, \alpha_2, \alpha_3, \ldots \alpha_n$ number of seconds. Assume that the DDoS attack is set off against the target machine at α_t which is inside the range of α, when the attack starts the normal traffic $T_n(t)$ so for will be increased to $T_n^*(t) > T_f$. The motive behind the attacker is to junk the packets beyond the processing capability of the server. Say the maximum request processing capability of the server is T_m then the attack is considered successful while it reaches $T_n^*(t) > T_m$. This is the point where the victim server collapses. Hence to avoid this, the DDoS monitoring has to be done instantly while $T_n^*(t) > T_f$.

Consider a random process { A(t),t = nΔ, n $\in$ N}, where Δ is a constant time interval, N is the set of positive integers, A(t) is a random variable and it is the aggregate throughput for incoming packets. A(t) is calculated during time interval {t - Δ, t} as follows:

$$A(t) = \sum_{i=1}^{CF} n_i, i = 1,2,3 \ldots CIF.$$ (1)

Here n_i represent total number of packet arrivals for a flow I in {t - Δ, t} and CIF represents cumulative incoming flow or total number of incoming flows.

Similarly the aggregate throughput for outgoing packets O(t) is calculated during time interval {t - Δ, t} as follows:

$$O(t) = \sum_{i=1}^{CF} n_i, i = 1,2,3 \ldots COF.$$ (2)

Here COF represents cumulative outgoing flow or total number of outgoing flows. However to confirm the attack the following equations are used

$$\frac{O(t)}{A(t)} \leq 0.90 \; thenalert \; the \; detection. \tag{3}$$

$$\frac{O(t)}{A(t)} \geq 0.90 \; thenitisharmless \; traffic. \tag{4}$$

Once the alert is raised this implies the possibility for attack flows amongst the flow. Following Flow specific detection is then used to segregate the DDoS flows.

3.3   Attack Mitigation Procedure

The goal is to detect the attack flows at various vantage points not only at the perimeter level. Therefore the characteristics of each and every flow are analyzed using goodput. Goodput is the application level throughput, i.e. the number of useful bits per unit of time, forwarded by the network from a certain source address to a certain destination, excluding protocol overhead and retransmitted data packetsGoodput is identified as appropriate method because the valid output or valid data doesn't flow or flows in insignificant proportions from the victim. Therefore the attack flow is detected using the following equation

$$\frac{Outgoinggoodputperflow}{IncomingThroughputperflow} \leq \varepsilon. \tag{5}$$

To detect the attack flow the goodput for each and every flow is calculated in shorter time window Δ because genuine flow always maintains healthy goodput rate. Hence if the goodput is low then that flow is decided as attack flow.Once the attack is confirmed not only the victim starts the filtering but it can alert the preceding hops through multicasting or broadcasting the attack flow details [6]. The preceding hop thus can filter the attack flows and also forward the alert to its preceding hop device. This will soothe the influx at victims end.

4   Result Analysis

To perform the analysis the backlog of moderate rate DDoS attack is chosen. Because this kind of attack is difficult to detect and even if it is detected it is even hard to segregate it from the legitimate traffic. Moreover if the mechanism can detect the moderate rate attack it can detect other attacks easily. After analyzing the traffic for more than a week using eqn (3) the normal traffic pattern is studied and the percentage of traffic received is graphed. It is tedious and unnecessary to present the result of various aspects of the analysis. Normally the overall traffic rate is 10000 pps (packets per second) and 20000 pps range. However 30000 pps mark is expected to happen during peak hours in the evening, happened in the afternoon for one day. Hence the graph for that particular day had been plotted and the result is given in fig.1.

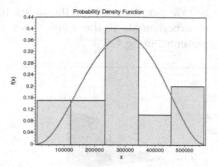

Fig. 1. Attack traffic distribution

According to eqn (4) the above shown traffic pattern has experienced DDoS attack. However the observed server cannot handle packets beyond 50000 pps at that time the drop has occurred tremendously and the packets range is distributed. However the packet range 30000 pps is at the peak which is something unusual. Moreover the flows at that peak region are analyzed for validity using eqn (5), but the result shows the annoying number of invalid flow as in fig.2.

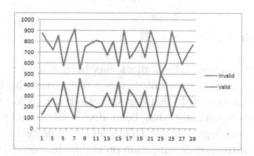

Fig. 2. Legitimate traffic against attack traffic

The traffic peak 30000 pps is analyzed with the step size of 1000 for validity using eqn (5). But majority of them had no valid data.

The simulation tool NS-2 is used to model the behavioral increase and the stability in attack traffic after it reaches 30000 pps range as in fig 3. It is because if the exponential increase in the drop after the 3000 pps.

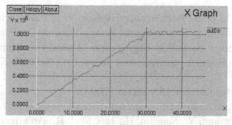

Fig. 3. Moderate Rate Constant slave set DDoS attack. Y axis 1 unit = 1 X 10^3 packets, X axis 1 unit = 1 *60 seconds.

However 20000 pps is 75% percent mark, if the influx traffic stays within this range no packet drop is experienced, if the range goes beyond then the drop intensifies. This result is presented in fig.4.

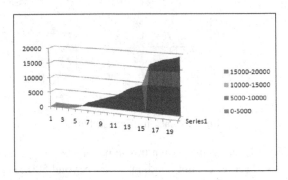

Fig. 4. Observation of packet drop above 75%

In the fig.4 the x-axis 1 is 76%, 2 is 77%, ... 20 is 95%. The drop almost starts at 76% and increases gradually. Hence the DDoS detection should be started at 75%.

5   Conclusion

In this paper various rates of DDoS attack has been discussed, then the method to model the legitimate traffic is presented, using that model the DDoS attack can be detected. The performance jiggle that happens when the packet rate consumes more than 75% of the sever capability has been discussed. Moreover a goodput based procedure to detect and segregate the DDoS attack is presented. Results shows that the DDoS attack confirmation & mitigation procedure handles DDoS effectively.

References

1. Zaroo, P.: A survey of DDoS attacks and some DDoS defense mechanisms. Advanced Information Assurance (CS 626)
2. Udhayan, J., Hamsapriya, T., Anitha, R.: Lightweight C&C based botnet detection using Aho-Corasick NFA. International Journal of Network Security & Its Applications (IJNSA) 2(4) (2010)
3. Cholda, P., Domzal, J., et al.: Performance Evaluation of P2P Caches: Flash-Crowd Case. In: Australian Telecommunication Networks & Applications Conference (2010)
4. Udhayan, J., Hamsapriya: Statistical Segregation Method to minimize the effects of false detection during DDoS attack. International Journal of Network Security 13(3), 152–160 (2011)
5. Best Practices for Performance in ISA Server (2006),
   http://technet.microsoft.com/en-us/library/bb794835.aspx
6. PyungKoo, P., HeeKyoung, Y., SangJin, H., JaeCheul, R.: An effective defense mechanism against DoS/DDoS attacks in flow-based routers. In: ACM International Conference on Advances in Mobile Computing and Multimedia, New York, USA (2010)

Integration Model for Multiple Types of Spatial and Non Spatial Databases

Mustafa Man[1], Mohd Shafry Mohd Rahim[2], Mohammad Zaidi Zakaria[3], and Wan Aezwani Wan Abu Bakar[4]

[1] Department of Computer Science, Faculty of Science & Technology, Universiti Malaysia Terengganu (UMT), 21030 Kuala Terengganu, Terengganu, Malaysia
mustafaman@umt.edu.my

[2] Department of Computer Graphics & Multimedia, Faculty of Computer Science & Information Systems, UniversitiTeknologi Malaysia (UTM), 81310 UTM Skudai, JohorBahru, Malaysia
shafry@utm.my

[3] Department of Fisheries Science, Faculty of Agrotechnology& Food Science, Universiti Malaysia Terengganu (UMT), 21030 Kuala Terengganu, Terengganu, Malaysia
zaidi@umt.edu.my

[4] Pre Sea Marine Engineering Department, Training & Education, Malaysian Maritime Academy (ALAM), 21030 Kuala Terengganu, Terengganu
aezwani@alam.edu.my

Abstract. Integration process of a various information in various database types requires a thorough understanding to carry out data extraction process in terms of its scheme and the structure. Due to this, a new model should be developed to resolve the integration process of this heterogeneous information in various database types and in various scattered and distributed locations. SIDIM is a model which covered processes such as pre-integration, scheme comparison, algorithm and intermediary software (middleware) development process and as well as post-integration. Emphasis are administered in algorithm development by using hybrid approach based on CLARANS approach's combination, abstract visualization and Catch Per Unit Effort (CPUE) to enable to achieve the required processed data or information in a quick, trusted and reliable manner. SIDIM will become a new engine to process information in various database types without changing any of the existing (legacy) organization system. To verify this model credibility, the case study related to fishing industry in Malaysia and artificial reef project are being made as a foundation for SIDIM efficiency testing.

Keywords: Spatial Information Databases Integration Model (SIDIM), Integration, Database, CLARANS Model, Abstract Visualization, Catch per Unit effort (CPUE).

1   Introduction

Recently, many research on information-seeking were more diverted on merging and unifying the spatial and non-spatial databases. The method of information searching is very much crucial among consumer. The consumer may requires information on some

V.V. Das, E. Ariwa, and S.B. Rahayu (Eds.): SPIT 2011, LNICST 62, pp. 95–101, 2012.

location and the updates on the change of that location are the major concern besides continuing to make a comparison through a visualization method which is based on map. The combination of both spatial and non spatial data is indeed important and crucial [1].Database technology is refers to wide range of approving technique for individual, industries or even government for daily operation. About 200 to 300 research papers were presented about similar issues in seminar, conference or even journal. Database technology and Database Management System are always in change. Online access becomes popular among users because it is faster and quicker. And today, data models for spatial and temporal data are most in need [2]. A broad spectrum of data is available through Web in distinct heterogeneous sources, stored under different formats and different type of databases and at different location or server: a specific database vendor format, length of data, image format, Step (CAD/CAM data), etc. Their integration is a very active field of research and development. To enable a specific tool to manipulate data coming from various sources especially different types of database format must be screened through a translation phase for example : the data (in the source format) needs to be mapped to the format expected by the application [3].There are several challenges that need to be faced in the process of merging and integrating the database from different sources and locations. It is required that these data, i.e., data from different sources to be in priority and can be selected prior to continuing the integration process. The objectives of our research;

1. How to produce one model to enable integration process various information data spatial and non spatial from various data base that the type different?
2. How the model that proposed afford to carry integration process various information data spatial and non spatial which differ the data base structure and in waiter environment which differ for environment on line?
3. How the proposed model can improve in terms of integration time?

Spatial Information Database Integration Model (SIDIM) is one of our prototypes which can integrate spatial and non-spatial data from various databases format and location. In principle, our model in this study is based on location coordinate technique in order to merge the predicted results based on location. The integration approach from various databases were used to give an impact analysis of information especially among spatial and non spatial data. The algorithm is developed using location integration technique in order to fasten the extraction process of spatial and non spatial data.

2   Related Work

Research on data integration is one of the most important element and is a 'hot issues' in the research of spatial data. Previous researches were more concentrated on developing a common form of information that is easier for the user to manage the database without consuming longer time. Integration is defined as a merger of various information from various sources that can provide benefits from the aspects of collection of the best information, less in processing time, resource conservation and data-sharing to various purposes. Information which will be combined or integrated must be staying in a state of analogous (uniform), but if the state of the information which will be consolidated is unequal, thus a form or modification process has to be executed on that particular information structure without damaging the original information.To place the information in various databases and at different or scattered location may contribute to difficulty in performing integration process. Thus a research to integrate 'every single piece into one' [5] is to be initiated as a kickoff start.Earlier integration method is called MULTIDATABASE in 1980. It is then followed by a mediator called as GARLIC. Later on, INFOSLEUTH is introduced. Then integration based on ontology which known as OBSERVER took place. After that, integration is based on peer to peer known as HYPERION. The journey lasts with web based integration method which is known as ACTIVE XML [6].The weaknesses of various databases in a common and typical organization can be prescribed as follows; High potential of incompleteness, inaccuracy of processed data, no control and monitoring of repeated data, conflict in task distribution to update data and inaccuracy of achieved data.

Interoperability is the key solution to solve the issue in integration. It allows heterogeneous data to communicate or interact from one application to another application by replying with the intended information. Interoperability is a complex feature because of the data source obtained is not in database format i.e. in email form or file attached only and external data source obtained through internet access in which the data is either unstructured or semi-structured which needs greater understanding in its semantic [7].

3   Research Methodology

SIDIM is an integrated spatial and non- spatial database designed to enable access and efficiency evaluation on artificial reefs based on the growth of phytoplankton and zooplankton for each dedicated artificial reefs area. The SIDIM is considered as a method, model or new idea to ensure the effectiveness and efficiency of artifcial reefs development project as a place for fish population and marine park.Since the high cost incurred to evaluate the development of artificial reef by hiring a special scuba task force, then the arrival of SIDIM is fit for the time. The SIDIM enables the integration of more than one database either within a similar or a different schemes. The research methodology consists of systematic process flow which is illustrated in figure 1.A few processes which have been subdivided that need to be taken prior to integration as in the 4 levels as depicted in figure 2 as follow:

i. Pre-integration: Process to assess database environment are used like Oracle example, MYSQL, ORACLE, and MS ACESSS and from other database.

ii. Scheme Comparison: Scheme comparison or structure for each this database is needed to facilitate integration process conducted. In the early stage, this process is made manually.

iii. Intermediary software development (middleware): an application shall be developed for integration process the data base workable.

iv. Post-Integration: Integration process assessment was being conducted from credibility process aspect and "interoperability".

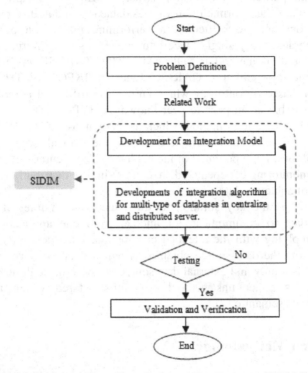

Fig. 1. Research Methodology Flow Chart for Integration Process of Multi Database Types

The focus of the research is on the algorithm development which enables multi database types in a distributed environment can be integrated into another database through online based on three-tier architecture.

A. Pre-integration Processes → 1st step

Like those mentioned previously, process of pre integration requires a study on present database environment. The researcher has already developed an application called ARPOS, funded under eSciencesFund (MOSTI) research grant in 2006 [8]. ARPOS database is in MYSQL and WiFISH database in MSSQL based. The system development uses .php software which is accessible through wired internet and wireless internet. Both of the databases are owned by different agencies namely Department of Fisheries (DOF) and LembagaKemajuanIkan Malaysia (LKIM) and were located in different location.

B. Scheme Comparison → 2nd step

The evaluation results of the two databases are found that the location (position) of artificial reef can be equal with the location of fish catches conducted. Due to this, the location based technique is a core and as a fundamental to determine the effectiveness development level of the artificial reef project development at a certain location and also within the timeline. The evaluation will be made to test for efficiency level and reliability of developed middleware in integrating process. The evaluation is carried out at the system user level. The process time is recorded to obtain and justify the information processing speed and interoperability is fulfilled.Other than processing time factor, evaluation of Catch Per Unit Effort or Ability Rate (CPUE) is also encountered in order to assess the whole project's efficiency for each dedicated artificial reef location. CPUE is defined as the level and efficiency degree between the catch in tan (t) and the ability of catch (frequency of fish catch) is being conducted [9],[10]. This method is based on variance and CPUE average CPUE. CPUE with non zero catch is modelled in the following formula:

$$\ln(CPUE)_{i,j,k,l} = \mu + \alpha_i + \beta_j + \gamma_k + t_l + \varepsilon_{i,j,k,l} \tag{1}$$

where μ is the variable, α_i is the year factor, β_j is the month factor, γ_k is the zone factor, t_l is the rate factor, and $\varepsilon_{i,j,k,l}$ is the random error component. Then the yearly value of CPUE is calculated in tone / total travelling trip that relates to statement below:

$$\ln(\frac{p}{1-p})_{i,j,k,l} = \mu' + \alpha'_i + \beta'_j + \gamma'_k + t'_l + \varepsilon'_{i,j,k,l} \tag{2}$$

Besides, if 'p' is defined as efficiency evaluator, then the yearly value of CPUE will relate to the calculation as follows:

$$CPUE_i = \exp(\mu + \alpha_i + 0.5\sigma^2)\exp(\mu' + \alpha'_i + 0.5\sigma'^2) \tag{3}$$

Assumption is made where an increase in CPUE trips with the catches can be influenced by the changes of boat's efficiency and the catch resources which represents either the fish catch is a success or otherwise. The result of integration process can determine the fish types with the catch area.

4   Testing and Evaluation

Evaluation and testing process for SIDIM model is conducted by comparing between manual data with a SIDIM processed data. The testing focused on the 'interoperability' feature in spatial and non-spatial data processing among the different types of database within a centralized server and compared with spatial and non-spatial data processing in a different types of database within a distributed server.The result obtained (as shown in Table 1) is compared either the two different servers (centralized or distributed) having a similar results or on the other way around. The comparison done will confirm whether each algorithm deployed at each particular steps has achieved the objectives or otherwise. Figure 2 shown the user interfaces of the system.

Table 1. An interoperability testing between different types of database in a centralized environment

Database Types	Types of Web Server	Interoperability Testing with Multi-types of Databases		
		MYSQL	ORACLE	MS Access
MYSQL	Apache	Yes	Yes	Yes
ORACLE	IIS	Yes	Yes	Yes
MS Access	IIS	Yes	Yes	Yes

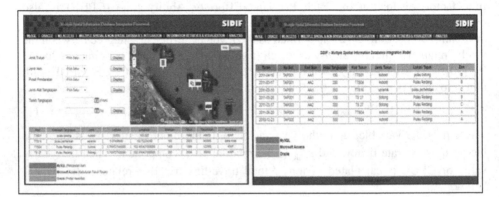

Fig. 2. System User Interfaces

5   Conclusions

SIDIM is a model design which is reusable in various types of database integration problem. The location based integration technique (longitude and latitude data) for artificial reef determination is very well conducted and can attain a satisfiable result. First they support data integration by allowing the resolution of different data representation conflicts. In addition, they permit the representation and use of query capabilities that may not be provided by any or some of the integrated GIS systems. As a result, we also tackle the problem of tools integration and extension. We hope that this tool could be extended to other domain as a solution for multiple types of database integration.

References

1. Ougouti, N.S., Belbachir, H., Amghar, Y., Benharkat, N.A.: Integration of Heterogeneous Data Sources. Journal of Applied Sciences 10(29), 2923–2928 (2010)
2. Elmasri, R., Navathe, S.: Fundamental of Database System, 5th edn. Addison Wesley (2006) ISBN: 0321369572
3. Abitebouly, S., Cluety, S., Milo, T., Mogilevskyz, P., Siméony, J., Zoharz, S.S.: Tools for Data Translation and Integration. Bulletin of the IEEE Computer Society Technical Committee on Data Engineering (1999)

4. Parent, C., Spaccapietra, S.: Issues and approaches of database integration. CACM 41(5), 166–178 (1998)
5. Ismail, W., Joseph, K.S.: Future IT trends for GIS/Spatial Information Management. Scientific Research and Essay 5(10), 1025–1032 (2010)
6. Patrick, Z., Klaus, R.: Three decades of data integration-All problems solved? In: IFIP Congress Topical Sessions 2004, pp. 3–12 (2004)
7. Kim, J., Peng, Y., Ivezic, N., Shin, J.: An Optimization Approach for Semantic-based XML Schema Matching. International Journal of Trade, Economics and Finance 2(1), 2010-023X (2011)
8. Mustafa, M., Yazid, M.S.M., Maizura, M.N., Khalid, S.: GIS spatial data visualization tools for artificial reefs distribution. In: The 3rd International Conference on Mathematics and Statistics (ICoMS-3) Proceeding 2008, pp. 25–38 (2008)
9. Raymond, T.N., Jiawei, H.: CLARANS: A Method for clustering objects for Spatial Data Mining. IEEE Transactions on Knowledge and Data Engineering 14(5), 1003–1015 (2002)
10. Stephans, A., MacCall, A.: A multispecies approach to sub setting logbook data for purposes of estimating CPUE. Journal of Fisheries Research, 299–310 (2004)

Access Control Based on Location and Time

Suresh Limkar[1], Nivedita Kadam[1], and Rakesh Kumar Jha[2]

[1] Department of Computer Engineering, GHRCEM, Pune, India
[2] Department of Electronics and Communication Engineering, SVNIT Surat, India
{sureshlimkar,Jharakesh.45,nivedita.kkadam}@gmail.com

Abstract. We propose an access control model that works like three factor authentication for getting access to our system. This system takes time and location into account to specify access control policies. We also discuss implementation techniques for location and time based policy specifications and the integration of these policies in standalone applications. This model enhances current security applications granting access to sensible information and privileges to execute orders only to entities that are in a trusted location with predefined time. Moreover this system authenticate authorized user but also time and location of the authorized user in both way i.e through GSM & GPS. The declarative nature of the model facilitates the analysis of policies and the evaluation of access requests: we present one case-study for clear understanding. This paper shows how computer and network security can be substantially improved through a new form of authentication based on geodetic location parameter received from GPS/ GSM along with the constraint of time.

Keywords: Cryptography, Encryption, Location based security, GPS, GSM, Biometric.

1 Introduction

We are moving towards an age of ubiquitous computing where location information will be an integral part of many applications. Denning, MacDoran [1] and other researchers [2], [3], [4], [5] have described how the use of location information can make applications more secure. Few examples will help to motivate our work. In a military application, if a computer containing top secret information is placed in a public place, then the computer should automatically become inaccessible. For instance, a user should be able to control or fire a missile from specific high security locations only. Verifying the location information and time parameter in addition to the checks that are performed by traditional methods of authentication and access control will improve the security of the underlying application.In this paper we propose one such formal model that is suitable for military applications. This paper shows how computer and network security can be substantially improved through a new form of authentication based on geodetic location and time. Location-based authentication has the effect of grounding cyberspace in the physical world so that the physical locations of network entities can be reliably determined.We illustrate how

V.V. Das, E. Ariwa, and S.B. Rahayu (Eds.): SPIT 2011, LNICST 62, pp. 102–107, 2012.
© Institute for Computer Sciences, Social Informatics and Telecommunications Engineering 2012

location parameter received from GPS (Global Positioning System) and GSM (Global System for Mobile Communication) impacts to enhances current security applications granting access to sensible information and privileges to execute orders only to entities that are in a trusted location with predefined time. Finally, we show how this location information can be used to determine whether a subject has access to a given system or not. The rest of the paper is organized as follows. We describe basic information related to our works in section 2, and introduce the proposed model with its operation and its security analysis in section 3. Then in section 4, we evaluate its efficiency and results in the form of screen shots of working model. We present a case study in 5. Section 6 concludes the paper.

2   Background History

Before moving towards the architecture of the proposed system first try to get the acquaintance with the basic technology that are used in this model.

A.GPS

The Global Positioning System (GPS) is a U.S. space based radio navigation system that provides reliable positioning, navigation, and timing services to civilian users on a continuous worldwide basis freely available to all. For anyone with a GPS receiver, the system will provide location and time. GPS provides accurate location and time information for an unlimited number of people in all weather, day and night, anywhere in the world. The GPS is made up of three parts: satellites orbiting the Earth; control and monitoring stations on Earth; and the GPS receivers owned by users. GPS satellites broadcast signals from space that are picked up and identified by GPS receivers. Each GPS receiver then provides three-dimensional location (latitude, longitude, and altitude) plus the time.

B. GSM

Global System for Mobile Communications, or GSM (originally from Group Special Mobile), is the world's most popular standard for mobile telephone systems. The GSM Association estimates that 80% of the global mobile market uses the standard.[6] GSM is used by over 1.5 billion people [7] across more than 212 countries and territories.[8] This ubiquity means that subscribers can use their phones throughout the world, enabled by international roaming arrangements between mobile network operators. GSM differs from its predecessor technologies in that both signaling and speech channels are digital, and thus GSM is considered a second generation (2G) mobile phone system. This also facilitates the wide-spread implementation of data communication applications into the system.Mobile positioning, which includes location based service that discloses the actual coordinates of a mobile phone bearer, is a technology used by telecommunication companies to approximate where a mobile phone, and thereby also its user (bearer), temporarily resides. The more properly applied term locating refers to the purpose rather than a positioning process. Such service is offered as an option of the class of location-based services (LBS). [9] The technology of locating is based on measuring power levels and antenna patterns and uses the concept that a mobile phone always communicates wirelessly with one of the closest base stations, so if you know which base station the phone communicates with, you know that the phone is close to the respective base station. GSM localization is the use of multilateration to determine the location of GSM mobile phones, usually with the intent to locate the user.

C. Biometric
[10] It consists of methods for uniquely recognizing humans based upon one or more intrinsic physical or behavioral traits. In computer science, in particular, biometrics is used as a form of identity access management and access control. It is also used to identify individuals in groups that are under surveillance.

Here in this model we are using two location based services to get the location of the object i.e. through GSM or GPS. Intention behind using two locations based services just because both have their own advantages and disadvantages.

3   Need of Location Based Security

Information security fundamentally depends on the ability to authenticate users and control access to resources. Existing user authentication mechanisms are based on information the user knows (e.g., password or PIN), possession of a device (e.g., access token or crypto-card), or information derived from a personal characteristic (biometrics). None of these methods are foolproof. Passwords and PINs are often vulnerable to guessing, interception, or brute force search. Devices can be stolen. Cryptographic systems and one-time password schemes can fail even when the algorithms are strong. Typically, their security reduces to that of PINs or passwords, which are used to control access to keys stored in files or activation of hardware tokens. Biometrics can be vulnerable to interception and replay. Geodetic location, as calculated from a location signature, adds a fourth and new dimension to user authentication and access control without changing the existing security mechanism. It can be used to determine whether a person is attempting to log in from an approved location, e.g., a user's office building or home. If a user is mobile, then the set of authorized locations could be a broad geographic region (e.g., city, state, country). In that case, the login location serves to identify the place of login as well as to authenticate it. If unauthorized activity is detected, system will not allow him to access it.Authentication through geodetic location has many benefits. It can be performed continuously so that a connection cannot be hijacked, for example, if a user forgets to logout or leaves the premises without logging out. It can be transparent to the user. Unlike most other types of authentication information, a user's location can serve as a common authenticator for all systems the user accesses.These features make location-based authentication a good technique to use in conjunction with single log-on. A further benefit of geodetic-derived location signatures is that they provide a mechanism for implementing an electronic notary function. The notary could attach a location signature to a document as proof that the document existed at a particular location and instant in time.

4   System Architecture

The scheme aims to develop an architecture that will provide access control system based on location and time obtained by GPS /GSM. The scenario of the proposed approach is presented in fig.1. There are two phases: administrator and end user phase. First, before end user want to get access to the system she has to register herself with the system. Administrator will do the registration. Below are the detailed functions of the administrator and end user.

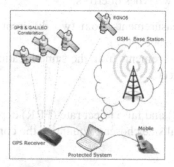

Fig. 1. System Architecture

A. Administrator
First every user needs to register with the administrator by providing its details like username, password, biometric identification, mobile number, and its location from which he would to access this system.

B. End User
One the end user completes its registration, then and only then he can access the system, otherwise he won't. Steps involved in authentication:

1. First end user need to enter his username password.
2. Once the first step is authenticated then next screen appears is to enter biometric credential.
3. Once the biometric credential of the end user is authenticated then next screen appears to enter pass code received on end users mobile. Passcode consist of alphanumeric message that end user need to enter in the text box.
4. Once the passcode is authenticated then it prompts for location check either through GSM or GPS
5. If user selects the GSM then mobile connected with end users system automatically send the users location info in the form of cell area, and get authenticate itself.
6. If user selects the GPS then GPS receiver connected with end user system automatically sends the GPS parameter i.e latitude, longitude, time and authenticates it.
7. While trying to provide location check either through GSM or GPS it automatically authenticate the user time too.

5   Security Analysis

The security analysis of a protocol is complicated as there are no standard metrics to precisely quantify the subject of security. To judge the performance and security of the proposed system, we developed an attack model. An attack model should provide possible failure modes due to the availability of the system. Furthermore, an attack model defines all possible attacks that might threaten the system. Whether a given systems is secure or not can depend dramatically on the attack model is considered.

Proposed system makes two types of errors:

a) FAR: Mistaking the measurements from two different locations to be from the same location, called false accept;

b) FRR: Mistaking the measurements from the same location to be from two different locations, called false reject.

Both false accept rate (FAR) and false reject rate (FRR) depend on the accuracy of the receiver and the grid interval size chosen to quantize the continuous location features.

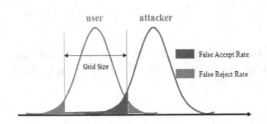

Fig. 2. False Accept and False Reject Ratio

Fig. 3. Pune Based Test Location

These two types of errors can be traded off against each other by varying the grid interval size. Ideally, both low FAR and low FRR are desired. Practically, a more secure system aims for low FAR at the expense of high FRR, while a more convenient system aims for low FRR at the expense of high FAR. The desired interval size is highly dependent on the final application.

6   Conclusion and Future Work

A novel improved access control based on time and location based service model based on GPS and GSM is proposed and implemented to overwhelm the defect of traditional access control model. This scheme enhances current security applications granting access to sensible information and privileges to execute orders only to entities that are in a trusted location. However, the security of our improved scheme has a pre-condition that is the radio frequency signal (GPS signal) is secure, and an adversary could not capture the radio frequency signal. The proposed scheme can be extended to the other application domains, e.g., Employees can access sensitive data only inside a specified geographical area, an email can be decrypted only in predetermined locations, critical operations could be performed only inside a predetermined zone, and managers can analyze in real time the locations from which employees or customers are accessing the enterprise network on a geographical map (if privacy policy allows it), and attestation (proof) of position and contextual data (e.g. time) which could be included in the digital signature of an email, providing information on where and under what conditions the email was written.

References

1. Denning, D.E., MacDoran, P.F.: Location-Based Authentication: Grounding Cyberspace for Better Security. In: Proceedings of the Computer Fraud and Security. Elsevier Science Ltd. (February 1996)
2. Scott, L., Denning, D.: Location Based Encryption Technique and some of its Applications. In: Proceeding of ION NTM 2003 (2003)
3. Jarusombat, S., Kittitornkun, S.: Digital Signature on Mobile Devices based on Location. In: International Symposium on Communications and Information Technologies, ISCIT 2006, APOS, pp. 866–870 (2006)
4. Liao, H.C., Chao, Y.H.: A new data encryption algorithm based on the location of mobile users. Information Technology Journal 7(1) (2008) ISSN 1812-5638
5. Liao, H.C., Lee, P.C., Chao, Y.H., Chen, C.L.: A Location-Dependent Data Encryption Approach for Enhancing Mobile Information System Security. In: The 9th International Conference on Advanced Communication Technology (ICACT 2007), Phoenix Park, Korea, February 12-14, pp. 625–628 (2007)
6. Zhou, J., Alshamsi, A.: GSM World statistics. GSM Association (2010) (retrieved June 08, 2010)
7. GSM Technical Data, Cellular.co.za (retrieved August 30, 2010)
8. Two Billion GSM Customers Worldwide. 3G Americas (June 13, 2006) (retrieved January 08, 2007)
9. Wang, S., Min, J., Yi, B.K.: Location Based Services for Mobiles: Technologies and Standards. In: IEEE International Conference on Communication (ICC), Beijing, China (2008)
10. Ratha, N.K., Connell, J.H., Bolle, R.M.: Enhancing security and privacy in biometrics-based authentication systems. IBM Systems Journal 40, 614–634 (2001)
11. Qiu, D.: Security Analysis of Geoencryption: A Case Study Using Loran. In: Proceedings of the 20th International Technical Meeting of the Satellite Division of The Institute of Navigation, ION GNSS (2007)

The Mapping Algorithm of Triangular Vertex Chain Code from Thinned Binary Image

Lili A. Wulandhari, Habibollah Haron, and Roselina Sallehuddin

Department of Modeling and Industrial Computing
Faculty of Computer Science and Information Systems
Universiti Teknologi Malaysia
81310 UTM Skudai, Johor Bahru, Malaysia
lili.wulandhari@gmail.com, {habib,roselina}@utm.my

Abstract. Image representation has always been an important and interesting topic in image processing and pattern recognition. In 1999, Bribiesca introduced a new two dimensional chain code scheme called Vertex Chain Code (VCC). VCC is composed of three regular cells, namely rectangular, triangular, and hexagonal. This paper presents the mapping algorithm that covers one of the VCC cells, the Triangular VCC cell. The mapping algorithm consists of a cell-representation algorithm that represents a thinned binary image into triangular cells, and a transcribing algorithm that transcribes the cells into Vertex Chain Code. The algorithms have been tested and validated by using three thinned binary images: L-block, hexagon and pentagon. The results show that this algorithm is capable of visualizing and transcribing them into VCC; it can also be improved by testing on more thinned binary images.

Keywords: Vertex Chain Code, Triangular Cells, Thinned Binary Image.

1   Introduction

Image representation is an important component in image processing and pattern recognition. One of the ways to simply and efficiently represent an image is by using chain code [1]. The first use of chain code was introduced by Freeman in 1961 that is known as Freeman Chain Code (FCC) [2]. This code follows the contour counter–clockwise and keeps track of the direction as we go from one contour pixel to the next. The codes involve 4–connected and 8– connected paths. In the 8-connected FCC, each code can be considered as the angular direction, in multiples of 45^0, through which we must move to go from one contour pixel to the next. Freeman [3] states that, in general, a coding scheme for line structures must satisfy three objectives. The three objectives are somewhat in conflict with each other, and any code necessarily involves a compromise among them.Bribiesca [4] introduced the Vertex Chain Code (VCC) in 1999; it complied with the three objectives that Freeman proposed. Some important characteristic of the VCC are: (1) The VCC is invariant

V.V. Das, E. Ariwa, and S.B. Rahayu (Eds.): SPIT 2011, LNICST 62, pp. 108–113, 2012.
© Institute for Computer Sciences, Social Informatics and Telecommunications Engineering 2012

under translation and rotation, and optionally may be invariant under starting point and mirroring transformation. (2) Using the VCC it is possible to represent shapes composed of triangular, triangular, and hexagonal cells. (3) The chain elements represent real values not symbols such as other chain code; are part of the shape; indicate the number of cell vertices of the contour nodes; and may be operated for extracting interesting shape properties. (4) Using VCC it is possible to obtain relations between contours and the interior of the shape. An element of VCC indicates the number of cell vertices, which are in touch with the bounding contour of the shape in that element position. In the Vertex Chain Code, the boundaries or contours of any discrete shape composed of regular cells can be represented by chains. Therefore, these chains represent closed boundaries. The minimum perimeter of a closed boundary corresponds to the shape composed of only one cell. An element of a chain indicates the number of cell vertices, which are in touch with the bounding contour of the shape in that element position [4]. This paper presents two algorithms that are used to derive the triangular cells of VCC from a thinned binary image and to transcribe the cells into Vertex Chain Code. The algorithms are tested and validated using three thinned binary images: L-block, hexagon, and pentagon.

2 The Mapping Algorithm of Triangular -VCC

2.1 The Cell-Representation Algorithm

Triangular cell is one of the basic cells in digital geometry. The structure of the triangular cell is much more complicated than rectangular one [5]. The triangular elements have alternating orientation; hence, the arrangement of peripheral elements will vary accordingly.As the previous explanation, triangular cell is more complicated than the rectangular one. It is not difficult to represent a thinned binary image into rectangular cell while to represent thinned binary image into triangular cell there are some rules must be considered. It is brought on by a condition as follows: It represents a thinned binary image that used two coordinate values, x and y. It has caused not every coordinate point is lied in the corner of the triangular, while every cell must be started from the corner, not in the middle of the triangle edge.Therefore, to avoid starting point in the middle of triangle edge, it is important to commit a step as follows: In this triangular cell system, every y = odd point. It causes every x point is in the middle of triangle edge. Therefore, for every cell that is started from this (x, y) point, they must be moved 0.5 point to the left. The cell-representation completely is given below (Table 1). It depends on the shape of triangle; upper or lower triangle and the representation is distinguished by where its position, in the right or left of the triangle. The Triangular cell-representation is created based on Table 1. The input is a thinned binary image that is defined as an array variable in MATLAB. The cell representation is moved in a clockwise manner. The algorithm is given below.

Table 1. Triangular Cell Representation

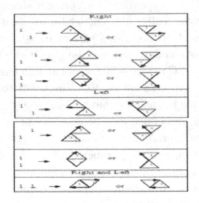

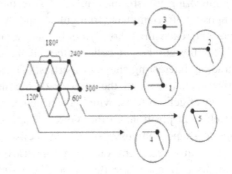

Fig. 1. Vertex Chain Code of Triangular Cell

Triangular Cell-Representation Algorithm:

1. Input: Thinned Binary Image (TBI)
2. Check number of TBI rows and columns
3. Divide the area of the image into 2 parts; left and right
4. Scan the thinned binary image from the top to the bottom, left to the right.
   If it finds code 1 and satisfy:
   - TBI (row, column) = TBI (row, column+1) = 1, or
   - TBI (row, column) = TBI (row+1, column) = 1, or
   - TBI (row, column) = TBI (row +1, column–1) = 1, or
   - TBI (row, column) = TBI (row+1, column+1) = 1
        Draw the segment of the cells according to Table 5.1, start from vertex of
        TBI (column, row).
5. Repeat step 4 until all of code 1 from the thinned binary image is represented on
   triangular cells.

However, the Triangular cell-representation algorithm is similar with the rectangular
one but triangular cell is more complicated. It is important to note that there is a
movement in the coordinate if the point touches the middle of triangle edge. The
result of this algorithm is used as the input of the next algorithm

2.2   The Transcribing Algorithm

Transcribing algorithm is used to transcribe the triangular cell into vertex chain code.
The Transcribing algorithm of triangular cell is not as complicated as the cell-
representation. If the cell representation has been obtained, the vertex chain code of
the thinned binary can be obtained. The algorithm is created based on Figure 1.There
are 5 different codes; 1, 2, 3, 4, and 5 for triangular cell. It depends on the corner that
is formed by each triangle in the cell. The algorithm to transcribe the triangular cell
into vertex chain code is given below. The code starts from the starting point that is
chosen continuously in a clockwise direction.

The Triangular Transcribing Algorithm

1. Input: Boundary of thinned binary image Cell-representation
2. Determine the starting point
3. Scan the boundary
   if180° is found, then VCC=3
   else if 240° is found then VCC=2
   else if 300° is found then VCC=1
   else if 60° is found then VCC=5
   elseVCC=4
   end
4. Repeat step 3 until the starting point is reached back.

3   Results and Discussion

3.1   Experimental Results

All the algorithms are tested and validated using three thinned binary images, L-block, hexagon, and pentagon. Table 2 shows the result of the experiment using the cell-representation and transcribing algorithm. Thinned binary images are transformed into triangular-VCC by using the cell-representation algorithm; The Triangular-VCC is transcribed into Vertex Chain Code using the transcribing algorithm. The entire algorithm is called Mapping Algorithm. The result of the experiment is analyzed to see how the algorithm works for the input. It will disclose that the algorithm is capable to represent the thinned binary image into the cell, and transcribe it into VCC.

Table 2. The Triangular Cells Mapping Result

NO	Thinned Binary Image	Triangular Cells	Triangular VCC
1			124151515241515151523415151515 152241514333333215152334515151 515143251514322334151514333 333151432515151515151514335 15151434
2			13333333234151515151515 1515151333333333323333 3333233333333331515151 5151515151515
3			224151515234151515152333 24242424242424133333333 33333333322424242424242 4233332515151432515151514

3.2   Result Analysis

Every experiment, no matter how careful it was done; there is an associated error inherent with the result of the experiment. It is difficult to get the exactly same result with the true value. The magnitude of the error is due to the precision of the experimental system.To determine the error associated to the experiment, scientists often refer to the precision and accuracy of the experiment measurement. The precision of the experiment is a measure of the reliability of the experiment, or how reproducible the experiment is. The accuracy of an experiment is a measure of how closely the experimental results agree with a true or accepted value. Related to the precision and accuracy, it is only close to the expected value, the error is still possible happen. The error could be calculated by error percentage formula. The error percentage calculated the error between our value measurements and the accepted value with the following equation:

$$\text{Error percentage} = \frac{|measured \ - Actual|}{Actual} x100\% \tag{1}$$

In this paper there are 3 kinds of error percentage calculated, namely cell-representation of thinned binary image based on code 1 number error percentage, cell-representation of thinned binary image based on coordinate error percentage, and cell-representation of vertex chain code error percentage. The error percentage is calculated by using Equation 1 and will be shown in the table below.

Table 3. Error Percentage of Triangular Cell-Representation from TBI Based on Total of Code 1

Kinds of Error Percentage	Error Percentage
Error Percentage of Cell-Representation from TBI Based on Total of Code 1	2%
Error Percentage of Cell-Representation from TBI Based on Coordinate	0.02%
Error Percentage of Cell-Representation from VCC	1%

4   Conclusion

The mapping algorithm has been tested and validated by using three thinned binary image objects, L-block, hexagon, and pentagon. Those thinned binary images have been represented as triangular cell and the cell has been transcribed into VCC. The results show that the cell-representation algorithm is capable of representing thinned binary image as triangular-VCC cells. Reciprocally the transcribing algorithm is capable of transcribing the triangular-VCC cells into Vertex Chain Code and the entire algorithm is called the Mapping Algorithm of Triangular Vertex Chain Code.

Acknowledgment. The authors sincerely thank to UniversitiTeknologi Malaysia (UTM) for the Short Term Grant Vote number 77316, and the Research Management Center (RMC), for their support in making this project success.

References

1. Wulandhari, L.A., Haron, H.: The evolution and trend of chain code scheme. ICGST International Journal on Graphics, Vision and Image Processing (GVIP) 8(III), 17–23 (2008)
2. Freeman, H.: On the encoding of arbitrary geometric configurations. IRE Trans. EC-10(2), 260–268 (1961)
3. Freeman, H.: Computer processing of line-drawing images. ACM Computing Surveys 6, 57–97 (1974)
4. Bribiesca, E.: A new chain code. Pattern Recognition 32(2), 235–251 (1999)
5. Deutsch, E.S.: Thinning Algorithms on Rectangular, Hexagonal, and Triangular Arrays. Communications of the ACM 15(9), 827–837 (1972)

Greening Digital Forensics: Opportunities and Challenges

Yap TzeTzuen, Ali Dehghantanha, Andy Seddon, and Seyed Hossein Mohtasebi

Asia Pacific University College of Technology and Innovation
Kuala Lumpur, Malaysia
ypjien@yahoo.com, {ali_dehqan,andy}@ucti.edu.my,
shmohtasebi@gmail.com

Abstract. Despite the fact that digital forensics involves strict procedures and principles, but as this paper presents, there are plenty of opportunities that can be practically employed in digital forensics to make this science greener. Virtualization can cost effectively reduce the number of workstations running forensic tools in the lab. Cloud computing not only facilitate managing and securing services but also decline the number of required network and cooling facilities. Forensic labs can also be optimized regarding environmental preservation. Using remote protocols and digitalizing paperwork procedures are environmentally helpful practices to accelerate investigation progress as well. Employing storage devices with optimal energy usage in digital forensics may highly reduce energy consumption. This paper studies established green technologies particularly in information technology field and suggests a framework for implementing compatible techniques in digital forensics to reduce greenhouse gas pollutants, limit carbon emissions, and preserve the environment.

Keywords: Green forensics, digital forensics, forensic lab.

1   Introduction

Recent years have witnessed a global intention of employing environmentally friendly products and technologies. Digital forensics, on the other hand, involves meticulous procedures, some deliberately redundant (e.g. duplicating data from digital evidence using different tools and storing several copies of that) to insure the accuracy of the investigation process. However a variety of green approaches and efforts might be adapted in digital forensics as well.This paper outlines the opportunities that can be taken for reducing environmental impacts of digital forensics in both forensic labs and crime scenes. It also encompasses challenges that confront with employing common green technologies in digital forensics. The remaining of this paper is organized as follows: Section 2 reviews virtualization and cloud computing, two notorious techniques being employed in green IT. It also delves into environmental conditions and electrical needs of forensics labs. Moreover, the section encompasses effective factors in energy consumption of storage devices. Section 3 proposes a framework for establishing the discussed methods in digital forensic labs. It also suggests some

V.V. Das, E. Ariwa, and S.B. Rahayu (Eds.): SPIT 2011, LNICST 62, pp. 114–119, 2012.
© Institute for Computer Sciences, Social Informatics and Telecommunications Engineering 2012

methods and techniques for implementing green digital forensic devices and forensic procedures. Section 4 analyses the proposed approach and the work is finally concluded in Section 5.

2   Literature Review

This section reviews the current state of the art of elements that affect greening digital forensics.

2.1   Virtualization

As stated in Gartner Data Center Conference, virtualization can promote hardware utilization by 5 to 20 times and enables organizations to decrease the number of servers and consequently reduce the power consumption [1].There are also some technologies can be employed for storage virtualization like IBM SAN Volume Controller (SVC) [2] that presents storage devices of a SAN coupled with a virtual pool as only one logical device[1].In addition to server virtualization that lowers costs, improves resource utilization, and increases availability, client virtualization can also be employed for the same benefits [1]. One of the challenges with regard to virtualization is any security threat that exploits a vulnerability of one of the running OSs may affect other OSs and services as well. Additionally, if a machine that provides several services, rather than one, goes down, then all services hosted on the machine will be shutting down [3]. Gartner has estimated that, by 2012, 60 percent of virtualized servers will be not as secure as physical machines that they have been replaced with [4]. Liu et al. [5] propose that a different IP is assigned to each virtual machine (VM) running on a machine. Each of VMs should be also separated from the rest using distinct virtual LANs (VLAN) and the only way a VM to connect to another VM should be through layer 3 network devices [5]. Using routers feature firewall for transmitting data between VLANs can minimize the risk of being infected by malicious software [5]. Even after applying this method still less network devices such as network interface controllers (NIC), cables, and switches are used [1].

2.2   Cloud Computing

Cloud computing optimizes and control resource usage by leveraging a measuring capability suitable for the type of service [6].Cloud computing environments are twofold, termed, public and private [7]. In public cloud computing environment, users communicate with servers using the Internet while private cloud computing environment is isolated from the outside world by means like firewall [7]. The common specification of two types is rather than equipping numerous workstations, strong servers with optimized configuration are run and managed.There are three types of cloud computing services as follows: (1) storage as a service, (2) processing as a service, and (3) software as a service [7]. In storage as a service as its name suggests, user stores their data in the cloud while in processing as a service user outsources intensive tasks to cloud [7]. Software as a service involves both of these services and allows user to put all their tasks to cloud [7].Baliga et al. [7] compared these types with regard to transport, storage, and processing which their results is presented in Table 1.

Table 1. High Energy Consumption in Cloud Computing with Regard to Cloud's Type

Factor	Software as Service	Storage as a Service	Processing as a Service
Transport	High frame rates	High download rate	Never
Storage	Never	Low download rate	-
Processing	Few users per server	High download rate	Medium to high encoding per week

Power Usage Effectiveness (PUE) and Data Center Infrastructure Efficiency (DCiE) are two metrics used for determining the energy efficiency of data centers, although they do not cover the whole scope of data center [1]. Equations (1) and (2), respectively, demonstrate how PUE and DCiE are calculated [8, 9].

$$PUE = \frac{\text{Total Facility Power}}{\text{IT Equipment Power}} \tag{1}$$

$$DCiE = \frac{\text{IT Equipment Power}}{\text{Total Facility Power}} \tag{2}$$

2.3   Environmental Conditions of the Lab

There are requirements specified for building and developing a digital forensic lab. These requirements and standards are stated in ASCLD/LAB and ISO/IEC 17025. One of the standards that the ASCLD/LAB requires for a laboratory to have is to provide a comfortable working environment for the employees [10]. One of the issues here is the cooling system in a lab. To save the cost of the electricity used by digital forensic lab, cooling fans or a good ventilation system is installed and can decline the waste of energy [1]. Unlike normal chemical lab systems can be designed to look alike of a normal office that has a low-velocity air handling system, resulting in substantial energy savings [11]. A proper energy saving lighting bulbs and tubes have the certification from the Energy Star program that promotes in protecting the environment and save money [17].

2.4   Storage Devices

Hard disk drives (HDD) are the most frequently used device being employed for storing data and HDD with high capacity typically use higher energy. There are models of HDDs in the market that use less energy and makes less heat. For instance, a Western Digital HDD consumes 5 watts less than a normal HDD [13]. Storage technologies like

NAND flash memory based SSD (Solid State Disk) in comparison with traditional HDDs waste less energy and at the same time provide more reliable services [14].Additionally, there are technologies which optimize power usage. MAID (Massive Array of Idle Disk) is an example that switches off idle HDDs [14, 15].

3   Proposed Approach

Our proposed framework is composed of four parts as follows as discussed in the rest of this section.

3.1   Virtualization and Consolidation

Installing multiple forensic tools with similar functionality on the same OS is deprecated [16]. The most elegant way to deal with these issues is employing VMs. Employing private cloud computing with optimal severs that provide services to multiple forensic investigators can significantly reduce the energy consumption.It also consolidates services and data and as a result it eases managing and securing them. As Table 1 demonstrates, in cloud computing energy consumption is dependent upon cloud type as well as the number of users. Since employing either virtualization or cloud computing will result in placing fundamental servers in data centers, improvement in cooling efficiency of data centers can conserve a considerable amount of energy.Metrics like PUE and DCiE can be employed for finding the efficiency of data centers.

3.2   Environmental Conditions of Lab

The heating, ventilation and air conditioning systems of a digital forensic lab can be designed similar of a normal office that requires low-velocity air system. Low-velocity air system consumes less amount of energy.Ventilation system can be installed for the digital forensic lab rather than using air conditioners, thus resulting in reducing the green house effect. Unlike air conditioning system, the usage of energy is lesser and there of no promoting of energy wastage by the ventilation system. Furthermore, to help in reducing the energy consumption of the lab, an energy saving lightning system should be installed. To maintain the energy consumption at a certain level and also to reduce the waste of energy on the digital forensic lab, energy recovery can be employed.

3.3   Storage Devices

Duplicating data stored on digital evidence and keeping several copies of them is an important stage in any digital forensics investigations. Therefore, using appropriate storage devices that consume less energy like modern HDDs and NAND flash memories can significantly reduce the overall power consumption in digital forensic investigations.Workstations connected to cloud environments do not need to have HDDs with high capacity since HDDs with higher capacity consume more energy.Optimizing energy consumption using technologies like MAID is helpful for those servers of forensic lab that need large disk arrays.

3.4   Forensic Devices

Replacing energy sources of these devices with renewable energy sources can effectively reduce environmental impacts.Additionally, as far as possible instead of using hazardous materials, recyclable ones should be employed. Batteries are an exemplar of these materials.Equipping digital forensic devices like data acquisition tools with remote functionality can speed up the investigation process and at the same time it reduces unnecessary traveling.Many manual paperwork tasks such as chain of custody forms can be digitalized using mobile applications run on tablets or smartphones that are already carried by investigators.

4   Analysis of Proposed Framework

Virtualization reducesrequired digital facilities in forensic labs.   Since in cloud computing servers are consolidated in data centers rather than being distributed in different parts of organization's building, optimizing cooling systems and the structure of data center can noticeable decline energy consumption.There are also factors like licensing that needed to be taken into consideration.

Consuming less energy means promoting less burning of bio-fuel that produces carbon's footprint. By using computers that have low power consumption than the normal ones, the electricity usage in the lab should be reduced. It is noted that these low power consuming equipments can perform better than the normal ones. Since the low power consumption computers can perform in a better speed, there is possibility that the time duration of an examiner to investigate digital evidences can be shorten. Equipping mobile forensic devices with remote access and using secure protocols for transmitting data may reduce travelling of investigators. Instead of using papers for recording investigation process tablets can be used to facilitate investigation progress.

5   Conclusion and Future Work

The proposed framework in the paper may not be the best but in the future, there is always a better solution that can be adapted into the digital forensic lab for the purpose of being environment friendly and also promoting the idea of going green. Another suggestion to reduce carbon's footprint is to adapting green procedures in the digital forensic lab. Certain duration of time is needed for the employees in digital forensic lab to become accustomed to the new procedures. Outstanding results can be seen after that period of time which reduces greenhouse effect and promoting green digital forensics.

References

[1] Lamb, J.: The Greening of IT: How Companies Can Make a Difference for the Environment. IBM Press (2009)

[2] IBM System Storage SAN Volume Controller, http://www-03.ibm.com/systems/storage/software/virtualization/svc

[3] Gorge, M.: Are we being greenwashed to the detriment of our organisations' security? Computer Fraud & Security 2008(10), 14–18 (2008)

[4] Gartner Says 60 Percent of Virtualized Servers Will Be Less Secure Than the Physical Servers They Replace Through 2012 (2010), http://www.gartner.com/it/page.jsp?id=1322414

[5] Liu, J., Lai, W.: Security analysis of VLAN-based Virtual Desktop Infrastructure. In: International Conference on Educational and Network Technology (ICENT), pp. 301–304 (2010)

[6] Mell, P., Grance, T.: The NIST Definition of Cloud Computing (Draft), National Institute of Standards and Technology (2011)

[7] Baliga, J., Ayre, R.W., Hinton, K., Tucker, R.S.: Green Cloud Computing: Balancing Energy in Processing, Storage, and Transport. Proceedings of the IEEE 99(1), 149–167 (2011)

[8] PUE Data Center Efficiency Metric - Data Center Benchmarks and Certifications, http://www.digitalrealtytrust.com/pue-efficiency.aspx

[9] What is data center infrastructure efficiency (DCIE) (2008), http://searchdatacenter.techtarget.com/definition/data-center-infrastructure-efficiency-DCIE

[10] The American Society of Crime Laboratory Directors/Laboratory Accreditation Board (ASCLD/LAB) (2011), http://www.ascld-lab.org/forms/intlrequirements.html

[11] Digital Forensic Investigator News, http://www.dfinews.com/article/architectural-and-engineering-design-requirements-digital-forensic-facility?page=0,0

[12] Ken, M., Michael, C.: Sustainable 'Green' Forensic Laboratory Design, Forensic Magazine (2006), http://www.forensicmag.com/article/sustainable-green-forensic-laboratory-design

[13] Velte, T., Velte, A., Elsenpeter, R.: Green IT: Reduce Your Information System's Environmental Impact While Adding to the Bottom Line, 1st edn., pp. 51–53. McGraw-Hill Osborne Media (2008)

[14] Zhang, X., Zhao, X., Lin, Y., Zeng, L.: Key Technologies for Green Data Center. In: 2010 Third International Symposium on Information Processing (ISIP), pp. 477–480 (2010)

[15] Colarelli, D., Grunwald, D.: Massive Arrays of Idle Disks For Storage Archives. In: ACM/IEEE 2002 Conference, p. 47 (2002)

[16] Jansen, W., Ayers, R.: Guidelines on Cell Phone Forensics, National Institute of Standards and Technology (2007)

[17] Energy Star, http://www.energystar.gov/index.cfm?c=about.ab_index

Error Propagation Analysis of Different Detectors for V-BLAST MIMO Channels

Shreedhar A. Joshi[1,*], T.S. Rukmini[2], and H.M. Mahesh[3]

[1] S D M College of Engineering Dharwad-580002, Karnataka, India
[2] R V College of Engineering, Bangalore-560069, Karnataka, India
[3] Bangalore University, Bangalore-560067, Karnataka, India
Shreedhar.j@rediffmail.com

Abstract. In a highly-scattering wireless environment, Vertical Bell Laboratories Layered Space-Time (V-BLAST) is a promising MIMO spatial multiplexing scheme, which can achieve high channel capacity without any increase in bandwidth and transmission power. In this paper a Parallel Interference cancellation (PIC) detection and ordered successive interference cancellation (OSIC) schemes are proposed to reduce the high computational complexity and large system delay caused by the pseudo inverse of channel matrix and the ordering process. The V-BLAST algorithms with ordered and un-ordered ZF / MMSE detectors are compared for the error propagation. The V-BLAST algorithm is combined with various Transmitter / Receiver antenna selection combination to achieve high channel capacity while sharing the spectral resources over a MIMO channel. The received signal after interference cancellation passes through linear equalization or parallel interference cancellation with low complexity. Simulation results shows, the proposed algorithms can decrease the computational complexity without performance loss.

Keywords: V-BLAST, OSIC, PIC, ZF, MMSE.

1   Introduction and Related Work

As a upcoming new 4G technology, MIMO (Multiple Input and Multiple Output) channels with Flat fading conditions are having multiple transmit and receive antennas offers relatively huge spectral efficiencies compared to SISO (Single Input and Single Output) channels [1][2][3]. As per the literature available, Capacity increases linearly with the number of transmit antennas as long as the number of receive antennas are greater than or equal to the number of transmit antennas. To achieve this capacity, Diagonal BLAST was proposed by Foschini [3]. This scheme utilizes multi-element antenna arrays at both ends of wireless link. However, the

---

* Corresponding author: Shreedhar A Joshi is a research student at R V Centre of Cognitive Technology (RVCCT) Bangalore and Department of Research in Electronics, Kuvempu University, Shimoga, Karnataka, India. This paper is a part of his Research work suggested by his guides, Dr. Rukmini T S, Dr. Mahesh H M.

V.V. Das, E. Ariwa, and S.B. Rahayu (Eds.): SPIT 2011, LNICST 62, pp. 120–125, 2012.
© Institute for Computer Sciences, Social Informatics and Telecommunications Engineering 2012

computational complexities of D-BLAST implementation led to V-BLAST which is a modified version of BLAST [4]. Two nulling criteria, namely Zero-Forcing (ZF) [5] and Minimum Mean Squared Error (MMSE) [8], are utilized as detection algorithms.Originally, the BLAST detection scheme was based on a successive interference cancellation [4] [5] [6]. A parallel interference cancellation scheme was also proposed later [7]. BLAST detectors including both SIC and PIC suffer from the error propagation problem, so that they lead to the poor energy efficiency which can be improved if the previously detected layers (symbols) were perfectly cancelled because the following layers depend highly on the result of the previous detected signals. The error propagation problem of BLAST detectors can be reduced with channel coding and interleaving [9] [10].

2   The Proposed V-BLAST Scheme with MIMO

The proposed V-BLAST scheme with MIMO channel is shown in Fig. 1. The received vector with size $n_R \ X1$ is modeled by

$$r = Ha + n. \tag{1}$$

H represents the channel matrix with dimension $n_R \times n_T$, whose element $h_{i,\,j}$ represents the complex fading coefficient for the path from transmit j to receive antenna i. These fading coefficients are modeled by an independent zero mean complex Gaussian random variable with variance 0.5 per dimension. a denotes the vector of transmitted symbols with dimension $n_T X\ 1$, n represents a complex vector of independent samples of AWGN over each received antenna with zero mean and variance σn^2.

The nulling matrix G is described in Equations 2 and 3 for the ZF and MMSE criteria with the form of pseudo-inverse of the channel matrix H:

$$G = (H^+\ H)^{-1}\ H^+ \tag{2}$$

$$G = (H^+ H\ +\ \sigma_n^2 /\ \sigma_d^2\ )^{-1}\ H^+ \tag{3}$$

Where $\sigma_n^2 /\ \sigma_d^2$ denote the inverse of signal-to-noise ratio at each receive antenna.
H^+ represents the conjugate transpose matrix of channel matrix H.

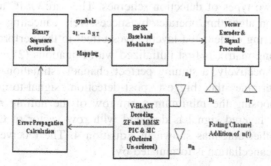

Fig. 1. Proposed System diagram of V-BLAST scheme in MIMO configuration

Figure.1 shows the proposed V-BLAST system model. Here the transmitted symbols are decoded first, and then the receiver needs to estimate the channel matrix. In this simulation, the fading channel characteristics are assumed to be known perfectly at the receiver. The transmitter consists of a binary random generator, a BPSK modulator and a vector encoder. The binary random generator generates the transmitted bits. These bits are modulated in the BPSK modulator. It is assumed that each symbol has an ideal rectangular pulse shape and may be sampled with a single point per symbol. The vector encoder maps the symbols to each antenna. In the channel block, the transmitted symbols undergo Rayleigh fading and additive noise. Rayleigh fading channel coefficients are generated with two independent Gaussian random variables with unit variance. The channel is assumed to be quasistationary, that is, the channel coefficients do not vary during the given time period. The receiver is made up of decoding processing and an error rate (BER) calculation block. Only SIC needs proper ordering process for interference cancellation (at each layers) using maximum iterations. But PIC does not need to consider the ordering issue since it cancels out all other paths of interference in the same stage (iteration). As shown in the figure.1, transmitted bits are demultiplexed into n_T parallel sub streams. Each sub stream is modulated using BPSK, interleaved and then assigned to a transmit antenna. As such, the number of layers is n_T and the spatial rate is b_{nT}. Since each layer is associated with a fixed transmit antenna, this architecture can accommodate applications with possibly different data rates and/or different users. The spatial diversity achieved by this scheme varies between one and n_R, depending on the detection scheme employed at the receiver. For instance, when interference cancellation and suppression is used, the first layer detected will have a spatial diversity of $n_R - n_T + 1$ because the other layers are suppressed. The last layer detected, on the other hand, will have a spatial diversity of n_R since the $n_T - 1$ previously detected layer is subtracted from the last layer, i.e., there is no suppression but rather cancellation.

The Receiver block consists of ordered and non-ordered ZF/MMSE detectors, which requires knowledge of the SNR at the receiver. Finally the BER is calculated by comparing the originally transmitted symbols with received symbols that are estimated at the receiver.

3   Comparison of OSIC and PIC

As per the previous surveys in the areas of symbol Interference cancellation schemes, there are mainly two types of detection schemes. They are OSIC and PIC schemes. The OSIC detection algorithm operates by successively canceling out one layer per iteration. The ordering of detected layers gives effect to the performance of the SIC detector. The nulling matrix is first initialized with Equations (2) and (3) for ZF and MMSE criteria respectively, assuming perfect channel estimation. For the ordering scheme, we determine the biggest post-detection signal-to-noise ratio. This corresponds to choosing the minimum norm row of the nulling matrix G in each iteration. First the layered signal is decoded with row vector of G suppressing the signals from all other antennas shown in Equation 4. The received signal after ith layer interference cancellation is formulated by

$$r_{i+1} = r_i - \text{est}(a_i)(H)_i \tag{4}$$

Where ai is the decoded symbols in the ith step. (H)i is the ith column of channel matrix. G is newly updated by nulling out the previous pseudo-inverse of the channel matrix. This procedure is repeated until symbols from all transmit antennas are decoded in a similar manner. The non-ordered scheme does not need to determine the largest post-detection SNR but chooses the row vector of nulling matrix randomly. The PIC-based V-BLAST detector does not obtain the gain with applying the ordering of the layers. In the first stage, all layers with Equation. (5) Are detected simultaneously.

$$\text{est (a)} = G \, r \tag{5}$$

Where G is the pseudo-inverse matrix of the channel matrix with size $n_T \, X \, n_R$, r is the received symbol vector and est (a) is a vector form of all detected layers. Equation (6) describes the cancellation process, which subtracts the interference of the other $(n_T \, X \, 1)$ layers. The received signal after first step interference cancellation is formulated by

$$r_k = r - \sum_{j=k} \text{est (a}_j) \, (H)_j. \tag{6}$$

Where rk is the received symbol vector applied with the interference cancellation of all but the kth layer, (H) j is the jth column vector of channel matrix and est(a_j) is the computed j^{th} layer symbol that is the jth element of the estimated symbol vector. In the second stage, the new nulling matrix is recalculated with the channel matrix nulling out the all but the kth layer. Therefore, the nulling matrix becomes a row vector with size $(1 \times n_R)$ as Equation. (7).

$$G_k = C \, H^+_k \tag{7}$$

By multiplying rk from Equation. (6) withGk from Equation. (7), the PIC-based V-BLAST detector recovers the all components of the transmitted symbol vector a.

4   Results and Discussions

Based on the effect of error propagation, OSIC and PIC detector schemes with MIMO V-BLAST are illustrated in this section using mat lab simulation results. Here, we compare the performance for ordered and non-ordered ZF/MMSE detection algorithms. The performance of individual layers of 4Tx X 4Rx MIMO systems is compared for error propagation. Figure 3 shows the simulated results of ZF / MMSE nulling algorithms with ordered and un-ordered algorithms. Here, the error propagation has improved for ZF-OSIC and MMSE-OSIC with ordered technique. The MMSE-SIC ordered technique works still better at maximum value of SNR (i.e. around 14 dB) compared to ZF-SIC. Similarly, figure 4 depicts the simulated results for PIC/OSIC detector techniques with 4Tx X 4Rx MIMO systems for ZF / MMSE methods. The improved performance of MMSE technique is adequate. Figure 5 displays 2Tx X 2Rx V-BLAST MIMO scheme simulation for with ordered ZF/MMSE-SIC in Rayleigh faded Channel. The simulation results with maximum SNR limits and its corresponding BER values are clearly seen from the performance comparison table. These results clearly show 8-10 dB improvement in SNR with respect to error propagation for MMSE detectors. In the ZF criterion, when a layer is detected, the interference coming from undetected layers is suppressed, whereas in the MMSE criterion, a compromise between interference suppression and noise reduction is achieved.

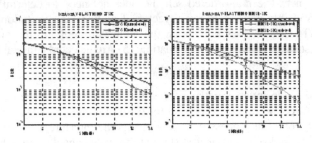

Fig. 2. Comparison of ZF & MMSE with SIC in unordered and ordered detectors

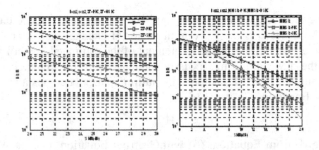

Fig. 3. Comparison of ZF, ZF - SIC and ZF-PIC MMSE, MMSE – SIC, MMSE-PIC

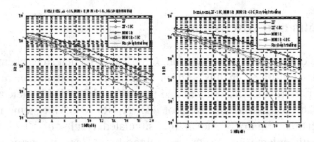

Fig. 4. Simulation results with ordered ZF-SIC and MMSE-SIC in Rayleigh faded Channel

Table 1. Performance with BER from all possible Interference Cancellation Detectors

SL.No	Type of the Detector	Maximum SNR limit	BER (Approximation)
1	ZF-SIC (Un-ordered)	14 dB	Nearly Equal to 10^{-1}
2	ZF-SIC (Ordered)	14 dB	Below 10^{-2}
3	MMSE (Un-ordered)	14 dB	Well Below 10^{-2}
4	MMSE (ordered)	14 dB	Below 10^{-3}
5	ZF-PIC	30 dB	Nearly Equal to 10^{-4}
6	MMSE-PIC	20 dB	Nearly Equal to 10^{-4}

5   Conclusions

As per the table, simulated results show the Ordered MMSE SIC performs better than un-ordered detectors. PIC method has also having limitation over OSIC nulling techniques. While both detection approaches are asymptotically equivalent, the ZF approach is less practical than the MMSE approach because the complete interference suppression achieved by ZF comes at the expense of enhancing the noise power, which leads to performance degradation. Another difference between the two schemes is that the constraint $n_R \geq n_T$, that is required for the ZF detector can be relaxed for the MMSE detector.

References

1. Li, D., Zhang, H.: Partial OSIC Detection for V-BLAST Systems. In: Pacific-Asia Conference on Circuits, Communications and Systems, pp. 376–379 (2009)
2. Foschini, G.J., Gans, M.J.: On limits of wireless communications in a fading environment when using multiple antennas. Wireless Personal Communications, 311–335 (1996)
3. Foschini, G.J.: Layerd space-time architecture for wireless communications in a fading environment when using multi-element antennas. Bell Labs Technical Journal (1996)
4. Wolniansky, P.W., Foschini, G.J., Golden, G.D., Valenzuela, R.A.: V-BLAST: Anarchitecture for realizing very high data rates over the rich-scattering wireless channel. In: URSI International Symposium on Signals, Systems and Electronics, pp. 295–300 (1998)
5. Golden, G.D., Foschini, G.J., Valenzuela, R.A., Wolniansky, P.W.: Detection algorithm and initial laboratory results using v-blast space-time communication architecture. IEE Electronic Letters 35(1), 14–16 (1999)
6. Baro, S., Bauch, G., Pavlic, A., Semmler, A.: Improving BLAST performance using space-time block codes and turbo decoding. In: GLOBECOM 2000, vol. 2, pp. 1067–1071 (2000)
7. Sellathurai, M., Haykin, S.: Simplified diagonal blast architecture with iterative parallel interference cancelation receivers. In: IEEE International Conference on Communications, vol. 10, pp. 3067–3071 (2001)
8. Wu, W., Chen, K.: Linear multiuser detectors for synchronous CDMA communication over Rayleigh fading channels. In: Seventh IEEE International Symposium, Personal, Indoor and Mobile Radio Communications, PIMRC 1996, vol. 2, pp. 578–582 (1996)
9. Sellathurai, M., Haykin, S.: Turbo-blast for high-speed wireless communications. In: Wireless Communications and Networking Conference, vol. 1, pp. 315–320 (2000)
10. Gozali, R.: Space-time codes for high data rate wireless communications. Ph.D. dissertation Virginia Polytechnic Institute and State University (2002)

Using Suffix-Tree to Identify Patterns and Cluster Traces from Event Log

Xiaodong Wang[2], Li Zhang[3], and Hongming Cai[1]

[1] School of Software, Shanghai JiaoTong University, Shanghai, China
[2] University of Mannheim, Mannheim, Germany
[3] IWW Institute, University Karlsruhe, Karlsruhe, Germany
wangxd.sjtu@googlemail.com, hmcai@sjtu.edu.cn, Li.Zhang@kit.edu

Abstract. Process mining refers to the extraction process models from event logs. Traditional process mining algorithms have problems dealing with event logs that are produced from unstructured real-life processes and generate spaghetti-like and incomprehensible process models. One means making traces more structural is to extract commonly used process model constructs (common patterns) in the event log and transform traces basing on such constructs. Another way of pre-processing traces is to categorize traces in event log into clusters such that process traces in each cluster can be adequately represented by a process model. Nevertheless, current approaches for trace clustering have many problems such as ignoring context process and huge computational overhead. In this paper, suffix-tree is firstly utilized for discovering common patterns. The traces in event log are transformed with common patterns. Thereafter suffix-trees are applied to categorize transformed traces. The trace clustering algorithm has a linear-time computational complexity. The process models mined from the clustered traces show a high degree of fitness and comprehensibility.

Keywords: Trace clustering, Suffix tree, Process mining.

1   Introduction

Today's information systems are logging events that are stored in so-called "event logs". For example, any user action is logged in ERP systems like SAP R/3, workflow management systems like Staffware, and case handling systems like Flower. An event log corresponds to a bag of process instances of a business process. A process instance is manifested as a trace which is an ordered list of activities. Process mining aims at a fine grained analysis of processes based on such event log [1]. It can deliver valuable and factual insights that show how processes are being executed in real life. Event logs are generally expected to be derived from well-structured processes. However, real-life business processes tend to be less structured than expected. Traditional process mining algorithms have problems with such unstructured processes and generate incomprehensible process models. In an event log, there can be instances where the system is subjected to similar execution patterns. Discovering of common patterns of

V.V. Das, E. Ariwa, and S.B. Rahayu (Eds.): SPIT 2011, LNICST 62, pp. 126–131, 2012.
© Institute for Computer Sciences, Social Informatics and Telecommunications Engineering 2012

invocation of activities in traces can promote comprehensibility of discovered process models. Another means to promote quality of process mining results is to categorize traces into clusters according to the prescribed characteristics of processes, so that complexities of traces in each cluster can be reduced and the resultant process models have more comprehensibility. In this paper a context aware approach to categorize traces into clusters is proposed. We first define patterns which commonly occur in traces. Suffix-tree is employed to discover common constructs (subsequences) in traces. Then the traces in event log are transformed as sequences of activities and patterns. A suffix-tree based approach is used to categorize transformed traces into clusters. This approach has a linear-time complexity and incorporates context information and execution order of processes during the trace clustering. We implemented the approach in the ProM framework[1] and evaluated the effectiveness of the approach through the goodness of mined process models.

2   Related Work

Greco et al. [2][3] proposed an approach to mine hierarchies of process models that collectively represent the process at different levels of granularity and abstraction. Jagadeesh et al. [4] proposed the definitions of context-aware patterns in traces and developed an iterative method of transformation of traces which can be applied as a pre-processing step for process mining techniques, yet the patterns were not fully considered for the clustering of transformed traces in this approach.Data clustering is one of the most important fields of data mining [5]. One of the most often used techniques for analyzing traces is to transform a trace into a vector, where each dimension of the vector corresponds to an activity. Song et al. [6][7] have proposed the idea of clustering traces by the combination of different perspectives of the traces as the feature vector. Though this combined approach might yield better results than before, such data modehas a few drawbacks. For example, the context information of process and execution order information are lost during the traces clustering. In [8][9], the generic edit distance based approach to trace clustering is proposed. However, the computational overhear of these approaches is still large.

3   Common Patterns in Traces

There are always special constructs in process models, such as loops and parallel constructs, etc. These constructs or abstract processes manifest themselves as different patterns in traces. Thereafter we need pre-process traces with such patterns, so as to improving the goodness of process mining results. In this section, we propose context-aware patterns of traces. The basic idea is to consider sub-sequences of activities that are conserved in and across traces, which signify some sets of common functionalities of process models. [10].

---

[1] ProM is an extensible framework that provides a comprehensive set of tools/plugins for the discovery and analysis of process models from event logs. See
http://www.processmining.org

Let $\mathcal{A}$ denote set of activities. $\mathcal{A}+$ is the set of all non-empty finite sequences of activities from $\mathcal{A}$. A trace, T is an element of $\mathcal{A}$. For $i \leq j, T(i,j)$ denotes the subsequence from the ith position to the jth position in the trace T. An event log $\mathcal{L}$, corresponds to a set of traces from $\mathcal{A}+$.

Simple loops manifest as the repeated occurrence of an activity or subsequence of activities in the traces. Thereafter, the tandem array of subsequence can be defined as:

Definition 3.1 Tandem Array: A tandem array in a trace T is a subsequence $T(i,j)$ of the form α^k with $k \geq 2$ where α is a sequence that is repeated k times. The subsequence α is denoted as a tandem repeat type.

Definition 3.2. Primitive Tandem Repeat (PTR): A tandem repeat is called a primitive tandem repeat if and only if α is not a tandem array.

Definition 3.3. Maximal Pair: A maximal pair in a sequence T. (1) is a pair of identical sub-words, extending s_1 and s_2 on either side would destroy the equality of the two strings ; (2) there are no two neighbor letters which are same in such string.

Definition 3.4. Maximal Repeat: A maximal repeat is defined as subsequence α that occurs in a maximal pair.

Definition 3.5. Primitive Repeat (PR): A primitive repeat is defined as a maximal repeat, which does not contain any other maximal repeat.

Considering an event log $\mathcal{L}=\{aabcdbbcda, dabcdabcbb, bbbcdbbbccaa, aaadabbccc, aaacdcdcbedbccbadbebdc\}$ over the alphabet $\mathcal{A}=\{a, b, c, d, e\}$, For the trace T_5 the set of primitive repeat is $\{a,c\}$; the set of maximal repeat is $\{bd, cb, db, dc, cdc\}$. The set of primitive repeats in trace T_5 is $\{bd, cb, db, dc\}$. Table 1 depicts the single repeats, non-single repeats and basic repeats in the entire event log $\mathcal{L}$.

Table 1. Primitive tandem repeat, maximal repeat and primitive repeat in event log

Primitive tandem repeat	Maximal repeat	Primitive repeat
$\{a, b,c,cd, dabc\}$	$\{bcd, bd, cb,db,dc,cdc\}$	$\{bd, cb,db, dc\}$

Process model contains special constructs, e.g. parallels, fork, join, etc. The execution order of activities in these constructs may vary from one process instance to another. Hence different patterns can share a common repeat alphabet. As to the above example, $[\{a, b, d, g, h\}]=\{abdgh, adgbh\}$.

Definition.3.6. Primitive Tandem Repeat Alphabet Set (PTAS): The primitive tandem repeat alphabet set is the alphabet set that corresponds to primitive tandem repeat.

Definition.3.7. Primitive Repeat Alphabet Set (PRAS): The features of this set are derived from primitive repeat set PR. The primitive repeat alphabet set is the alphabet set that corresponds to primitive repeat.

With the aforementioned sets of patters PTR, PR, $PRAS$, each trace is transformed into feature sequences. The repeated activities subsequences in a trace are replaced by the feature alphabet sets which occur at the same place.

4   Clustering Traces with Suffix Tree

Suffix tree can be also applied to find feature repeats, since it allows a particularly fast implementation of many import string operation. Simple repeats that exist across the traces in the event log can be discovered by concatenating the traces in the event log with a special delimiter. In this paper, we focus on patterns that manifest as primitive tandem repeats or primitive repeats, as we use such patterns to transform traces so as to improve the quality of trace clustering.

Trace Transformation with Feature Sets: Any clustering technique relies on four concepts: data representation model, similarity measures, clustering model and clustering algorithm that generates the clusters using the data model and similarity measures [11]. In our approach suffix-tree model is employed as data model for trace clustering. As above mentioned, traces cannot be directly used to construct suffix-tree because of special constructs in processes. Here the traces are transformed based on the feature sets which are defined in section 3.2.

Definition.4.1. Featured Trace (ft): A featured trace is a trace from event log, whose repeats are replaced by corresponding pattern sets.

Concretely, tandem repeated subsequences are replaced by primitive tandem repeats and primitive tandem alphabet sets; other repeated subsequences are replaced by primitive repeats and primitive repeat alphabet set.

Clustering Traces with Suffix Tree: After transformation of traces, suffix tree is used to cluster featured traces. Zamir and Etzioni proposed Suffix Tree Clustering algorithm (STC) for Web-document clustering [12]. In our context, a phrase is an ordered sequence of one or more letters and feature alphabet sets. The logical steps of clustering traces analogically include identifying base clusters and combining base clusters into final clusters. A differentia between trace clustering and document clustering is that the number of activity types is finite. Therefore a trace is often made up of many repeated subsequences. For this reason such repetitious occurrence of subsequence should be considered during the clustering.*Identifying Base Clusters*: As presented in section 4.1, traces in event log are transformed into featured traces. The identification of base clusters can be viewed as the creation of an inverted index of phrases for featured trace collection. We treat featured traces as strings of letters and patters sets, thus suffixes contain one or more letters and feature alphabet sets. Figure 1 shows the suffix tree of the examples in section 3.

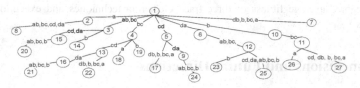

Fig. 1. Building base clusters through suffix tree

Combining Base Clusters: After identifying base clusters, similar base clusters are combined. One subsequence may appear in more than one trace, and traces may share more than one common subsequence. To avoid the proliferation of nearly identical clusters, the high overlapped base clusters should be merged. Thereafter we use an equivalent of a single-link algorithm to group base clusters into end clusters. For the above example, the end clusters are *{{1,2},{1,3},{2,3}}*.

5   Evaluating the Goodness of Clusters and Experiments

In this section we introduce the criteria to evaluate the goodness of clusters in our approach and corresponding experiments result. To evaluate the significance of the clusters formed, one can compare the process models that are discovered from the traces within each cluster. Good clusters tend tocluster trace such that :(1)The process models mined show a high degree of fitness. (2)The process models mined are less complex [8]. To evaluate the result of trace clustering, the approach was implemented as a plug-in in the framework of ProM. An event log of telephone repair is employed as data set. This event contains a total of 1104 process instances. Random subsets of this data set are chosen for analysis. For each sub set of instances, three clustering techniques are applied for clustering (1) k-gram model approach; (2) Generic edit distance approach; (3) Suffix-tree approach. Process models of clusters were generated through the Alpha++ mining algorithm [13]. The fitness of process model was calculated in the Conformance Checker plug-in in ProM. Petri-Net Complexity Analysis plug-in was used to generate metrics of control flows, such as join, split, arcs in process models. Figure 2a depicts weighted average fitness of the process models mined from the trace clusters. Figure 2b shows the execution time of clustering with three techniques. It shows that our approach has approximate linear computational complexity.

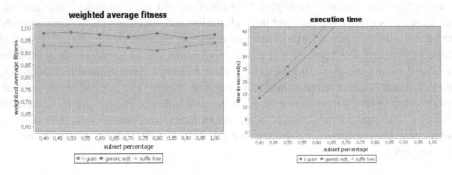

Fig. 2. Weighted average fitness of three trace clustering techniques and execution time of experiments

6   Conclusions and Future Directions

In this paper, a suffix tree based approach for trace clustering is proposed. Patterns of subsequence in traces are introduced to aid to representing traces in clustering. Based on pattern sets, traces are transformed so as to be clustered with suffix tree. It was shown that the proposed approach has good clustering results and is faster than other trace clustering algorithms. Identifying such activities' relationship can improve the efficiency of process mining and help discovery more semantic information of process models.

Acknowledgment. This research is supported by the National Natural Science Foundation of China under No.70871078, 71171132, the National High Technology Research and Development Program of China ("863" Program) under No.2008AA04Z126, and Shanghai Science and Technology Projects 09DZ1121500.

References

1. van der Aalst, W.M.P., Weijters, A.J.M.M., Maruster, L.: Workflow Mining: Discovering Process Models from Event Logs. IEEE Trans. Knowl. Data Eng. 16(9), 1128–1142 (2004)
2. Greco, G., Guzzo, A., Pontieri, L.: Mining Hierarchies of Models: From Abstract Views to Concrete Specifications. In: van der Aalst, W.M.P., Benatallah, B., Casati, F., Curbera, F. (eds.) BPM 2005. LNCS, vol. 3649, pp. 32–47. Springer, Heidelberg (2005)
3. Greco, G., Guzzo, A., Pontieri, L.: Mining Taxonomies of Process Models. Data Knowl. Eng. 67(1), 74 (2008)
4. Jagadeesh Chandra Bose, R.P., van der Aalst, W.M.P.: Abstractions in Process Mining: A Taxonomy of Patterns. In: Dayal, U., Eder, J., Koehler, J., Reijers, H.A. (eds.) BPM 2009. LNCS, vol. 5701, pp. 159–175. Springer, Heidelberg (2009)
5. Jain, A.K., Murty, M.N., Flynn: Data Clustering: A Review. ACM Computing Surveys 31(3), 264–323 (1999)
6. Song, M., Günther, C.W., van der Aalst, W.M.P.: Trace Clustering in Process Mining. In: Ardagna, D., Mecella, M., Yang, J. (eds.) BPM 2008 Workshops. LNBIP, vol. 17, pp. 109–120. Springer, Heidelberg (2009)
7. Greco, G., Guzzo, A., Pontieri, L., Sacca, D.: Disco-covering Expressive Process Models by Clusering Log Traces. IEEE Trans. Knowl. Data Eng., 1010–1027 (2006)
8. Jagadeesh Chandra Bose, R.P., van der Aalst, W.M.P.: Context Aware Trace Clustering: Towards Improving Process Mining Results. In: Proceedings of the SIAM International Conference on Data Mining, SDM, pp. 401–412 (2009)
9. Song, M., Günther, C.W., van der Aalst, W.M.P.: Trace Clustering in Process Mining. In: Ardagna, D., Mecella, M., Yang, J. (eds.) BPM 2008 Workshops. LNBIP, vol. 17, pp. 109–120. Springer, Heidelberg (2009)
10. Bose, R.P.J.C., van der Aalst, W.M.P.: Trace Clustering Based on Conserved Patterns: Towards Achieving Better Process Models. In: Rinderle-Ma, S., Sadiq, S., Leymann, F. (eds.) BPM 2009. LNBIP, vol. 43, pp. 170–181. Springer, Heidelberg (2010)
11. Hammouda, K.M., Kamel, M.S.: Efficient phrase-based document indexing for web document clustering. IEEE Transactions on Knowledge and Data Engineering 16(10), 1279–1296 (2004)
12. Zamir, O., Etzioni, O.: Web document clustering: a feasibility demonstration. In: Proceedings of the 21st Annual International ACM SIGIR Conference on Research and Development in Information Retrieval, pp. 46–54 (1998)
13. Wen, L., van der Aalst, W.M.P., Wang, J., Sun, J.: Mining Process Models with Non-Free Choice Constructs. Data Min. Knowl. Discov. 15(2), 145–182 (2007)

Multiband Curvelet-Based Technique
for Audio Visual Recognition over Internet Protocol

Sue Inn Ch'ng[1], KahPhooi Seng[2], Fong Tien Ong[1], and Li-Minn Ang[1]

[1] University of Nottingham Malaysia Campus
JalanBroga, 43500 Semenyih, Selangor, Malaysia
{keyx9csi,keyx1ofe,Kenneth.Ang}@nottingham.edu.my
[2] Sunway University
No. 5, JalanUniversiti, Bandar Sunway, 46150 PetalingJaya, Selangor, Malaysia
Jasmine.Seng@nottingham.edu.my

Abstract. The transmission of the entire video and audio sequences over an internal or external network during the implementation of audio-visual recognition over internet protocol is inefficient especially when only selected data out of the entire video and audio sequences are actually used for the recognition process. Hence, in this paper, we propose an efficient method of implementing audio-visual recognition over internet protocol whereby only the extracted audio-visual features are transmitted over internet protocol. To extract the robust features from the video sequence, a multiband curvelet-based technique is employed at the client whereas a late multi-modal fusion scheme using RBF neural network is employed at the server to perform the recognition across both modalities. The proposed audio-visual recognition system is implemented on several standard audio-visual databases to showcase the efficiency of the system.

Keywords: curvelet transform, multiband technique, internet protocol, windows sockets.

1 Introduction

An audio-visual (AV) recognition system is a multi-modal biometric system that recognizes a person based on the person's audio (voice) and visual (face) data. However, most of these systems [1],[2],[3] are localized and does not permit remote authentication or recognition to be done. To solve this problem, a method of implementation over internet protocol (IP) is required. The works in [4] uses Java Media Framework API (JMF) to stream the video and audio data of the subject acquired from the client to the server where the recognition process is done. Based on the study carried out in these papers, it can be noted that this method of implementation is highly ineffective as the system is susceptible to packet losses when the network conditions are poor. According to the results reported in [4], the packet loss phenomenon has an adverse effect on the performance of the audio-visual recognition system. To overcome this drawback, the later work in [5] uses multi-frame technique to compensate the loss

V.V. Das, E. Ariwa, and S.B. Rahayu (Eds.): SPIT 2011, LNICST 62, pp. 132–138, 2012.
© Institute for Computer Sciences, Social Informatics and Telecommunications Engineering 2012

of information by utilizing the information contained from several frames during the recognition process. Although there is an improvement in the performance compared to using one frame for testing, there is still a slight degradation in the performance of the system implemented over internet protocol compared to the performance of the same system in its standalone state. This is because the actual problem of packet loss was not addressed but a solution to mitigate the effects of packet loss was only done. Furthermore, it is noted that the entire video and audio sequences are transmitted over the network in the above-mentioned systems while only several frames of the data are used for the recognition process at the server. This process is highly inefficient as it is a waste of network resources which is limited especially in the case of mobile networking.The use of curvelet transform [6] for face recognition has been widely explored in the works of [7-9]. These works show that curvelet transform is a viable alternative to wavelets as the latter has limited directional representation and requires more wavelets for edge representation. However, the earlier works of curvelet for face recognition only deals with face recognition on a general basis and does not particularly delve into the problem of specific visual variations such as illumination variation. The more recent work in [10] uses multiband technique to extract illumination invariant features from the decomposed curveletsubbands to improve the performance of the system to illumination variation. Nonetheless, the isolated illumination invariant features which are extracted from the high frequency subbands are less effective against expression variation because the illumination variation affects the low frequency components whereas the expression variation affects the high frequency components [11, 12]. Hence, by solely selecting the high frequency subbands to solve illumination variation will cause the current system to be susceptible to expression variation and vice versa. To overcome this problem, the work in [13] proposed a fusion scheme to harvest the benefits of both high and low frequency subbands to solve expression and illumination variations. However, the work in [13] is based on wavelets.

Hence, in this paper, we extend our previous work [10] to extract expression invariant features from the decomposed curvelets using multiband curvelet-based technique. The extracted expression and illumination invariant features are then applied to two separate radial basis function neural networks to be classified. Subsequently, the score adaptive fusion used in [13] is used to combine the classification scores of the expression and illumination invariant features. In addition to the extension of the multiband curvelet-based technique to cover expression and illumination variations, a more efficient method of implementing the overall audio-visual system over internet protocol is also proposed. The proposed implementation reduces the load on the network by transmitting only the extracted audio and visual features over internet protocol. The performance of the proposed audio-visual recognition system over internet protocol is tested with CUAVE, XM2VTS and VIER database.The outline of the paper is as follows: Section 2 describes in detail the architecture of the audio-visual system over internet protocol. The simulation results showcasing the performance of the proposed multiband curvelet-based technique and the proposed system over internet protocol is provided in Section 3. Finally, Section 4 concludes the paper.

2   Proposed AV Recognition System over Internet Protocol

The proposed audio-visual system consists of a client and server. At the client, the video of the test subject to be recognized is first captured using a webcam. The data is then demultiplexed into video and audio streams. Subsequently, the proposed multiband curvelet-based technique and MFCC[14]+LDA[15] are applied to the streams to extract the visual and audio features respectively. These extracted features are then sent to the server using the application program created using C++ and Windows Socket (WinSocks) [16]. Since the data size of the extracted features are small in comparison with the original video and audio stream, Transmission Control Protocol (TCP) is opted as the transport protocol between server and client compared to User Datagram Protocol (UDP). The use of TCP is advantageous in this case as it employs acknowledgement and retransmission to ensure that the received data stream is uncorrupted. Hence, the issue of packet loss is eliminated. At the server, the received data is passed to the RBF neural networks to be classified. To combine the audio-visual scores and the scores of the different feature sets, the three-level fusion scheme proposed in [5] is used. Figure 1 shows the block diagram of the overall proposed AV recognition system over internet protocol. The process of the proposed multiband curvelet-based technique is as follows: First, the video frames are decomposed to their subband representations using Fast Discrete Curvelet Transform (FDCT) via Wrapping [17]. The multiband selector is then applied on the decomposed curvelet to select the expression and illumination invariant features. The multiband selector uses the Average Unmatched Similarity Measure (AUMSV) and between-within class ratio to determine the level of representation contained by each subband. To determine which subbands contain the expression invariant features, we use the findings in [11, 12] to minimize our search to the approximate curvelets at different scales. Based on our simulation results on the Yale and AR database, the expression invariant features were located at the approximate subband for scale 2 and scale 3 whereas the illumination invariant feature were located at (2,1) and (2,2). Hence, in the following evaluations, the approximate subbands for scale 2 and scale 3 and the subbands at (2,1) and (2,2) are concatenated together to form the optimal curveletsubbands for expression (Curve_E) and illumination (Curve_I) respectively.

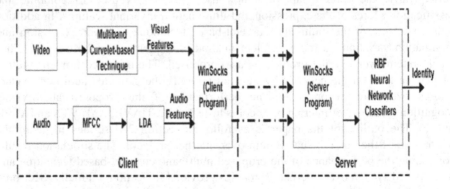

Fig. 1. Block diagram of the proposed AV recognition system over internet protocol

During the implementation over IP, the visual features (both Curve_E and Curve_I) and audio features are combined to form a singular matrix, F, prior to transmission. At the server, these features are demultiplexed back to their original form by using the received sizes of the features to reshape the received data before it is applied to the corresponding neural network for classification.

3   Results and Discussion

There are two experiments carried out in this section. The aim of the first experiment is to showcase the effectiveness of the proposed multiband curvelet-based method to other methods, particularly gradientfaces[18], dual optimal multiband features[13] and eigenfaces[19]. This is done by first evaluating the isolated optimal curveletsubbands for expression (curve_E) and illumination (curve_I) and subsequently its fusion state using the method proposed in [13]. The experiments were carried out on three standard databases namely AR database[20], Yale database [21] and ORL database[22]. Two training samples were used for each of the databases. Only images with even lighting and neutral expressions were chosen to be used as the training samples. For the case of Yale and ORL databases, the rest of the images were used as the testing samples. These images contain a mixture of facial expressions and illumination variation. On the other hand, two images containing illumination variation and two images containing expression variations were chosen as the testing samples for the AR database. The classifier used throughout the performance evaluation including for the other methods is RBF neural network classifier. The weight value for the adaptive decision fusion used to combine both feature sets in the proposed curvelet-based multiband feature technique and dual optimal multiband features is set to 0.6 as described by the original paper. Table 1 shows the recognition rate obtained for the individual feature sets and the performance of the proposed multiband curvelet-based method while Table 3 shows the performance comparison results of the proposed method to other techniques.

From Table 1, it can be seen that by using the method of fusion proposed in [13], a higher recognition rate can be achieved compared to the individual feature sets. This shows that the fusion method proposed by Wong et. al. is effective in solving the problem of adverse effect of compensating one variation for the other. However, based on the simulation results in Table 2, it can be seen that the performance of the original DOMF method can be further improved with the use of curvelets instead of wavelets.

Table 1. Recognition performance (%) for individual feature sets and the fusion set

	Curve_E	Curve_I	Fusion Set
AR	69.50	68.50	80.25
Yale	75.00	65.00	88.15
ORL	86.56	62.19	83.44

Table 2. Recognition performance (%) of the proposed method compared to other techniques

	Gradientfaces	DOMF	PCA	Multiband Curvelet-based Method
AR	76	78.5	30.8	**80.3**
Yale	86	83.7	76.3	**88.2**
ORL	71.9	83.4	58.1	**83.4**

The aim of the second experiment is to evaluate the performance of the proposed audio-visual recognition system over IP. This experiment was carried out on the CUAVE [23], XM2VTS [24] and UNMC-VIER [25] audio-visual database. For the visual parts of the experiment on the CUAVE and XM2VTS database, the first five frames were taken for training and the sixth frame was taken for testing. On the other hand, for VIER database, the five frames of the video from the controlled environment with neutral expression were used for training. One test image with facial expression and one with illumination variation were then used as the testing samples. For the audio part of the experiment, five training samples and one testing sample of each subject speaking the utterance "zero" was used for all the databases. The fusion weights between the two modalities are set to 0.5 whereas the weight value for the adaptive fusion between the features set is set to 0.6. To evaluate the effectiveness of the proposed AV system over internet protocol, the link capacity at the client and server was set according to 10Mbit/s and 380Kbit/s respectively. This is the same settings used in [5]. For reference purposes, the standalone system was also evaluated. The performance of both systems is reported in Table 3. Based on the results obtained, it can be seen that the implemented system over internet protocol is unaffected by the network conditions. This is due to the type of transport protocol used which removes packet loss completely. Hence, the data received at the server is unaffected by the network conditions as compared to the works in [4, 5].

Table 3. Recognition performance (%) of the proposed system and its standalone counterpart

	Standalone			Proposed System		
	Audio	Visual	Combined AV	Audio	Visual	Combined AV
CUAVE	83.33	100.00	100.00	83.33	100.00	**100.00**
UNMC-VIER	71.54	95.12	97.56	71.54	95.12	**97.56**
XM2VTS	75.00	100.00	100.00	75.00	100.00	**100.00**

4   Conclusion

In this paper, an audio-visual recognition system over IP using multiband curvelet-based technique was proposed. The proposed system uses WinSocks programming to implement a reliable transmission process between the client and server. To improve the efficiency of the transmission, only the extracted audio and visual features are used. A multiband curvelet-based technique is used in the proposed system to extract robust features that is invariant to illumination and expression variation. The simulation results of the proposed system shows that the proposed system is unaffected by the network conditions and has similar results to that of its standalone counterpart.

References

1. Chibelushi, C., Deravi, F., Mason, J.S.: Voice and facial image integration for speaker recognition. In: Proc. IEEE Int. Symp. Multimedia Technologies Future Appl. IEEE, Southampton (1993)
2. Brunelli, R., Falavigna, D.: Person identification using multiple cues. IEEE Trans. Pattern Anal. Machine Intell. 10, 955–965 (1995)
3. Jourlin, P., et al.: Integrating acoustic and labial information for speaker identification and verification. In: Proc. 5th Eur. Conf. Speech Communication Technology, Rhodes, Greece (1997)
4. Yee Wan Wong, K.P.S., Ang, L.M.: Audio-visual authentication or recognition System Insusceptible to Illumination Variation over Internet Protocol. IAENG International Journal of Computer Science Mag. 36(2), IJCS_36_2_0
5. Ch'ng, S.I., et al.: Robust Video Authentication System over Internet Protocol. International Journal of Biometrics 3(4), 322–336 (2011)
6. Candes, E.J., Donoho, D.L.: Curvelets, multiresolution representation, and scaling laws. In: Proc. SPIE 2000, vol. 4119(1) (2000)
7. Aroussi, M.E., et al.: Local appearance based face recognition method using block based steerable pyramid transform. Signal Processing (91), 38–50 (2010)
8. Rziza, M., et al.: Local curvelet based classification using linear discriminant analysis for face recognition. International Journal of Computer Science 4(1), 72–77 (2009)
9. Mandal, T., Wu, Q.M.J., Yuan, Y.: Curvelet based face recognition via dimension reduction. Signal Process. 89(12), 2345–2353 (2009)
10. Ch'ng, S.I., Seng, K.P., Ang, L.-M.: Curvelet-based illumination invariant feature extraction for face recognition. In: 2010 International Conference on Computer Applications and Industrial Electronics, ICCAIE (2010)
11. Ekenel, H.K., et al.: Multiresolution face recognition. Image Vision Comput. 23(5), 469–477 (2005)
12. Nastar, C., Moghaddam, B., Pentland, A.: Flexible Images: Matching and Recognition Using Learned Deformations. Computer Vision and Image Understanding 65(2), 179–191 (1997)
13. Wong, Y.W., Seng, K.P., Ang, L.-M.: Dual optimal multiband features for face recognition. Expert Systems with Applications 37(4), 2957–2962 (2010)
14. Campbell Jr., J.P.: Speaker recognition: a tutorial. Proceedings of the IEEE 85(9), 1437–1462 (1997)
15. Lu, X.: Image Analysis for Face Recognition (2003)
16. Comer, D.E.: Internetworking with TCP/IP vol.1: Principles, Protocols, and Architecture, 4th edn. Prentice Hall Internation Inc., Upper Saddle River (2000)
17. Candes, E.J., et al.: Fast discrete curvelet transform. SIAM Multiscale Model Simul. (2007)
18. Taiping, Z., et al.: Face Recognition Under Varying Illumination Using Gradientfaces. IEEE Transactions on Image Processing 18(11), 2599–2606 (2009)
19. Turk, M., Pentland, A.: Eigenfaces for face recognition. Journal of Cognitive Neuroscience 3(1), 71–86 (1991)

20. Martinez, A.M., Benavente, R.: The AR face database (1998)
21. University, Y.:
    http://www.cvc.yale.edu/projects/yalefaces/yalefaces.html
22. The ORL in Cambridge, U.:
    http://www.cl.cam.ac.uk/research/dtg/attarchive/
    facedatabase.html
23. Patterson, E.K., et al.: CUAVE: A new audio-visual database for multimodal human-computer interface research. In: Proc. ICASSP (2002)
24. Messer, K., et al.: XM2VTSDB: The Extended M2VTS Database. In: Second International Conference on Audio and Video-based Biometric Person Authentication (1999)
25. Wong, Y.W., et al.: The Audio-Visual UNMC-VIER Database. In: Proceedings of the International Conference on Embedded Systems and Intelligent Technology (ICESIT 2010) (2010)

A New Framework in Solving Tailing and Necking Problems of Thinned Binary Image

Sabarina Abu Bakar, SitiSophiayati Yuhaniz, HairudinAbd Majid,
and Habibollah Haron

Department of Modeling and Industrial Computing
Faculty of Computer Science & Information Systems
Universiti Teknologi Malaysia
Johor Bahru, Johor, Malaysia
sabarinaAB@gmail.com, {sophia,hairudin,habib}@utm.my

Abstract. A framework for solving tailing and necking problem in thinned binary image (TBI) is proposed. Tailing and necking are some of the classical problems occurred in thinned binary image. Artificial Neural Network (ANN) approach has been selected to be implemented in this study for obtaining a better thinned binary image. The identified TBI with tailing and necking problem are represented in a n x n dimensions of matrix and will be undergo a training of different set of neural network models that have been develop by using multiple layer perceptron and back propagation algorithm with different numbers of hidden layers. The experimental works show promising results.

Keywords: Tailing, necking, thinning, neural network.

1   Introduction

Thinning is a fundamental preprocessing step in image processing. This process reduces a large amount of memory usage for structural information storage [1]. Not all objects can be thinned. Thinning is only useful for objects that consist of lines, not useful for objects with shapes that enclose a significant area [2].Thinning is also defined as the process of reducing the width of a line-like object from several pixels into one pixel thick. The resultant image is called thinned binary image (TBI) or skeleton. Thinning algorithms can be classified into two types which are sequential and parallel. Both categories use iterative approach, which mean the pixels on the pattern are deleted successively until only one pixel thick skeleton is obtained. In parallel algorithm, the deletion of pixels depend only on the results of the previous iterations. On the other hand, the sequential algorithms operate on a single pixel at a time, and the deletion of pixels depend upon the preceding processing result. However, there are few properties that need to be preserved while doing a thinning in order to get a good skeleton (TBI) which are:

i.   The process does not remove the end points,
ii. The process does not break the line connectivity, and
iii. The process does not cause excessive erosion of the region

V.V. Das, E. Ariwa, and S.B. Rahayu (Eds.): SPIT 2011, LNICST 62, pp. 139–142, 2012.

Thinning is an important process, thus many algorithms have been developed since 1970's until present day. Many researches in thinning algorithm have been presented by many researchers. Stefanelli and Rosenfeld [3] investigated whether parallel thinning algorithm can be applied in digital pictures or not. The relative performance of the thinning algorithms was explained by Deutsch [4]. He compared three algorithms that had been applied to triangular, rectangular and hexagonal arrays. Zhang-Suen [5] enhanced the parallel thinning algorithm and came out with a faster parallel thinning algorithm than Stefanelli and Rosenfeld [3]. They used binary images as their application domain. In 1986, Lu and Wang [6] explored the study of parallel thinning algorithm in digital pattern and they improved the fast parallel algorithm by Zhang-Suen [5] and Stefanelli-Rosenfeld [3]. Many other researches have been conducted afterwards in order to get a better thinning algorithm by many researchers [7]. The application domains are not focused on digital patterns only but applied in differential domain like shape arrays, freehand sketch line, 3D object, fingerprint and the most popular application domain is handwritten character. One of the famous applications of thinning is character recognition, which is broadly used in the field of document analysis.

2   The Framework

In particular, the research concerns on the study of using ANN in solving tailing and necking problems of TBI. In this case, TBI of handwritten character are used as an input data. The TBI of handwritten character is obtained from a thinning process that has been conducted by Engkamat [8]. This input data is in the form of m x n matrix that consists of 0 or 1 which stand for binary image. Figure 1 shows the steps involved in each stage that are listed and explained in the remaining section.

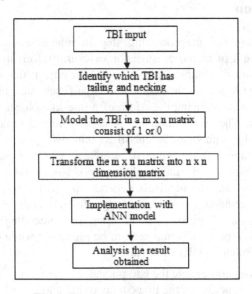

Fig. 1. The framework of the research

The first step is to identify the TBI of handwritten characters with tailing and necking and without tailing and necking. The identified handwritten characters will become the targets in the ANN training. The TBI with tailing and necking will be transformed from m x n matrix into n x n matrix dimensions in the next step. This process is to model the input training for ANN architecture. Figure 2 shows the design of input for ANN.

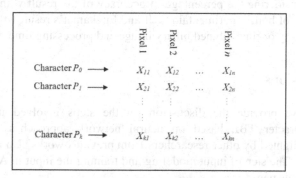

Fig. 2. Input data design

The next step is to implement the thinning algorithm in the ANN model by training the ANN model so it can fix the tailing and necking problems for each input data. The data are divided into three parts which are used for training, validating and testing in ANN learning algorithm. This algorithm is executed in MATLAB program.The training consists of a few different set of neural network models. These models use different numbers of hidden layers. The goal is set using Model Performance Evaluation (MSE) value. Figure 3 show the example of one of experimental results obtained from the training process.

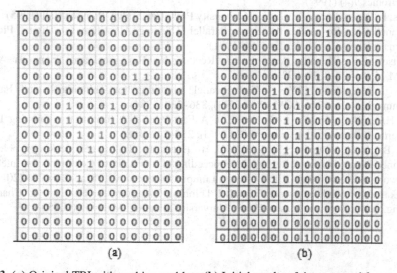

Fig. 3. (a) Original TBI with necking problem (b) Initial results of the proposed framework

From Figure 3, it can be seen that the trained ANN model has generated a new TBI from the original TBI with necking problem. In the example above, the necking problem in the original TBI is reduced. However, it produces separated pixels.The final stage of the research framework concerns on analyzing the result obtained. The result must be transform into n x n matrix first before we can change it back into m x n matrix which means the real form of binary image. The performance of the model is calculated by considering the percentage of accuracy of the result with target output. The performance of both experimental result and Engkamat's result will be compared based on the quality of final thinned binary image and processing time obtained.

3   Conclusions

In this paper we provide the discussion on the steps involved in modeling a handwritten character TBI, based on neural network approaches. Several other approaches highlighted by other researchers from previous works also been discussed in the beginning. The step of input modeling and training the input in ANN model are also outlined in this paper.

Acknowledgment. The authors honorably appreciate Ministry of Higher Education (MOHE) for the funding of the FRGS grant and Research Management Center (RMC), University Technology Malaysia (UTM) for the support in making this projects success.

References

1. Peng, Z., Zhang, L.: A Neural Network Hardware Model for Image Thinning. Journal of Electronics 9(4) (1992)
2. Pitas, I.: Digital Image Processing. University Press Cambridge, Prentice Hall (1995)
3. Stefanelli, R., Rosenfeld, A.: Some Parallel Thinning Algorithm for Digital Pictures. Journal of the ACM 18(2), 255–264 (1971)
4. Deutsch, E.S.: Thinning Algorithm on Rectangular, Hexagonal and Triangular Arrays. ACM 15(9), 827–837 (1972)
5. Zhang, T.Y., Suen, C.Y.: A Fast Parallel Algorithm for Thinning Digital Patterns. Communications of the ACM-IPCV 27(3), 236–239 (1984)
6. Lu, H.E., Wang, P.S.P.: A Comment on A Fast Parallel Algorithm for Thinning Digital Patterns. Communications of the ACM 29(3), 239–242 (1986)
7. Abu Bakar, S., Yuhaniz, S.S., AbdMajid, H., Haron, H.: Tailing and Necking Problems in Thinned Binary Image: A Review. In: Proceeding of International Conference on Intelligent Network and Computing (ICINC), Kuala Lumpur, Malaysia, vol. 1, pp. 248–251 (2010)
8. Engkamat, A.: Enhancement of Parallel Thinning Algorithm for Handwritten Characters Using Neural Network. Master Thesis, Universiti Teknologi Malaysia (2005)

Implementation and Performance of Threshold Cryptography for Multiple Escrow Agents in VoIP

Abdullah Azfar

Department of Computer Science and Information Technology (CIT),
Islamic University of Technology (IUT), Board Bazar, Gazipur 1704, Bangladesh
azfar@iut-dhaka.edu

Abstract. This paper focuses on improving the accessibility and security of multiple escrow agents by dividing the session master key into M chunks and escrowing the chunks with M escrow agents. Using threshold cryptography the key can be regenerated by gathering any N-out-of-M chunks. This N-out-of-M approach increases the security of the session master key as at least N chunks of the session key are needed to regenerate the session key. Disclosure of less than N chunks does not threat the security of the session key. On the other hand, failure of a single escrow agent does not affect the availability of the session key as long as N escrow agents are working. For a highly sophisticated session, the user might define a higher value for M and N. For a less confidential or less important session, the value of M and N might be smaller.

Keywords: Key escrow, VoIP, Escrow Agents, Threshold Cryptography, Shamir's Secret Sharing.

1   Introduction

An escrow agent is a trusted third party (TTP) with whom users store their session master key. The term key escrow refers to storing the cryptographic key with a TTP or escrow agent [1]. Using a Key escrow agent in conjunction with Voice over IP (VoIP) communication ensures that law enforcements agencies (LEAs) can retrieve the session key used to encrypt data between two users in a VoIP session. However, the use of a single escrow agent has some drawbacks. A fraudulent request by an evil employee from the LEA can lead to improper disclosure of a session key. The problem with a single escrow agent becomes even more critical as a failure of the escrow agent can delay or even make it impossible to reveal the session key.With threshold cryptography [2] approach, the session key is divided into several parts and each part is stored in different escrow agents. For (N, M) threshold cryptography, there will be M escrow agents with each escrow agent stores their own secret part. If at least N escrow agents reveal their secret parts, then the session key can be generated. The secret shares in threshold cryptography do not have any explicit relation with each other. If one escrow agent is compromised by an attacker, only the secret portion stored by that escrow agent is revealed. The complete key can be

V.V. Das, E. Ariwa, and S.B. Rahayu (Eds.): SPIT 2011, LNICST 62, pp. 143–150, 2012.

generated only if N escrow agents' keys are compromised. Additionally, if one or more escrow agents are not functioning, the key can still be generated as long as N escrow agents are functioning. This gives extra reliability for key retrieval.In this paper, we have split the session key of a VoIP session into five chunks and escrowed them to five escrow agents. The threshold value is set to three as the session key can be regenerated by combining any of the three chunks out of the five chunks. This is the first approach of threshold cryptography in the context of the escrowing of VoIP session key.The rest of the paper is organized as follows: related works are reviewed in section 2. The design and implementation issues of splitting the session key are discussed in section 3. The performance measurements and discussion are done in section 4. Finally, some conclusions are drawn in section 5.

2   Related Works

RomanidisEvripidis at the Royal Institute of Technology (KTH) addressed the issues of key escrow [3]. The escrow agent stores the session key and some related data. The LEA is assumed to have recorded a communication session between two users. The escrow agent reveals the key to the LEA upon a legal request from the LEA. He pointed out that there is a problem when using a single escrow agent as any evil person either in the LEA or in the escrow agent can reveal the session key.The problem of forgery by a single escrow agent can be overcome by signing the hashes of the data with the user's private key and storing the final hash with the escrow agent. This proposed solution has been implemented by Md. SakhawatHossen at the Royal Institute of Technology (KTH) [4]. Md. SarwarJahanMorshed addressed the issues of a LEA when retrieving a session key and performing decryption of a captured session [5].

3   Design and Implementation Issues

As we are interested in splitting the key into M chunks and then retrieve the key from N-out-f-M chunks, a suitable algorithm for this would be Shamir's Secret Sharing Algorithm [7][7]. Shamir's secret sharing is an N-out-of-M threshold scheme based on polynomial interpolation. At least N participants must provide their shares in order to decrypt the secret. Shamir's Secret Sharing algorithm is scalable because the number of chunks can be changed. As a result, it is possible to increase or decrease the value of M or N for an implementation.We have used Minisip [8] as our user agent. Minisip is an open source Voice over Internet Protocol (VoIP) user agent (UA). It is based on the Session Initiation Protocol (SIP) [9] and special security features are included in it. The user agent is responsible for splitting the keys. The escrow agents will only store the escrowed information. The splitting operation is performed in the user agent and the user agent stores the values in files. Upon successful connection with the escrow agent, the user agent escrows the split values. This is shown in Fig. 1.

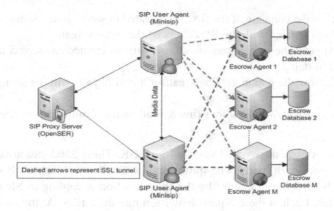

Fig. 1. General architecture of M Escrow agents

According to the thesis of Hossen [4] and Morshed [5], they have escrowed the session master key, i.e., the Traffic Encryption Key (TEK) Generation Key (TGK) along with the pseudo-random number (Rand), last signed hash and Crypto Session Bundle (CSB) ID value. This key is exchanged by the key agreement protocol MIKEY [10]. This TGK along with some security parameters are used to generate the session keys for encryption and integrity protection.In our case, we have extended the escrow operation from one escrow agent to multiple escrow agents. Thus, the parameters being escrowed remained the same. But question arises which parameters should be split and then escrowed. The reason behind splitting the key is to enhance security and availability of the key. Splitting the Rand, last signed hash and CSB ID value enhances the security, but it is not really necessary to do so. If we rather only split the TGK and replicate the Rand, last signed hash and CSB ID value to M escrow agents, then our purpose is served. As this implementation is an N-out-of-M system, no one can retrieve the TGK value without having at least N chunks. This increases the security and confidentiality. Again, the availability increases as even if few escrow agents are not working, the key is retrievable from N escrow agents.

3.1   Implementation of Split Operation

The procedure of splitting the key into chunks and escrowing them can be depicted by a general algorithm. The algorithm works according to the following steps:

Step 1: Create five files for temporarily storing the key chunks.

Step 2: Divide the TGK into two parts.

Step 3: Invoke the split function for each of the parts.

Step 4: Each part is split into five subparts. Store each of these split parts into the files created in step 1. The five subparts created from the first part will be the first entries in the five files. Five subparts created from the second part will be the next entry in the files. Separate them with a separator "%".

Step 5: Create a temporary string with the Rand, signed hash, CSB ID value and the names of the escrow agents. Separate them with "%" symbol.

Step 6: Read the contents of the first file created in step 1 into a string.

Step 7: Form a string with the IP address of the escrow agent.

Step 8: Append the user id, password and strings created in steps 5 and 6 to the string created in step 7.

Step 9: Escrow the parameters by creating a curl object with the string formed in step 8.

Step 10: Repeat steps 6 to 9 four times, read values from different files each time in step 6.

There are 256 bytes in the base 64 value of the TGK. These 256 bytes are divided into 2 equal (128 bytes each) parts. The split function is called for each of these parts and each part is divided into 5 chunks by the split function according to Shamir's Secret Share algorithm. Each of these 5 parts is written into the 5 files. At the end of the split operation, we get 5 files. Each of the files contains 2 subparts of the TGK. These 2 parts are separated by a "%" symbol.An URL is formed with the IP address of the first escrow agent, user name and password of the user appended by the contents of the first file. The signed hash value, rand value, CSB ID values are appended into the URL separated by a "%" symbol without any modification. We have used secure HTTP (HTTPS) to escrow the session master key. The key is transferred along with the URL of the escrow agent by appending a key value pair in addition to the key value pairs used to provide the user name and password for authentication to the escrow agent. To escrow the session master key with the escrow agent from the user agent we have used libcurl [11]. We have used third party code written by B. Poettering [12] for splitting the key licensed under the GNU General Public License [13]. We have modified the code according to our need to integrate with Minisip.

3.2   Implementation of Combine Operation

This subsection discusses about the general approach of how we have designed our system to retrieve the key chunks from the escrow agents and combine them in order to get the TGK. The general algorithm is as follows:

Step 1: Login to the escrow agent by providing user id and password by a web based form.

Step 2: Provide the target user id, start time and end time of target session for which the session key has to be retrieved.

Step 3: For authenticated user, read the first escrow agent database and fetch the two parts of the split TGK, Rand, CSB ID value, last signed hash value and names of the escrow agents.

Step 4: Write the values read in step 3 into a temporary file. Separate the values by a "%" symbol.

Step 5: Repeat step 3 and 4 for four other escrow agents. For each escrow agent, write the retrieved values in separate files.

Step 6: Read any three files until the first separator "%" is found.

Step 7: Invoke the combining function with the values fetched in step 6. At theend of this step we get the first half of the TGK.

Step 8: Read the same three files read in step 6 starting after the first "%" symbol until the next "%" symbol is found.

Step 9: Invoke the combining function with the values fetched in step 8. At the end of this step we get the second half of the TGK.

Step 10: Merge the two halves of the TGK to get the session key.

A php script has been written in order to fetch the information from the escrow agents. The php script runs five times and invokes the escrow agents one after another. Upon successful invocation on the escrow agents the script fetches the two split parts of the TGK, Rand, CSB ID, the signed hash value and the names of the escrow agents and writes them into files separated by a "%" symbol. After invoking five escrow agents, the LEA is provided with five text files. This text files are stored and are inputs to the combining function.

4   Performance Measurements and Discussion

For the purpose of measuring the performance of the escrow operations we used the experimental setup as shown in fig. 2.

Fig. 2. Experimental setup for escrow operations

We have used one machine as SIP user agent and another machine as the SIP proxy server and other user agent. We have used a third machine configured as escrow agents along with escrow databases. The escrow agents machine was connected to the user agent via SSL tunnel. The escrow agents machine had five databases and five escrow agents defined in it. We have used SuSE version10.3 of Linux,on DellT7570with Intel® Pentium® D CPU processor clocked at 2.80GHz and configured with2048MB of memory as the SIP user agents and proxy server.The base 64 TGK value consists of 256 bytes. We have divided this value into two equal halves. Then we executed the split function ten times for each of the halves and each time the split function was executed hundred times. In a normal execution, the split function is called twice, once for the first half of the TGK, and again for the remaining half of the TGK value. In our experiment, we executed the split function one hundred times for the same TGK value. The procedure was repeated ten times with ten different TGK values. As a result we have ten measurements for each of these hundred calls.Fig. 3 shows a box plot of the measured execution time of the split function for the first half of the base 64 TGK value. The reason for this large number of outliers in round 2 is unknown. But we can make some assumptions based on the following facts: The time to compute the split is data dependent - i.e., for different values of a key it takes different amounts of time, the computer is multitasking - thus the CPU is being allocated to other processes, and the computer is also servicing interrupts from various devices.

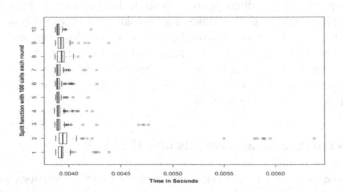

Fig. 3. Execution time for split function applied to the first 128 bytes of the TGK

Fig. 4 shows the box plot for the execution time of the split function for the second half of the TGK value encoded in base 64 (i.e., the last 128 bytes). The scale for this figure is quite different for the previous figure, due to the one extreme outlier at 0.1 seconds in round 10.

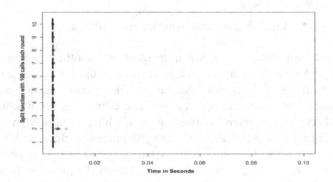

Fig. 4. Execution time for split function applied to the last 128 bytes of the TGK

Table 1 shows the statistical data found from the time required to split the first 128 bytes and last 128 bytes of the base 64 TGK value using 1,000 calls of the split function. Here, the unit of time is seconds.

Some observations can be made from table 1. First, the mean time to execute the split function for the first half of TGK encoded in base 64 is 0.0039 seconds and the mean time to execute the split function for the second half of the TGK encoded in base 64 is 0.004 seconds. So, the mean time to execute the split function for escrowing the TGK encoded in base 64 is the sum of these two values i.e. 0.0079

Table 1. Statistical data to split two halves of TGK encoded in base 64

	First 128 bytes	Last 128 bytes
Count	1000	1000
Mean	0.0039	0.004
Median	0.0039	0.0039
Mode	0.0038	0.0038
Standard Deviation	0.00019	0.003
Sample Variance	3.72056E-08	9.38E-06
Minimum	0.0038	0.0038
Maximum	0.0063	0.1
Confidence Level (95.0%)	3.82489E-07	6.07E-06

seconds or 7.9 milliseconds. The next observation is that the median values are identical in both experiments. The third and final observation is that the minimum time required to execute the split operation is same for both experiments. This means that the time to split the original 256 byte based 64 encoded TGK is 2 * 0.0038 seconds or 7.6 milliseconds.

5   Conclusions

This paper focused on a proposal, implementation, and evaluation of a multiple key escrow agent model that allows escrowing the session keys into M escrow agents. Shamir's secret sharing algorithm was used to implement threshold cryptography. This is the first approach of using Shamir's secret sharing algorithm for dividing the session key of a VoIP session. The session key was divided into M chunks and each of the chunks was escrowed to the M escrow agents. An N-out-of-M key retrieval mechanism was implemented. This allowed to retrieve the key by retrieving at least N chunks out of M chunks where the value of N is always less than or equal to the value of M. Practically, the system was implemented with 5 escrow agents with a threshold value of 3. This increased the security as if an LEA officer wants to retrieve the key chunks for a session, he or she has to convince at least 3 escrow agents. In case of fraudulent request, it is difficult to convince all those 3 escrow agents with a fraudulent notice. On the other hand, the reliability of the key being retrieved properly increased as if any of the 2 escrow agents are unavailable for some reason, the remaining 3 escrow agents can provide the key chunks.

Acknowledgments. This work was a part of a Master thesis project in the Department of Communication Systems (CoS) in the Royal Institute of Technology (KTH), Sweden. We would like to thank Professor Gerald Q. Maguire Jr. for his continuous support and guidance throughout the project.

References

1. Abelson, H., Anderson, R., Bellovin, S.M., Benaloh, J., Blaze, M., Diffie, W., Gilmore, J., Neumann, P.G., Rivest, R.L., Schiller, J.I., Schneier, B.: The Risks of Key Recovery, Key Escrow, and Trusted Third-Party Encryption (1997),
   http://www.schneier.com/paper-key-escrow.pdf
2. Zhou, H., Mutka, M.W., Ni, L.M.: Multiple-key cryptography-based distributed certificate authority in mobile ad-hoc networks. In: Global Telecommunications Conference, GLOBECOM 2005, vol. 3. IEEE, St. Louis (2005)
3. Evripidis, R.: Lawful Interception and Countermeasures: In the era of Internet Telephony, School of Information and Communication Technology (COS/CCS), 2008-20, Royal Institute of Technology (KTH), Stockholm (2008),
   http://web.it.kth.se/~maguire/DEGREE-PROJECT-REPORTS/
   080922-Romanidis_Evripidis-with-cover.pdf
4. Hossen, M.S.: A Session Initiation Protocol User Agent with Key Escrow: Providing authenticity for recordings of secure sessions, Department of Communication Systems (CoS), Royal Institute of Technology (KTH), TRITA-ICT-EX-2010:1, Stockholm (2010),
   http://web.it.kth.se/~maguire/DEGREE-PROJECT-REPORTS/
   100118-Md._Sakhawat_Hossen-with-cover.pdf
5. Morshed, M.S.J.: VoIP Lawful Intercept: Good Cop/Bad Cop, Department of Communication Systems (CoS), Royal Institute of Technology (KTH), TRITA-ICT-EX-2010:28, Stockholm (2010), http://web.it.kth.se/~maguire/DEGREE-PROJECT-REPORTS/100221-Muhammad_Sarwar_Jahan_Morshed-with-cover.pdf
6. Shamir, A.: How to share a secret. Communications of the ACM 22(11) (1979)
7. RSA Laboratories, http://www.rsa.com/RSALABS/node.asp?id=2259
8. MiniSIP homepage, http://www.minisip.org
9. Rosenberg, J., Schulzrinne, H., Camarillo, G., Johnston, A., Peterson, J., Sparks, R., Handley, M., Schooler, E.: SIP: Session Initiation Protocol, IETF RFC 3261, IETF Network Working Group (2002)
10. Arkko, J., Carrara, E., Lindholm, F., Naslund, M., Norrman, K.: MIKEY: Multimedia Internet KEYing, IETF RFC 3830, IETF Network Working Group (2004)
11. Libcurl-the Multiprotocol File Transfer Library, http://curl.haxx.se/libcurl/
12. Shamir's Secret Sharing Scheme, http://point-at-infinity.org/ssss/
13. GNU General Public License, http://www.gnu.org/licenses/gpl.html

Error Recovery Mechanism for iSCSI Protocol Based Mobile NAS Cluster System

Shaikh Muhammad Allayear[1], Sung Soon Park[2], Md. Nawab Yousuf Ali[3], and Ullah Mohammad Hasmat[4]

[1,2,3,4] Dept of Computer Science and Engineering
[1,3] East West University, Bangladesh
[2,4] Anyang University, Korea
{allayear,nawab}@ewubd.edu, {sspark,raju}@anyang.ac.kr

Abstract. In this paper, we proposed an error recovery module for iSCSI protocol based NAS (Network Attached Storage) system in wireless network environment, which ensures reliability and efficiency data transmission.

Keywords: iSCSI Protocol, Network Storage, wireless network.

1   Introduction

A NAS system is usually a specially designed device providing clients with files on a LAN; it is widely used to bridge the interoperability gap with many advantages.However, NAS supports only file I/O protocol such as NFS and CIFS, block-level storage applications are not available on NAS with the performance of NFS and CIFS is only a fraction of the exported storage system. To this day, they continue to have limited network, CPU, memory, and disk I/O resources due to their single server design, which binds one network endpoint to all files in a file system.Now, the iSCSI storage has emerged. iSCSI is an Internet Protocol-based storage standard for linking data storage facilities, and presents storage to servers as disk targets[1], which, from the perspective of the application, appear to be storage attached locally to the server. It presents storage space as virtual block-level devices, operating systems and applications have the ability to put their own file systems on them, which is something not possible with NAS.In current age mobile appliances are going to be used in more area as the time goes by. Due to their mobility, they should be small and use a flash memory to store the data. So it is very difficult to store large data and install large software [2],[3],[4],[5],[6],[7].To alleviate these problems and access mass storage we developed MNAS [6], an iSCSI based NAS Cluster system, for providing the allocation of a mass storage space to each mobile client through networks. The system offers to its users the possibility of keeping large size of data and database in a secure and safe space. But in wireless environment data may losses due to bad channel characteristics, interference or intermittent connectivity due to handoffs (mobile appliance). ISCSI over TCP performance in such networks suffers

V.V. Das, E. Ariwa, and S.B. Rahayu (Eds.): SPIT 2011, LNICST 62, pp. 151–156, 2012.

from significant throughput degradation and [1]very high interactive delays. Therefore, in this paper we propose error recovery module for iSCSI protocol based mobile NAS cluster system.The organization of this paper is as follows. In section 2, we described the motivations of iSCSI data transmission and parameters in wireless environment. In Section 3, error recovery method has described. Experiments and Analysis has described in section 4 and finally we conclude this paper in section 5.

2   Motivation

When we use iSCSI protocol in network with wireless and other lossy links in order to offer mobile NAS services with this situation, it suffers from significant non-congestion-related losses due to several reasons such as a bit errors and handoffs. So mobile NAS services in wireless networks needs several schemes designed to improve the performance of TCP as a try.Communication over wireless link is often characterized by sporadic high bit-error rates, and intermittent connectivity due to handoffs. TCP reacts to packet losses as it would in the wired environment and it drops its transmission window size before re-transmitting packets and resets its retransmission timer. These measures result in an unnecessary reduction in the link's bandwidth utilization, thereby causing a significant degradation in performance in the form of poor throughput and very high interactive delays [6].Since iSCSI runs on a TCP network, it requires new strategies to evade the forceful decrease of transmission rate from TCP congestion control mechanism without changing existing TCP.The iSCSI Data-In PDUs are passed to the TCP layer, since the iSCSI PDU is a SCSI transport protocol over TCP/IP. When the iSCSI Data-In PDU size is greater than the MSS (maximum segment size) of TCP layer, the PDU will be further fragmented into smaller segments. The iSCSI Data-In PDU is generally larger than the MSS in size. If some segments of parts of an iSCSI Data-In PDU are lost due to the high bit error rate in wireless networks, TCP layer would require re-transmitting the segments. At that time all the other segments of those parts of an iSCSI Data-In PDU must wait for being reassembled into an iSCSI Data-In PDU in TCP buffer. It decreases the performance of the system due to the reducing of the available capacity of TCP buffer. The sender can transmit data segments, which are allowed by the receiver using TCP flow control mechanism. In a wireless network with high bit error rate, the more size of iSCSI PDU is increased by the MRDSL (MaxRecvDataSegmentLength) parameter, the more segments would have to wait due to the lost of some segments of parts of an iSCSI PDU in TCP buffer. The performance of the system thus decreases more in both write and read operation. In addition, a wireless link generally becomes a bottleneck portion in an end-to-end TCP connection because of its narrowbandwidth, it also one the cause of performance falling to the storage system for mobile applications.

---

[1] This research (Grants No.2009-0075576) was supported by Basic Science Research Program through the National Research Foundation of Korea (NRF) funded by Ministry of Education, Science and Technology.

[2] This work (Grants No. 47504) was supported by Business for Cooperative R&D between industry, Academy and Research Institute funded Korea small and Medium Business Administration 2011.

3   Error Recovery Module in iSCSI Protocol for Mobile NAS Cluster System

The error recovery module was implemented MNAS (Mobile NAS Cluster System)[6]. A storage management tool was placed on top of it. The storage management tool is used to allocate server's storage to each client to pre-defined extent. Figure 1 shows the architecture of error recovery module.

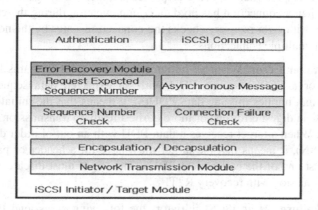

Fig. 1. Architecture of Error Recovery Module of MNAS (Mobile NAS Cluster System)

For the mobile appliances, it is very important because of high error rate in the wireless network. The following two considerations prompted the design of much of the error recovery functionality in iSCSI [7],[8].

– An iSCSI PDU may fail the digest check and be dropped, despite being received by the TCP layer. The iSCSI layer must optionally be allowed to recover such dropped PDUs.
– A TCP connection may fail at any time during the data transfer. All the active tasks must optionally be allowed to continue on a different TCP connection within the same session.

Considerable Errors. The iSCSI initiator and the iSCSI target organize the iSCSI system. iSCSI initiator is used on a mobile device, PDAs in this paper, iSCSI target has one or more mass storage devices.In wireless environment, many kinds of errors can be happened. However, iSCSI error recovery considers the errors on iSCSI protocol layer. iSCSI error recovery module considers following two errors in this paper.

– Sequence Number Error: When the iSCSI protocol transmits iSCSI Command PDU or Data PDU that has a sequence number, some PDU can be lost. So iSCSIPDU receiver (an initiator or a target) cannot get the valid PDU, it will get the PDU with an out of order.

– Connection Failure: If iSCSI target or initiator cannot communicate each other via a TCP connection, we define this situation, "connection failure".

3.1   Error Recovery Procedure

iSCSI protocol with error recovery checks the sequence number of every iSCSI PDU. If iSCSI target or initiator receives an iSCSI PDU with an out of order sequence number, then it requests an expected sequence number PDU again. In Connection failure case, when a connection has no data communication during the engaged time, iSCSI protocol with error recovery checks the connection status by the nop-command. We assume the multiple connections.

Sequence Number Error. When an initiator receives an iSCSI status PDU with an out of order or a SCSI response PDU with an expected data sequence number (ExpDataSN) that implies missing data PDU(s), it means that the initiator detected a header or payload digest error one or more earliest ready to transmission (R2T) PDUs or data PDUs. When a target receives a data PDU with an out of order data sequence number (DataSN), it means that the target must have hit a header or payload digest error on at least one of the earlier data PDUs. The target must discard the PDU and request retransmission with recovery R2T.

Connection Failure. At an iSCSI initiator, the following cases lend themselves to connection recovery

– TCP connection failure: The initiator must close the connection. It then must either implicitly or explicitly logout the failed connection with the reason code "remove the connection for recovery" and reassign connection allegiance for all commands still in progress associated with the failed connection on one or more connections. For an initiator, a command is in progress as long as it has not received a response or a Data-in PDU including status.
– Receiving an Asynchronous Message that indicates one or all connections in a session has been dropped. The initiator must handle it as a TCP connection failure for the connection(s) referred to in the Message.
   At an iSCSI target, the following case lend themselves to connection recovery

TCP Connection Failure. The target must close the connection and, if more than one connection is available, the target should send an Asynchronous Message that indicates it has dropped the connection. Then, the target will wait for the initiator to continue recovery.

4   Experiments and Analysis

We use the iSCSI initiator on Microsoft Windows CE.net 4.20 emulator version 4.0.2 for the convenience of experiments though it is available on real mobile devices like PDA. The iSCSI target is on the Linux kernel version 2.4.18 (Red hat 8.0). We experiment with the 100Mbps Ethernet and the private network for no interference. Also we make the error for the experiments by ourselves.

Experiment for Sequence Error and Connection Failure. PDU loss is generated factitiously for this experiment and round trip time (RTT) of PDU is about 0.4 second. We use iSCSI write Command PDUs for 1 Mbyte data in this experiment. The experiment progress is:

- Initiator sends iSCSI PDUs to write 1Mbyte data.
- Several PDUs would not be sent by the PDU loss rate during the transmission.
- Target checks the PDU loss by the sequence number checking, and then it requests the PDU of the expected sequence number.

We consider an error recovery failure that target cannot receive the PDU of the expected sequence number during the time (RTT $\times 2 + \alpha = 1$ second).

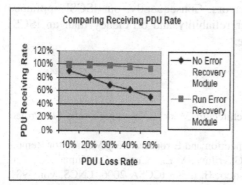 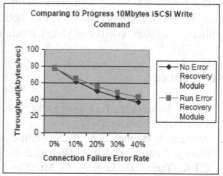

Fig. 2. Comparing the iSCSI PDU Receiving Rate. In this figure Y-axis is representing the PDU Receiving Rate and X-axis is representing the PDU Loss Rate.

Fig. 3. Comparing to Progress 10Mbytes iSCSI Write Command. In this figure Y-axis is representing the throughput and X-axis is representing the connection failure error rate.

Figure 2 shows that PDU receiving rate is drastically decreasing without an error recovery module. However, the case of running our error recovery module just has about 8% PDU loss at 50% PDU loss rate. We assumed following factors for the experiments of connection failure:

- PDU loss is not considered.
- When iSCSI module without an error recovery has a connection failure, it reconnects after 60 seconds (Linux version 2.4.2 TCP Timeout). When iSCSI module has an error recovery, it reconnects by an error recovery module. We did not consider the time to reconnect by TCP or an error recovery module.
- Connection failure error rate is 0%, 10%, 20%, 30% and 40%. 10% Connection failure error rate is defined that 1/10 connections of all connections has connection failure during the time (DefaultTime2Wait + DefaultTime2Retain = 22 seconds) [8].

– We experimented with 4 connections and a connection failure can be happened concurrently.
– We experimented iSCSI write commands because iSCSI read commands have similar characters with iSCSI write commands.

Figure 3 shows that writing progress with our error recovery module has better throughput than writing progress without an error recovery module. Increasing the connection failure error rate, the difference of throughput becomes larger. Result showed that the difference of throughput on 40% error rate was above 6 Kbytes/sec.

5   Conclusion

In this paper, we describe the implementation of the error recovery module for iSCSI protocol based Mobile NAS Cluster system. According to experiments, iSCSI appliance with our error recovery module can transfer data stably and efficiently in wireless network which can have many errors. Consequently, our iSCSI appliance with the error recovery module has better reliability and efficiency than an iSCSI appliance without an error recovery module.

References

1. SAM-3 Information Technology – SCSI Architecture Model 3, Working Draft, T10 Project 1561-D, Revision 7 (2003)
2. Allayear, S.M., Park, S.S.: iSCSI Multi-connection and Error Recovery Method for Remote Storage System in Mobile Appliance. In: Gavrilova, M.L., Gervasi, O., Kumar, V., Tan, C.J.K., Taniar, D., Laganá, A., Mun, Y., Choo, H. (eds.) ICCSA 2006. LNCS, vol. 3981, pp. 641–650. Springer, Heidelberg (2006)
3. Kim, D., Ok, M., Park, M.-S.: An Intermediate Target for Quick-Relay of Remote Storage to Mobile Devices. In: Gervasi, O., Gavrilova, M.L., Kumar, V., Laganá, A., Lee, H.P., Mun, Y., Taniar, D., Tan, C.J.K. (eds.) ICCSA 2005. LNCS, vol. 3481, pp. 1035–1044. Springer, Heidelberg (2005)
4. Park, S., Moon, B.-S., Park, M.-S.: Design, Implement and Performance Analysis of the Remote Storage System in Mobile Environment. In: Proc. ICITA 2004 (2004)
5. Ok, M., Kim, D., Park, M.-S.: UbiqStor: A Remote Storage Service for Mobile Devices. In: Liew, K.-M., Shen, H., See, S., Cai, W. (eds.) PDCAT 2004. LNCS, vol. 3320, pp. 685–688. Springer, Heidelberg (2004)
6. Allayear, S.M., Park, S.S.: iSCSI Protocol Adaptation With NAS System Via Wireless Environment. In: International Conference on Consumer Electronics (ICCE), Las Vegus, USA (2008)
7. Allayear, S.M., Park, S.S., No, J.: iSCSI Protocol Adaptation with 2-way TCP Hand Shake Mechanism for an Embedded Multi-Agent Based Health Care Service. In: Proceedings of the 10th WSEAS International Conference on Mathematical Methods, Computational Techniques and Intelligent Systems, Corfu, Greece (2008)
8. RFC 3270, http://www.ietf.org/rfc/rfc3720.txt

Generation of Bangla Text from Universal Networking Language Expression

Md. Nawab Yousuf Ali[1], Shaikh Muhammad Allayear[1], M. Ameer Ali[1],
and Golam Sorwar[2]

[1] Department of Computer Science and Engineering, East West University, Bangladesh
[2] Southern Cross University, Australia
nawab,allayear@ewubd.edu, ameer7302002@yahoo.com,
golam.sorwar@scu.edu.au

Abstract. This paper presents a work on generating Bangla sentences from an interlingua representation called Universal Networking Language (UNL). UNL represents knowledge in the form of semantic network like hyper-graphs which contains disambiguated words, binary semantic relations, and speech act like attributes associated with the words, assisted by the semantically rich lexicon and a set of analysis and generation rules. We have developed a set of generation rules for converting UNL expression to Bangla sentences. Our experiment shows that these rules successfully generate correct Bangla sentences from UNL expressions.

Keywords: Interlingua, Universal Networking Language, Universal Word, Morphology, DeConverter, Generation Rules.

1   Introduction

A significant part of the development of any machine translation (MT) system is the creation of lexical resources that the system will use. Dictionaries are of critical importance in MT. They are the largest components of an MT system in terms of the amount of information they hold. Generation of natural language from a machine processable, precise knowledge representation has to grapple with the problem of redundancy and impreciseness inherent in any natural language. In the UNL system [1], natural language analysis is carried out by two tools: EnConverter (EnCo) [2] and DeConverte (DeCo) [3]. Both tools are associated with a word dictionary of the native language and a set of language specific analysis and generation rules. EnCo converts a natural language text into corresponding UNL expressions whereas DeCo converts UNL expressions to a variety of natural languages. We have worked on various types of simple sentences. For brevity, in this paper we present the steps to construct a simple affirmative sentence. In our earlier work [4], [5-6], we have shown how to convert Bangla sentences into UNL expressions. In this paper we present a set of generation rules to convert UNL expressions into Bangla sentences. By using these generation rules along with a supporting word dictionary Bangla . Analysis of Hindi

V.V. Das, E. Ariwa, and S.B. Rahayu (Eds.): SPIT 2011, LNICST 62, pp. 157–163, 2012.

grammar for parts of speech tagger has been performed by Chakrabarti and Bhattacharyya [7], Chakrabarti*et al.* [8] and Singh *et al.* [9] and generation of Hindi from UNL has been analyzed by Dwivedi [10]. Hindi grammar has been analyzed to create UNL based MT system for Hindi language. Hindi generation rules for Hindi EnConverter have been created by analyzing Hindi grammar by Giri [11], Dave *et al.* [12], and Bhattacharyya *et al* [13]. The analysis of Tamil morphology for the development of Tamil EnConverter for EnConversion of Tamil to UNL has been performed by Dhanabalan*et al* [14]. Similar kinds of works have been done in many other countries such as French, Spanish [15], Chinese, English, Russian, and German [16]. For Bangla language processing, research has been done for morphological analysis of Bangla words [17], parsing methodology for Bangla sentences [18] and dictionary development of Bangla words[19]. Suffix, prefix and inflexions are discussed in [20]. No previous attempt has been made to convert Bangla texts into UNL expressions and UNL expressions to Bangla texts.

Section 2 explains the different stages in the generation process and outlines the format of dictionary entries. After proposing the generation rules and illustrating the experimental results in section 3, we summarize the paper with some concluding remarks in section 4.

2   Stages in the Generation Process

The generation process consists of three main stages morphological generation of lexical words, function words insertion, and syntax planning. In morphological analysis, Bangla nouns inflect for number and case, and can be described as having major categories of the forms based on the oppositions direct-oblique and singular-plural. They can be categorized into masculine and feminine gender in terms of their agreement with adjectives and verbs. In UNL, plural nouns are represented using the attribute *@pl,* and singular ones remain unspecified (absence of *@pl*refers to a singular noun). Gender and vowel endings are stored in the UNL-Bangla dictionary. The morphological rules based on word paradigms generate a noun form using all this information, *viz.,* lexical, relational, and UNL attributes.Bangla verbs inflect based on vowel ended and consonant ended roots [6]. Inflections are marked either on the main verb or on its auxiliaries that appear as free morphemes.

Roles of Root and Verbal Inflexion in the Formation and Meaning of a Verb. A root contains the core meaning, which relates with the action or state of the verb, whereas verbal inflexion (VI) defines the formation of the verb and reflects person, tense (in case of finite verb) and other properties [7].

Variations of Roots. For development of the lexicon for UNL compatible Bangla Word Dictionary and rules for morphological and semantic analyses, Vowel Ended and Consonant Ended roots have been divided into several groups [6]. It has been observed that some of the roots change their forms when they combine with some specific VIs to make verbs. All the variations of a root appear in the lexicon at different entities, though they all contain same UW but in case of grammatical attributes we use ALT (for first alternative), ALT1(for second alternative) and ALT2 (third alternative) etc. and rest of the attributes will be the same for all variations.

UNL encodes case information by using relation labels assigned as per the properties of the connected nodes. Consider, for example, the translation of sentence, 'আমি কলম দিয়ে চিঠি লিখচ্ছি', pronounce as "Ami kolom die chitthi likhchhi" means *I am writing a letter with a pen*. Here, the case marke 'দিয়ে' *(diye)* and 'ছি' *(chhi)* are inserted to derive the relation 'কলম', *kolom* (pen) and 'লিখচ্ছি', *likhchhi* (writing) have with the verb 'write'. Given a node along with all its lexical attributes from the UNL Bangla dictionary, an appropriate case marker is inserted. Similarly, other function words like- conjunctions, disjunctions, particles, *etc.*, are also inserted to represent clausal information.

Dictionary Format. Each entry of the Word Dictionary is composed of three kinds of elements: the **Headword (HW)**, the **Universal Word (UW)** and the **Grammatical Attributes** [4], [16].

Data Format: **[HW]{ID}"UW"(Attribute1, Attribute2,...)<FLG, FRE, PRI>**

According to the dictionary format some examples are as follows:

[আমি]{ }"i(icl>person)"(PRON,HPRON, P1,SG,SUBJ)<B,1,1>
[ভাত]{ }"rice (icl>food)"(N)<B,0,0>

The entries in parentheses are morpho-syntactic and semantic attributes of Bangla words which control various generation decisions choosing special case makers.

3   Conversion of UNL Expression to Bangla Texts

A set of generation rules is to be used to generate native language sentences from UNL expressions. The DeConverter finds the most suitable rule to create a native language sentence. A set of native language sentences from UNL expressions will finally be generated after applying all the necessary rules. Among the various types of generation rules described in [3], *Attribute changing* (:) rule plays an important role to insert words and morphemes from node-nets of UNL expressions into node-list for making the sentences. Attribute changing rule is used to rewrite the attributes of the nodes in both left and right Generation Windows. If any rewriting action occurs in the node of the Left Generation Window, the position of the Generation Window moves to the left so that the Right Generation Window will always be placed on the rewritten node. It is also used for insertion node. In that case, either node in the Generation Window must be indicated as being an inserted node. If the left node is an inserted node, the Right Generation Window will move so that it is placed on it after the rule application.

3.1   Proposed Rules

In this section, formats of some generation rules have been proposed that are to be used for converting UNL expressions to Bangla sentences. We define format of rules to insert subjective pronouns for agent (agt) relation of both alternative and not alternative roots. We also define rules to insert subjective pronouns for thing with attributes (aoj) relation of both alternative and not alternative roots. Format of rules is also defined to insert verbal inflexions at the end of roots for first, second and third persons. Finally, format of rules to insert nouns before roots and to insert articles for singular and plural are defined. For example, the format of rules to insert subjective pronouns of alternative roots for agent relation is defined as follows,:"HPRON,(x)P,SUBJ, [^] @respect, | [^]@contempt, | [^]HON, [^] NGL :: agt:"{ROOT,VEND,[^]@present|@progress|@complete,VEG(y),ALT,#AGT,^(x)p:(x)p::}P10;Here, the grammatical attributes 'HPRON' for human pronoun, '(x)P' indicates person and the value of 'x' denotes first, second or third person., 'SUBJ' for subject of a sentence, @respect for respected person, @contempt for neglected person, 'agt' for agent relation, 'ROOT' for verb root, 'VEND' for vowel ended root, @present for present tense, @progress for continuous tense, @complete for perfect tense, VEG(y) for vowel ended group, where 'y' denotes group number, 'ALT' for alternative root '#AGT' indicates that the corresponding root involves with agent relation. and 'p' is the temporary attribute for person to prevent recursive operations. Similarly, the format of rules to insert noun before roots is defined as follows,:"N,[^]@pl,^SUBJ:SUBJ:agt:"{ROOT,VEND,#AGT,^3p,[^]sg|pl:3p,sg|pl::}P 10; Here, N denotes noun, 'sg' for singular and 'pl' for plural numbers. Within the limited scope of this paper we avoided presenting all the format of rules. Interested readers are referred to [21], for a detailed description of format of all the rules.

3.2   Experimental Results

This section describes the conversion procedures and the experimental results of the UNL expressions into Bangla sentence. The UNL expressions of the sentence, *John has eaten a mango with spoon* is shown in Table 1 by using Russian and English language server [22]. In the UNL expressions, *agt*(agent), *obj* (object) and *ins* (instrument) are the **semantic relations**. The relaters eat(icl>consume>do,agt>living_thing,obj>concrete_thing), John(icl>name,iof>person,com>male)), mango(icl>edible_fruit>thing)) and spoon(icl>cutlery>thing) are the **Universal Words (UWs)** [1]. These are language words with restrictions mentioned in parentheses for the purpose of denoting a unique sense. *icl* stands for *inclusion* and *iof* stands for *instance of*. Attribute @entry typically attached to the main predicate. We have used a DeConverter [23] tool for our experiment. The tool takes as its input a UNL expression file (Table 1), a set of generation rules (Table 3) and a dictionary file (Table 2) and generates sentence of the target language.

Table 1. UNL expressions of the sentence 'John has eaten mango with a spoon'

agt(eat(icl>consume>do,agt>living_thing,obj>concrete_thing).@entry.@present,john (icl>name,iof>person,com>male))
obj(eat(icl>consume>do,agt>living_thing,obj>concrete_thing).@entry.@present,spoo n(icl>cutlery>thing).@indef)
ins(eat(icl>consume>do,agt>living_thing,obj>concrete_thing).@entry.@present,man go(icl>edible_fruit>thing))

Table 2. Dictionary entries for respective Bangla sentence

[জন]{ } "John (iof>person)"(N, NPRO, 3P, SG,SUBJ)<B,1, 1>

[চমচ] { }"spoon(icl>cutlery>thing)"(N,#INS,CEND)

[আম] { } "mango(icl>edible_fruit>thing)"(N,NCOM, #OBJ,CEND)<B,0,0>

[এ]{ }"eat(icl>consume>do,agt>living_thing,obj>concrete_thing)"(ROOT,VEND,#AGT, #OBJ, VEG1)<B,0,2>

[এছ] { }"VI" (VI,VEND,3P,PRS,CMPL,CHL)

[ছিল] { }"INF"(INF, 3RD, CEND)

Table 3. Generation rules for converting UNL expression to Bangla sentence

Rule 1: (Noun insertion)
:"N, SUBJ,^@pl,::agt:"{ROOT,VEND,#AGT,^3p,^sg:3p,sg::}P10;
Rule 2: (Right shift)- R{:::}{SUBJ:::}
Rule 3: (Blank insertion)- :{SUBJ,^blk:blk::}"[],BLK:::"P10;
Rule 4: (Right shift)- R{:::}{SUBJ:::}
Rule 5: (Right shift)- R {SUBJ:::}{:::}
Rule 6: (Noun insertion)
:"N,^ins:ins:ins:"{ROOT,VEND,#INS:::}P9;
Rule 7: (Right shift)- R{:::}{N,INS:::}
Rule 8:(Insertion rule of case maker)
:{N,INS:::}"[[INF]],INF,CEND:::"P10;
Rule 9: (Right shift)- R{:::}{N,INS:::}
Rule 10: (Right shift)- R{N,INS:::}{:::}
Rule 11:(Blank insertion)- :{INF,^blk:blk::}"[],BLK:::"P10;
Rule 12:(Blank insertion)- :{N,INS,^blk:blk::}"[],BLK:::"P10;
Rule 13:(Right shift)- R{:::}{N,INS:::}
Rule 14:(Right shift)- R{N,INS:::}{:::}
Rule 15:(Right shift)- R{:::}{INF:::}
Rule 16:(Right shift)- R{INF:::}{:::}
Rule 17: (Noun insertion)
:"N,^obj:obj:obj:"{ROOT,VEND,^#AGT,#OBJ:::}P9;
Rule 18: (Right shift)- R{:::}{N,#OBJ:::}
Rule 19:(Blank insertion)- :{N,#OBJ,^blk:blk::}"[ ],BLK:::"P10;
Rule 20: (Right shift)- R{:::}{N,#OBJ:::}
Rule 21:(Right shift)- R{N,#OBJ:::}{:::}
Rule 22:(Right shift)- R{:::}{ROOT,VEND:::}
Rule 23: (Verbal inflexion insertion)
:{ROOT,VEND,3p,#AGT,@present,@complete,^@progress,^kbiv:kbiv::}
"[[KBIV]],KBIV,VEND,3P,PRS,CMPL,^PRGR"P10;
Rule 24: (Right shift)- R(V:::}{:::}

These generation rules will be applied to the nodes in the node-list for operation on them and/or inserting nodes from the Node-net into the Node-list.

Rule 1 describes when root "খে" (khe) is in the RGW (Right Generation Window) the noun "জন" (John) is to be inserted in the RGW. Rule 2 is applied to shift the windows of DeConverter to right. The blank insertion rule (rule 3) is applied to insert a blank space between noun and root. After applying right shift rules (rule 4, 5), rule 6 is to be used to insert noun "চামচ", *chamoch* (spoon) in the RGW. If the noun "চামচ" is in the RGW, the windows will be shifted to right by applying rule 7. The case maker insertion rule (rule 8) is to be applied to insert 'দিয়' (diye) on the right side of the RGW. Two right shift rules 9 and 10 are to be applied to shift the windows two steps right followed by two blank insertion rules 11 and 12 to insert blank spaces between case maker and root, and noun "চামচ", and case maker respectively. Subsequently, noun 'আম', *aam* (mango) is to be inserted into the node-list (rule 17) after applying right shift rules 13, 14, 15 and 16. To make a blank space between noun, 'আম', and root, rule 19 is to be applied after using right shift rule 18. Finally, right shift rules 20, 21 and 22 are to be applied followed by a verbal inflexion insertion rule (rule 23). The right shift rule 24 completes the sentence generation processes of DeConverter. After completing the deconversion procedures, DeCo generates the following Bangla sentence, জন চামচ দিয় আম খেয়েছ.

We have experimented different types of simple sentences by varying subjects, persons as well as tenses. Our experiment showed that Bangla sentences are generated correctly by the proposed generation rules.

4   Conclusions

We have proposed a set of generation rules to generate Bangla sentences from UNL expressions. The paper also focused on the dictionary formats of Bangla words and case makers considering grammatical and semantic attributes using standard dictionary format of UNL. We have analyzed various types of simple Bangla sentences. By using the generation rules we successfully translated correct Bangla text from UNL expressions. It is now possible to generate any simple Bangla sentence from UNL expressions. Our long term plan is to develop a mechanism which will allow us to translate any language into corresponding Bangla texts through UNL expressions. This paper focused only on simple sentences. Currently, we are experimenting on both compound and complex sentences and respective generation rules. Our generation rules are defined by following standard formats so that generation rules of other languages can be benefited from our formats. Completion of the generation rules for all types of sentences will be a major step towards developing a generic Bangla language translator.

References

1. Uchida, H., Zhu, M., Senta, T.C.D.: Universal Networking Language, UNDL Foundation, International environment house, 2005/6, Geneva, Switzerland
2. EnConverter Specification, Version 3.3, UNL Center/UNDL Foundation, Tokyo 150-8304, Japan (2002)

3. DeConverter Specification, Version 2.7, UNL Center, UNDL Foundation, Tokyo 150-8304, Japan (2002)
4. Ali, M.N.Y., Das, J.K., Abdullah Al Mamun, S.M., Nurannabi, A.M.: Morphological Analysis of Bangla words for Universal Networking Language. In: ICDIM 2008, London, England, pp. 532–537 (2008)
5. Ali, M.N.Y., Sarker, M.Z.H., Das, J.K.: Analysis and Generation of Bengali Case Structure Constructs for Universal Networking Language. IJCA International Journal of Computer Applications, 34–41 (March 2011)
6. Ali, M.N.Y., Sarker, M.Z.H., Farooque, G.A., Das, J.K.: Conversion of Bangla Sentence into Universal Networking Language Expression. IJCSI 8(2) (March 2011)
7. Chakrabarti, D., Bhattacharyya, P.: Syntactic Alternation of Hindi Verbs with Reference to Morphological Paradigm. In: Language Engineering Conference, Hyderabad, India (December 2002)
8. Chakrabarti, D., Sarma, V., Bhattacharyya, P.: Hindi Verb Knowledge Base and Noun Incorporation in Hindi. In: Third Global WorldNet Conference, Jeju Island, Korea (January 2006)
9. Singh, S., Gupta, K., Shrivastava, M., Bhattacharyya, P.: Morphological Richness Offsets Resource Poverty- an Experience in Building a POS Tagger for Hindi. In: COLING/ACL, Sydney, Australia (July 2006)
10. Vijay, D.: Generation of Hindi from Universal Networking Language. IIT Bombay M Tech Thesis
11. Giri, L.: Semantic Net Like Knowledge Structure Generation from Natural Languages. IIT Bombay B Tech Dissertation (2000)
12. Deve, S., Bhattacharyya, P.: Knowledge Extraction from Hindi Text. JIETE 18(4) (2001)
13. Deve, S., Parikh, J., Bhattacharyya, P.: Interlingua Based English Hindi Machine Translation and Language Divergence. Journal of Machine Translation (JMT) 16(4), 251–304 (2001)
14. Dhanabalan, T., Saravanan, K., Geetha, T.V.: Tamil to UNL EnConverter. ICUKL, Goa, India (2002)
15. Gilles, S., Christian, B.: UNL-French Deconversion as Transfer & Generation from an Interlingua with Possible Quality Enhancement through Offline Human Interaction. Machine Translation Summit-VII, Singapore (1999)
16. Ali, M.N.Y., Das, J.K., Abdullah Al Mamun, S.M., Choudhury, M.E.H.: Specific Features of a Converter of Web Documents from Bengali to Universal Networking Language. In: ICCCE 2008, Kuala Lumpur, Malaysia, pp. 726–731 (2008)
17. Asaduzzaman, M.M., Ali, M.M.: Morphological analysis of Bangla Words for Automatic Machine Translation. In: International Conference on Computer and Information Technology, Dhaka, Bangladesh, pp. 271–276 (December 2003)
18. Asaduzzaman, M.M., Ali, M.M.: A Knowledge Based Approach to Bangla-English Machine Translation for Simple Assertive Sentences. International Journal of Translation 15, 77–97 (2003)
19. Islam, M.S.: Research on Bangla Language Processing in Bangladesh: Progress and Challenges. In: 8th ILDC, Dhaka, Bangladesh (June 2009)
20. Khairunnahar, K.: Morphological Analysis of Bangla Prefix. The Dhaka University Journal of Linguistic 1(2), 157–168 (2008)
21. http://www.ewubd.edu/~nawab
22. http://www.unl.ru/deco (last access: July 20, 2011)
23. http://www.undl.org/ (last access: July 20, 2011)

GISOS: A Model for Rectifying Complexities and Mitigating the Risks of Global Information System Development

Ahdieh Sadat Khatavakhotan, NavidHashemi Taba, and Siew Hock Ow

Department of Software Engineering, Faculty of Computer Science and Information Technology, University of Malaya, 50603, Kuala Lumpur, Malaysia
Khotan@siswa.um.edu.my, {nhtaba,show}@um.edu.my

Abstract. A global information system (GIS) connects companies in various countries. Although GIS professionals have produced many facilities for connectivity, only a few have developed a comprehensive GIS model to overcome the obstacles. Complexities, ambiguity as well as other risks are among GIS development difficulties. To develop an efficient and effective decision-making process, critical performance is essential. This article presents a comprehensive model to concur with the GIS development obstacles. The model is based on satisfying GIS critical factors and consists of four components. GISOS covers a large spectrum form global feedback processing to global maintenance facilities. Applying GISOS model facilitate GIS development and improves the performance of global systems.

Keywords: Global Information System, IT risk management, GIS model, Software development process.

1 Introduction

According to Turban, Rainer, and Potter [1], International information systems that connect companies in various countries is referred to Global Information System (GIS). In one look each global organization requires a powerful GIS to satisfy the information requirements. Scholars' studies showed that many types of organizations such as Multinational Companies (MC), International Companies (IC), and Virtual Global Companies (VGC) need GIS. The latter case refers to joint ventures with different places of business partners. The non-physical nature of VGC (the magic common acronym for Virtual Global Companies and Virtual Global Communications) provides the flexibility to follow one-time mission such as efforts to control the Gulf of Mexico oil spill after failure of controls in last year [2].

2 Global Information System Critical Factors

Kadiyala and Kleiner [3] stated that a global information system with the permanent improvement feature and continuously upgrade the technologies, provides competitive

V.V. Das, E. Ariwa, and S.B. Rahayu (Eds.): SPIT 2011, LNICST 62, pp. 164–169, 2012.
© Institute for Computer Sciences, Social Informatics and Telecommunications Engineering 2012

advantage to a business. In addition, a well designed decision-making has significant positive effects on process performance improving in a global organization. To develop an efficient and effectiveness decision-making process, considering critical performance critical factors is essential. Figure 1 shows some common critical factors of GIS. Costs, culture, location, and strategic emphasis are some critical factors for improving performance [4].

Fig. 1. GIS Critical Factors

3   World Wide Web a Common Solution for GIS

Manu [5] states that from the storage, retrieval, and global accessing perspective, WWW provides a common solution for making a global information system. According to Raisinghani [6], global organizations need incorporating new applications and adapting to new business requirements. Web services, besides providing rapid connection ability, enable the organization to access a variety of communication devices as well as using existing infrastructure. Gerth and Rothman [7] believed that accessing to global markets and the global workforce made the world flat. From another point of view, Zwass [8] stated that Web provided new opportunities in digital democracy but its capabilities are not discovered nor used yet.

4   Global Information System Obstacles Simplifier (GISOS) Model

Global organizations are facing many complex issues [9]. The complexity of GIS has root in Cultural Differences, Economic, and Political Differences, and transfer of data across international borders [1]. Environment, culture, and structure are three dimensions in each business. Every problem in aforementioned dimensions influences the business performance and each potential solution a problem in one dimension has to consider the possible impacts on other dimensions [10]. According to Laurentiu, and Tantau [11], the critical IT risks has a significant direct relations with the size of processes. Therefore, many of potential risks in GIS development process have roots in complexities. GISOS is using an ambiguity rectifying approach to reduce the complexities as well as risk consequences.

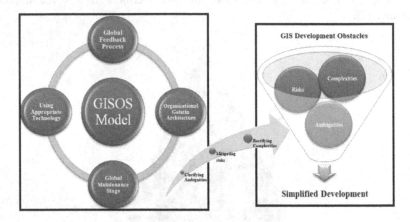

Fig. 2. GISOS Model

Figure 2 is a pictorial view of the GIS Obstacles Simplifier (GISOS) model proposed in this article. The GISOS model in this article focused on core applicable technologies as well as the strategic decisions to facilitate the GIS implementation. Gehaniand Gehani [12] believe that two innovative wings of each organization are employees' competencies and external strategic alliances with supplier and distributors. According the Nielson [13] familiarity with values, customs, and the local regulations is mandatory for understanding a specific culture. From another point of view, Performance improving has significant positive effects on decision-making process in a global organization. Developing the GISOS model with the aforementioned features will satisfy the critical factors for improving performance [4].

5   GISOS Components

The proposed model in this article has four important components. The collaboration between components make a significant effects on reducing ambiguity, complexity, and potential risks of GIS development. GISOS components influence each other in a bidirectional approach and facilitate the complexity rectifying as the main common task.

5.1   The Appropriate Technology

The segmentation is an appropriate strategy to reduce the complexities in a global organization. By segmentation roles, duties, and responsibilities would be cleared.

Therefore, one of important mission of the GIS is classification the responsibilities of each segment and providing the necessary informative resources. Another mission of the GIS likely is mapping the segments in the correct way. The aforementioned mapping will share the knowledge and experiences as well as information between segments and will fill the possible technological technical, structural, and technological gaps.Designing decision making process in organizations has a strong relationship with objective satisfaction [14]. Opposite the decentralized process for decision making in multinational organizations, the main control in global organization is placing in parent organization [9]. Therefore, providing technological environment for concurrent centralized and decentralized decision-making is mandatory.

5.2   Global Maintenance

GIS needs Maintenance stage is the most important phase of each IS development methodology [15]. Spokoiny, and Shahar [16] stated that in a large scale, manipulating data is a complex domain-meaningful concept. Changing data set in a real-time manner and through a knowledgebase active time-oriented database, likely is one important part of every GIS. The freedom in decision making by local offices of a global organization is not a reasonable cause for ignorance in maintenance stage of GIS development.According to Biehl [17], at the global level and to provide organization services such as finance and supply chain management, companies require robust GIS with a flexibility characteristic. A reliable maintainable ICT backbone, well-designed communication and interaction as well as Internet-based information technology [18].Failure in meeting objectives in organizations, likely has root in ineffective communications [19].

5.3   Global Feedback Process

Based on scholars' studies, developing a global feedback control system is an essential part of a GIS. Neth, Khemlani, and Gray [20] explained that a global feedback controller will aggregate the individual feedbacks and cover their gaps. Therefore, an integrated feedback system provides the flexibility as the major characteristic of a GIS.Global feedback system makes a GIS empower to adapt with global changing through providing global information about the current situations of each region as well as successes or failures of managerial decisions and procedures. Magniez, Brombacher, and Schouten [21] emphasized that an efficient feedback system is an indicator to reveal the GIS innovation abilities.

5.4   Organizational Gelatin Architecture

Finally, Global sourcing has major impacts on GIS, and its mobile nature forced global organization leaders to prepare their enterprise form all related aspects [22]. In this way, enabling the GIS structure capacity to accept, analyze, and use the feedback to shift in totally new state is so important. Gelatin architecture that mentioned in current subtitle refers to capability of structural changes of a GIS[23].

6   Conclusion

Solving complex problem requires simple approaches. Using complicated tools or methods likely will increase the complexity degree The GISOS model provides a clear roadmap to concur the complexities and potential risks of global information system development process.. In a global information system development paying attention to appropriate methodology, especially maintenance phases, is too important to neglect. The adequate maintenance stage supporting the rapid change in GIS configuration, even the structure of the global organization could be applicable in the global level.Global feedback process is another essential suggestion of the proposed model in this article to improve the GIS performance and productivity. Each feedback process in a GIS requires a prior design in GIS development stages. Based on flexibility nature of global organization a global feedback process, as a self-instrument will empower GIS to reassess as well as improve the capabilities.

References

1. Turban, E., Rainer, R.K., Potter, R.E.: Introduction to Information Technology. John Wiley & Sons, Inc. (2003)
2. Jackson, R.A.: The state of CONTROL. Internal Auditor 67(5), 35 (2010)
3. Kadiyala, R., Kleiner, B.H.: New developments concerning business information systems. Management Research News 28(11/12), 164–170 (2005)
4. Bienko, M., Mankins, M.C., Rogers, P.: The decision-driven organization. Harvard Business Review 6, 54–62 (2010)
5. Manu, A.: The Imagination Challenge. Strategic Foresight and Innovation in the Global Economy. Pearson Education (2007)
6. Raisinghani, M.S.: Web Services for Global Information Systems: Opportunities and Challenges. Journal of Global Information Technology Management 7(3), 1–4 (2004)
7. Gerth, A.B., Rothman, S.: The future IS organization in a flat world. Information Systems Management 24(2), 103–111 (2007)
8. Zwass, V.: The web-internet compound as the infrastructure of digital government. Business Process Management Journal 12(1), 7–12 (2006)
9. Lan, Y.: Global information society: operating information systems in a dynamic global business environment. Idea Group, Hershey (2005)
10. Higgs, R.C., Smith, M.E., Mechling, G.W.: Making better business decisions. Supervision 71(2), 12–15 (2010)
11. Laurentiu, F., Tantau, A.: Aspects of IT Risk Management for a Company. Annals of the University of Oradea, Economic Science Series 17(2), 141–146 (2008)
12. Gehani, R., Gehani, R.: Mary Parker Follett's constructive conflict: A psychological foundation of business administration' for innovative global enterprises. International Journal of Public Administration 30(4), 387–404 (2007)
13. Neilson, G.L., Martin, K.L., Powers, E.: The secrets to successful strategy execution. Harvard Business Review 1(8) (2008)
14. Hill, C.W.L.: Global strategy, global business, 2nd edn. McGraw-Hill Irwin, New York (2003)
15. Pressman, R.: Software engineering: a practitioner's approach, 7/e. McGraw-Hill (2009)

16. Spokoiny, A., Shahar, Y.: An active database architecture for knowledge-based incremental abstraction of complex concepts from continuously arriving time-oriented raw data. Journal of Intelligent Information Systems 28(3), 199 (2007)
17. Biehl, M.: Success factors for implementing global information systems. Communications of the ACM 50(1), 52–58 (2007)
18. Darling, J.R., Beebe, S.A.: Effective entrepreneurial communication in organizational development: Achieving excellence based on leadership strategies and values. Organizational Development Journal 25(1), 76–93 (2007)
19. Grover, S.M.: Shaping effective communication skills and therapeutic relationships at work: The foundation of collaboration. AAOHN Journal 53(4), 177–182 (2005)
20. Neth, H., Khemlani, S., Gray, W.: Feedback Design for the Control of a Dynamic Multitasking System: Dissociating Outcome Feedback From Control Feedback. Human Factors 50(4), 643–651 (2008), doi:10.1518/001872008X288583
21. Magniez, C., Brombacher, A., Schouten, J.: The use of reliability-oriented field feedback information for product design improvement: a case study. Quality & Reliability Engineering International 25(3), 355–364 (2009), doi:10.1002/qre.973
22. King, W.R.: The IS organization of the future: impacts of global sourcing. Information Systems Management 24(2), 121–127 (2007)
23. Kettinger, W., Marchand, D., Davis, J.: Designing enterprise it architectures to optimize flexibility and standardization in global business. MIS Quarterly Executive 9(2), 95–113 (2010)

A Novel Model to Improve the Efficiency of the Think Tank Room Approach for Knowledge-Based IT Environments

NavidHashemi Taba, Ahdieh Sadat Khatavakhotan, and Siew Hock Ow

Department of Software Engineering, Faculty of Computer Science and Information Technology, University of Malaya, 50603, Kuala Lumpur, Malaysia
Khotan@siswa.um.edu.my,
{nhtaba,show}@um.edu.my

Abstract. Thinkers in IT management and IT industry with slight difference in opinion have put forward various categories of staff members. Strategists, high ranking, or candidates for key positions use the *Think Tank Room* term to indicate they have preplanned and reliable programs. In reality, if scientists lacking work experience, or strategists unfamiliar with contingencies of the day occupy such think tank rooms, the undoubtedly the disadvantages of the room are much more than its advantages. The Collaborate Think Tank Room (CTTR) model, proposed in this article, compensate the disadvantages of traditional think tank room model by using a collaborative approach. The model has four stages, conducting *Setting, Getting Using,* and *Doing* (SGUD). To clarify the advantages of using the suggested model, two real cases of professional fields are explained.

Keywords: IT management, Think Tank Room, IT risk management, Collaborative model, Collaborative criteria, Knowledge-based IT environment.

1 Introduction

Long ago, management approaches considered staff members as similar to other tools and devices [1]. There is no place for the erroneous thought that the staff members of an organization are used to produce the end product or services; or they should be considered as a means to be used more economically, even if it exists in reality [2]. In each organization, the most important department is now human resources [3]. Therefore, individuals are considered as a resource, which should be attended to the way the other resources are.Thinkers in management and industry science like Waren [4], with slight difference in opinion, have put forward various categories of staff members.They are referred to as blue collars in some cases and as white collars in others, as leaders in some, and as followers as others; sometimes as order givers and sometimes as order takers. What is attended to less is that experts in organizations can be more fruitful than managers require or know.

V.V. Das, E. Ariwa, and S.B. Rahayu (Eds.): SPIT 2011, LNICST 62, pp. 170–175, 2012.
© Institute for Computer Sciences, Social Informatics and Telecommunications Engineering 2012

2   Think Tank Room and Lack of the Real Experiences

2.1   Think Tank Room Definition

The term Think Thank Room has for long been used [1]. Hart, and Vromen [5] stated: "The term think tank is a verbal container which accommodates a heterogeneous set of meanings." Strategists, high ranking, or candidates for key positions use this term to indicate they have preplanned and reliable programs. However, in reality, if scientists lacking work experience, or strategists unfamiliar with contingencies of the day occupy such think tank room rooms, the undoubtedly the disadvantages of the room are much more than its advantages [2]. The collaboration and obtaining the professionals' real experiences could be assumed as the silver bullet to compensate the weak points of the Think tank room conceptual models.

2.2   Think Tank Room Theoretical Frameworks

Although, the brain storm and collaborative decision making is suggested, analyzed, and emphasized by many of scholars, there is a lack of research study about the think tank room in IT environment field [5]. The real role of IT and the exact position of thinkers in automated systems are not clear and a series of case studies are required to clarify the current as well as future situations of IT environments [7]. Researches show that establishing, developing, and institutionalizing a think tank room using high professional thinkers will change the catastrophic treats to eye-catching opportunities [6].

3   The Collaborative Think Tank Room Model (CTTR)

Concentrating on the expressed opinions by Nemeth [8], Morris et al. [9], and McAlearney et al. [10] shows that the idea of a CTTR model can cover the weak points and decrease the negative effects made by the presence of the experts in any types of decision making process. Figure 1 is An static presentation of the suggested model by this article. The CTTR model has four critical stages (SGUD):

Setting Collaboration Criteria. Setting the criteria for collaboration is the first stage that could be the starting stage of the model [11]. Each problem has common as well as unique specifications. Clarifying the problem characteristics and the constraints is a essential step to set the collaboration criteria. Defining and focusing on the collaboration criteria will avoid wasting the valuable resources such as the time and work force. Determining the communication styles and meeting procedure will satisfy the aforementioned criteria.

Getting Reliable Reports on the Current Situation. The up-to-date integrated information system will help decision makers to make appropriate decisions as well as measure it [12]. Developing an effective knowledge base as well as comprehensive database including historical data is recommended in this stage. Generating brief comprehensive reports provides an efficient atmosphere and assists the think tank room members in their duties.

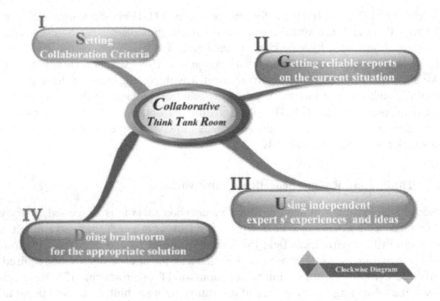

Fig. 1. SGUD stages of CTTR model

Using Independent Experts' Ideas. Exploiting the employed professionals occurs some advantages as well as some disadvantages. Using independent reliable experts as the think tank room members compensates the disadvantages and reduces the risks of dependants' professionals. Independent professionals will provide insights by sharing the outlook perspectives [13].

Doing Brainstorm for the Appropriate Solution. Gathering various ideas is not sufficient for making correct decision. Brainstorm between think tank room members reveal the benefits and disadvantages of ideas. Leading and controlling the brainstorm meetings is so important issue that could be done through a collaborative digital charter as a creative tool [14].

4   Collaboration Matrix for CTTR Model

CCTR means every expert can cooperate as much as his ability, knowledge, experience and expertise, and benefit from others' as much as he needs. To implement the collaboration model, a matrix of subjects and collaboration will be assist managers. The line of aforementioned matrix is the subjects, which should be collaborated. The column of the matrix belongs to the knowledge workers, whose knowledge and experience can be used. The entries belong to the role of knowledge worker in that corresponded subject or activity (Table 1).

Table 1. Collaborative sample matrix for CCTR model

SUBJECTS	KNOWLEDGE WORKERS			
	KW $_1$	KW $_2$	...	KW $_n$
S $_1$	Consulter	...	...	
S $_2$	Resource provider			
...	...	...	...	...
S $_m$	Relative experiences	...	...	...

5   Two Professional Cases for Implementing CCRT Model

Physicians and retail loan officers are considered as knowledge workers for a couple of reasons [15]. They are in close contact with the clients and in touch with hard facts due to the nature of their jobs. Strict rules drawn up for loan allocation purposes indicate the rate of clients. Information available to this group is not comparable to that derived from opinion polls and samplings or simulations. The most important reason behind this is that such information is documented. No opinion is acceptable without proof. It means if a loan applicant talks about his family status, financial resources, and provides no proofs; his claim will not be accepted.The case is a little different about physicians. The difference is not in the importance of the matter but in the type of the resources used. McAlearney et al. [10] emphasized that physicians are not only analysts, but also their ability in diagnosis and giving medication completes the treatment process. It means that one of the most important sources for the physicians to help them decide is the remarks made by the patients. Physicians suppose that their patients are the people who have lost their physical or mental health or have referred to them to check their health status; otherwise, they wouldn't have referred to physicians. Therefore, if all tests show that a patient is healthy, yet the patient feels aches, physicians shall not stop treatment. On the other hand, physicians can depend upon their knowledge and ask key questions, or rely on the existing models and diagnose the physical conditions of the patient. The important point is that the patient is not done when treatment process is done; rather a new process has already started. This new process is seeking the reasons of the disease and uprooting it. Suppose a patient afflicted with a hard-to-cure disease refers to a doctor. His remedy shall consist of treatment along with removing its social effects or preventing the disease to be epidemic.According to CCTR mode, physicians can express their ideas in making decisions related to the development of the hospitals regarding their human resources. In a same way, loan officers can express their opinions on the developments made through years. Loan officers are somehow like doctors. They receive the terms and conditions from the above on one hand and evaluate the conditions of the applicants on the other. If the files available to these two groups are updated in a knowledge-based system, they can be a good back up for the short term and medium term plans. In long term, good information can be extracted through refining information and using deductive scientific methods.

6   Conclusion

The suggested CTTR model is focused on the presence of knowledgeable practitioners. Real updated information, unlike unreal one can back up strategic plans. The first Stage of CTTR model is setting collaboration criteria through arranging an appropriate collaboration charter. Other stages are focused on the using integrated information system and involving professional knowledge workers. Knowledge workers are the most appropriate people to prepare and submit this information. Besides, their inferences are correct because they are experts and in touch with the case.Using CCTR model supports the organizations to make the best decisions through pro-action approach. If knowledge workers get involved in decision-making and planning processes, the inconvenient consequences of decisions could be reduced. Using CCTR plans can be saved from being single angled, dogmatic, and merely theoretical; and change them into multilateral flexible and applicable plans.

References

1. George Jr., C.S.: The History of Management Thought. Prentice-Hall, Inc., Englewood Cliffs (1968)
2. Wanna, J.: Independence and Responsiveness – Re-tying the Gordian Knot. Australian Journal of Public Administration 67(3), 340–344 (2008), doi:10.1111/j.1467-8500.2008.00591.x
3. Caldwell, C., Truong, D., Linh, P., Tuan, A.: Strategic Human Resource Management as Ethical Stewardship. Journal of Business Ethics 98(1), 171–182 (2011), doi:10.1007/s10551-010-0541-y
4. Waren Daniel, A.: The History of Management Thought. John Wiley & Sons, Inc. (2005)
5. Hart, P., Vromen, A.: A New Era for Think Tanks in Public Policy? International Trends, Australian Realities. Australian Journal of Public Administration 67(2), 135–148 (2005), doi:10.1111/j.1467
6. Zou, P.X.W., Redman, S., Windon, S.: Case Studies on Risk and Opportunity at Design Stage of Building Projects in Australia: Focus on Safety. Architectural Engineering and Design Management 4(3), 221–238 (2008)
7. Costello, T.: A New Management Framework for IT. IT Professional Magazine 12(6), 61–64 (2010)

8. Nemeth, C.J.: Managing Innovation: When Less Is More. California Management Review 40(1), 59–74 (1997)
9. Morris, S.A., Marshall, T.E., Rainer Jr., R.K.: Impact of user satisfaction and trust on virtual team members. Information Resources Management Journal 15(2), 22; Hospital Topics 83(2),11–18 (2005)
10. McAlearney, A., Fisher, D., Heiser, K., Robbins, D., Kelleher, K.: Developing Effective Physician Leaders: Changing Cultures and Transforming Organizations. Hospital Topics [serial online] 83(2), 11–18 (2005)
11. De Gregorio, F., I-Huei, C.: Do stronger links with practice make perfect? International Journal of Advertising 28(3), 555–589 (2009)
12. Bell, M., Farrier, S.: Measuring Success in e-Learning - A Multi-Dimensional Approach. Electronic Journal of e-Learning 6(2), 99–109 (2008)
13. Dubois, D.: Representation, propagation, and decision issues in risk analysis under incomplete probabilistic information. Risk Analysis: An Official Publication of the Society For Risk Analysis 30(3), 361–368 (2010)
14. Brafield, P.: Brainstorm: software and habitus in digital design. Digital Creativity 21(2), 112–126 (2010), doi:10.1080/14626268.2010.483688
15. Senn, G.F.: Physicians at the CFO's door: what's your response to requests for new technology? HFM (Healthcare Financial Management) 64(3), 92–98 (2010)

A Non-greedy Local Search Heuristic
for Facility Layout Problem

Rajesh Matai[1], Surya Prakash Singh[2], and Murari Lal Mittal[3]

[1] Management Department, BITS Pilani, India
[2] Department of Management Studies, IIT Delhi, India
[3] Department of Mechanical Engineering, MNIT Jaipur, India
{rajeshmatai73,surya.singh,mlmittal.mnit}@gmail.com

Abstract. This paper proposes a non-greedy local search heuristic for solving facility layout problem. The proposed heuristic works on non-greedy systematic pair wise exchange of two facilities, that is 2-exchange local search based on non-greedy strategy. Pair wise exchanges are accepted if the objective function value after the exchange is lowered or smaller than the average objective function increment divided by an intensity factor. Proposed heuristic is tested on commonly used Nugxx series problems and computational results show efficiency and effectiveness of proposed heuristic.

Keywords: Local search, Facility Layout Problem, Quadratic Assignment Problem.

1 Introduction

The facility layout problem (FLP) is an important problem of industrial engineering and well researched problem. It was first formulated as quadratic assignment problem (QAP) by Koopmans and Beckman [5]. Later, Sahni and Gonzalez [8] showed QAP is a NP-complete problem. To achieve global optimum for QAP branch-and-bound, cutting planes or combinations of these methods, like branch-and-cut and dynamic programming are used. However, results by these exact algorithms are modest. Diponegoro and Sarker [2] reported that instances of the QAP of sizes larger than 20 cannot be solved optimally in a reasonable computational time. Therefore, interest of researchers and practitioners lies in the application of heuristics and meta heuristics approaches to solve QAP. Some of the well known heuristic approaches applied in the past and available in literature are CRAFT, HC-66, ALDEP, CORELAP, SABLE etc. But the performance of these heuristics is good only for small or moderate sized problems. As the problem size increases the solution quality decreases. In addition of applying heuristics, now-a-days meta-heuristic approaches like Simulated Annealing (SA), Tabu Search (TS), Ant Colony Algorithm (ACO) and Genetic Algorithm (GA) are also widely applied to solve FLP. A good amount of work on FLP can be found in Kusiak and Heragu [6], Heragu [4], Heragu and Kusiak [3], Singh and Sharma [9] and Matai *et al.* [7]. This paper proposes a local search heuristic based on non-greedy strategy for solving the FLP.

V.V. Das, E. Ariwa, and S.B. Rahayu (Eds.): SPIT 2011, LNICST 62, pp. 176–181, 2012.
© Institute for Computer Sciences, Social Informatics and Telecommunications Engineering 2012

2   Problem Formulation

Consider the problem of locating 'n' facilities in 'n' given locations. Each location can be assigned to only one facility, and vice versa. F_{ik} is the flow between facilities 'i' and 'k', and D_{jl} is the distance between locations 'j' and 'l'. The FLP has been formulated as follows:

$$\text{Min TF} = \sum_{\substack{i=1 \\ i \neq k}}^{n} \sum_{\substack{j=1 \\ j \neq l}}^{n} \sum_{k=1}^{n} \sum_{l}^{n} F_{ik} * D_{jl} * X_{ij} * X_{kl} \tag{1}$$

$$\sum_{i=1}^{n} X_{ij} = 1 \quad \forall \ j = 1, \ldots, n \tag{2}$$

$$\sum_{j=1}^{n} X_{ij} = 1 \quad \forall \ i = 1, \ldots, n \tag{3}$$

$$X_{ij} \in \{0,1\} \quad \forall \ i, j = 1, \ldots, n \tag{4}$$

$X_{ij} = 1$ if facility $'i'$ is located/assigned to location $'j'$ and $X_{ij} = 0$ if facility $'i'$ is not located/assigned to location $'j'$, where $'n'$ is the number of facilities.

3   Non-greedy Local Search Heuristic

The proposed heuristic works on non-greedy systematic pairwise exchange of two facilities in the neighbourhood locations rather than exchange of facilities randomly. The neighbourhood NB(r) is defined as all assignments that can be reached from a given assignment when r elements are exchanged. For pairwise exchange algorithms, the size of a neighbourhood is $[NB(2)] = \frac{1}{2} n(n-1)$. Two alternatives exist for neighbourhood search process. First, choose the next potential facility for exchange randomly. Second, explore the neighbourhood in a systematic way having all the possible exchange elements ordered ("shuffled"). The precise order is irrelevant, it is only essential that the neighborhood is explored thoroughly. Proposed heuristic uses later approach that is systematic (ordered) neighbourhood search and this systematic neighbourhood search is based on the non-greedy strategy. The key idea is, pair wise exchanges are accepted if the objective function value after the exchange is lowered or smaller than the average objective function increment divided by an intensity factor. The average objective function increment divided by an intensity factor is called threshold value and evaluated from equation (5) given below.

$$\tau = \left(\frac{\sum \Delta Z^+}{C} \right) \Big/ \varepsilon \tag{5}$$

$$\Delta Z = Z(P_c) - Z(P_i) \tag{6}$$

$$\Delta Z^+ = \Delta Z \text{ if } \Delta Z > 0 \tag{7}$$

Where, P_i is the initial random solution and P_c is current solution after pairwise exchange of two facilities and ΔZ is the current difference of the objective function value of current solution ($Z(P_c)$) and initial random solution ($Z(P_i)$). ε is the intensity factor which lies in the interval of [0,1]. C is the total number of increments of objective function value (i.e. when $\Delta Z > 0$) or number of times when objective function value of current solution is more than old solution after pairwise exchange. From equation (5) it can be seen that τ is the average objective function increment (in C number of increments) divided by the factor (ε). The acceptance rule can be finally defined as: the solution in the heuristic during pair wise exchange is accepted if and only if equation (8) does hold. Table 1 shows few other acceptance rules used and available in the literature.

$$\Delta Z < 0 \text{ or } \Delta Z < \left(\frac{\sum \Delta Z^+}{C}\right)\Big/ \varepsilon \tag{8}$$

Table 1. Decision Rule: Comparison of Greedy descent and SA with the Proposed Heuristic

Algorithm	Rule (Conditions)
Greedy descent	$\Delta Z < 0$
Simulated Annealing	$\Delta Z < 0$ or $random[0,1] < e^{-\Delta Z / t}$
Non-Greedy Local Search	$\Delta Z < 0$ or $\Delta Z < \left(\frac{\sum \Delta Z^+}{C}\right)\Big/ \varepsilon$

The main feature of SA is its ability to escape from local optimum. If the current solution (P_c) has an objective function value smaller (supposing minimization) than that of the initial solution (P_i), then the current solution is accepted. Otherwise, the current solution can also be accepted if the value given by the Boltzmann distribution shown in equation (9) is greater than a uniform random number in [0,1], where t is the 'temperature' control parameter. The solution in the SA during pair wise exchange is accepted if equation (10) does hold.

$$e^{-\Delta Z / t} \tag{9}$$

$$\Delta Z < 0 \text{ or } random[0,1] < e^{-\Delta Z / t} \tag{10}$$

Proposed heuristic also try to escape from local optimum using non-greedy approach, however acceptance rule of candidate solution in proposed heuristic is different [equation (8)] than SA [(equation (10)]. In SA 'temperature' is the control parameter however in proposed local search heuristic 'intensity factor' is the control parameter. We present a pseudo code in figure 1 to better understand the proposed approach.

Input: n, P_i , K, Iterations, ε

/n- number of facility or problem size/

/ P_i – initial random solution for proposed heuristic/

/K- maximum number of trials of the size of neighbourhood /

/Iterations- number of times heuristic is run/

/ε- initial value of the intensity factor, ε[0, 1] /

$P_b = P_i$ /best solution treated so far/

$h_\varepsilon = \dfrac{\varepsilon}{\max\left(1, \dfrac{Kn(n-1)}{2} - 1\right)}$ /intensity *quantum*/

Sum = 0 /sum of the positive differences of the objective function value/

C = 0 /counter of the positive differences of the objective function value/

t = 0 /current trial number/

for (m=1, m<*Iterations*, m++) /for loop for number of Iterations/

for(k=1, k<K, k++) /for loop for the number of iterations/

    for(i=1, i<n-1, i++) /for loop for pair wise exchange of facilities/

        for(j=i+1, j<n, j++) /for loop for pair wise exchange of facilities/

        $P_n = N_2(P_i, i, j) / P_n$ - new solution of pair wise exchange

        $\Delta Z = Z(P_n) - Z(P_i)$ /difference of objective function value/

        if ΔZ <0 **then** exchange = **TRUE**   /start if loop/

          else *Sum* = *Sum* + ΔZ , C = C +1

                 $\varepsilon_c = \varepsilon - (t-1)h_\varepsilon$ /current intensity level/

           if $_{\Delta Z} < \left(\dfrac{Sum}{C}\right) \Big/ _\varepsilon$ **then** exchange = **TRUE**

                               elseexchange = **FALSE**

        end   /end of if loop/

        t = t +1 /next trial number/

    end/end of for loop for the pair wise exchange of facilities/

end/end of the for loop for the K number of trials of size of neighbourhood search/

return P_b / return best solution value after each Iteration/

end /end of for loop for number of Iterations/

return P_b/ return best solution value after all Iterations/

Fig. 1. Pseudo code for Non-Greedy Local Search heuristic

Since the size of a neighbourhood is $[NB(2)] = \frac{1}{2}n(n-1)$ therefore, in each iteration the total number of swaps examined are $K\frac{n(n-1)}{2}$.

4   Computational Experience

The proposed heuristic has been coded in C and tested on a Core2duo machine having processor speed 2.2 GHz with RAM of 2.96 GB. Proposed heuristic is executed for 500 number of iterations keeping default value of K equal to 10. In each iteration a new random solution is generated which is improved by pair wise exchanges. Heuristic performs K times n(n-1)/2 swaps in each iteration. Different solutions are produced in each iteration and one best solution is selected from all iterations as final solution. To prove the effectiveness of our proposed algorithm, comparison was made with optimal values of the fifteen commonly used test problems of Nugxx series taken from QAPLIB (Burkard*et. al.* [1]) available at http://www.seas.upenn.edu/qaplib. A comparative analysis of the solutions obtained from the proposed heuristic with the optimal solutions available in literature are tabulated along with the percentage deviation from optimal solutions (Table 2). In addition to this, computational time of the proposed heuristic approach (in CPU seconds) is also reported for each problem instance tested in the paper. Out of the 15 test problems, proposed heuristic provides optimal solution for 14 problems and very small deviation (0.048%) from optimal for Nug30 problem.

Table 2. Solution of Instances with series Nugxx

S. No.	Instance	Optimal	Proposed Heuristic solution	% deviation	CPU
1	Nug12	578	578	0.00	0.702
2	Nug14	1014	1014	0.00	0.812
3	Nug15	1150	1150	0.00	2.671
4	Nug16a	1610	1610	0.00	3.406
5	Nug16b	1240	1240	0.00	3.406
6	Nug17	1732	1732	0.00	1.781
7	Nug18	1930	1930	0.00	5.484
8	Nug20	2570	2570	0.00	8.375
9	Nug21	2438	2438	0.00	20.171
10	Nug22	3596	3596	0.00	12.281
11	Nug24	3488	3488	0.00	70.218
12	Nug25	3744	3744	0.00	202.921
13	Nug27	5234	5234	0.00	227.625
14	Nug28	5166	5166	0.00	637.562
15	Nug30	6124	6154	0.48	646.937

5   Conclusions

In this paper a new non-greedy local search heuristic for finding a quality solution in reasonable computational time for the FLP is presented. Computational results suggest proposed non-greedy local search is an effective and efficient approach for solving FLP.

References

1. Burkard, R.E., Karisch, S., Rendl, F.: QAPLIB - a quadratic assignment problem library. J. Glob. Opt. 10(1), 391–403 (1997)
2. Diponegoro, A., Sarker, B.R.: Machine assignment in a nonlinear multi-product flowline. J. Oper. Res. Soc. 54, 472–489 (2003)
3. Heragu, S.S., Kusiak, A.: Machine layout: An optimization and Knowledge Based Approach. Int. J. Prod. Res. 28(4), 615–635 (1990)
4. Heragu, S.S.: Recent models and techniques for solving the layout problem. Eur. J. Oper. Res. 57(2), 136–144 (1992)
5. Koopmans, T.C., Beckman, M.: Assignment problems and the location of economic activities. Economet. 25(1), 53–76 (1957)
6. Kusiak, A., Heragu, S.S.: The facility layout problem. Eur. J. Oper. Res. 29(3), 229–251 (1987)
7. Matai, R., Singh, S.P., Mittal, M.L.: Facility Layout Problem: A State-of-the-art Review. Vilak. XIMB J. Manag. 7(2), 81–106 (2010)
8. Sahni, S., Gonzalez, P.: P-Complete approximation problems. J. ACM 23(3), 555–565 (1976)
9. Singh, S.P., Sharma, R.R.K.: A survey on various approaches to solve facility layout problem. Int. J. Adv. Manu. Tech. 30, 425–433 (2006)

Modelling Uncertainty Factors in Environmental Issues on Late Delivery for Construction Industry: A Propose

Zirawani Baharum[1], Noorfa HaszlinnaMustaffa[1], Mohd Salihin Ngadiman[1],
and Azliza Yacob[2]

[1] Dept of Modelling & Industrial Computing, FSKSM,
University Technology Malaysia, Skudai, Johor
zirawani@gmail.com, {noorfa,salihin}@utm.my
[2] Faculty of Computer, Media and Technology, TATI University College,
Kemaman, Terengganu
azliza@tatiuc.edu.my

Abstract. A very limited research of fixing uncertainties in environmental issues (EI) actually encountered biggest problems for company, especially in late delivery (LD) of project completion for construction industry (CI). Uncertainty could be happens causes by many factors which known or unknown, statically to totally ignorance. Many factors of uncertainties have been modelled in previous research by ignored factors in EI. However, in the real cases all the factors must be manage even it is in-deterministic. Therefore, the modelling of uncertainty factors in EI for CI is very important to be studied, and it will be considered to be used as guidance for decision makers while they are facing with the problems that related to uncertainties. The uncertainty of EI can split into 2 categories; acts of God and acts of humans.. Preliminary result of conceptual model for uncertainty factors in EI is presented according to previous case study.

Keywords: Modelling, Uncertainty, Environment Issues, Construction Industry.

1 Introduction

In deflation economy condition nowadays, construction companies are keen to achieve project substance goal such as profit (budget of cost and time) and client-satisfactions. In other words, they need to minimize the total project cost and the project completion time in order to get an optimum profit in any construction projects. It is a very crucial for company to achieve high customer satisfaction preventing the bad-performance in LD. They have to strive with many issues and causes that can lead to potentially loss in profits and become as non-achievement in their quality performances. The problem becomes more complicated for the large project as uncertainties (in project outcomes) is dependent on the project size scale. The uncertainties that occur either in planning, designing, scheduling, constructing or production of product, will impact to bad performance such as LD on construction schedule for construction project development. Most of the researches for uncertainty issues deal with the field of industry where all the parameters are considered known and can be measured. Common factors such as

V.V. Das, E. Ariwa, and S.B. Rahayu (Eds.): SPIT 2011, LNICST 62, pp. 182–187, 2012.

machine failure, resource breakdown, material and labour shortage always relate as issues in manufacturing industry. On the other hand, the problems are different for CI. The construction work is often effect by the soil condition, unpredictable weather, accident, lack of labour skill and erosion. The uncertainty issues in real plants need to give more attention since many of the parameters that are associated in the whole project's timelines are basically unknown and immeasurable. Therefore, the model of uncertainties for each company need to be specialized and the investigation about the causes and the effects that underlying a major problem to that company has to be identified uniquely. The details and deep research are important and needed for measuring and ensuring of good performances. Objective of this paper is to propose the methodology to develop the uncertainty model as a guideline for the construction industry (CI) to deal with the uncertainties, especially in EI on project completion (late delivery). Following these introductory remarks, is Section 2 that provides the definition of uncertainty in CI and the ideas of how to determine causes and previous classification factors of uncertainty in CI. Section 3 represented the conceptual model of uncertainty factors, and the model was assumed as initial findings for this research. Section 4 discusses on propose methodology to develop the model of uncertainty in EI, follow by last section for conclusion and future research.

2   The Uncertainty

The uncertainty can be defined as an expression of the degree to which a value is unknown. Uncertainty can be resulted from lack of information or from disagreement about what is known or even knowable. Uncertainty also refers to measuring the degree of differences between the models and the real systems' values respective or between the estimation of variables and their true values. The uncertainty can be caused by the errors associated with the model itself and the uncertainties of the model inputs [1]. Different people were interpreted uncertainty differently. In CI, uncertainty also can be referred as complexity and risky of environmental.

The concept of uncertainty will be used as guides to company and researcher for the first step to understand the behaviours and characters of uncertainties that happen in their company or project development. The three-dimensional concept; nature, level and location important to be determined before any model of uncertainty has been developed or applied. It may have many types of sources, from quantifiable errors in the data to ambiguously defined concepts or terminology, or uncertain projections of human behaviour. Uncertainty can therefore be represented by quantitative measures or qualitative statements that normally by estimation. A range of values calculated by various models is the example of quantitative measurement and reflecting the judgement of a team of experts for a qualitative statements approach. Uncertainty experts agree that there are different dimensions of uncertainty related to model-based decision support exercises, and [2] has chosen to distinguish three dimensions of uncertainty, which are location, nature and type/level. Through the uncertainty concept, the ideas how to characterise the uncertainty can be learned.

The location of uncertainty is an identification of where uncertainty manifests itself within the whole complex model. In simple word, location means the place of the improper or a factor of causes comes from. Then, nature is questioning of whether the uncertainty is due to the imperfection of our knowledge or is due to the inherent variability of the phenomena being described. It also has to define whether it can be reduced or not. Level of uncertainty is the knowledge that knows about the uncertainty along the spectrum between deterministic knowledge and total ignorance. CRES report meeting ministry of Climate and Energy, Geological Survey of Denmark and Greenland has discussed about the level of uncertainty and found out 5 types of uncertainties, which are statistical, scenario, qualitative, recognise ignorance and epistemic arrogance [3]. Figure 1 shows the level of uncertainty.

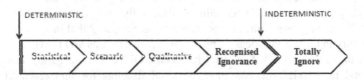

Fig. 1. The Uncertainty; From "Know" to "Un-Known"

Uncertainty generally can originate from many aspects and causes, such as machining failure, labour skills, material shortage, irregular cash flow, bureaucracy and red tape, severe weather condition, unpredictable local condition, acts of God – disaster, erosion, and etc. However, same causes could not result the same effects according to differentiate field of industry. Some of industries such manufacturing which involve in-building operation could be ignored all the causes of EI such as weather condition. However, in CI area, most of their works are in open-air environment that needs to chew over EI as a very big issues and major challenges to the project development. Several researches were distorted the terms of level/type of uncertainty to our human language to make it easy to understand. The type of uncertainty classified according to its sources (location), which are design, procurement, material handling, operation residual and others [4]. While, [5] has identified 5 types of uncertainty which are technical, acts of God, financial and economical, statutory clearance risk, and organizational risk. Every researcher has their own classification, causes, effects or factors of uncertainty because of the difficulties in generalise the uncertainty fix to all industry. All the causes have to identify based on single case study that match with the industry. Besides, high probabilities of the un-tackled uncertainty existed because of in-deterministic or un-known factors. Consequently, we split them to 2 categories of in-deterministic level (previously totally ignore) for EI which are acts of human and acts of God - unpredictable weather, disaster, and etc.

3   Factors of Uncertainty in Environmental Issues – Preliminary

Clearly known, uncertainties were a problematic issue causing border line in exploit profit to organizational. It is factorable, reasonable, vulnerable and unstable. Many of researchers put their own factors of uncertainty and try to solve it depends on what kind of that uncertainties. In addition, [1] have defined several factors of uncertainty according to problems tackle by several researchers. Yet, it is not enough if we assumed only the listed factors of uncertainties that always facing in industries, either manufacturing, construction or other types of industry. For example, in [1] research paper, he presented that [6] stand for quantity uncertainty while [7] confront of resource breakdown as the uncertainty factor, whereas [4] defined severe weather and soil condition as the factors of uncertainty that not listed. More factors, reasons and causes that give impacts on project construction performance are discusses in [9] particularly weather conditions which leading uncertainty in the planning stage. Causes and factors are different for each different location of cases. Thus, the research and investigation should be customized based on the company's requirements uniquely. Figure 2 shows the premilinary factors according to our observations and conversations with construction engineers and contractors. In other cases, company that facing the same causes and factors can be applied the same model of uncertainty into their business.

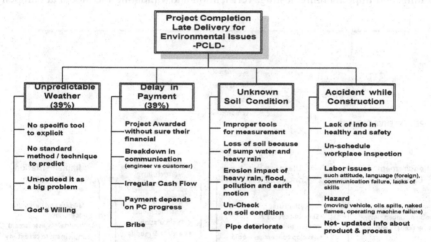

Fig. 2. Initial Factors of Uncertainty in Environmental Issues – Conceptual Model

In this research, model of uncertainty for LD will be developed considering model-based decision support specialized to the pipeline CI/our case study company. The model would operate as guidance for CI in managing and handling uncertainty of project development. As for the result, the project development will be delivered on or in time as scheduled. This uncertainty model should constructive with decision-making support by communicating the uncertainty using science engineering/project management interface. Model-based decision support use to get the systematic and graphical overview of the essential features of uncertainty in relation. It is also clearly shown through Walker's uncertainty matrix [2].

4   Proposed Methodology of Uncertainty Model

Uncertainty Matrix (UM) is the one of 14 popular techniques and tools represented by [9]. UM is adopted via [2] to get a systematic and graphical overview of the essential features of uncertainty in relation to the use of models in decision support activities. But, the model is still confused and frequent lack of mutual understanding as noted in their research publication paper. Inspire by this UM approach, this development of modelling will takes into account the factors that are rarely been existed in EI according to 2 types of uncertainty as mentioned previously; act of God and act of humans (Also refer to Figure 2 as factors in this research). The proposed research methodology encompasses of four main stages, namely requirement definition and specification, diagnosing and conceptualising, modelling and constructing, implementing and validating as shown in Figure 3. Tasks and activities that might be performed amongst the phases are include of understand the key factor determination and definition of objective, scope and collecting of data, defining the most effective and efficiency technique for identifying the factors facing in EI in CI, diagnosing and analysing causes and effects, construct a business model, develop the model of uncertainty – do modelling, and implementing, testing, verification and validating the model at company.

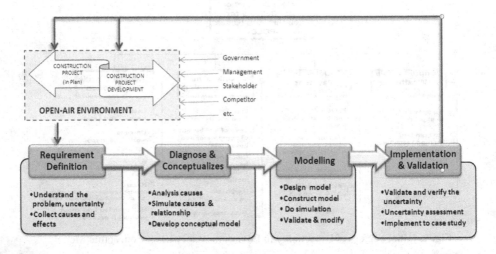

Fig. 3. The Methodolgy Research

A process modelling will involve several phases and many activities need to as well as identification of actors. A typical modelling study will involve many actors either in the management team or construction team. Thus, four different types of actors will be involved in the development of the environment uncertainty model. There are manager, stakeholders/public, reviewer, and modeller directly or indirectly. The five associate roles are collaborating in future works, hence while designing and constructing this model. The decision maker consist of 1.*The manager or user* (person faced with the problem *or* decision and take action then responsible for the consequences), 2.*The intermediary* (person who helps the user, perhaps as a more substantial "staff assistant" to interact and make suggestions), 3.The *builder or facilitator* (assembles the necessary capabilities from the generator to "configure" the specific the model with which the user/intermediary interacts directly), and 4.*The technical supporter* (develops additional information system capabilities or components when they are needed as part of the generator).

5   Conclusion

The terminology and classification of uncertainties represented with the aim of research to make researcher or manager clearly acknowledge and make out their problem. The concept of uncertainty gives an assistant for the researcher to get more understanding about the underlying factors of uncertainty in modelling the CI. It is very important to identify the nature, level and source (location) of uncertainties to structure the relationship of the causes and effects, and clarify the factors. The investigations of the causes have to determine uniquely based on the selected case study and all the collectible data need to be conceptualise by comprehensive analysis. Not all cases can use the existing models or tools because of the fluctuate parameters (causes and effect) and many elements that needed to be considered. The conceptual model was developed to provide the initial findings for this research. Additionally, the methodology of proposed uncertainty model is discussed in details as guideline of the researcher. Furthermore, the actors and their roles towards the development of the model also presented. Next, the structure of causes and effects for the uncertainty can be constructed using a simulation and testing. Later, the modelling process will take over and we assume this research willpower give their contributions in decision making model-based implement for CI.

References

1. Wazed, M.A., Ahmed, S., Yusoff, N.: Uncertainty Factors in Real Manufacturing Environment. Australian Journal of Basic and Applied Sciences 3(2), 342–351 (2009)
2. Walker, W.E., Harremoes, P., Van Der Sluijs, J.P., Van Asselt, M.B.A., Janssen, P., Krayer, M.P.: Defining Uncertainty: A Conceptual Basis for Uncertainty Management in Model-Based Decision Support. Integrated Assessment 4(1), 5–7 (2003)
3. Refsgaard, J.C.: CRES Annual Meeting reportof Geological Survey of Denmark and Greenland Ministry of Climate and Energy. Svendborg (November 17-18, 2010)
4. Polat, G., Ballard, G.: Waste in Turkish Construction: Need for Lean Construction Techniques (2004) White paper via,
   http://www.iglc2004.dk/_root/media/13080_067-
   polat-ballard-final.pdf
5. Prasanta, K.D.: Decision Support System for Risk Management: A Case Study. Management Decision 39(8), 634–649 (2001)
6. Koh, S.C.L., Saad, S.M.: Development of a Business Model for Diagnosing Uncertainty in ERP Environments. International Journal of Production Research 40 (2002)
7. Koh, S.C.L., Gunasekaran, A.: A Knowledge Management Approach for Managing Uncertainty in Manufacturing. Industrial Management and Data Systems 106, 439 (2006)
8. Shahin, A., Abourizk, S., Mohamed, Y., Fernando, S.: A Simulation-Based Framework for Quantifying The Cold Regions Weather Impacts on Construction Schedules. In: Proceedings of the 2007 Winter Simulation Conference, pp. 1798–1804 (2007)
9. Refsgaard, J.C., Jeroen, P., Anker, L.H., Peter, A.V.: Uncertainty in the Environmental Modelling Process - A Framework and Guidance. Environmental Modelling & Software 22, 1543–1556 (2007)

Statistical Process Control Method Based on Weight Percent of Al-Si Alloy for Melting and Holding Process in Die Casting

Marcel Fedak, Pavol Semanco, and Milan Micko

Faculty of Manufacturing Technologies of Technical University of Kosice, Bayerova 1,
080 01 Presov, Slovakia (Slovak Republic)
{marcel.fedak,pavol.semanco,milan.micko}@tuke.sk

Abstract. We proposed a conceptual method of how to control liquid state of Al-Sialloys in holding process of the die casting. Given that, we determine the characteristic of the holding furnace based on weight percent (wt %) of the certain alloys and their elements. An Experimental case study deals with the application of the proposed method in company that produces castings by the die-casting technology.

Keywords: die casting, chemical analysis, alloy, weight percent, SPC.

1 Introduction

The die casting technology is the widest technique for producing castings from aluminum alloys. High cadency of casting production by this technology causes high intensity of melting and replenishment of molten metal into melting holding furnaces [1]. The critical parameters include quality of liquid alloy, which means their chemical composition, etc. [2] and [3]. These parameters impact the final properties of castings produced in pressure die-casting process. The cold chamber die-casting machine employs holding furnace that has to hold molten metal preparatory to casting [4]. The melting and holding process of non-ferrous metals is carried out in the induction stationary crucible furnaces [5]. Our objective is to present method to control melting and holding process in holding furnace. Subsequently in Section 3, we applied our method in the specific condition. The last part gives an overall assessment and possible future direction to extend this method in a practical sense.

2 Proposal of Statistical Process Control Method

We assume that with proposed method, the company will be able to measure the process more effective in quality way on the basis of determining the characteristics of the holding furnace. We can also determine the ideal balanced weight percent of given elements in every layer. The particular steps of the given method are as follows:

V.V. Das, E. Ariwa, and S.B. Rahayu (Eds.): SPIT 2011, LNICST 62, pp. 188–190, 2012.

1. Ensure degassing and the removal of oxide layers that is emerging at the surface of the liquid alloy.
2. Determine the number of the samples, referred as n, where the first sample is carried out before the casting process. ($n=10$).
3. Determine the interval between sampling (see Eq. 1), referred as i, based on capacity, q, and utilization, u, of the furnace.

$$i = \frac{u \times q}{n-1}$$ (1)

4. Carry out sampling from the layer that is in the range of 50 to 70 mm below the surface of the molten metal.
5. Perform the visual control of the samples. If it is found that sample was contaminated by surface layer of the liquid alloy, the sample must be excluded. If there are 3 or more excluded samples in a row or more than 4 in total, it is necessary to repeat the sampling from the start.
6. Adjust the surface of the sample after solidification by grinding to analyze.
7. Carry out the chemical analysis using spectrophotometer.
8. Process the measured values to determine variation trend index of element content, denoted as k (see Eq. 2), where m stands for weight percent of certain element.

$$k = \frac{m_n - m_1}{u \times q} \quad \begin{cases} k > 0; \text{increasing trend in wt\%} \\ k < 0; \text{decreasing trend in wt\%} \end{cases}$$ (2)

9. Create charts for each element where x-axis presents number of castings and y-axis stands for weight percent of the certain element. From the charts we can determine the optimal number of cast parts with quality required.

3   Experimental Case Study for Demonstrating Proposed Method

We used our method to investigate variations of chemical composition in specific layers of liquid alloy vertically during the die casting process. In our three-experiment study, we observed the variations of liquid alloy composition, and also investigated a time span of estimated variations of selected elements in alloy that are defined by standards (EN 1706). The furnace uses an induction heating with capacity of 150 kg of the liquid alloy. The utilization of the furnace is 70 %, which stands for approximately 80 cast parts. The chemical analysis was performed for each sample by spectrophotometer SPECTROLAB JR.CCD 2000. We also analyzed volume of Al, Si, Fe, and Mn expressed in weight percent.The calculated values of k for Si (-0.0084), Fe (-0.0011) and Mn (-0.0024) point at decreasing trends of all three elements, which means the gradual deterioration of casting parts. In the Fig. 1 depicts charts with variation of the content for each element that is expressed by weight percent. We can assume the decreasing trend of the weight percent for silicon, ferrite, and manganese.

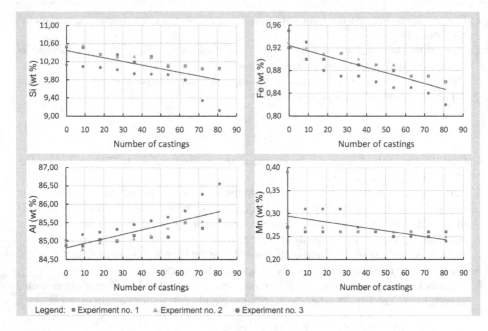

Legend: ■ Experiment no. 1   ▲ Experiment no. 2   ● Experiment no. 3

Fig. 1. Weight percent of Si, Fe, Mn, and Al in Al-Si alloy depending on the casted parts

4   Conclusions

The experimental case study demonstrated the application of the method in the company that produces casting parts by die-casting technology. It is recommended to use the proposed method in combination with standards that can lead to an increase in quality of casting parts. Future research work will be focused on monitoring the impact of the changes for selected mechanical properties such as: permanent deformation, ductility and hardness of the casting. It extends the experimental study on others types of Al-based alloys.

References

1. Zolotorevskii, V.S., Belov, N.A., Glazoff, M.V.: Casting aluminum alloys. Elsevier (2007)
2. Ragan, E., et al.: Liatiekovov pod tlakom. VMV, Presov (2007)
3. Fedak, M., Semanco, P.: Monitoring of chemical composition of aluminium alloys AlSi in the maintenance furnace. In: Fabian, S. (ed.) Scientific Papers: Operation and Diagnostics of Machines and Production Systems Operational States, vol. 3, pp. 139–144. RAM-Verlag, Ludenscheid (2010)
4. Malik, J., et al.: Špecialnetechnologie v zlievarenstve HF. TU, Kosice (2010)
5. Kaufman, J.G., Roy, E.L.: Aluminium alloy castings. ASM International, USA (2004)

Security and Privacy Enabling Solution for Vehicular Networks

Upasana Singh and Pardeep Singh

Computer Science and Engineering
NIT Hamirpur
Hamirpur, India
upasananith@gmail.com, pardeep@nitham.ac.in

Abstract. Vehicular Ad-Hoc Network, better known as VANET is a promising new technology which combines the capabilities of different wireless networks in vehicles enabling Intelligent Transportation System (ITS). Vehicular Ad-Hoc networks provide communication between on-board unit (OBU) already integrated in the vehicles and road-side units (RSUs) consisting of on-board sensors, processing modules, and wireless communication modules. Immense amount of research is going on both by industry and academia. In vehicular communication because of the high speed of vehicles frequent handovers occur and hence there is always a requirement of secure and fast authentication for a seamless handover to take place. In this paper we propose an authentication scheme that will not only provide security and privacy but also will reduce the storage and communication overhead increasing the efficiency.

Keywords: Vehicular Networks, Security, Privacy, Authentication, VANET.

1 Introduction

VANETs are the providers of traffic safety and efficiency including several other applications like public services and infotainment. A large amount of research is being done to enhance the capabilities of VANETs. Among which a significant amount of work is dedicated to communication in vehicular networks. The vehicular communication could be Intra-Vehicular communication or Inter-Vehicle Communication. In Intra-Vehicular communication the On-Board Unit (OBU) communicates with several Electronic Control units (ECU). The Inter-Vehicular Communication could be Vehicle-to-Vehicle (V2V) and Vehicle-to-Infrastructure (V2I) communication. For communication in VANETs various wireless technological standards are being developed like Dedicated Short Range Communication (DSRC). Since a rich set of tools are offered to drivers and authorities, a formidable set of exploits and attacks becomes possible. Hence for communicating in vehicular networks every entity has to be authenticated. Also for carrying out communication some keys have to be agreed upon. When a node moves from one RSU's coverage area to another, re-authentication is required in the new security domain, which is called the security handover problem. This realm combines both communication and

V.V. Das, E. Ariwa, and S.B. Rahayu (Eds.): SPIT 2011, LNICST 62, pp. 191–194, 2012.

security.The security of vehicular networks is crucial, because these systems can make anti-social and criminal behavior easier, in ways that will actually endanger the benefits of their deployment. And hence in order to have secure vehicular communication message and entity authentication has to be done, and also message integrity and confidentiality has to be maintained while preserving user's privacy and anonymity.In this paper we have proposed an authentication and key agreement protocol for vehicular networks. The paper is organized in the following way: Section 2 describes the related work. Our proposed solution is given in Section 3 with its security analysis. Finally section 4 concludes the paper.

2   Related Work

In case of vehicular networks a balance has to be made between the security and privacy for its proper functioning. Security and privacy related problems have been discussed by many researchers. While most of them addressed both security and privacy some of them fail to do so. Although communication in vehicular networks has to be real-time constrained, most of the proposals incur communicational overhead. Various techniques have been used to secure vehicular communication like symmetric key cryptography, asymmetric key cryptography, ECC, Id-based cryptography, and some times in combination with some hardware.A secure communication architecture is proposed in [1] based on a public key infrastructure (PKI) and a virtual network controlled by cluster-heads but their approach produces a remarkable overhead and the use of cluster-heads can create bottleneck. The importance of privacy and secure positioning was considered in [4] and proposed the use of Electronic License Plates (ELP) to identify vehicles. Although they recognize the importance of conditional privacy, they do not provide any specific solution to the problem. To the best of our knowledge, there are few articles that consider both security and conditional privacy preservation in VANETs. In this line, [3] gave a foundational proposal of using pseudonym based approach using anonymous certificates and the public key infrastructure (PKI).The anonymous certificates are used to hide the real identities of users. This scheme required extra communication and had storage overhead. Also privacy could be invaded by logging the messages containing a given key and tracking the sender until her identity is disclosed. GSIS presented in [6], is a conditional privacy-preserving scheme using group signatures and ID-based signatures. In it a single membership manager is used to issues secret member keys to the vehicles. The conditional anonymity claimed applies only to the vehicles amongst the peer, with an assumption that the infrastructure points are trusted. An alternative way was proposed in [7] to overcome the limitation of pre-storing a large number of anonymous certificates while preserving conditional privacy. They proposed a group signature based scheme, making an assumption that vehicles and RSUs are able to collaborate actively. Every vehicle gets a short-time anonymous certificate from a RSU after running a Two-round protocol when passing by the RSU. In order to prevent link ability of the messages, the vehicle should change the anonymous certificate regularly by interacting with RSUs. These frequent interactions may affect the network's efficiency. The group based schemes could not be applied properly due to certain limitation as the difficulty in election of group leader due to the non-availability of a trusted entity among the peer vehicles; also there may be too few cars in the vicinity to create a group.

3   Proposed Algorithm

Vehicular networks consist of several entities. A trusted authority (TA)is one which could be a law enforcement authority (or a group of authorities) that could trace and disclose the identity in case of accident or crime.AAA server is authentication, authorization and accounting server which authenticates the vehicle when it first enters the network and establishes the keys to be used.Road Side Units (RSU) which act as the access points or access routers.And the On-Board Units (OBU)which are installed on vehicles, at RSUs and AAA server.In our solution we will be using terms vehicle and mobile node interchangeably, similarly Access router (AR) and Road Side Unit (RSU) interchangeably. We have divided the Solution in two phases starting with mutual authentication and key agreement phase, next verification phase.Each vehicle is given a unique identity UID and password PSW by the TA. When the vehicle enters a network it enters UID and PSW in the OBU which generates a pseudoidentity ID_A as;$ID_A = (UID \quad PSW)$.

3.1   Mutual Authentication and Key Agreement

The AAA server chooses two large primes p and q and keeps them secret, it than computes $n = (p.q)$.When the vehicle first enters the network it sends ID_A to the AAA server. AAA server than computes $J_A = f(ID_A)$ and sends J_A to the vehicle where f( ) is a pseudorandom function. AAA chooses a secret s such that $1 \leq s \leq n-1$ and computes $v = (J_A.s)^2 mod\ n$and makes it publically available. AAA selects and sends a shared secret 'g' to the vehicle. After which both AAA server and vehicle choose respective secret numbers a and b such that $1 \leq a$ and b $\leq g-2$ each co-prime to g-1. They respectively compute $(a^{-1}\ mod\ g-1)$ and $(b^{-1}\ mod\ g-1)$. **AAA server chooses a secret 'k'** such that $1 \leq k \leq g-1$, and computes $(k.a)\ mod\ g$and sends to the vehicle. Vehicle than multiplies the received value by b and sends it to AAA. AAA than multiplies the received value by $(a^{-1}mod\ g-1)$ which undoes its previous multiplication and sends it back to the vehicle. Vehicle than multiplies the received value by$(b^{-1}\ mod\ g-1)$ which results in $K\ mod\ g$. This $K\ mod\ g$ is the shared secret key between the AAA and the vehicle which is used as the Master key (MK). This key will not be used for any kind of encryption it will only be used for deriving handover encryption key. The AAA computes handover encryption key (HEK) using the MK as HEK = (MK||IDMN||IDAR) and sends the HEK to the corresponding AR.

3.2   Verification Phase

Before the vehicle attaches to the new RSU and disconnects from the previous one, previous RSU is responsible to send V's related authentication information to the new one. Whenever a vehicle enter the vicinity of an RSU and have to communicate its identity must be verified. For verification vehicle sends IDA and $x = (JA.r)2$ mod n to the NAR(RSU) . NAR than randomly select a challenge bit e=0 or 1 and send to vehicle. The vehicle than compute $y=(ID_A.r)\ mod\ n$ if e=0 and if e=1 than $y = (ID_A.r.s)\ mod\ n$ and sends it to NAR. NAR than computes J_A from ID_A using f and $y^2 = (x.v^e)\ mod\ n$. If both the values of y received and calculated are same than the verification is successful.

3.3   Security Analysis

Denial of Service attack: Our proposal suggests a secure binding update authentication scheme using a security association between AR and MN. The scheme provides not only mutual authentication between MN and ARs, but also guarantees secrecy between ARs.Passive attack: Even if the attacker performs a passive attack, hecan't succeed as after verification both vehicle and the RSU will compute their session keys based on their secret shared information that attacker can not compute. Moreover the session key is computed by both vehicle and the RSU instead of transmitting. Therefore the proposed protocol is safe against the passive attack.Man in middle attack: It is a kind of active attack. Since no information about the secret key is revealed so the solution is safe against the man in middle attack. Even if the adversary intercepts the signals 'g' sent by the RSU in the verification process the adversary would not be able to face the real time challenge, so the solution is safe against the man in middle attack.

4   Conclusion

Vehicular networks are the vital solution to secure and efficient transportation system proving different types of applications to the vehicles. In order to take full advantage of the vehicular networks the communication must be secured meeting all the security requirements. Our proposed solution provides security and privacy both using symmetric key cryptography reducing the computation and storage required.

References

1. Blum, J., Eskandarian, A.: The threat of intelligent collisions
2. Gollan, L., Meinel, C.: Digital Signatures for Automobiles. Technical Report, Institute for Telematike 6(1), 24–29 (2004)
3. Raya, M., Hubaux, J.: Securing vehicular ad hoc networks. Journal of Computer Security, Special Issue on Security of Ad Hoc and Sensor Networks 15(1), 39–68 (2007)
4. Lin, X., Sun, X., Ho, P.: GSIS: A secure and privacy preserving protocol for vehicular communications. IEEE Trans. Vehicular Technology 56(6), 3442–3456 (2007)
5. Lu, R., Lin, X., Zhu, X.: ECPP: Efficient conditional privacy preservation protocol for secure vehicular communications. In: IEEE INFOCOM 2008, pp. 1229–1237 (2008)
6. Zhang, C., Lu, R., Lin, X.: An efficient identity based batch verification scheme for vehicular sensor networks. Journal IEEE INFOCOM 2008, 246–250 (2008)

Clause Boundary Identification for Tamil Language Using Dependency Parsing

R. Dhivya[1], V. Dhanalakshmi[2], M. Anand Kumar[1], and K.P. Soman[1]

[1] Centre for Excellence in Computational Engineering and Networking,
Amrita School of Engineering, AmritaVishwaVidyapeetham, Coimbatore, India
[2] Department of Tamil, SRM University, Kattankulathur
{r.dhivya23,dhanagiri}@gmail.com,
anandkumar@yahoo.co.in, kp_soman@amrita.edu

Abstract. Clause boundary identification is a very important task in natural language processing. Identifying the clauses in the sentence becomes a tough task if the clauses are embedded inside other clauses in the sentence. In our approach, we use the dependency parser to identify the boundary for the clause. The dependency tag set, contains 11 tags, and is useful for identifying the boundary of the clause along with the identification of the subject and object information of the sentence. The MALT parser is used to get the required information about the sentence.

Keywords: Natural Language Processing (NLP), Dependency parser, Clause boundary, Parts of Speech (POS), Shift reduce parser, MALT.

1 Introduction

Clause boundary identification plays a major role in various NLP tasks. If the sentence length is too long, it is split into many simple clauses, which makes the translation process an easy one. If the sentences are connected using connectives or separated by comma, the clauses can be split easily. In other cases, the process is tedious. So, the dependency parser is used, to identify the boundaries of the clauses, using the MALT tool.

2 Related Works

Clause boundary identification is a significant work in NLP tasks in the last few years. R. Vijay Sundar Ram and SobhaLalithaDevi[1] identified the clause boundary using the Conditional Random Fieldsand used a hybrid approach. Fredrik Jorgensen[2] detected the clause boundaries by classifying coordinating conjunctions in spoken language discourse as belonging to either the syntactic level or discourse level of analysis. Hyun-Ju Lee et al. [3] proposes a method for Korean clause boundary recognition by recognizing the ending points of clauses first, and then identify the starting points by considering the typological characteristics of Korean.

V.V. Das, E. Ariwa, and S.B. Rahayu (Eds.): SPIT 2011, LNICST 62, pp. 195–197, 2012.

Tomohiro Ohno et al. [4]proposed a technique for clause-by-clause basis by identifying the clauses based on clause boundaries analysis, analyzes the dependency structures of them, and tries to decide the dependency relations with another clause. Tomohiro Ohno et al. [5]identified clause boundaries in two levels, one is the clause level and the other one is the sentence level. Dan Lowe Wheeler[6] presented a paper for machine translation through clausal syntax for his thesis, which is a tree to tree translation from English to Chinese that predicts the English clause structure from Chinese clause structure.

3   Proposed Method

The input sentences are first tokenized and given to the POS tagger and chunker. It is then preprocessed to the parser input format and then passed to the parser. The parsed output is then converted to a digraph format which serves as the input to the tree viewer. The tree viewer generates the tree structure forthe parser output. The block diagram for the parsing system is given in Figure 1.

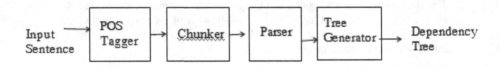

Fig. 1. Block diagram of the proposed method

4   Dependency Tag Set

The tag set developed for the Dependency Parsing has 11 tags, which is listed in Table 1.

Table 1. Dependency Tagset

S.No.	Tag	Description
1	<ROOT>	Head Word
2	<N.SUB>	Nominal Subject
3	<D.OBJ>	Direct Object
4	<I.OBJ>	Indirect Object
5	<NST.MOD>	Spatial Time Modifier
6	<CL.SUB>	Clausal Subject
7	<CL.DOBJ>	Clausal Direct Object
8	<CL.IOBJ>	Clausal Indirect Object
9	<SYM>	Symbols
10	<X.CL>	Clause Boundary
11	<X >	Others

5 Tool Used for Dependency Parsing

The tool used for Dependency Parsing is the MALT Parser Tool[7].In our model, we have considered the following features: word index, word, POS tag, chunk tag, dependency head and dependency relation.The word index, word, POS tag and the chunk tag are in the first four columns. The dependency head and the dependency relation should be in the 7th and 8th column respectively. The rest of the features are marked '_'. The output is given to the GraphViz tool to generate the tree structure.GraphViz is an open source tool that generates the tree structure from a digraph file.

6 Results and Conclusion

The parser is trained using the sentences of different patterns collected from various Tamil grammar books and so the training data covered almost all the patterns available for simple sentences and limitedcomplex sentences. The developed model showed better accuracy for the sentences of smaller length.So, including the complex sentences in the training data will improve the accuracy of the clause boundary identification.

References

1. Ram, R.V.S., Lalitha Devi, S.: Clause Boundary Identification Using Conditional Random Fields. In: Gelbukh, A. (ed.) CICLing 2008. LNCS, vol. 4919, pp. 140–150. Springer, Heidelberg (2008)
2. Jorgensen, F.: Clause Boundary Identification in Transcribed Spoken Language. In: Nivre, J., Kaalep, H.-J., Muischnek, K., Koit, M. (eds.) NODALIDA Conference Proceedings, pp. 235–239 (2007)
3. Lee, H.-J., Park, S.-B., Lee, S.-J., Park, S.-Y.: Clause Boundary Recognition Using Support Vector Machines. In: Yang, Q., Webb, G. (eds.) PRICAI 2006. LNCS (LNAI), vol. 4099, pp. 505–514. Springer, Heidelberg (2006)
4. Ohno, T., Matsubara, S., Kashioka, H., Kato, N., Inagaki, Y.: Incremental Dependency Parsing of Japanese Spoken Monologue Based on Clause Boundaries. In: Proceedings of 9th European Conference on Speech Communication and Technology, pp. 3449–3452 (2005)
5. Ohno, T., Matsubara, S., Kashioka, H., Maruyama, T., Tanaka, H., Inagaki, Y.: Dependency Parsing of Japanese Monologue Using Clause Boundaries. Springer (2007)
6. Wheeler, D.L.: Machine Translation through Clausal Syntax: A Statistical approach for Chineese to English, Technical Report, Massachusetts Institute of Technology (2008)
7. MALT Parser website, http://www.maltparser.org/userguide.html

An Approach to Understand Secure MANET Routing Using OPNET

Virendra Singh Kushwah[1], and Gaurav Sharma[2]

[1] Department of Computer Science
Hindustan Institute of Management and Computer Studies, Farah, Mathura, India
[2] Department of Computer Science
GLA University, Mathura, India
{kushwah.virendra248,gauravsharma53}@gmail.com

Abstract. Mobile Ad-Hoc Network (MANET) is a wireless network without infrastructure. Self-configurability and easy deployment feature of the MANET resulted in numerous applications in this modern era. Efficient routing protocols will make MANETs reliable. The open and dynamic operational environment of MANET makes it vulnerable to various network attacks. A common type of attacks targets at the underlying routing protocols. Malicious nodes have opportunities to modify or discard routing information or advertise fake routes to attract user data to go through themselves. The aim of the research is to prevent network using secure routing protocols and to study the performance of the secure network.

Keywords: Secure, OPNET, ad hoc, routing.

1   Introduction

Mobile Ad-hoc network is a set of wireless devices called wireless nodes, which dynamically connect and transfer information. When a wireless node plays the role of intermediate node, it serves as a router that can receive and forward data packets to its neighbour closer to the destination node. Due to the nature of an ad-hoc network, wireless nodes tend to keep moving rather than stay still [1] [4]. Therefore the network topology changes from time to time. MANET has various potential applications. Some typical examples include emergency search-rescue operations, meeting events, conferences, and battlefield communication between moving vehicles and/or soldiers.

2   Literature Review

It is understandable that most security threats target routing protocols – the weakest point of the mobile ad-hoc network. There are various studies and many researches in this field in an attempt to propose more secure protocols [1] [2]. However, there is not a complete routing protocol that can secure the operation of an entire network in

V.V. Das, E. Ariwa, and S.B. Rahayu (Eds.): SPIT 2011, LNICST 62, pp. 198–200, 2012.

every situation. Typically a "secure" protocol is only good at protecting the network against one specific type of attacks [3].Many researchers have been done to evaluate the performance of secure routing protocols in comparison with normal routing protocols [3] [4]. One of the objectives of this research is to examine the additional cost of adding a security feature into non-secure routing protocols in various scenarios. The additional cost includes delay in packet transmission, the low rate of data packets over the total packets sent, etc.It is well known that the real-world network does not operate in an ideal working environment, meaning that there are always threats and malicious actions affecting the performance of the network. Thus, studying the performance of secure routing protocols in malicious environments is needed in order to effectively evaluate the performance of those routing protocols [5] [6].

3   Simulation Setup

In this paper, simulation set up of a network with 30 wireless nodes moving at random, each with various speed between 1 and 10 meters per second. Each of the objects can move at a random direction, stop for some time (per the *pause time*), and then change its direction at random and move again. The *traffic pattern* models the voice data transferred from one node to the other [1] [4]. The data is sent at a rate of 2 kbps to represent compressed voice data. The number of data source nodes is chosen based on the assumption that a half of the nodes send the data and a half of the nodes receive the data. The destination of data is determined at random to mimic the real situations. The simulation scenario is summarized below:

Table 1. SimulationSetup Parameters

Sr. No.	Parameters	Value
1	Simulation Area	1000 M x 1000 M
2	Mobility Model	Random Waypoint
3	Simulation Time	10 Min
4	Number of Nodes	30
5	Node speed	1-10 m/second
6	Type of traffic	Constant Bit Rate (voice)
7	Packet size	512 bytes (or ~ 4096 bits)
8	Sending frequency	4 packets/second
9	Traffic destination	Random

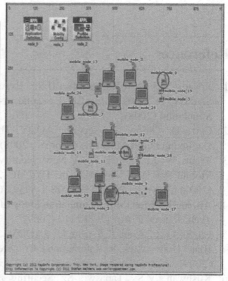

Fig. 1. Simulation Environment with 30 nodes

4   Result and Analysis

The simulation is done using AODV protocol into OPNET[4] Simulator. The 30 nodes in which 26 are free nodes and 4 are attackers. A scenario is set up for data collection. This scenario is run 10 times with 10 different values of the mobility *pause time* ranging from 1 to 10 seconds. The data is collected according to two metrics – *Packet Delivery Fraction* and *Normalized Routing Load* [1] [3]. In general, the actual values of the performance metrics in a given scenario are affected by many factors, such as node speed, moving direction of the nodes, the destination of the traffic, data flow, congestion at a specific node, etc. It is therefore difficult to evaluate the performance of a protocol by directly comparing the acquired metrics from individual scenarios. In order to obtain representative values for the performance metrics, we decided to take the average values of multiple simulation runs [1] [4] [5].

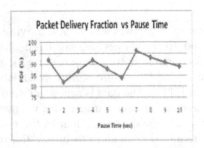

Fig. 2. PDF vs. pause time values in benign environment   **Fig. 3.** NRL vs. pause time values in benign environment

References

1. Juwad, M.F., Al-Raweshidy, H.S.: Experimental Performance Comparisons between SAODV & AODV. In: IEEE Second Asia International Conference on Modelling & Simulation (2008)
2. Cerri, D., Ghioni, A.: Securing AODV: The A-SAODV Secure Routing Prototype. IEEE Communications Magazine (February 2008) 0163-6804/08 © 2008 IEEE
3. Tsaur, W.-J., Pai, H.-T.: A New Security Scheme for On-Demand Source Routing in Mobile Ad Hoc Networks. In: IWCMC 2007, Honolulu, Hawaii, USA, August 12-16 (2007) Copyright 2007 ACM 978-1-59593-695-0/07/0008
4. Ali, M.H., Odah, M.K.: Simulation Study of 802.11b DCF using OPNET Simulator. Eng. & Tech. Journal 27(6), 1108–1117 (2009)
5. Lu, S., Li, L., Lam, K.Y., Jia, L.: SAODV: A MANET Routing Protocol that can Withstand Black Hole Attack. In: International Conference on Computational Intelligence and Security (2009)
6. Kushwah, V.S., Tapaswi, S.: Securing Nodes in MANETs Using Node Based Key Management Scheme. In: Proceeding of the IEEE Xplore 2010 International Conference on Advances in Computer Engineering– ACE 2010, Bangalore, India, June 21-22, pp. 228–231 (2010)

Synchronization of Health Informatics
with "AADHAAR" (UID: Unique Identification)

Nitin Vohra and N.K. Jain

Centre for Development of Advanced Computing (CDAC), Department of Information
Technology, Ministry of Communications & Information Technology, Government of India
{nitinvohra,nkjain}@cdac.in

Abstract. Healthcare providers are facing challenges to make unique
EMRacross hospitals. In existing scenarios there is no concept of centralized
repository and no mechanism to map records. To prevent duplicity of records
various checks are available in rolled out applications but it depends on
information keyed. Slight deviation in records may lead to duplicate
registration. This 'identity silos' increase overall cost of identification and
extreme inconvenience. WHO provide HL7 standards to exchange data between
heterogeneous applications, but most of applications do not support HL7. In all
scenarios the aim to maintain Unique EMR is lost. It can be prevented by
identify a compulsory field which is unique to identify patient record. With the
advent of AADHAAR we can check the duplicity of record and get EMR
according to unique IDacross hospitals. Since AADHAAR is not mandatory in
Hospital applicationsbecause ofguidelines, as a challenge we introduced UID in
GNCTD, PGIMER and AROGYA Hospital projects.

Keywords: Hospital Management Information System(HMIS), UID,
AADHAAR, EHR, EMR, LUCENE, HI (Health Informatics).

1 Introduction

HI is a discipline at the intersection of information science, computer science, and
health care. It applies to the areas of nursing, clinical care, dentistry, pharmacy, public
health and biomedical research. Research in the field of electronics instruments
making dreams come true of researchers in the field of HI, HMIS is one example.

AADHAAR is a 12-digit unique number (Fig. 1) which the Unique Identification
Authority of India (UIDAI) will issue for all residents. The number will be stored in a
centralized database and linked to the basic demographics and Biometric information,
photograph, ten fingerprints and iris of each individual. [1]

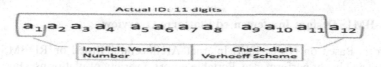

Fig. 1. UID (Unique Identification Number Format)

V.V. Das, E. Ariwa, and S.B. Rahayu (Eds.): SPIT 2011, LNICST 62, pp. 201–204, 2012.

HMIS is used in hospitals with the objective of streamlining the treatment flow of a patient, allowing doctors and other staff to perform to their best ability, in an optimized and efficient manner. Modeled on a unique combination of a 'patient centric and medical staff centric' paradigm it is beneficial to the recipients and the providers of healthcare. It provides an accurate, medical record of the patient. EHR is the ultimate goal of those who see the value of information systems in the care of patients. However much remains to be done in the areas of data exchange/interoperability, data entry, user interfaces, database design and security before the full benefits of EHR's can be realized [2]. The HL7 communication standard is developed for the Health Care domain and facilitates the exchange of messages between Health Care Information Systems [3]. Patients are mobile and visitmultiple health service providers. At present medical record number is issued and maintained by a practitioner or a provider organization; it is inadequate to support the national healthcare system. In our country about 15-20 per cent of patients are brought to the hospital in an unconscious state. Doctors have to find out their medical records, but by then it is often too late in case of emergency. "In order to uniquely identify an individual across multiple health organizations, a reliable Healthcare System is required and the best would be AADHAAR.

2   Industry Initiative (Previous Work in the Field / Literature Review)

The basic health care delivery system in India is implemented through the Primary Health Centers. In providing healthcare services the ANMs are made to maintain number of records in registers. Keeping this as the key information, CMC Limited designed a project using state-of-the-art technology, mobile devices which were handed to the ANMs for capturing data at the doorsteps of the rural people. The system covers the health care delivery at two levels. Data is electronically transferred upwards in the department hierarchy for strategic planning and decision-making. [4]

3   UID in HMIS

3.1   Requirement

Existing system with no Central Repository and absence of Patient's Unique Identifier was the biggest challenge. At present patients are mobile, visit multiple providers and treated by multiple health organizations. Patient Identifier is unique only within a provider organization which is inadequate to support the national healthcare system.

3.2   HMIS Design: Implemented Platform Overview

System is Based on N-tier J2EE Internet Architecture, Based on RDBMS for easy retrieval and better performance, Portable across a variety of platforms. (Fig. 2)

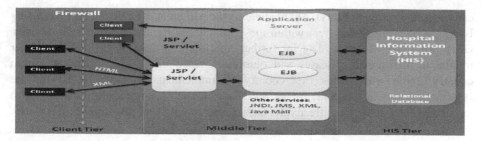

Fig. 2. HMIS Architecture

Patient information captured using Registration process of the HUIDS application and based on the National Health ID maintained in the system Unique Patient Information is stored in the Database, which is at the Hospital level point and then stored in Central Repository through boot model of cloud computing making it possible to run remote applications on "cloud" of computers [5], limits the Duplicity of records by implementation of LUCENE Technology, ensures smooth and fast retrieval and updating of Patient Historical medical information every healthcare point. (Fig. 3)

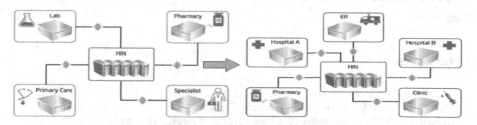

Fig. 3. Health Information Network

The Five basic functions that a Healthcare UID System supports are:

1. Complete computerization of hospital's operations.
2. Centralizing data storing and retrieving capabilities. (Fig. 3)
3. Manual and automated linkage of various clinical records from different practitioners, sites of care to form a lifelong view of patient records.
4. Accurate identification functions and DIS-Identification functions (under principle of Information security: confidentiality, integrity, availability).[6]
5. Reduce healthcare operational cost and enhance the health status of the nation.

4   Benefits of UID

Data collected can be used for surveys; this will provide a platform to roll out schemes like RSBY (RASHTRIYA SWASTHYA BIMA YOAJANA). Data can be used by companies ,institutions, service providers (such as developing a system which can be used to provide FIRST Aid medical to the patient at the place of accident using I-version of healthcare system within the Ambulances by use of Hand held devices. Govt. will have access to data for further analysis and drawing up plan for better treatments to rampant diseases and outbreaks based on specific locations within country. India will be the first country to implement a unique ID HealthCare Information system (HUIDS) for its residents on such a large scale. Enabling it to target and deliver services effectively, higher returns on social investments in country.

5   Conclusion

Health informatics with UID will be a big success for developing a reliable Health care Information system under which UID will allow hospitals and clinics to track patient's medical records and get their medical histories. This way, patients may not take duplicate tests or treatments and in case of emergencies doctors will have access to critical information like patient is allergic to which medicine and insurance coverage etc. mapping of health related data with 12 key numbers of UID will speed up the process of treatment and will avoid cumbersome paperwork.

Acknowledgment. The Author expresses gratitude to UIDAI and seniors for their Guidance.

References

1. http://uidai.gov.in/
2. Carter, J.H. (ed.): Electronic Health Records, 2nd edn.
3. Koisch, J.: HL7 Interoperability Paradigms, http://www.hl7.org/
4. http://www.cmcltd.com/industry_practices/ e-Governance/ihc.shtml
5. Sullivan, D.: The Definitive Guide to Cloud Computing. Cloud Computing: An enabler of IT in Indian Healthcare Sector, Study Report by Zinnov Management consulting
6. Whitman, M.E., Herbert: Principles of Information Security, 3rd edn.

Image Steganography Optimization Technique

Bassam Jamil Mohd[1], Sa'ed Abed[1], Bassam Al-Naami[2], and Sahel Alouneh[3]

[1] Computer Engineering Department, Hashemite University Zarqa, Jordan
{bassam,sabed}hu.edu.jo
[2] Bio-medical Engineering Department, Hashemite University Zarqa, Jordan
b.naami@hu.edu.jo
[3] Computer Engineering, German-Jordan University, Amman, Jordan
sahel.alouneh@gju.edu.jo

Abstract. This paper presents a novel steganography technique which combines Discrete Cosine Transform (DCT) and Least Significant Bit (LSB). The objective is to maximize the capacity and invisibility of the secret image with minimal modification to the cover image (at most k-bits per block). The secret image is transformed to frequency domain using DCT. An algorithm is employed to construct the optimum quantization to embed the DCT coefficients in k-bits. The k-bits are then hidden in the LSBs of the cover image. The performance (capacity and peak signal-to-noise ratio) of the proposed method is compared with LSB.

Keywords: Steganography, Image Processing, Quantization.

1 Introduction

Steganography is the art and science of hidden communication. The objective of steganography is to communicate information in a undetectable manner such that when the messages are observed by unintended recipient there will not be enough evidence that the messages conceals additional secret data. A steganography system consists of three elements: cover-object (which hides the secret message), the secret message and the stego-object (which is the cover-object with message embedded inside it.) Many different digital cover-file formats can be used such as text, audio, image and video. However, given the proliferation of digital images, especially on the internet, and the large redundant bits present in the digital representation of an image, images are the most popular cover objects for steganography [1].One of the main image stegnography techniques is the Least Significant Bit (LSB) where the values of one or more of least significant bits to embed the secret information. Another technique is the Transform (DCT)-based steganography which embed the secret information in the frequency domain. LSB and DCT based steganography vary in their performance with respect to capacity a security. Typically, LSB is easily detectable [2] and has larger capacity [3]. On the other hand DCT-based

V.V. Das, E. Ariwa, and S.B. Rahayu (Eds.): SPIT 2011, LNICST 62, pp. 205–209, 2012.

steganography has higher peak signal-to-nose ratio (PSNR) [3] and is more robust against statistical attacks 1].Reference [4] examined and evaluated LSB steganography techniques to hide messages in 8-bit and 24-bit formats. It evaluated the techniques for 2, 4, and 6 LSBs for .png and .bmp formats. Reference [4]presented an image steganography based on LSB, DCT, and compression techniques on raw images to enhance the security of the payload. The LSB algorithm is used to embed the payload bits into the cover image followed by applying DCT on the stego-image. Finally, quantization and run length coding algorithms are used for compressing the stego-image to enhance its security. Furthermore, [5] compared LSB steganography with embedding secret message in the LSB of the DCT coefficient. It demonstrated that PSNR of DCT&LSB is higher than LSB only. However, the amount of secret information in DCT&LSB is much smaller.This paper proposes an image steganography technique which combines the benefits of DCT and LSB steganography and mitigates their weaknesses. This is accomplished by embedding quantized DCT coefficients of the secret image in k-bits of cover image LSBs. An algorithm is designed to calculate an optimum quantization. The rest of the document is organized as follows. Section-2 describes the system model, illustrates the technique steps and explains proposed algorithm. Section-3 discusses some experimental results. Finally, section-4 presents concluding remarks and some future trends.

2   Proposed Model

The secret image (denoted as SEC) has a size of size N×N, and the cover mage (denoted as CVR) has a size M×M pixels. The model processes 8×8 pixel blocks of the SEC and CVR images. For each block (i) from CVR (referred as CVR_blocki) k bits are embedded, where k is determined based on the maximum distortion and accepted PSNR for the CVR. The rest of the section explains how to embed/extract secret message and discusses the optimization algorithm.

2.1   Embedding and Extracting Methods

Fig. 1 (a) illustrates the embedding method of the SEC image in CVR image. The SEC is divided into 8×8 blocks of pixels, where each block is transformed to the frequency domain using DCT. Next, the DCT coefficients are processed according to optimized quantization to represent DCT coefficients in k bits per block. The k bits are them embedded in an 8×8 cover message using LSB technique. Fig. 1 (b) demonstrates the extraction of the SEC from the stego-image. Initially, the k bits per block are extracted from the CVR least significant bits. Next, the DCT coefficients are constructed by applying reverse process of the optimum quantization on the k bits. Finally, Inverse Discrete Cosine Transform (IDCT) is applied on the DCT coefficients to retrieve secret image.

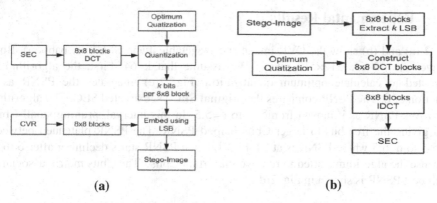

Fig. 1. Embedding (a) and Extracting (b) Methods

2.1.1   Optimum Quantization

The quantization step calculates the optimum quantization which provides the best PSNR for SEC image. The objective is to pack as much information about the SEC in k bits (per block per color layer), which accomplished by the below algorithm. The algorithm is applied on colored images (for CVR and SEC images), where each pixel is described by three values ranging from 0 to 255. It is also assumed that the CVR image is colored image. The algorithm inputs are the SEC DCT coefficients (represented by C matrix) and k. The output of the algorithm is a matrix (Cbits), which determines the number of bits allocated for the DCT coefficients. Therefore, Cbits (i,j) states the number of bits used to quantize DCT coefficient C(i,j).

Hence, the dynamic range for C(i,j) is expressed as:

$$\text{Dynamic range} = [\ -2 \ \text{Cbits}(i,j)-1 \ , \ (2 \ \text{Cbits}(i,j)-1-1) \ ]$$

If C(i,j) is outside the rage, during the quantization it will be saturated to the closer of the limits of the dynamic rage. The algorithm searches for the optimum Cbits matrix. The algorithm consists of the following steps:

- The "average" or "weight" of C(i,j) across the blocks is determined:

- $$C_w (i, j) = \frac{1}{B} \sum_1^B C (u, v)$$

- whereB is the number of 8×8 blocks in SEC image. The k bits are distributed amongst the DCT based on Cw values. Larger Cw's are rewarded more bits than smaller Cw's.
- Next, the algorithm attempts to take bits from smaller owners of the bits and award them to larger owners. This accomplished by set Cbits(i,j) to zero if it is less than (δi), and redistributing the bits to other Cbits.
- Select Cbits associated with best PSNR.

Determining the min/max/step for δ requires examining many simulation runs. However, reasonable results suggest Min/Max values of 0/7.0/0.1.

3   Experimental Results

Fig 2 (a) and (b) show the CVR image (i.e. vegetables) and SEC (i.e. baboon). Both images are of size 512×512 pixels. We assume that k=64. First, the algorithm is executed to calculate optimum quantization. Fig. 2(c) illustrates the PSNR as a function of δ. The PSNR compares the original SEC vs. extracted SEC. The algorithm improves PSNR as it moved from δ=0 to δ=5.5. In this interval, pruning small Cbits and giving the free bits to larger Cbits helped PSNR. The PSNR plateaued between δ=5.5 to δ=6.5 where PSNR is at 21.45 dB. Then PSNR starts declining after δ=6.5, because the algorithm started to remove important Cbits. The Cbits matrix associated with best PSNR is shown in Fig. 2(d).

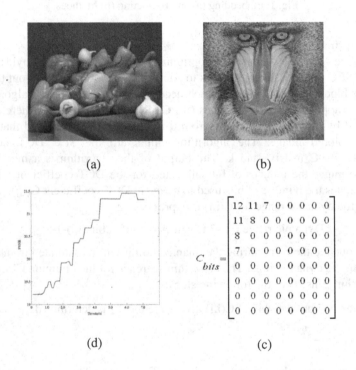

(a)   (b)

$$C_{bits} = \begin{bmatrix} 12 & 11 & 7 & 0 & 0 & 0 & 0 & 0 \\ 11 & 8 & 0 & 0 & 0 & 0 & 0 & 0 \\ 8 & 0 & 0 & 0 & 0 & 0 & 0 & 0 \\ 7 & 0 & 0 & 0 & 0 & 0 & 0 & 0 \\ 0 & 0 & 0 & 0 & 0 & 0 & 0 & 0 \\ 0 & 0 & 0 & 0 & 0 & 0 & 0 & 0 \\ 0 & 0 & 0 & 0 & 0 & 0 & 0 & 0 \\ 0 & 0 & 0 & 0 & 0 & 0 & 0 & 0 \end{bmatrix}$$

(d)   (c)

Fig. 2. The Cover Image (a) Secret Image (b)PSNR(c) and C$_{bits}$ matrix (d)

Fig. 3 shows the stego-image and extracted image. The PSNR for the stego-image compared with CVR is 51.1 dB, which is considerably high. In fact 51.1 dB implies that ~1% of CVR data have been modified after embedding the SEC.Since only 1% of the CVR image data is modified with unknown quantization (except for the intended recipient), the embedded message is securely encrypted. Hence, the proposed steganography method provides high level of imperceptibility for the secret image.When compared with LSB, the proposed method provides better security since

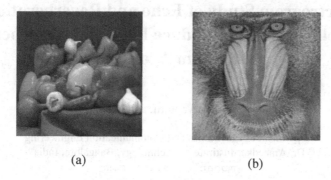

(a)   (b)

Fig. 3. The stego-image (a) and recovered SEC image (b)

the quantization serves as an encryption. Additionally, the proposed method is superior in terms of capacity and PSNR.

4   Conclusion

In this paper, we have presented a steganography technique which is based on LSB and DCT methods. Existing LSB_DCT steganography methods suffer from limited poor PSNRStego as number of LSBbits increases. Furthermore, some of the existing methods have capacity issues.The proposed method embeds the entire SEC image while balancing the PSNR for CVR and SEC images by calculating an optimum quantization for SEC DCT coefficients. Moreover, the quantization improves imperceptibility for the secret message.

References

1. Morkel, T., Eloff, J., Olivier, M.: An Overview of Image Steganography. In: The Fifth Annual Information Security South Africa Conference (ISSA 2005), Sandton, South Africa (June/July 2005)
2. Wang, H., Wang, S.: Cyber warfare: Steganography vs. Steganalysis. Communications of the ACM 47(10), 76–82 (2004)
3. Walia, E., Jain, P., Navdeep: An Analysis of LSB & DCT based Steganography. Global Journal of Computer Science and Technology 10, 4–8 (2010)
4. Deshpande, N., Sneha, K., Jacobs, D.: Implementation of LSB Steganography and Its Evaluation for various Bits. In: 2006 1st International Conference on Digital Information Management, pp. 173–178 (2007)
5. Raja, K., Chowdary, C., Venugopal, R., Patnaik, L.: A Secure Image Steganography using LSB, DCT and Compression Techniques on Raw Images. In: 3rd International Conference on Intelligent Sensing and Information Processing, pp. 170–176 (2005)
6. Walia, E., Jain, P., Navdeep: An Analysis of LSB & DCT based Stegnography. Global Journal of Computer Science 10, 4–8 (2010)

Spectrogram Study of Echo and Reverberation– A Novel Approach to Reduce Echo and Reverberation in Room Acoustics

Pushpalatha G.S., Shivaputra, and Mohan Kumar N.

Department of Electronics and Communication Engineering
Dr. Ambedkar Institute of Technology, Bangalore, India
mohan.ait@live.com

Abstract. This paper presents new approach to enhance the quality of sound signal perceived by the listener in a concert hall considering Spectrogram and Single Spectrum Plot. We simulate a natural concert hall using Digital Echo and Schroeder Reverberator models. We analyze the results using Spectrogram and Single Spectrum Plots and finally propose a model for better analysis of room acoustics.

Keywords: Acoustics, Echo, Reverberation, SIMULINK®, Single Spectrum Plot and Spectrogram.

1   Introduction

An Echo is a reflection of sound, arriving at the listener some time after the direct sound. This is followed by a group of closely packed reflections with decaying amplitude referred to as Reverberation. The display of the magnitude of the Short-Time Fourier Transform (STFT) is usually referred to as the Spectrogram. However, since the STFT is a function of two variables, the display of its magnitude would normally require three dimensions. Often, it is plotted in two dimensions, with the magnitude represented by the darkness of the plot. In the STFT magnitude display, the vertical axis represents the frequency variable (ω) and the horizontal axis represents the time index(n) [5]. In this paper, we perform digital implementation of Echo and Schroeder Reverberator models using SIMULINK® to obtain Spectrograms of input and output signals. For each Spectrogram, we determine Single Spectrum Plot and finally compare the Single Spectrum Plot obtained for output signal against input Single Spectrum Plot to obtain the Error Plot. From the Error Plot analysis, we propose a model to analyze Echo and Reverberation to improve quality of sound signal perceived.

2   Literature Review and Audio Effects Used in Sound Production

Echo can be implemented digitally using FIR or IIR filter. It can be Single or Multiple Echo Filters [5]. There are several models proposed for Reverberation which include

V.V. Das, E. Ariwa, and S.B. Rahayu (Eds.): SPIT 2011, LNICST 62, pp. 210–213, 2012.

the algorithms proposed by Schroeder, Moorer, Gardner, Dattoro [2] and Jot [3]. Schroeder Reverberator forms the basis for all other Reverberator models. In this paper, we concentrate mainly on FIR Single Echo Filter, Schroeder's Comb Reverberator and Allpass Reverberator. Echoes are simply generated by delay units. The direct sound and a single Echo appearing after R (delay parameter) sampling periods later can be generated by FIR filter [5] whereas the gain parameter α with $|\alpha| < 1$ represents the signal loss caused by propagation and reflection. Schroeder's Comb Reverberator has a delay cell with an output redirected to the input. In second Reverberator model, Schroeder replaced Comb Filter with an Allpass Filter to develop more realistic Reverberation. According to Schroeder, approximately 1000 Echoes per second are necessary to create a Reverberation that sounds natural and free of flutter [1].

3   Digital Implementation and Analysis Using SIMULINK®

We implement Digital Echo and Reverberator models using SIMULINK®. The Echo – Simulink model is represented in Fig. 1. Fig. 2 represents Comb Filter Reverberator and Fig. 3. represents Allpass Reverberator. Fig. 4 represents the proposed Error Detection Model.

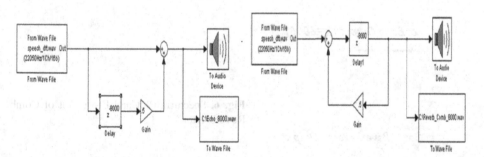

Fig. 1. Echo Model   **Fig. 2.** Comb Filter Reverberator

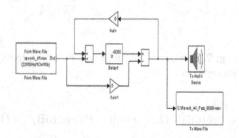
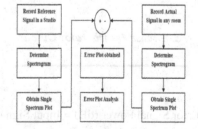

Fig. 3. Allpass Reverberator   **Fig. 4.** Error Detection Model

We use PCM 16 bit signed, 352 kbps, 22050 Hz speech signal as input signal in all three existing models and for each model we run the simulation for 8 seconds and record their corresponding output samples. We determine Spectrogram for input and output samples to obtain Single Spectrum plot. Table 1 represents the Spectrograms obtained for the input and output of Echo, Comb Reverberator and Allpass Reverberator respectively. For each Single Spectrum Plot, power difference between input and output signal is determined using Equation 1.

Table 1. Spectrograms

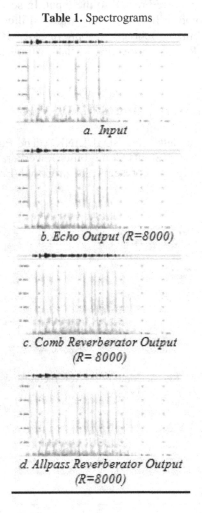

a. Input

b. Echo Output (R=8000)

c. Comb Reverberator Output (R= 8000)

d. Allpass Reverberator Output (R=8000)

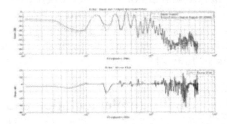

Fig. 5. Specturm Plot and Error Plot of Echo Filter

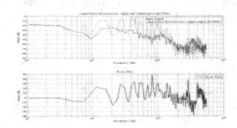

Fig. 6. Specturm Plot and Error Plot of Comb Reverberator

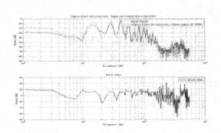

Fig. 7. Specturm Plot and Error Plot of Allpass Reverberator

Error Signal Power (dB) = Input Signal power (dB) – Output Signal Power (dB)   (1)

The magnitude of Error Signal obtained from Equation 1, indicates the amount of power variation between input and output signal. We refer to this as Error Plot. Error Plot is simply the power difference between input and output power levels for all frequencies at a particular time index. Fig. 5, Fig. 6 and Fig. 7 represents the Single Spectrum Plots and Error Plots. Ideally, Equation 1 will yield 0 dB values if the listener perceives the sound signal with the same magnitude as that of the original signal without any reflections and decay in signal magnitude. But in all practical cases, we get some difference in values due to sound reflections and decay in signal magnitude. We refer to this as Error Value. In Echo spectrogram, the reflected signals will have considerable magnitude when compared to direct sound. But in Reverberation Spectrogram the amplitude of reflected signals decays with time. In both Reverberator models the entire spectrum gets shifted with increase in delay parameter but in Allpass Reverberator some spectrum is fixed due to feed-forward path which produces natural reverberation.From Figure 5 we can observe that Echo Error plot has almost 0 dB values for frequencies less than 10 KHz. But from Figure 6 and Figure 7 we observe that Reverberation Error plots has almost 0 dB values for frequencies less than 1 KHz. It must be reduced to 0 dB for better audio signal perception.

4   Conclusion

This paper provides clear distinction between Echo and Reverberation using Spectrogram and Single Spectrum Plot in a natural concert hall. From simulation analysis we conclude that sound signal perception can be enhanced if input and output signal power variations match together even with variations in delay parameter. This paper also lays the foundation for further research work in the field of room acoustics to increase the quality of sound signal perceived by the listener at any point in the room by getting the values of Error Plot to almost 0 dB for all frequencies with varying delay parameters. This methodology can be used to improve acoustic design.

References

1. Schroeder, M.R.: Natural Sounding Artificial Reverberation. JAES 10(3), 219–223 (1962)
2. Dornean, I., Topa, M., Kirei, B.S.: Digital Implementation of Artificial Reverberation Algorithms. Acta Technica Napocensis 49(4) (2008)
3. Beltrán, F.A., Beltrán, J.R., Holzem, N., Gogu, A.: Matlab Implementation of Reverberation Algorithms. Journal of New Music Research 31(2), 153–161 (2002)
4. Moorer, J.A.: About this Reverberation Business. Computer Music Journal 3(2) (1978)
5. Mitra, S.K.: Digital Signal Processing, 3rd edn. Tata McGraw-Hill Companies (2006)
6. Spectrogram Version 5.0, http://smedor.com/gram50.zip

Web Content Management System for Schools

Shaha T. Al-Otaibi[1] and Samir El-Masri[2]

[1] College of Computer and Information Sciences, Princess Nora Bint Abdulrahman University, Riyadh
[2] College of Computer and Information Sciences, King Saud University, Riyadh

Abstract. The Content Management System (CMS) changes the perspective towards the web design process through allowing easily nontechnical users to manage contents of their web sites. It has a wide range of features that will satisfy the school communication needs that are well served by dynamic web sites. Consequently, the main goal of this work is designing an appropriate framework for the School Content Management System (SCMS). This system adopts CMS features for creating, editing, organizing, and publishing content relating to different schools' activities. These activities include school administrative works, course management, and classroom management.

Keywords: CMS, WEM, UWE, UP.

1 Introduction

A few years ago, the administration of website such as updating, or adding new contents needs assistance from IT companies or web designer. Today with a few skills in computer, it is easy for nontechnical users to create and manage a comprehensive websites through using the CMS applications. They used for creating, editing, organizing, and publishing content of the website. The use of CMS for managing educational portal makes school's activities become more reliable and easy to perform. It should support schools from the following perspectives: Communication, CMS will enhance the communication between students and school faculty. The dynamic website keeps up the communication with coursework while away from the school and the forum modules provide an online interaction where students and teachers can discuss course materials, as well as events at the school. Usability, CMS for schools should be facilitating the tasks to optimize user's time spent in managing their website. Determining the appropriate utilization of modules, menus, managers, the visual design and physical place of the interface elements can improve the user's capability to navigate successfully through the tasks. Content Publishing, the CMS should be made easy to publish and manage all school website contents. Furthermore, schools need specific modules that serve the educational activities for the school's community. For example, Course Management which provides a full range of features to help teachers planning and managing the course contents. As well as, it assists students to conduct online learning. In addition to, Classroom Management which encourages the alternative collaborative learning. It provides features including modules for assignments, chat, forums, and quizzes.

V.V. Das, E. Ariwa, and S.B. Rahayu (Eds.): SPIT 2011, LNICST 62, pp. 214–224, 2012.
© Institute for Computer Sciences, Social Informatics and Telecommunications Engineering 2012

There are a lot of CMSs in the market, some of them released as an open-source software. Unfortunately, many systems have more functionality and most of them useless function for the school community. The huge number of functionalities complexes the use of these systems and they become not user-friendly for nontechnical persons. In addition, other systems miss the essential functions that needed to handle school activities such as course and classroom modules. Of course, some of them provide an opportunity to add customized features or integrate with other systems, which offer some features needed for educational systems. However, the school faculty in most cases misses the technical skills that required to understand these features. These reasons orient the CMS users to establish a customized CMS which satisfy their needs through easy and direct interface. The contribution of this paper is the design of CMS Framework for schools. It determines the fundamental requirements that should be offered by CMS that serve the school community and should be fulfilled the above perspectives. The rest of this paper is organized as follows: Section 2 presents the literature review. Section 3 defines the problem statement of this research. Section 4 presents the framework development and describes the key functions of SCMS. Section 5 discusses some issues related to the proposed framework. Finally, a conclusion of this paper in Section 6.

2   Literature Review

This research has been studying the existing CMSs and investigated some experiences of schools which already migrated for using CMSs to manage their websites. As well as, it reviewed the literatures that related to managing the school website's contents. At the beginning of this section, we will provide an overview of the two popular open-source CMSs that can be used to manage the school's website:

1. Joomla, which is considered the most powerful CMS. It is very widely used by users and includes many features, which allow users to create a website and manage their content. Joomla established JoomSchools which is a reasonable CMS that provides both primary and secondary schools with the ability to modify their websites. There are thousands of functions that can be used for school. The standard package includes modules such as email, calendar, document manager, file Repository, menu. Besides, optional modules such as room and resource online booking, e-Learning (LMS), and discussion Forum [27].
2. Drupal, which is used to create the personal blogs, as well as, enterprise applications. It includes thousands of add-on modules that assist to build any website. It recently incorporates the school administration module that responsible for storing information of students, faculty and non-academic staf\f. This module enables parents to view information of their kids. It contains some other modules for managing classes, lessons, class lists, and rooms booking [25].

Nowadays, many schools around the world already started the migration to CMS to gain advantages of Information Technology (IT). The Queensland (a state of Australia) education ministry used Joomla [23] to move their schools from fixed websites to a CMS and help schools to publish and managed their content by offering many pre-installed templates [7]. Additionally, the program for the technology modernization of Portuguese schools that aim to improve the educational environment by developing school portals, that offering content publishing, course management, and virtual learning environments [20]. Moreover, the Malaysian Smart School is one of leading schools in using IT in education and management, these schools provided an educational portal to enable the knowledge sharing and improving the learning process [6, 8]. We have not found related works regarding the CMS for schools, but there are many literatures present some issues related to the school CMS. The web service oriented resource-based system named E-School which is a platform independent. The E-School simplifies the interaction between the students, teachers, administrators and the policy makers. Furthermore, the system provides management for reading materials, references, student reports, multimedia tools, central databases, and helps to standardize the education in both urban and rural institutes [3]. A school resource management system is a platform designed to help primary schools in developing and sharing the school's resources. These resources refer to digital teaching materials include documents, video, pictures, and other coursework materials [4]. In addition, a Web-based course plays a vital role in the educational system; the web-course platforms presented in [5,11] organize all course resources and realize the overall process of building a web-based course. The web-based learning system of computer course [9] that supports teachers in lesson preparation, teaching process, and implementation of online assessment as well as, a discussion, and providing student self-learning. Additionally, the platform that uses learning object to organize all the resources and content related to the web-course. It performs the whole process of building a web-based course, from creating a new course, editing the course content to publishing the course content [1].

Moreover, a classroom management is the powerful ability for any teacher, and can only be accomplished by establishing an effective interaction among teachers and students. Reference [10], constructed a web-based classroom management system using the concept of E-commerce technologies as well as, using the tools for building a dynamic website. Furthermore, the author [12] designed a Web-based teaching system for information retrieval. This system characterized by the active teaching which improves the student's ability in searching the Internet information resources. At the same time, it is helping teachers to monitor the overall affairs of students' learning process, and is providing content flexibility to optimize the effectiveness of teaching.

3   Problem Statement

All schools in Saudi Arabia's educational system already used computerized management system to achieve school administrative functions, and most of school have its own website to publish school information. The website has extremely limited or out-of-date information. Typically, school website contains only general information that is updated each semester. If data from the management system wants to be published on the web, it should be manually transmitted to the website by website designer such as grading result at the end of semester. Additionally, teachers and students are missing the effective interaction; Teachers cannot upload their course materials on the website while the students cannot use it for supporting their learning. Furthermore, parents lack the ability to follow up their child's learning progress or check their attendance. Consequently, these systems loosely comply the current school needs. In order to address the above problems, this paper proposes the use of CMS solutions, which have a wide range of features that will satisfy the school community needs. Using CMS in schools ranges from managing school activities and creating teacher blogs, to extended community discussion forums, to online course offerings. We aim to design framework of SCMS that satisfy school needs and present required functions through user-friendly interface.

4   System Development

The next step is the selection of the methodology - which will apply of the framework design. There are several approaches have been proposed in the field of web engineering. Though, the CMS is an application which merges the Web technology and manages the unstructured data. The existing approaches for the requirements engineering of Web applications fail to implement the CMS system [19]. We apply the engineering method developed specifically for CMS-based web applications which built by merging components of two methods: UML-based Web Engineering (UWE) and the Unified Software Development Process (UP). This Engineering Method (WEM) proposed by Souer in [16,19] and it was applied successfully in several cases for WCM systems [16].

4.1   System Analysis

The definition phase of WEM defines the actual requirements analysis and specification [19]. A school's environment composed of psychological, social, and academic dimensions. The interaction among students, teachers, administrators, parents, and the community help to shape a school's environment [18]. This definition gives an overview of all school components. The school system requirements acquired by collecting information for existing system specifications, documents evaluation, and literatures investigation. These requirements covered all schools activities which relating to students, teachers, and administrators. Thus, the derivation of the accurate requirements will assist in developing a framework for school CMS. Several problems found and converted into the overall needs.

4.2   System Design

System design is the core of this paper and it is usually considered a crucial for the success of any system. The SCMS is a framework for a tool that will help in building dynamic websites for schools. It will be used, to create, edit, manage, and publish content at runtime in an organized fashion. Content managed may include blogs, documents, images, audio, and video files. Figure 1. depicts the system architecture of SCMS. The CMS gets and puts all its contents and the corresponding metadata into its database. Different users connect to the CMS by standard browser clients. If users have access rights, then they can create and manage web contents. Otherwise, they can only browse web pages depending on their privileges.

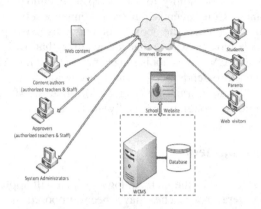

Fig. 1. System Architecture for SCMS

According to the objective and the design principle, the SCMS framework should include the following main functions: system and members manager, web pages manager, file manager, page editor, template editor, and module manager. The description of SCMS components is presented below.

1. **System and Members Manager.** This manager organizes and maintains the system information. It is handling the database backup and the system configuration functions such as themes, website title, language, date format, and user privilege. There are four types of WCMS members: system administrator, faculty and staff members, students, and parents. Each type of users has different access rights. The system administrators have the highest privileges. They can add or approve different users, and give other users the creating and managing privileges. Faculty and staff members can create, edit, manage and publish contents in a different format such as text, graphics, video, documents, etc. Students can browse the web contents and have additional functionality, such as submitting assignment or quizzes. Parents can view their child's record to follow up their learning progress or check their attendance.

2. **Web pages Manager.** This manager handles sections, categories, and web pages of the web sites. Section refers to a collection of web pages that can display in a menu. Category allows to create an extra hierarchal in the website menu and categorize pages within a section. Through this manger, the authorized users can create, edit and delete sections, categories, and web pages.

3. **Files Manager.** Files uploaded from the user's computer on to the server where the SCMS manager is running. Files can be organized by different categories, such as text, picture, flash, video and audio. It allows to create directories for different categories. From there, teachers can upload their lecture notes and laboratory experiments in audio and video format. Authorized users can be added these files to web pages and to course contents or to classroom activities.

4. **Page Editor.** The SCMS should be offered a fully featured editor to edit pages. The resultant files should be compatible with any web browser.

5. **Template Editor.** This editor helps nontechnical persons to create sophisticated templates for the website. It should provide easy tools and menus to handle the layout of different parts of the webpage. Additionally, any SWCM system should be offered preinstalled Templates.

6. **Module Manager.** Module is a program that can perform a determined function in the webpage. These functions include school administration, course, classroom, test, send email and messages, search, calendar, forum, links, news, and etc. The authorized users can use these functions in their web pages by selecting the module name from modules list. The following paragraphs present the key modules in SCMS:

   1. **School Administration Module.** School resources and records management are daily functions for school administration staff. Records for students, faculty and non-academic staff intended to store in the central database server. Student records keep general information, attendance, and medical records, as well as, grading information. The authorized users are responsible for adding a new record and updating existing record information. These records used to generate reports and perform statistical analysis. Parent can monitor their child's learning progress. Additionally, faculty and non-academic staff records include general information, contact numbers, and qualification. Through this module, faculty members can create personal web pages or blogs to publish their news and external information related to teaching courses. The business process model for student record management presented in Figure 2. Furthermore, this module handles room reservation which responsible for assigning rooms to subjects in school's schedule and determining teacher who will conduct this lecture

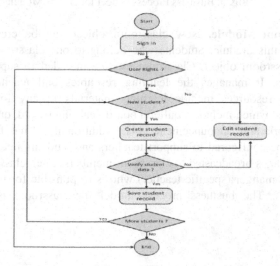

Fig. 2. Business Process Model for student record management

2. Course Module. Authorized teachers can create a new course or modify existing one. This process includes adding the basic information about the course, course index, course contents, polices, grading system, and calendar events. The course contents can be added from the files repository which are uploaded to the system from file manager. The following process is the course content approval and publishing which accomplished by authorized staff. The business process model for course module presented in Figure 3.

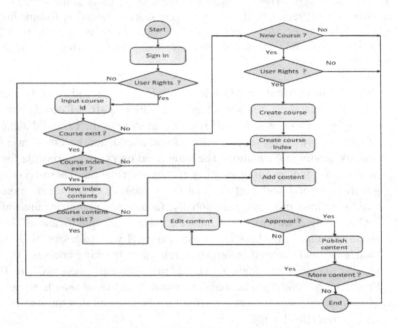

Fig. 3. Business Process Model for course Module

3. Classroom Module. New classroom object can be created and managed through this module. Students who belong to one classroom should be added to a classroom object. Classroom module intended to support different class activities. It manages the learning resources and teaching activities. The learning resources include learning materials in any format and teaching activities, which include a bulletin board, learning record, quizzes, assignments, homework and announcement [14]. Additionally, Chat for each classroom should be configured to support teachers and students interaction. In addition to, messages broadcasted to classroom members. Each classroom administrated by class manger (specific teacher) who is responsible for managing classroom activities. The business process model for classroom is shown below in Figure 4.

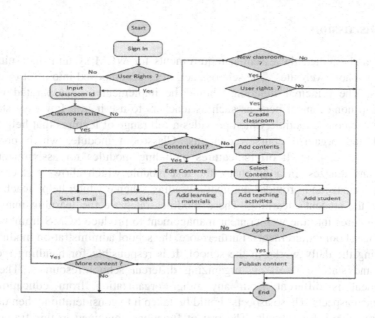

Fig. 4. Business Process Model for Classroom Module

4.3   Presentation Design

This phase is part of WCM implementation. It is related to the construction of the visual presentation of the website. The presentation usually developed by an external graphical designer such as XHTML prototype [16]. Additionally, the implementation consists of using other technologies to support CMS-based Web applications. We intended to use eXtensible Markup Language (XML) [24] to support CMS framework. There are many areas in CMS where XML plays an important role such as communication, authoring, interoperability, storage, query processing, and publishing [21]. In communication, a number of XML based interaction formats designed to maintain the flow of information between different groups. There is a need to pass messages among different system modules and different groups of user. These messages can be carried out using XML Remote Procedure Call (XMLRPC), the Rich Site Summary (RSS) and NewsML [3,21]. Additionally, the use of XML-aware editor as part of a CMS will simplify the authoring of school information. The Interoperability, where most of the schools already have school management system. There is a need to connect the CMS with other information systems. The solution is the use of web service platforms, such as Sun's J2EE or Microsoft's NET [21]. Furthermore, The XML schema and the XML DTDs can be used to determine the set of rules for the data storage [3]. Finally, we can use the XQuery [27], the XML-based query language to create the query response. Then, the result can be published by Extensible Stylesheet Language Transformation (XSLT) [28] which offers a separating of the presentation from the contents to support multiple published formats depends on user preferences.

5   Discussion

This research studied the essential requirements for WCM system that suitable for managing school web sites. The school's activities decomposed into a set of coherent functions. The principal functions should be implemented in separated modules, which help nontechnical persons such as teachers to use it in a few easy steps. For example, the course module which provides a full range of features that help teachers to build and organize course's contents. Classroom module, which provides a collaborative learning. It offers features including modules for assignments, chat, forums, and quizzes. In addition to, the test module which allows test creation in different formats and provides automatic grading scheme which helps teacher easily to assess the student's learning. These modules integrate the learning management system features into the web content management to produce SCMS framework that fulfills the school requirements. Furthermore, the school administration module which is handling the daily works in the school. It is responsible for handling records of student and staff, as well as, organizing different school resources. The school environment is different from any other organization from educational and pedagogical aspects. These aspects should be taken into consideration when designing WCM framework for schools. The rest of functions contained in this framework is shared with other WCM systems. These functions provide website creation and content development as well as to offer communications tools.

6   Conclusion

In conclusion, this paper presented a flexible and scalable framework for school content management system. Based on the study of school requirements, we proposed a design of the framework that supports the content management and activities accomplishment. The proposed framework provides an effective management process that needed to create and manage website contents. The SCMS is employed an easy and flexible tools that suitable for nontechnical users such as school staff. It used the customized modules to incorporate educational and pedagogical features to our framework. For example, the course module helps teachers to build and to organize course's contents. Classroom module offers features including modules for assignments, chat, forums, and quizzes. Additionally, the test module allows test building and provides automatic grading system which helps teacher easily to evaluate the student's learning. Furthermore, the school administration module assist school administration staff to accomplish school's daily work. For example, school resources and records management are daily functions in the school environment. These features represent the main difference between WCM system that suitable for the school environment and other general WCM systems. We perceive that the essential functions of any WCM system included in this framework. Finally, we plan as a continuation of this research to present an implementation for the proposed framework.

References

1. Omar, Y., Sahari, N.: Futuristic Model for School's Content Management Systems: A Beginning. IEEE (2010)
2. Brumbulli, M., Topçiu, B., Dalaçi, A.: SMIS: A Web-Based School Management Information System. In: International Scientific Conference Computer Science (2008)
3. Sultana, A., Sultana, I.: E-School: A Web-Service Oriented Resource Based E-Iearning System. In: 2010 International Conference on Networking and Information Technology. IEEE (2010)
4. Chengi, Y., Wang, Y., Tongi, S., Wangi, F., Zhengi, Z.: Design of School-based Resource total management system. In: 2nd International Conference on Education Technology and Computer, ICETC (2010)
5. Chengi, Y., Wang, Y., Tongi, S., Wangi, F., Zhengi, Z.: Design of Web-based Course: Developing Platform Based on Learning Object. In: International Conference on New Trends in Information and Service Science (2009)
6. Joseph, Z., Gibbs, D.: Series: Globalisation, Comparative Information technology: Languages, Societies and the Internet. Comparative Education and Policy Research 4 (2009)
7. Web Content Management System (CMS) for Schools, Release 2008 Q3.1, Version: A.6 (October 2008)
8. Muhammad, Z., Zain, M., Murugaiah, P., Atan, H., Idrus, M.: Management Practice in Malaysian Smart School: Tasks and Support Analysis of the ICT Implementation. In: Proceedings of the IEEE International Conference on Advanced Learning Technologies (ICALT 2004). IEEE (2004)
9. Xu, J., Wu, J., Wan, Z., Xu, X., Chen, Y.: Web-based Learning of Computer Courses Resources: Design and the Management Policy Based on Campus Network. IEEE (2010)
10. Zeng, B., Feng, S., Zhang, J.: Web-Based Class Management System Using E-commerce Technology. In: Third International Symposium on Electronic Commerce and Security. IEEE (2010)
11. Siew, O., Shepherd, J.: WebCMS: A Web-based Course Management System. In: Proceedings of the 13th International Workshop on Database and Expert Systems Applications. IEEE (2002)
12. Qiuhui, X.: Design of Web-based Teaching System for Information Retrieval. IEEE (2009)
13. Yu-Fang, Yong-sheng, T.Z.: Design and Implementation of College Student Information Management System Based on Web Services. IEEE (2009)
14. Liu, T.-Y., Tan, T.-H.: The Design and Implementation of Web-Based Instruction System for High School– WISH and Executing Status. In: Proceedings of the IEEE International Conference on Advanced Learning Technologies, ICALT 2004 (2004)
15. van de Weerd, I., Souer, J., Versendaal, J., Brinkkemper, S.: Situational Requirements Engineering of Web Content Management Implementations. In: Proceedings of SREP 2005, Paris, France (August 2005)
16. Souer, J., Luinenburg, L., Versendaal, J., van de Weerd, I., Brinkkemper, S.: Engineering a Design Method for Web Content Management Implementations. In: Proceedings of iiWAS 2008. ACM, Linz (2008)
17. Ralyté, J., Deneckère, R., Roland, C.: Towards a Generic Model for Situational Method Engineering. In: Eder, J., Missikoff, M. (eds.) CAiSE 2003. LNCS, vol. 2681, pp. 95–110. Springer, Heidelberg (2003)
18. Baldwin, B.: School Environment Analysis. Louisiana Principle Intership (1994)

19. Souer, J., van de Weerd, I., Versendaal, J., Brinkkemper, S.: Situational requirements engineering for the development of content management system-based web applications. Int. J. Web Eng. Technol. (IJWET) 3(4), 420–440 (2007)
20. Education Appliance enabling school 2.0, Case Study: Portuguese Public Schools Deploy the Critical Links education appliance in the Largest School Modernization Project Worldwide (2009)
21. XML and content management system,
    http://www.steptwo.com.au/papers/kmc_xmlandcms/index.html
22. cms4schools, http://www.cms4schools.net/
23. Joomla, http://www.joomla.org/
24. XML, http://www.xml.org
25. Drupal, http://drupal.org/
26. Sharepoint,
    http://sharepoint.microsoft.com/en-us/Pages/default.aspx/
27. XQuery, http://www.w3.org.TR11xquery/
28. XSLT, http://www.w3.org.TR11xslt

Performance Evaluation: Ball-Treeand KD-Tree in the Context of MST

Hazarath Munaga[*] and Venkata Jarugumalli

Dept. of Information Technology
University College of Engineering
JNTUK, A.P. India
{hazarath.munaga,venkata.jarugumalli}@gmail.com

Abstract. Now a day's many algorithms are invented / being inventing to find the solution for Euclidean Minimum Spanning Tree (*EMST*) problem, as its applicability is increasing in much wide range of fields containing spatial / spatio – temporal data viz. astronomy which consists of millions of spatial data. To solve this problem, we are presenting a technique by adopting the dual tree algorithm for finding efficient EMST and experimented on a variety of real time and synthetic datasets. This paper presents the observed experimental observations and the efficiency of the dual tree framework,in the context of kd-tree and ball-tree on spatial datasets of different dimensions.

Keywords: Euclidean Minimum Spanning Tree (EMST), dual Tree, kd-tree, ball-tree.

1   Introduction

Minimum Spanning Tree (*hereinafter*, MST) is the one of the oldest and most thoroughly studied problem in computational geometry [1]. The Minimum-weight Spanning Tree or simply MST problem is one of the well-known optimization problems for finding minimum weighted spanning tree for both undirected and directed graphs. MST have many applications in computer design, communication, transportation and some other problems that can apply directly/indirectly are wireless network connectivity, clusteringand classification of different data namely spatial data. In literature, several authors proposed a variety of greedy algorithms[2, 3, 4]. The general drawback with these greedy algorithms is that these cannot handle large amount of data and performance bottleneck will happened and later some more advanced algorithms are developed to solve this problem [5].In this paper, authors evaluated the performance of dual tree algorithmic framework [6] using single linkage clustering [7] and compared the performance of the dual tree framework in the context of kd-tree and ball-tree. As per the Ref. [8] theoretically single-linkage clustering provides optimal clusters.

---

[*] Dr MHM Krishna Prasad, Associate Professor & Head.

V.V. Das, E. Ariwa, and S.B. Rahayu (Eds.): SPIT 2011, LNICST 62, pp. 225–228, 2012.

2   Related Work

Many of the MST Algorithms are utilized Tarjan's Blue rule[10] to find the minimum weight edge. Using this rule many of the greedy algorithms are developed viz. Prims with $O(m+nlogn)$ and Krushkal with $O(mlogn)$ time complexity's respectively. In Dual-Tree Boruvka's Algorithm,the efficiency of the Boruvka's algorithm mainly depends on the adopted nearest neighbor technique. If we find nearest neighbors efficiently by using some intelligent data structure like spatial trees,kd-tree, ball tree or any spatial tree, the performance of the Boruvka's algorithm can be enhanced. For example, for the query set Q and reference set R, then for each point $q \in Q$ and $r \in R$ such that $d(q, r)$ must be minimized and call it as nearest neighbor pair. Native approach will take $O(n^2)$ run time for finding nearest neighbor pair for n number of components[11]. Hence, in this paper, authors adopted the algorithms proposed by [7] to evaluate the performance of Dual Tree Boruvka and compared with kd-tree and ball-tree.

KD-tree[12] is one of the space partitioning tree for organizing k-dimensional data points. For building this kd-tree of n points it takes $O(n \log n)$ if we use the linear median finding algorithm described by [13] and for adding new point to the balanced tree it takes $O(log n)$ and for removing a point from tree takes $O(log n)$, because of removing a point from tree the balance of the tree will change then we need to rebalance the tree so for both adding and removing point from tree will take same time complexity of $O(log n)$.

Ball Tree[14] is also binary tree data structure for maintaining spatial data hierarchically like kd-tree and oct-tree [15]. Each node in the ball-tree referred as ball contains a region of Euclidean points bounded by a hyper-sphere and interior balls are small containing their children balls. One can specify the ball $n+1$ float values as co-ordinates and r radius as its center. Like kd-tree the ball tree also uses top down approach for building the tree recursively from top to down by choosing the split dimension and splitting value to find these values,balls are sorted along each dimension and store the cost in an array. Best dimension and split location can be found in $O(nlog(n))$, so, time complexity to construct the ball-tree is $O(n(log n)^2)$.

3   Implementation

In this paper, authors adopted Dual-tree Boruvka in the context of kd-tree and ball-tree for finding the EMST. Experiments are performed on synthetic datasets and real time datasets [9]. Both algorithms are implemented and incorporated in weka3.6.4 [16] and compiled with the jdk1.6. Following Table and Fig. 1 shows the observations.

Table 1. Performance of *kd-tree* and *ball-tree* for 50 dimensions

Operation Instances	Build		Insertion		Deletion		N-NN Search	
	kd-tree	ball-tree	kd-tree	ball-tree	kd-tree	ball-tree	kd-tree	ball-tree
10000	187	1203	188	1187	218	1172	31	47
25000	547	3469	531	3468	516	3454	96	110
50000	1344	7906	1172	8094	1156	8093	118	219
100000	2578	16547	2750	16437	2812	16485	391	422
200000	5937	36672	5688	36703	5640	36375	875	907

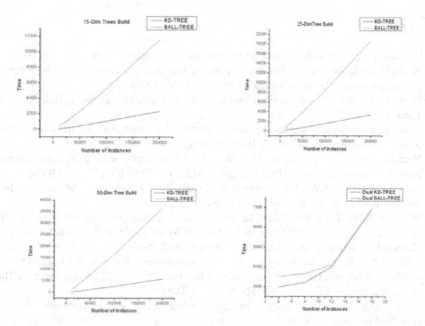

Fig. 1. (a) time taken for building kd-tree and ball-tree for 15-dimensions (b) time taken for building kd-tree and ball-tree for For 25-dimensions (c) time taken for building kd-tree and ball-tree for 50-dimensions of data; (d) Comparison of dual tree algorithm using both kd-tree and ball-tree.

From the above results, one can easily observe that the computational time for constructing ball-tree takes more time than the kd-tree, and as the dimensionality increases the performance of kd-tree is also increases when compared with ball-tree. Figure-1(d) shows the performance of DualTreeBoruvka using kd-tree as well as ball-tree for varying dimensions on real-time datasets obtained from SDSS. Both algorithmic performance is nearly equal but overall performance differs with creation of tree structure, i.e., kd-tree takes $O(n \log n)$ and ball-tree takes $O(N(\log N)^2)$ for n points in Euclidean space. Finally, from the experimental results, authors conclude that DualTreeBoruvka on kd-tree performs faster than the DualTreeBoruvka on ball-tree for finding Euclidean MST.

4   Conclusion

In this paper,authors compared kd-tree and ball-tree based dual tree Boruvka algorithm for finding Euclidean Minimum Spanning Tree (*EMST*). For finding efficient EMST, authorsadopted dual tree algorithm and experimented on a variety of real time and synthetic datasets of various dimensions. From the experimental observation, authors conclude that the *kd-tree performs faster than the ball-tree for not only constructing the tree and also for solving the EMST problem. Moreover, the kd-tree based dual tree Boruvka is giving good results than the ball-tree based dual-tree Boruvka.*

References

1. Preparata, F., Shamos, M.: Computational Geometry. Springer, New York (1985)
2. Nesetril: OtakarBoruvka on minimum spanning tree problem Translation of both the 1926 papers, comments, history. Discrete Math. 233, 3–36 (2001)
3. Prim, R.C.: Shortest connection networks and some generalizations. J. Bell Sys. Tech., 1389–1401 (1957)
4. Kruskal, J.B.: On the shortest spanning subtree of a graph and the traveling salesman problem. Proc. Am. Math. Soc. 7, 48–50 (1956)
5. Narasimhan, G., Zachariasen, M., Zhu, J.: Experiments with computing geometric minimum spanning trees. In: Proceedings of ALENEX 2000, pp. 183–196 (2000)
6. Gray, A., Moore, A.W.: N-body problems in statistical learning. In: Advances in Neural Information Processing Systems, pp. 521–527 (2001)
7. William, B.M., Parikshit, R., Alexander, G.: Fast Euclidean Minimum Spanning Tree: algorithm, analysis, and applications. In: 16th ACM SIGKDD International Conference on Knowledge Discovery and Data Mining, pp. 603–612 (2010)
8. Balcan, M., Blum, A., Vempala, S.: A discriminative framework for clustering via similarity functions. In: 2008 Proceedings of the 40th Annual ACM Symposium on Theory of Computing, pp. 671–680. ACM, New York (2008)
9. Sloan Digital Sky Survey, http://sdss2.lib.uchicago.edu/dr7/en/ (accessed on January 15, 2011)
10. Tarjan, R.E.: Data Structures and Network Algorithms. In: Society for industrial Applied Mathematics, vol. 44 (1983)
11. Graham, R.L., Pavol, H.: On the history of the Minimum Spanning Tree Problem. J. IEEE Ann. Hist. Comput. 7, 43–57 (1985)
12. Moore, A.W.: An intoductory tutorial on kd-trees. Technical Report No. 209, Computer Laboratory. University of Cambridge (1991)
13. Cormen, T.H., Leiserson, C.E., Rivest, R.L., Clifford, S.: Introduction to Algorithms, 3rd edn. MIT Press and McGraw-Hill (2009)
14. Omohundro, S.M.: Five Balltree Construction Algorithms, ICSI Technical Report TR-89-063 (December 1989)
15. Warren, M.S., Salmon, J.K.: A parallel hashed Oct-Tree N-body algorithm. In: Proceedings of the ACM/IEEE Conference on Supercomputing, pp. 12–21 (1993)
16. Machine Learning Group at university of Waikato, http://www.cs.waikato.ac.nz/ml/weka/ (accessed on August 25, 2010)

Analysis of M-Ary Modulation with M-Ary LDPC Coding for DVC

N.M. Masoodhu Banu[1] and S. Sasikumar[2]

[1] Professor Sethu Institute of Technology,
Kariapatti, Tamilnadu, India
banumobeen@yahoo.com
[2] Professor Rover College of Engg and Technology,
Perambalur, Tamilnadu, India
sonopoppy@gmail.com

Abstract. In this paper we consider the issue of Distributed Video Coding (DVC) over practical channel which involves Gaussian noisy channel. Since the research on DVC over practical channel with respect to modulation is still incomplete this paper does a comprehensive study on DVC modulation techniques to fill the gap. It discusses the suitability of M-Ary modulation to DVC on the basis of energy consumption. The study covers both theoretical and practical aspects through the practical implementation of DVC encoder and decoder, the performance in terms of bit error rate, decoder complexity and data rate of M-Ary modulation techniques used with M-Ary LDPC coding

Keywords: DVC, M-Ary modulation, M-AryLDPC codes, S/W and WynerZiv coding.

1   Introduction

In a video compression process, one of the main tasks at the encoder side is motion estimation which is to extract the temporal correlation between frames which is a more complex process and leads to encoder complexity ten times more than the decoder. Distributed video coding is a new video coding paradigm where the encoder decoder complexity is reversed. The main reason behind DVC attraction is that the applicability of this new paradigm in the widely used video uplink applications such as wireless video cameras and video conferencing using mobile devices, applications. DVC is based on the information theoretic ideas of Slepian-Wolf and Wyner-Ziv theorems.The idea behind DVC goes back to the 1970s when Slepian and Wolf [1] proved that, if the source Y is compressed to its entropy limit H(Y), X can be transmitted at a rate very close to the conditional entropy H(X|Y), provided that Y is available at the receiver as side information for decoding X. Since H(X,Y) = H(Y) + H(X|Y), X and Y can be independently encoded and jointly decoded without any loss in the compression efficiency, compared to the case where both sources are jointly encodedand decoded. The application of this concept to lossy source coding is known

V.V. Das, E. Ariwa, and S.B. Rahayu (Eds.): SPIT 2011, LNICST 62, pp. 229–235, 2012.

as the Wyner-Ziv coding [2]. In practical DVC systems, a subset of frames, known as key frames, is usually compressed using traditional intra coding techniques. Frames following each key frame, known as Wyner-Ziv (WZ) frames, are then compressed either by sending the parity bits or syndrome bits. At the receiver side the previous frames are interpolated to give side information. Within the DVC framework there are multiple issues to be solved, here we restrict ourselves to discuss i) Compression rate ii) BER (Bit Error Rate) and iii) Data rate with respect to parity and syndrome approach. With the same base channel code (n, k) the two approaches gives different compression rate. The syndrome code's compression rate is n − k/n which is much better than parity approach. With respect to error correction, parity approach can correct x number of bit error out of kbits while syndrome approach can correct same x number of bit error out of n bits. In short while the syndrome approach performs well in noiseless scenario the parity approach performs well in practical noisy channel conditions [3]. As there are other issues with parity approach as we discuss in section 4, which decreases the performance of parity approach, we choose the syndrome approach as an optimized one and hence we analyze the higher order modulation for syndrome based DVC.The reminder of the paper is as organized as follows, section 2 briefs DVC background, section 3 rationalizes the need for higher order modulation, section 4 discusses the higher order modulation approach section 5 evaluate the need for syndrome approach, and section 6 concludes with simulation results.

2   Reviews on DVC

DVC is a new compression technique where the correlation between two signals is utilized. The concept emerged from Slepian Wolf theory [5] which dates back to 1970s. Given two statistically dependent sources X and Y being separately compressed to its limit $H(Y), H(X), X$ can be transmitted at a rate very close to the conditional entropy $H(X/Y)$. This leads to effective compression of X with much less operational complexity, provided that Y is perfectly recovered at the receiver as side information. This characteristic of less complexity finds application in wireless sensor based multimedia and multimedia over low powered portable devices.The Slepian Wolf problem has been solved by two major research groups using two approaches namely DSC using syndromes (DISCUS) and DSC using parity (DISCUP). The optimality of DISCUS approach is proved in [4]. But thisapproach does not consider the practical channel with noise and it also does not consider the two channels involved for the channel code design.However if the syndrome based compressed bits are transmitted over noisy channel it is considered to be inefficient for the reason of loss of error resilience. It estimates a wrong sequence even for one bit of error in the syndrome. Recent developments [5] in S/W coding reveal that syndrome method also can provide better error resilience, but addresses only puncturing of syndromes and not the channel noise problems. This paper addresses the syndrome technique with channel noise problems.

3   Higher Order Modulation for Total Power Reduction

The basic need of a DVC system is less power consumption at the encoder as it finds its major application in Wireless sensor networks (WSN) and low power compression devices. At various levels of system design, various ways of optimizing it, from encoder complexity to wireless transmission models.As it is known that some of the modulation schemes are energy efficient than the others [6], it indeed becomes important in a WSN to use the optimum modulation scheme so as to increase energy efficiency and at the same time maximize data rates and minimize the bit error probability. This would result in reduction in the usage of battery and improvement in the system performance. The choice of a good modulation scheme is critical for reliable communication in a WSN.Several papers have studied the effect of modulation technique on power and efficiency. In [7] an optimal strategy to decrease the transmission energy per bit is studied. In [8] it is showed that M-Ary will be energy efficient than binary for small transmission on time. Optimum transmits on time and constellation size for different modulation techniques has been analyzed for both Rayleigh and AWGN channel in [9]. All these papers view modulation schemes from circuit standpoint rather than the traditional perspective ofEb/N0. Based on these analyses, we find M-Ary modulation is a low power high data rate transmitter.

4   M-Ary Modulation and M-Ary LDPC Codes

Non binary LDPC GF (q) codes are defined by similar sparse binary LDPC matrices except the fact that the members of the matrices are 0 to q-1.The LDPC codes designed over GF (2) has shown to approach near Shannon performance limit, when decoded using Belief propagation algorithm at the cost of large block lengths. But for small block lengths the error performance can be improved by increasing q [10][11]. To avoid bit errors and to increase spectral efficiency in data transmission it is efficient to combine non binary LDPC codes with higher order modulation in wirelesscommunication. As said in section 3 it also decreases the total power required in case of wireless sensor transmission.These non binary LDPC codes can be conveniently combined with multilevel modulation, which are capable of supporting high data rate transmission. It is beneficial to consider non binary QAM or QPSK schemes with equivalent matching non binary LDPC as it avoids symbol to bit de mapping (BPSK) or one grouping of bits to another grouping of bits to form another symbol (M-Ary PSK/QAM). Using LDPC with field order equal to the size of the constellation has a clear advantage as the encoder and modulator directly works with same symbols.

5   Encoding with Syndrome Technique

5.1   Problem Formulation

The comparative analysis between parity based and syndrome based DVC over noiseless environment is well explained in [12]. The factors for comparison are i) the compression rate ii) space partitioning code design iii) general implementation strategies iv) ability to handle source correlation. While the author discusses more on compression rate, space partitioning and implementation strategies favoring syndrome approach over noiseless channel he recommends parity based approach over noisy channel on the ground that parity approach has better ability to handle source correlation. But we put forth some of the other things which the author has not considered to prove syndrome technique is better.

5.2   Further Discussions and Solutions

Ourdiscussions are based on encoder complexity, ability to handle bit error and decoder complexity. For (n, k) LDPC parity check matrix to achieve the same compression rate approaching the S/W limit, the parity approach should have the code dimensions $(2n - k, n)$ [13] [14]. Firstly this dimension increases the complexity of both encoder as well as decoder due to longer channel code length. Secondly the parity check matrix factor graph will have short cycles in the design due to longer code length for the same number of check nodes. This can be explained with an example, we consider (7,4) syndrome code and the equivalent parity code should be (10, 7) to achieve the same compression rate. For the syndrome approach the number of check node is 3 for total of 7 variable nodes, while for parity approach 3 check nodes for 10 variable nodes. The theory is that as the number of bits participating in the check node increases its error correcting capacity increases, when it is done in parity method, 10 nodes instead of 7 has to join only 3 check nodes which results in short cycles which further increases the error rate. The bit error correcting capacity is more for parity check approach with respect to the hamming distance [12]. But the author does not take in to account the longer coderequired to achieve the same compression rate. With longer code length both approaches has the same bit error correcting capacity. We explain with the simple example here. Syndrome approach takes (7,4) code for code rate of 3/7 and its error correcting capacity is one out of 7 bits. To achieve the same code rate and error correction parity approach needs (10,7).

The compression rate cannot go below $1/2$ for parity approach if the code has to approach S/W limit [13]. As we need a variable rate code for DVC application, this gives the greatest limitation in the video transmission over variable correlation parameter channel. Finally we consider a point called channel estimation error in favor of syndrome approach, which no author has considered so far. The channel estimation error plays a role in the bit error in an indirect way, in parity approach both the parity bits and side information are involved in the initial log likelihood ratio side (LLR) calculation. As the parity bits and side information bits both belongs to different channel two different channel parameter estimation need to be done. The transmission channel estimation error leads to parity bit error which subsequently results in information bit error in decoding. The syndrome approach suffers from only single channel estimation error. This can be explained with the Belief propagation decoding algorithm for parity and syndrome approach. The algorithm described in

[15] is explained here with respect to the difference. While the step 1 and step 2 is same for both the techniquesthe step three is given by

$$\tanh\left(\frac{t_{j.m}^{out}}{2}\right) = (1 - 2s_j)\prod_{i=1,i\neq m}^{r_j} \tanh\left(\frac{t_{i.m}^{in}}{2}\right)$$

m = 1,2, ... r_j & i = 1,2, ... $n - k$ .The factor $1 - 2s_j$ accounts for the syndrome factor.In Parity approach the variable node is formed by side information which is under virtual channel and parity information under the actual channel.But in syndrome approach the syndromes are not the part of variable node and hence not involved in LLR calculation; this reduces the channel estimation error and hence we conclude syndrome approach is optimal for both noiseless and noisy S/W problem from the above discussions

6   Simulation Setup and Results

6.1   Simulation Setup and Results

As our research is to focus on modulation techniques for DVC rather than DVC itself, we simulated the DVC setup by image files in order to reduce the complexity of coding work. For a DVC setup to be created with bmp image, we need one actual frame and side frame. We simulated the side frame by corrupting the image with different cross over probabilities. AWGN channel is considered for wireless transmission. A LDPC matrix of (20000, 10000) for GF (2)-BPSK, (9000, 6000) for GF (4) -QPSK /QAM and (6000, 4000) GF (8)-8PSK is considered for Slepian wolf coding.Simulation results in Figure 1shows the Q2 LDPC DVC coding of parity and syndrome approaches. We see that the syndrome approach is as good as parity approach at higher SNR and lower SNR. This means that we have still room for improvement with syndrome approach for same compression ratio when we take in to account the LLR estimation going wrong in real time scenario. Figure 2 results show that the gray labeling of bit sequence improves a little less than one db coding gain. Similar results apply for 8 PSK 8 Ary LDPC. Figure 3 gives the comparison results of Q(2) Q(4) and Q(8) LDPC coded modulation results. We see that though higher modulation increases the Bit error rate the higher order LDPC coding reduces the bit error rate in such a way that almost 10db coding gain we geton comparing between Q(2) and the higher order one. But between Q(4) and Q(8) we get very little coding gain like 3 db. With respect to our simulations we believe that combination of M-Ary LDPC with M-Ary modulation syndrome based DVC will work comparatively with parity approach in a noisy environment. Our next work is to prove that syndrome approach in a noisy environment outperform parity approach when LLR estimation goes wrong in parity approach and also to combine a different labeling technique other than gray labeling.

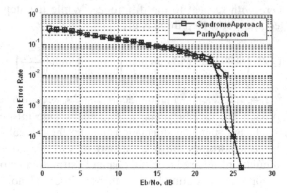

Fig. 1. Bit Error Probability Curve for Parity and Syndrome Approaches

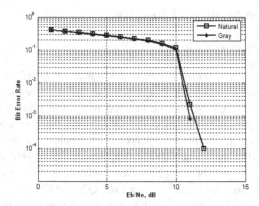

Fig. 2. Bit Error Probability Curve for 4Ary LDPC coded 4Ary Modulation

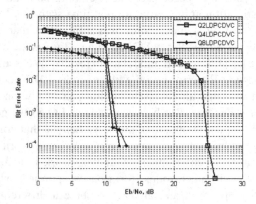

Fig. 3. Comparison of higher order LDPC coding with Binary LDPC

References

1. Slepian, D., Wolf, J.K.: Noiseless coding of correlated information sources. IEEE Transaction on Information Theory 17-19, 47 (1973)
2. Wyner, Ziv, J.: The Rate-distortion Function for source coding with side information at the decoder. IEEE Transaction on Information Theory 22(1), 1–10 (1976)
3. Cappellari, L., De Giustiar, A.: A Unified Perspective, A.: on Parity- and Syndrome-Based Binary Data Compression Using Off-the-Shelf Turbo Codecs. Xiv:0902.0562v3 [cs.IT] (August 2, 2010)
4. Pradhan, S.S., Ramachandran, K.: Distributed source coding using syndromes (DISCUS), Design and Construction. In: Proc. IEEE DCC, pp. 158–167 (March 1999)
5. Wyner, A.: Recent results in the Shannon theory. IEEE Trans. Inform. Theory IT-20, 2–10 (1974)
6. Sklar, B.: Digital Communications Fundamentals and Applications, 2nd edn. Prentice Hall (January 2001)
7. Verdhu, S.: Spectral efficiency in wideband regime. IEEE Trans. on Information Theory 48, 1319–1343 (2002)
8. Shih, E., Cho, S.H., Rexmin, Sinha, A., Chandrakasan, A.: Physical layer driven protocol and algorithm design for energy efficient Wireless sensor networks. In: MOBICOM 2001, Rome, Italy, July 15-21 (2001)
9. Mukesh, S., Iqbal, M., Jianhual, Z., Ping, Z., Inam-Ur-Rehman: Comparative Analysis of M-ary Modulation Techniques for Wireless Ad-hoc Networks. In: SAS 2007 IEEE Sensor Application Symposium, San Diego, California (2007)
10. Davey, M., Mackay, D.: Low density parity check codes over GF(q). In: Liveris, et al. (eds.) Information theory Workshop 1998, pp. 70–71 (1998)
11. Thambu, K.: Wyner-Ziv Video Coding with Error-Prone Wireless Fading Channels. Crown (2010) 978-1-4244-7265-9/10/ $26.00 c_
12. Tan, P., Xie, K., Li, J.: Slepian Wolf coding using parity approach and syndrome approach, 1-4244-1037-1/07/$25.00 C2007 IEEE
13. Xue, G., Zhang, W., Hao, C.: Syndrome based error resilience scheme of distributed joint source channel coding. In: Proceedings of ICCTA 2009 (2009)
14. Cappellari, L., De Giustiar, A.: A Unified perspective on parity and syndrome based binary data compression using off the shelf turbo codes. Xiv 0902-0562v3 [CS-IT] (August 2, 2010)
15. Declereq, D., Fossorier, M.: Decoding algorithm for non binary LDPC codes over GF(q). IEEE Trans. Communication 55, 633–643 (2007)
16. Ye, F., Men, A., Zhang, X.: An Improved Wyner-Ziv Video Coding for Sensor Network, 978-1-4244-8331- 0/11/$26.00 2011 IEEE
17. Distributed Image Codin. Wireless Multimedia Sensor Networks: A Survey. In: Third International Workshop on Advanced Computational Intelligence, Suzhou, Jiangsu, China, August 25-27 (2010)

Subband and MSF Performance Comparison for AEC

O.P. Sahu[1], Sanjeev Kumar Dhull[2], and Sandeep K. Arya[2]

[1] Department of ECE, National Institute of Technology, Kurukshetra
opsahu_2011@yahoo.com
[2] Department of ECE Guru Jambheshwar University of Science and Technology
Hisarsanjeev_dhull_ap@yahoo.co.in, arya1sandeep@rediffmail.com

Abstract. We have designed and simulated two techniques for acoustic echo cancellation. These systems are based upon a least-mean-square (LMS) adaptive algorithm and uses multi sub and sub band technique. A comparative study of both methods has been carried out.

Keywords: LMS, Multiple subfilter, Sub band, AEC, ERLE.

1 Introduction

Acoustic echo cancellation (AEC) [1] is used in teleconferencing and its purpose is to provide high quality full-duplex communication. The main part of an AEC is an adaptive filter which estimates the impulse response of the loudspeaker-enclosure-microphone (LEM)[2] system. There are various adaptive algorithms for the AEC filter update, these are the least mean square, normalized least mean square (LMS, NLMS), affine projection (AP) [3][4]and recursive least squares (RLS) algorithms. As the echo cancellation environment is not stationary therefore echo reduction in rooms with long reverberation time is necessary. Hence, the signal processing methods are in demand in industry. The technique used in earlier stages was echo suppression .Due to some disadvantages of echo suppression echo cancellation came into picture and the process of Acoustic echo cancellation [15] is achieved with the help of adaptive filter which models the LEM system. The purpose of an acoustic echo-canceller is to reduce the amount of sound which a far-end teleconference transmits from returning to them. This paper is organized in four sections. Section two describes the simulation model of AEC in matlab using sub band and msf approach. Further, section three discusses the results. In the end section four concludes the paper.

2 Subband and Multiple Sub Filters

In order to obtain a full-duplex hands-free communication, in for instance a car, it is necessary to perform an acoustic echo cancellation of the far-end speaker. The echo cancellation must be adaptive and follow variations in the acoustic channel. The filter length of the acoustic canceller can be typically between 500-1500 FIR taps. Filter

V.V. Das, E. Ariwa, and S.B. Rahayu (Eds.): SPIT 2011, LNICST 62, pp. 236–242, 2012.
© Institute for Computer Sciences, Social Informatics and Telecommunications Engineering 2012

lengths of these sizes gives a large computational burden even with a simple adaptive Filter algorithm such as LMS[6]. These filters also suffer from long convergence time, especially if the reference signal spectrum has a large dynamic range i.e. a large eigen value spread in the corresponding signal covariance matrix. Sub-band techniques give a twofold advantage: the computational burden is essentially reduced by the number of sub-bands[7] and it is also possible to get a faster convergence because the spectral dynamic range in each sub-band will be smaller. In this paper we present an implementation of AEC using sub-band adaptive Filter and multiple sub filter methods.

2.1   Analysis of Sub-Band and MSF Adaptive Filters

The delay less attribute of this technique comes from the fact that the new adaptive weights are computed in sub-bands and then transformed to an equivalent full-band filter with means of an FFT. The filter works in real time on the loudspeaker signal. The coefficients are calculated separately in each band. They can be calculated either by employing the error signal $\mathcal{C}(k)$ or the microphone input signal $d(k)$. If the signal $d(k)$ is used a local error signal in each band must be created and the calculations must not be performed in real time. This will however give somewhat lower suppression because the algorithm is blind towards the real error signal. The full band signal is divided into several sub-bands signals by using a polyphase FFT technique. The outputs from the sub-band filters are only down sampled by a factor D=M/2. This means that even sub-bands are centered at dc while odd sub-bands are centered at one half of the decimated sampling frequency, see in Fig.2. This fact must be considered in the poly phase filter bank. Since, we only consider full-band filters with real coefficients; it is enough to calculate M/2 complex sub-band signals. The rest can be found by utilizing the complex conjugate symmetry. If we have a N tap full-band filter, the filter length in each sub-band will be N/D. A N/D points FFT will be calculated on the adaptive weights in each sub-band [11][15]. These are then stacked to form a 0-(N/2-1) point array. The array is then completed by setting point N to zero and using the complex conjugate of points 1-(N/2-1) in reverse order. Finally, the N point array is transformed by N point inverse FFT to obtain the full-band filter weights.

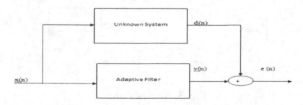

Fig. 1. Full Band version of Adaptive Filter

Fig.1 depicts the full-band version of an identification system, where $x(n)$ represents the input data, which is common to both unknown system and adaptive filter. The desired signal $d(n)$ contributes to the error minimization by subtracting from it the output of the adaptive filter y (n). Adaptive identification is a procedure that learns more about the model as long as a new pair of measurements is received, updating the knowledge in order to incorporate the newly received information. The error signal e (n) ideally should be equal to the near-end signal $x(n)$. Classical full-band cancellers are unattractive for real time processing and their computational requirements exceed the capabilities of present day DSPs. Fig.2 depicts the sub-band adaptive filtering (SAF) for M sub-bands. Using analysis filter banks, the original signal isdecomposed into M signals $(x0(n), x1(n)...xM-1(n))$ bysubdividing its spectra. Adaptive filtering[19] is then performedin these sub-bands by a set of independent filters $(h0(n)$, $h1(n),..., hM-1(n))$. The outputs of these filters are subsequentlycombined using a synthesis filter bank to reconstruct the full bandoutput.

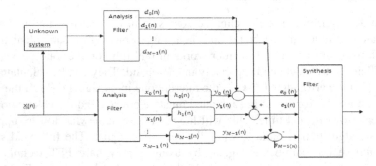

Fig. 2. Sub-band system

To ease the processing, down-sampling (L↓) and up-sampling (L↑) can be inserted between the analysis and synthesis filter banks[11]. The analysis(Fig.3) filter bank design problem reduces to the design of a single prototype non-recursive filter $P(z)$, the analysis filters being modulated versions of the prototype. Ideal analysis filters are band-pass filters with normalized centre frequencies $\omega m = 2$ $m/M, m = 0... M -1$, and with bandwidth 2 / M.

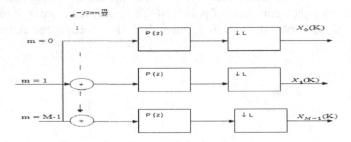

Fig. 3. Analysis filter

The ideal filters have unit magnitude and zero-phase in the pass-band while the stop-band magnitude is zero. While zero phase filters involve non causality, the requirements need to be relaxed by using linear phase filters. The choice is to use FIR filters that have linear phase, but not ideal magnitude requirements. This approximation leads to aliasing effects. The design of synthesis Fig.4 filter banks reduces also to the design of a single synthesis prototype filter $Q(z)$. When designing the synthesis filter bank, the focus is on the performance of the analysis-synthesis filter bank as a whole.

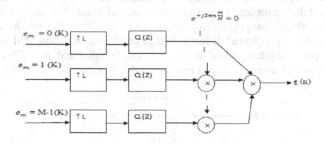

Fig. 4. Synthesis filter

Achieving zero residual error (no alias effect) requires the sub-band filters and sub-band models to have an infinite tap size. Since we always use FIR sub-band filters and sub-band models, residual errors are unavoidable. This implies that in the design of a sub-band identification system, there is a tradeoff between asymptotic residual error and computational cost.

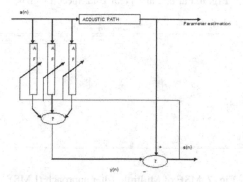

Fig. 5. Multiple sub filter echo cancellation

As shown in Figure.5 we can do echo cancellation by multiple sub filter structures also.The aim of the paper is to compare these two techniques. The system capability can be represented by the output error, but for accurate meaure Echo Return Loss Enhancement (ERLE) is the basic formula to compute the performance; it is defined as the ratio of the power of the desired signal over the power of the residual signal:

$$\text{ERLE} = -10 \log_{10} \frac{E(d^2(n))}{E(e^2(n))}$$

3   Simulation Results

The next work is to do simulations of multiple filter and sub band model. For simulations comparisons we are taking far end and near end speech signals. ERLE is the main comparison parameters for this approach. Simulations are carried by estimating correct values of time delay, gain and step size and order of filter. We have calculated true estimate of time delay using GAE algorithm and comparing the results as shown in different figures. We have plotted different ERLE graphs for full band.MSF and Sub band strucuture.The filter length required in case of single full band is 1075. Filter length required in MSF is 194 where as it has been reduced to 8 in case of sub band structure.

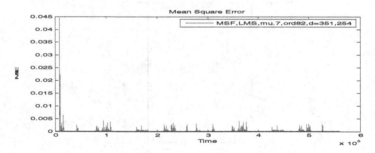

Fig. 6. Far end and Near End Speech signal

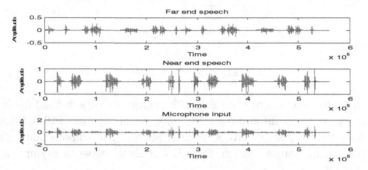

Fig. 7. MSE of Multiple filter approach (LMS)

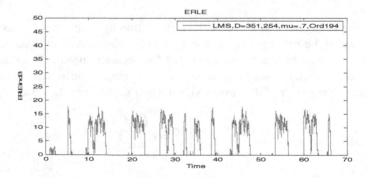

Fig. 8. ERLE for MSF using LMS

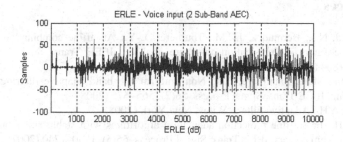

Fig. 9. ERLE for two subband

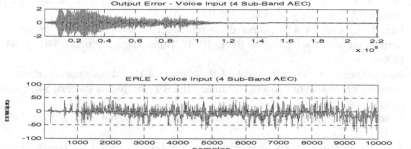

Fig. 10. ERLE for 4 Subband

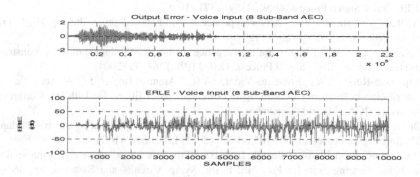

Fig. 11. ERLE for 8 subband

4   Conclusion

No doubt multiple sub filter converge faster than full band but Suband design of echo canceller converge faster than multiple sub filter design and filter length required in subband is also less as compared to multiple subfilter design.

References

1. Bershad, N.J., Bermudez, J.C.M., Tourneret, J.-Y.: An affine combination of two LMS adaptive filters —Transient mean-square analysis. IEEE Trans. Signal Process. 56(5), 1853–1864 (2008)
2. Petraglia, M.R., Batalheiro, P.B.: Non uniform sub band adaptive filtering with critical sampling. IEEE Trans. Signal Process. 56(2), 565–575 (2008)
3. Sayed, A.H.: Adaptive Filters. Wiley, New York (2008)
4. Ding, H.: Fast affine projection adaptation algorithms with stable and robust symmetric linear system solvers. IEEE Trans. Signal Process. 55(5), 1730–1740 (2007)
5. Ni, J., Li, F.: A variable regularization matrix normalized sub band adaptive filter. IEEE Signal Process. 16(2), 105–108 (2009)
6. Lee, K.A., Gan, W.S., Kuo, S.M.: Sub band Adaptive Filtering: Theory and Implementation. Wiley, Hoboken (2009)
7. Lee, K.A., Gan, W.S.: Inherent décor-relating and leastperturbation properties of the normalized sub band adaptive filter. IEEE Trans. Signal Process. 54(11), 4475–4480 (2006)
8. Arenas-Garcia, J., Figueira-Vidal, A.R., Sayed, A.H.: Mean-square performance of a convex combination of two adaptive filters. IEEE Trans. Signal Process. 54(3), 1078–1090 (2006)
9. Sondhi, M.M.: The history of echo cancellation. IEEE Signal Process. Mag. 23(5), 95–98 (2008)
10. Kao, C.C.: Design of echo cancellation and noise elimination for speech enhancement. IEEE Trans. Consumer Electronics 49(4), 1468–1473 (2003)
11. Courville, M.D., Duhamel, P.: Adaptive filtering in sub bands using a weighted criterion. IEEE Trans. Signal Process. 46(9), 2359–2371 (1998)
12. Pradhan, S.S., Reddy, V.U.: A new approach to sub band adaptive filtering. IEEE Trans. Signal Process. 47(3), 655–664 (1999)
13. Lee, K.A., Gan, W.S.: Improving convergence of the NLMS algorithm using constrained sub band updates. IEEE Signal Process. Lett. 11(9), 736–739 (2004)
14. Azpicueta-Ruiz, L.A., Figueiras-Vidal, A.R., Arenas-García, J.: A.:Acoustic echo cancellation in frequency domain using combinations of filters. In: 19th Int. Congress on Acoustics (ICA), Madrid (September 2007)
15. Ohno, S., Sakai, H.: Convergence Behavior of the LMS algorithm in sub band adaptive filtering. Signal Processing 81, 1053–1059 (2001) ISBN 0165-1684
16. Brennan, R., Schneiderm: A flexible filter bank Structure for extensive signal manipulation in digital Hearing aids. In: Proc. IEEE Int. Symp. Circuits and Systems, pp. 569–572 (1998)
17. Chao, J., Kawabe, S., Tsujii, S.: A new IIR adaptive echo canceller. IEEE Journal on Selc. Areas in Corn. 12, 1530–1539 (1994)
18. Widrow, B., Stearns, S.: Adaptive Signal Processing. Prentice-Hall, Englewood Cliffs (1985)
19. Kellermann, W.: Analysis and design of multirate systems for cancellation of acoustical echoes. In: Proc. Int. Conf. Acoust., Speech, Signal Proc., New York, pp. 2570–2573 (1988)
20. Gilloire, A., Vetterli, M.: Adaptive filtering in sub-bands. In: Proc. Int. Conf. Acoustic. Speech, Signal Proc., New York, NY (April 1988)
21. Irina, D.: Marina.:Subabd Adaptive Filtering, pp. 810–813. IEEE (2009)

Information Technology Phenomenon in Thailand

Wilawan Phornphatcharaphong

Faculty of Informatics, Mahasarakham University, Thailand
wilawan.c@msu.ac.th

Abstract. Since Information Technology spreads in various groups of people and tasks in Thailand, the researcher tries to review this important situation. The objective was Explore the application of Information Technology in Thailand in five dimensions: Policy, Theory, Applications types, Contents, and users. The content analysis approach was used to discussion of IT phenomenon. The sampling was 83 research documents that were recent published in August 2011. The result found that The National Education Act (81.93%) was mostly influenced factor of IT Policy /Plan in Thailand, the theory of Learning (87.95%) was the mostly influenced factor of IT Concept or Theory, IT application mostly was Courseware (49.40 %), IT contents were language mostly (53.66%), and mostly IT users were students (89.16%). Finally, the idea of IT phenomenon in Thailand will be as the case study for the other countries to review their IT applications further.

Keywords: Information Technology Applications, IT usage, IT situation.

1   Introduction

Thailand, the only Southeast Asian nation never to have been colonized by European powers, is a constitutional monarchy whose current head of state is HM Bhumibol Adulyadej. Thailand is the 50th largest country in the world; most nearly equal in size to Spain or roughly equivalent in size to France or Texas. The vast majority (roughly 80%) of Thailand's nearly 65 million citizens are ethnically Thai. The remainder consists primarily of peoples of Chinese, Indian, Malay, Mon, Khmer, Burmese, and Lao decent. Of the 7 million citizens who live in the capital city, Bangkok. More than 92% of the population speaks Thai language, the official language. As a result of its cosmopolitan capital city and established tourism infrastructure, English is spoken and understood throughout much of Thailand. [20]. Information Technology (IT) in Thailand found in 1987 when the Asian Institute of Technology (AIT) in Thailand entered into an agreement with the Department of Computer Science at the University of Melbourne in Australia to operate Internet email service on a regular basis, as send and collect mail. Until 2007, 8.4 million internet users out of Thailand's overall population, and by early 2008, mobile penetration was around 82 percent of population.   Although Thailand is still in the early stages of its technological developments, the government of Thailand's information and communication technology plans for the years 2000 to 2010 is *"to promote the increase in internet usage for both its citizens and business sectors."* The information infrastructure is

V.V. Das, E. Ariwa, and S.B. Rahayu (Eds.): SPIT 2011, LNICST 62, pp. 243–248, 2012.

becoming more universal and less expensive. Security, privacy protection, and trust are being enhanced so that consumers will have more trust and confidence, and will try different products and services in the future. These developments are creating great opportunities E-Commerce solution providers, and E-Commerce-related service. [19]. For the year 2011-2020, Thai government plans for the years as "*Smart Thailand 2020*" that technology will allow Thailand to meet 3 goals : Stronger Economy, Social Equality, Environmental Friendly. Then, the development process based on three levels. For the basic level : including ICT Human Resources and ICT Competent Work force, ICT Infrastructure, and ICT Industry. For the middle level : including Smart Government. The advanced level : including Stronger Economy (Smart Agriculture and Smart Services), Social Equality (Smart Health, Smart Learning), and Environmental Friendly (Smart Environment as ICT for Green & Green ICT). [9]. Since Information Technology spreads in various groups of people and tasks in Thailand, the researcher tries to review this important situation. Then, the idea of IT phenomenon in Thailand will be the case study for the other country to compare or take the advantage points for supporting of Information Processing and computer in their country.

2   Objective

Explore the application of Information Technology in Thailand in 5 dimensions, Policy /Plan, Concept/Theory, Applications types, Contents , and users.

3   Methodology

There are two phases of research and spent for one year to complete the project.

Phase 1: Content Analysis approach. This phase were took about nine months to explore the application of IT in Thailand by using the content analysis approach. The sampling was 83 research documents that were published recently in August 2011. The tool was the explore forms that divided in five categories: 1) IT Policy /Plan, 2) IT Concept/Theory 3) Type of IT applications 4) IT Contents 5) IT users

Phase 2 : Analysis data and discuss of information system application for three months. Percentage was used for calculated.

4   Result

4.1   IT Policy /Plan

From the eighty three research documents, The National Education Act (81.93%) was mostly influenced by factor of IT Policy /Plan in Thailand. For the other influenced factors were Government Policy (12.05%), and Educational Technology Plan (6.02%). From the National Educational Act, noticed that "The National Education Act of Thailand will prepare people for new social requirements. It will encourage Thais to develop towards more analytical and independent thought. The knowledge-based and learning society will help fine new solutions for the global era". [22]. In year 2011, Miss Yingluck Shinawatra, a prime minister, presented the government policy for a short period as one year and long term period as four years. For a short term-immediately plan, the government focuses on "Tablet PC for students aged 6-7 years old". [11] Now, the tablet in Thailand was the hot issue for discussion among government, entrepreneur, teachers, and parents in positive and negative way. Most teachers and parents were serious that tablet will be influenced on children' health and behavior -playing game, chat. On the other side, government agreed with the successful educational dimensions of new technology–motivate learning, mobile library, critical thinking, then the experimental tablet project began in readiness primary schools in Thailand and government supports mostly for educational content production. Besides, there are many systems that support government policy to reach as e-government role -one stop service, such as Citizens ID Card system, E-Revenue system, E-Procurement system, and e-Auction system. [12]

4.2   IT Concept/Theory

From the eighty three research documents, the theory of Learning (87.95%) was the mostly influenced factor of IT Concept or Theory in Thailand. Next, theory or concept of IT was skills concept (8.43%), Human resource development concept (2.42%), and Ethics concept (1.20 %). For Learning Theories involve with Blended Learning, Cased-Based Learning, Constructivist Learning, Project-Based Learning, Collaborative Learning, and Game-Based Learning. For Skills Concept related with reading skill, writing skill, searching skill, and critical thinking skill. The example of information system to support learning concept was E-learning system. E-learning focuses on building learning and teaching among online environment. The system included input, process and output factors. Input factors were student, teacher, objective, resource, educational media, knowledge based, communication & activity, and evaluation. Process factors were the learning and teaching situation that build up input factors. Output factor was learning achievement from evaluation. [14] Today, the example systems that support learning concept, skills concept, and ethics concept was as Virtual Learning Community for Thai Muslim Youth –the social networking LMS based on collaborative of Muslim youth and Muslim head of community. Every member will brain storm in social network for creating one project for developing Muslim community. [7]

4.3   Type of IT Applications

From the eighty three research documents, mostly type of IT application was Courseware (49.40%). Next, IT application were Information System (24.10%), Game (16.86%), and Social Network (9.64%). IT tools were applied in different styles such as Professional Home Pages language (PHP), MySQL program, Adobe Flash CS Software, Adobe Dreamweaver CS Software, Adobe Photoshop software, Adobe Illustrator software, Sony Sound forge software. Information System tools were as LMS, CMS, and Moodle. Most system based on more OS : Windows server, Linux Server, Cent OS Server, Free BSD Server, Ubuntu Server, Mac OSX 10.4. Communication tools were as FACEBOOK, for chat, e-mail, forum, blog, wiki. Storytelling practice websites were applied, for example, Voice Thread, Scrapbook, Lino. Presentation programs were Microsoft PowerPoint, Adobe Presenter 7, and Adobe Captivate 5. The mostly main system was E-learning system, applied new tools for communication & activity –social media, game. The examples were E-learning : Implement of Game-Based Learning in Higher Education– Multimedia Online Role-Playing Game or MMORPG [4], Video Conferencing System for online teaching and learning by Red5 – Flash streaming server, the open source [13], Reflecting Writing of Goodness via Weblog –self concept goodness and other goodness [1], Web-based information system for evaluation of Boyscout activities - using concept of System Development of Life Cycle (SDLC) and developing with PHP language and MySQL database [16], The development of Management Information System for Publishing Company -both operational and management level and developed with MySQL database for connection, HTML, PHP, AJAX, JAVA application development for linking via internet [6], and Development of Automatic Online Item Analysis system – for analyzed discrimination, difficulty, and reliability of testing questionnaires by using PHP, MySQL, JavaScript, Apache Web Server. [23]

4.4   IT Contents

For the IT contents were described as the concept of Dewey idea, that contents were divided in 10 subjects (000-900) - 000 computer, 100 Philosophy, 200 Religious, 300 Social Science, 400 Language, 500 Pure Science, 600 Apply Science, 700 Art & Entertainment, 800 Literature, 900 History- Mostly IT content, from the forty one research documents of Courseware, was language (53.66%). Next were computer (24.39%), Pure Science (14.63%), Apply Science (12.20%), Religious & Social Science (9.76%). The contents of language areas were Japanese, Thai, and English. Besides, the social science contents were education and community, computer contents were network, data processing. Science contents were physics, environment. Applied science content was business document. Last, religious was the content about ethics, Buddhism, and goodness. The example systems that contained specific contents were E-learning system of Effecting Game-based Learning in Teaching English Reading Skill -Eternal story with English Vocabulary[15], Online Morality and Ethics Encouragement Learning System–e-learning system applied Buddhism fables [24]. The other systems that contained in different contents were The development of e-learning on Electronic Data Processing– computer subject [25], Creating of e-learning on Computer Mathematics[8], e-learning for Business Document Subject -business student [18], Create the RT e-learning Courseware [21], and Development of Advertisement Creation instruction [5].

4.5   IT Users

Mostly researches were focus on the Students and Teachers. Students were chosen as a main sampling (89.16%) and the other groups were Teacher (6.03%), Employee (2.41%), Blind (1.20%), and Deaf (1.20%). The example of information system for disability such as The e-learning system for development of Sign Language Animation of students with Hearing Deficiency – cartoon animation classifies in five sections: things, animal and nature, religious and place, vehicle, other [2]. The system for teacher was Teacher Electronic Porfolio Management System : CUFolio – based on self assessment concept and individual development planning by using ASP.NET and PostgreSQL Database[3]. Today, there was one interesting project, named

Openmind Projects , that introduced the overseas volunteer to develop IT in Thailand : helping with e-learning projects, IT and website projects, and teaching [10]. The project will be responsibility for three tasks: 1) Help a poor teenagers to use a computer and help them to get a better job in the future. 2) Help poor farmers to use computers and Internet and help them to sell their products without middlemen who make the money. 3) Help poor villagers to use computers and Internet and help them to develop community based eco tourism and sell it without tour operators who keep the profits. The project could help the youth to be good at technology and help all the other part of users, poor farmer and villagers, in Thailand.

5   Conclusion

The government of Thailand promoted the increase in internet usage for both its citizens and business sectors. These developments will create great opportunities of E-Commerce solution providers, and E-Commerce-related service. The result of the research found that mostly factors related the IT phenomenon as The National Education Act, the theory of Learning, type of IT application was Courseware, IT content was language, IT user mostly was students. Then, Thailand applied more techniques of IT tools: Professional Home Pages language (PHP), MySQL, Adobe Flash CS, Adobe Dreamweaver CS, Adobe Photoshop, Adobe Illustrator, Sony Sound forge, Moodle. Windows server, Linux Server, Cent OS Server, Free BSD Server, Ubuntu Server, Mac OSX 10.4., Microsoft PowerPoint, Adobe Presenter 7, and Adobe Captivate 5, website of Voice Thread, Scrapbook, Lino, and Facebook. Moreover, most users were generally as student, employee, blind and deaf. However, Thailand still be received the contact project from IT volunteer oversea.

Acknowledgement. Mahasarakham University Development Fund, and Faculty of Informatics.

References

1. Dangjamroon, A., Onjaree, N.: Effects of Using a Virtuous Project-Based Model Using Cooperative-Learning Method on the Web and Reflective Writing of Goodness Via Weblog, to Development Respect Characteristics of Seventh Grade Students. In: National e-Learning Conference, pp. 221–229. TCU, Thailand (2011)
2. Komkeing, T., Phanitha, W., Pratchayanan, N.: The Development of Sign Language Animation in Web-Based Instruction Toward Learning Achievement of Sixth Grade Students with Hearing Deficiency. In: National e-Learning Conference, pp. 262–269. TCU, Thailand (2011)
3. Korraneekit, P., Phitak, S.: Teacher Electronic Portfolio Management System: CUFolio. In: National e-Learning Conference, pp. 230–236. TCU, Thailand (2011)
4. Lonhajarassang, T., Natthanan, K.: Successful Implementation of Learner-Centered Game-Based Learning in Higher Education. In: National e-Learning Conference, pp. 131–132. TCU, Thailand (2011)

5. Meecharoen, S., Pornphon, C.: The Development of Online Lesson through Synectics Instruction on Advertisement Creation. In: National e-Learning Conference, pp. 489–496. TCU, Thailand (2011)
6. Noibanjong, S., Suwanna, S., Pharote, T.: The Development of Management Information System for Publishing Company. In: National e-Learning Conference, pp. 532–537. TCU, Thailand (2011)
7. Nootchamee, K.J., Surachai, P.: Virtual Learning Community for Thai Muslim Youth. In: National e-Learning Conference, pp. 190–197. TCU, Thailand (2011)
8. Nuanphaka, N., Suwanna, S.: Creating of e-learning on Computer Mathematics, Higher Diploma Level Department of Business Computer, Ratchaburi Technical College. In: National e-Learning Conference, pp. 465–472. TCU, Thailand (2011)
9. National Electronics and Computer Technology, http://www.ict2020.in.th
10. Openmind Projects, http://www.openmindprojects.org
11. Paliament-government statement, http://www.techmoblog.com
12. Prince of Songkla University-Thai e-government, http://vclass.mgt.psu.ac.th
13. Prugthawee, B.: Innovation of Video Conferencing Systems for Teaching and Learning by Red5. In: National e-Learning Conference, pp. 60–65. TCU, Thailand (2011)
14. Roungrong, P.: http://www.thaiwbi.com
15. Soothathoton, P., Phatcharakan, I.: Effects of Integrating Game-based Learning in Teaching English Reading Skill of the First Year Chiang Mai University Student. In: National e-Learning Conference, pp. 133–140. TCU, Thailand (2011)
16. Sriwapee, K., Nithida, B., Suwanna, S.: Development of Web-Based Information System for Evaluation of Boyscout for Students at Mahasarakham Technical College. In: National e-Learning Conference, pp. 612–619. TCU, Thailand (2011)
17. Tangphiw, S., Nithita, B., Suwanna, S.: The development e-learning lesson on Business Document Subject. In: National e-Learning Conference, pp. 532–537. TCU, Thailand (2011)
18. Thailand Chapter of the Internet Society, http://www.isoc-th.org
19. Tourism Authority of Thailand, http://www.tourismthailand.org
20. Treewithayarat, P., Wanna, T.: The Comparison of Using the Appropriate Software to Create the RT e- learning Courseware. In: National e-Learning Conference, pp. 598–604. TCU, Thailand (2011)
21. The Education Council, http://www.edthai.com
22. Wanothayaphitak, S.: A Development of Automatic On-line Item Analysis System. In: National e-Learning Conference, pp. 553–561. TCU, Thailand (2011)
23. Wongwatkit, C., Suriyong, L.: A Development of Online Morality and Ethics Encouragement Learning System. In: National e-Learning Conference, pp. 412–420. TCU, Thailand (2011)
24. Worranam, I., Nithida, B., Suwanna, S.: The Development of e-Learning on Electronic Data Processing Subject for Students of Vocational Certificate level. In: National e-Learning Conference, pp. 510–516. TCU, Thailand (2011)

Black Hole Combat Using Node Stability System in MANET

Ranajoy Chatterjee[1] and Mukti Routray[2]

[1] Faculty of Computer Science and Engineering, Indic Institute of Design and Research,
Bhubaneswar, Orissa, India
[2] Faculty of Computer Science and Engineering, Silicon Institute of Technology,
Bhubaneswar, Orissa, India
{ronychatterjee,muktiroutray}@gmail.com

Abstract. MANET (Mobile Ad hoc Network) is a form of ad hoc network consisting of mobile nodes. The behavior of such network is autonomous and it gets connected to several types of network by using wireless connection. As no nodes in this network infrastructure are stationary, nodes link each other to participate in transmission. However nodes in the family may turn bad (malicious) or external attacking nodes disrupt secured routing bringing instability to network and sometimes increasing threat to applications of importance for e.g. both military and civilian applications. In both the above cases the nodes needs to be punished. In this paper we use a Node Stability System (NSS) to propose methods of identification of singular and co-operative Black hole nodes and provide steps to recover the network from such vulnerabilities.

Keywords: DTMS, Black Hole Attack, Node Stability System.

1   Introduction

One of the major characteristics of a Mobile Ad hoc network is the absence of a fixed infrastructure (no access points or base stations) or centralized administration. A group of wireless nodes(mobile computers) which may directly co-operate with each other by transmitting packets and from a network or sometimes collecting data or information from various sensors and then connecting to the network to distribute the data among several nodes for distributed processing forms an ad hoc network. The network should be much more adaptive since unlike wired transmission the nodes are often significantly mobile thereby inducing a significant topological change. [7]The attacker[10] sometimes prevents the useful packets from reaching the destination by use of Rushing Attacks[2][1][8][9] ARIADNE ensures limiting the attacking power by preventing the attacker form injecting packets resulting in routing loops. [5]. A DTMS [6] based DSR (Dynamic Source Routing) is empowered to detect and eliminate any kind of malicious packet dropping. [6][7]Therefore our major aim by developing this system infrastructure is to combat such intrusions[4] and devise strategies using the proposed system.

V.V. Das, E. Ariwa, and S.B. Rahayu (Eds.): SPIT 2011, LNICST 62, pp. 249–254, 2012.

2   Node Stability System

As mentioned earlier, we propose a NSS as an efficient and robust defense mechanism for MANETs where we go for reliability based calculation and reserve it for further interpretation.We allot FID to each and every participating node in the network before forming the network. We assume that this id is intended only for the members of the network and this FID is hidden from any outsider, passerby or intended hackers.

We represent the initial Node Security Value to be

$$NSV=N/X^2$$

Where, 'X' is the total number of nodes having FID, and 'N' is the total number of good nodes in the network after time Tk. Therefore at the time of initialization the nodes are set with an initial Node Security Value of 0.5. This NSV is broadcasted to several other nodes at periodic intervals for regular update to the Node Security Table. When any node xi is added then there is to be an authentication check whether the node can be a member of the family. If found good a family id is generated for this new node and the NSV for all the nodes are set once again in the next time interval after new node xi joined the network.At its stability of NSV=0.5, each node builds up its own Node Security Table where the participating node is assigned a Node Security Level which is given negligible weightage of c as a knowledge parameter, where the total NSL for a node xi is calculated by node xj which can be given as

Current $NSL=c\ NSL_{prev} + (1-c)\ NSL_{Tk}$
Where $NSL_{Tk}=NSV * NSL_e$
Where $NSL_e= 1-[1/(\{(S/(S+U))*Wis\}+2)]$, When $S \geq U$
And $NSL_e= [1/(\{((U-S)/(S+U))*Wiu\}+2)]$, When $S<U$

Here, S represents the number of successful interactions, U represents the number of unsuccessful interactions, Wis and Wiu represents the weight of net successful and unsuccessful interactions respectively, chosen arbitrarily depending on the number of interactions taking place.This Node security level determines the stability of each node. In case the level of any node drops to zero it is termed to be as a 'Black hole' and further marked as a bad node.The source node transmits a Route Request packet to all the family members. Then it randomizes a timer to collect the Route Replies. In each Route Reply the Node Security level of the responding node to it and also the node of its next hop's level is checked. On getting routes having the same NSL, the routes having least hop counts is taken if not then the route with the node having highest NSL is selected.Good nodes are awarded and bad ones are punished. When the destination sends acknowledgement on receiving data packets it goes on incrementing the NSL en route all the nodes to the source. In absence of acknowledgement the intermediate node's NSL will be decremented.

A proper check has to be maintained to see the Node Stability Point of NSV=0.5. When NSL falls to 0 then the node is termed as a bad node and NSV of each and every node becomes less than the Node Stability Point. It is now an alarming situation. Each and every node should now no longer select the above detected node for routing, and hence the node is identified as bad node and eliminated from the network. Trial for recovery of such node can be ttaken up periodically. On the contrary NSV is also considered to be instable in the range of $0.5 \leq NSV < 1$, as the value rises with the event of addition of unauthenticated nodes (nodes without family id). In the above range there must be a periodic attempt by the nodes not in the family to get itself identified and all other nodes too should advocate the same cause so that NSV once again must tend to gain the Node Stability Point. When NSV reaches 1 it means the network has grown to the size where non family members are of the same size of the present family members. This is now a critical situation where the nodes must stop sending any packets and generates a massive alarm before shutting themselves down.

3   The Defense Mechanism

3.1   Related Works

Cases for elimination of collaborating black hole have also been dealt [11] with PCBHA [3] with modifications to AODV protocol. Also modification to DSR has enabled a Trust Based Scheme wherein a Trust factor is induced with a greater stress on the recommendation factor.In the method of route selection, a second chance is given to the nodes that were misbehaving previously to operate so that they have to work good to be trusted.[12]

3.2   Working of NSS

3.2.1   Response Collection
The incoming responses are collected in the Response table . The fields would be source address, destination address, next hop, hop count, TTL, destination sequence number, source and destination header addresses. The collection will be done till timer expires.

3.2.2   Choosing a Route
A valid route is selected from the method as under.A Node Security table is maintained which holds the NSL of the participating nodes. NSL for the responded node and also the next hop would be recorded. If the mean M of their levels is found to be above the specified threshold then the node is considered to be reliable. On receipt of the RREPs the one with the highest NSL is taken into consideration and the route is selected. If Nodes are found of same NSLs the one with minimum hop count is selected.

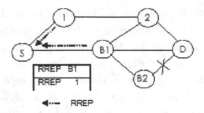

Fig. 1. Response Collection

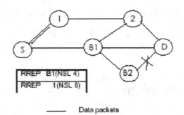

Fig. 2. Response Selection on the basis of NSL for a route to forward data

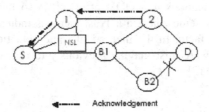

Fig. 3. Receipt of Acknowledgement and updating of NSL

As shown in the above figures the source S chooses RREP-1 after checking the NSL values

3.2.3   NSL Updating
On receipt of data packets every destination nodes sends an acknowledgement. On receipt of acknowledgement the Source node S increments the NSL of the Next node and awards it to be a good node. On the contrary if within the expiry of the timer the intermediate node fails to give any acknowledgement (In the above Figure B1 and B2 acts as the co-operative Black holes) then it decrements the NSL Value of that node and also the next hop of the intermediate node to identify the collaborating attack. And the rest nodes are informed in the network. Periodically the NSL value is shared among the participating nodes.

3.2.4   Eliminating Black Hole

When NSL drops to 0, it proves that it has dropped all the packets forwarded to it and we call this node as the bad node. This simultaneously decrements the NSV to form instability in the network. Alarm packets are sent across all the nodes in the network and the node is eliminated.

Algorithm for the above system is as follows.

```
RREP: Route Reply
NEXT : Next Node
NSL refers to the current NSL computed above.


On receipt of RREP
Mean NSL = NSLNext + NSLNext Hop
Route with highest Mean NSL is selected
NSLNext> THRESHOLD and NSLNext hop >
THRESHOLD
      {
           send data packets
      }
else
     {
          repeat till a max TTL.
          Still if not done then declare the route invalid.
     }
On Timer EXPIRY
                  if Data ACK is received
            {
                  Next NSL is incremented
                  NSL packets broadcasted for other nodes information
            }
                      if Data ACK is not received
            {
                  Next NSL and Next Hop NSL is decremented
                  NSL packets broadcasted for other nodes information
            }
  if (NSL = 0)
       {
           Node is eliminated from the NS Table
           NSV of Sender is checked for Node Stability.
       }
```

4   Conclusion and Future Work

In this paper we have presented an effective method to combat with misbehaving nodes in MANET. And also we have given stress on maintaining stability in such a network. Not a massive change in the existing protocol structure is appreciable. But for stability of these networks NSS might prove to be a road to further solutions in this area.Our future work aims at probing more into the structure of MANETs with elimination of further adversities regularly.

References

1. Nguyen, H.L., Nguyen, U.T.: A study of different types of attacks on multicast in mobile ad hoc networks. In: Proceedings of the ICNICONSMCL 2006 (2006)
2. Mölsä, J.V.E.: Increasing the dos attack resiliency in military ad hoc networks. In: Proc. IEEE MILCOM, Atlantic City, New Jersey, USA (2005)
3. Tamilselvan, L., Sankaranarayanan, V.: Prevention of Blackhole Attack in MANET. In: The 2nd International Conference on Wireless Broadband and Ultra Wideband Communications. IEEE (2007)
4. Aad, I., Hubaux, J.-P., Knightly, E.W.: Impact of Denial of Service Attacks on Ad Hoc Networks. IEEE Transactions on Networking, Reference: LCA-ARTICLE-2007-011
5. Hu, Y.-C., Perrig, A., Johnson, D.B.: Ariadne: A Secure OnDemand Routing Protocol for Ad Hoc Networks. In: Proceedings of the Eighth Annual International Conference on Mobile Computing and Networking, MobiCom 2002 (2002)
6. Choudhury, S., Roy, S.D., Singh, S.A.: Trust Management in Ad Hoc Network for Secure DSR Routing. In: CISSE 2007, December 3-12 (2007)
7. Johnson, D.B., Maltz, D.A.: The dynamic source routing protocol for mobile ad hoc networks. Internet Draft, Mobile Ad Hoc Network (MANET) Working Group, IETF (October 1999)
8. Hu, Y.-C., Perrig, A., Johnson, D.B.: Rushing Attacks and defense in Wireless Ad Hoc Network Routing Protocols. In: ACM Workshop on Wireless Security (WiSe 2003), San Diego, CA, pp. 30–40 (September 2003)
9. Choudhury, S., Roy, S.D., Singh, S.A.: Countering Sinkhole and Black hole attacks on Sensor Networks using Dynamic Trust Management System. In: CISSE 2008 (2008)
10. Wood, A.D., Stankovic, J.A.: A Taxonomy for Denial-of-Service Attacks in Wireless Sensor Networks
11. Ramaswamy, S., Fu, H., Sreekantaradhya, M., Dixon, J., Nygard, K.: Prevention of Cooperative Black Hole Attack in Wireless Ad Hoc Networks
12. Bansal, S., Baker, M.: Observation-based cooperation enforcement in ad hoc networks (July 2003), http://arxiv.org/pdf/cs.NI/0307012

Design and Implementation of Fuzzy Controller for Estimating the Attitude of Unmanned Aerial Vehicles

S. Roopashree[1], K.M. Deepika[2], and Shubha Bhat[1]

[1] Department of Computer Science and Engineering, Dayananda Sagar College
of Engineering, Affiliated to VTU, Bangalore-560078, India
{roopashree.patil,shubha22}@gmail.com
[2] Department of Information Science and Engineering, NitteMeenakshi Institute
of Technology, Affiliated to VTU, Bangalore-560064, India
km.deepika4@gmail.com

Abstract. This paper describes the design of Compact, accurate and inexpensive Fuzzy Logic Controllers and Fuzzy Inference Systems which estimates the attitude of Unmanned Aerial Vehicles(UAV).Attitude refers to parameters of Unmanned Aerial Vehicle such as latitude, longitude and altitude and angles of rotation known as pitch and roll. A Soft Computing technique called Fuzzy Logic is used to design the Fuzzy Logic Controllers and Fuzzy Inference Systems. Visual simulation tool and Aerosim (Aeronautical Simulation Set) Flight gear interface are used for Simulation purpose.

Keywords: Unmanned Aerial Vehicle (UAV), Soft Computing Techniques, Fuzzy Logic (FL), Fuzzy Inference System (FIS).

1 Introduction

An Unmanned Aerial Vehicle (UAV) is an aircraft that flies without human crew. One of the critical Capabilities for making UAV autonomous and practical is the precise estimation of its position and orienatation.The position and orientation of UAV is termed as attitude (Latitude-Longitude,Altitude,Heading,roll and pitch. Usually UAV relies on GPS (Global Positioning System) and INS (Inertial Navigation System) to determine its position and orientation, but if the GPS signal for reasons like adverse weather conditions and hostile jamming becomes unavailable or corrupted, the state estimation solution provided by the INS alone drifts in time and will be unusable after sometime. GPS signal can also be unreliable when operating close to obstacles due to multipath reactions. Therefore when GPS and INS cannot predict and correct the position of UAV, Fuzzy Logic Controllers helps to predict the precise position and orientation of UAV autonomously and in turn helps in navigation of UAV.The objective of this paper is to demonstrate the design and implementation of an Fuzzy Inference System (FIS) which in turn are fed as input to three modular Fuzzy Logic Controllers named as Latitude-Longitude FLC, Altitude FLC and Heading FLC to predict the position of UAV and helping in autonomous navigation of UAV .To design Fuzzy Inference System a Soft Computing technique called the Fuzzy Logic is explored. Literature review has revealed the fact that Fuzzy Logic

V.V. Das, E. Ariwa, and S.B. Rahayu (Eds.): SPIT 2011, LNICST 62, pp. 255–261, 2012.

Controllers are designed to control the attitude of UAVs but have failed to give accurate results due to burden of many rules in the controller. Techniques such as Kalman filtering and steady state Genetic algorithms are used to design FIS, but they require a prior mathematical model to estimate the flight parameters, where as Fuzzy logic does not require any reference or pre-existing model to estimate the flight parameters.In section 2 the general structure of Fuzzy Logic Controller is explained. The Design of FIS which is used by FLC is explained in section 3. The results are discussed in section 4 Conclusion and future enhancements are discussed in Section 5.

2   Fuzzy Logic Controller

When a UAV navigates from one waypoint to another the attitude (Flight Dynamic Parameters) of the UAV varies. Therefore Fuzzy Inference Systems are designed which in turn used by modular FLCs to estimate the attitude of UAVs. The general structure of FLC is shown below.

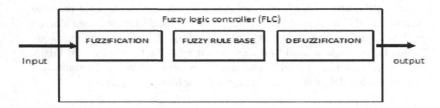

Fig. 1. General structure of Fuzzy Logic Controller

The block diagram of the generalized Fuzzy Logic controller consists of three elements

1) Fuzzification block: transforming input physical values into linguistic variables
2) Fuzzy Rule Base: containing rules to estimate and control UAV parameters.
3) Defuzzification block: transforming output linguistic variables into physical values to control the Flight Parameters.

The three modular Fuzzy Logic Controllers consists of three modules. First module is Latitude-Longitude FLC.Second module is altitude FLC and third module is heading FLC. Latitude-Longitude FLC determines the position of UAV along UAV.Altitude Module estimates the current altitude (height) of UAV .Altitude module has its inputs as altitude error, change of altitude error and airspeed. These inputs are used in design of FIS which controls the Fuzzy Logic Controller output parameters such as elevator, throttle and scaling and in turn helps in controlling Altitude of UAV. The third module is the heading module which has inputs as the change of heading error and airspeed, these inputs are used in design of FIS which controls the Fuzzy Logic Controller output parameters such as Heading and Roll angle and in turn helps in controlling the angles of rotation of UAV. The proposed Fuzzy Logic Controller which comprises of three modules is shown in Fig.2. The three modular FLC is responsible for the estimation and control of Altitude, Latitude-Longitude and Heading of UAV.

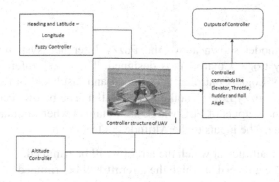

Fig. 2. Fuzzy Logic Controller comprising three modules

3   Simulation Environment

A Simulated environment in MATLAB and Aerosonde Model from Flight gear interface has been used for Simulation. The derived Aerial Controller model is shown in Fig.3. It consists of following Subsystems.

1) Fuzzy Logic Controller: It is composed of combination of Altitude, Latitude-Longitude and Heading Fuzzy Logic Controllers.
2) Scaling Embedded Matlab Function: it contains aircraft states as the input and calculates the scaling factor.
3) Altitude Embedded Matlab Function: it takes scaling as the input and calculates the change in altitude.
4) ErrorCalc Embedded Matlab Function: It Contains two inputs called Altitude and Airspeed. This block contains conditions to Control the Elevator and throttle of Aircraft.

The Functional model Altitude fuzzy logic controller is shown below:

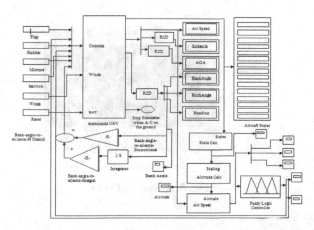

Fig. 3. Demonstrating the Aerosonde Simulation Model for Estimation of altitude of Unmanned Aerial Vehicles

4   Results

Considering the model shown above the Fuzzy Inference system for all the three modules of Fuzzy Logic Controllers is designed. The Fuzzy Inference System (FIS) for Altitude Fuzzy Logic Controller is designed and displayed in the Graphical User Interface (GUI) of Fuzzy Logic Toolkit using Matlab.The below section also explains about the command outputs of FLC which are obtained when simulation model is run for a specified time. The inputs to the Altitude controller are:

> Altitude: The altitude at which the aircraft will be trimmed.
> Airspeed: The airspeed at which the aircraft will be trimmed.
> Altitude Error: It is the difference between the desired altitude and the current altitude of the airplane.
> Change of Altitude: The error indicates whether the, aerial vehicle is approaching the desired altitude or if it is going away from it.

The graphs of inputs are shown below:

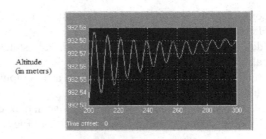

Simulation Time in seconds

Fig. 4. Altitude of UAV

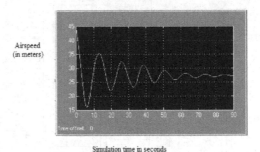

Simulation time in seconds

Fig. 5. Airspeed of UAV

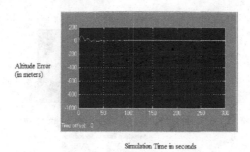

Altitude Error
(in meters)

Simulation Time in seconds

Fig. 6. Altitude error

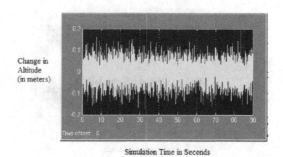

Change in
Altitude
(in meters)

Simulation Time in Seconds

Fig. 7. Change of Altitude Error

The command outputs to the Altitude controller are:

➤ Elevator: The initial guess for the elevator position at trim condition.
➤ Throttle: The initial guess for the throttle position at trim condition.
➤ Scaling: This is the factor that indicates uniform change in altitude from one
   waypoint to another. Constant scaling in maintained when flight is navigating from
   one waypoint to another.

The graphs of command outputs are shown below:

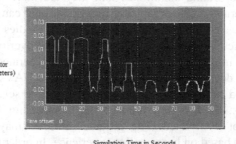

Elevator
(in meters)

Simulation Time in Seconds

Fig. 8. Elevator of UAV

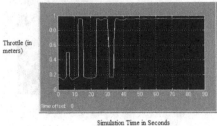

Throttle (in meters)

Simulation Time in Seconds

Fig. 9. Throttle of UAV

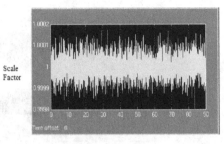

Scale Factor

Simulation time in Seconds

Fig. 10. Scaling of UAV

5   Conclusion and Future Enhancements

The purpose of this paper is to demonstrate the Fuzzy Logic Controller which is used for Waypoint Navigation and Control of Small Aerial Vehicles. Fuzzy Logic is the best and promising technique to control Aerial Vehicles when precise mathematical models are not available. Fuzzy logic controllers have the following advantages over the conventional Controllers. Experiments show comparable results with conventional systems like Kalman filter and particle filter. They are cheaper to develop, they cover a wider range of operating conditions, and they are more readily customizable in natural language terms. A self-organizing fuzzy controller can automatically refine an initial approximate set of fuzzy rules. Simulation Studies have shown adequate overall performance but sometimes controllers may be overloaded with many inputs and outputs which in turn increase the rules that are generated to control the attitude of UAVs and thus degrade the tuning of parameters of UAVs. To overcome the rule expansion a method called Combs method is employed to select minimum number of inputs and outputs. This in turn reduces the membership functions and thus the Controllers are not overloaded. The attitude of UAV may oscillate because the controller design is based on human pilot experience. In order to achieve better results the Controller can be designed on flight performance observations.

Acknowledgement. This work has been jointly supported by Neeta Trivedi, Scientist F, Head of AIEL and VikramJain,Scientist B, Aeronautical Development Establishment (ADE), and DRDO Bangalore. I also would like to thank our head of the department Dr. Ramesh Babu D.R, Prof. K.A.Ramakrishna, Vindhya P Malagi, Research Fellow for their critical reviews and comments.

References

1. Metev, S.M., Viejo, V.P.: Laser Assisted Micro technology, 2nd edn. Springer, Berlin (1998); Osgood, Jr., R. M.(ed.)
2. Verbrugge, H.B., Bruin, P.M.: Fuzzy control and Conventional control 90, 151–160 (1997)
3. Kowalski, T.O., Shabbats, K., Jaszczak, K.: The Influence of Parameters and Structure of PI-Type Fuzzy-Logic Controller 131, 251–264 (2002)
4. Doitsidis, L., Valavanis, K.P., Tsourveloudis, N.C., Kontitsis, M.: A Framework for Fuzzy Logic Based UAV Navigation and Control. In: Proceedings of the Conference on Robotics and Automation. IEEE (2004)
5. Špink, O., Kroupa, S., Hanzalek, Z.: Control System For Unmanned Aerial Vehicles. In: Proceedings of the AIAA Guidance Navigation and Control Conference, OGI School of Science and Engineering, Austin, USA (2004)
6. McLain, T., Goodrich, M.A.: Autonomous Vehicle Technologies for Small Fixed-WingUAVs. Journal of Aerospace Computing 2 (January 2005)
7. Mahmood, M.M., Chowdhury, S., Ihsan, R., Yousaf, U.M., Afifi, M.W., Chuwdhury, I.M.: UAV Autopilot Design for the AUVSI, UAS International Competition. In: Proceedings of the ASME 2009 International Design Engineering Technical Conferences (2009)
8. Ervin, J.C., Alptekin, S.E., De Turris, D.J.: Optimization of the Fuzzy Logic Controller for an Autonomous UAV (2005)

Tamil to Hindi Machine Transliteration Using Support Vector Machines

S. Keerthana[1], V. Dhanalakshmi[2], M. Anand Kumar[1],
V.P. Ajith[1], and K.P. Soman[1]

[1] Computational Engineering and Networking,
Amrita Vishwa Vidyapeetham,
Ettimadai, Coimbatore
[2] Department of Tamil, SRM University, Kattankulathur
{keerthana.keerthi,dhanagiri,ajith12485}@gmail.com,
anandkumar@yahoo.co.in, kp_soman@amrita.edu

Abstract. Transliteration is the process of replacing the characters in one language with the corresponding phonetically equivalent characters of the other language. India is a language diversified country where people speak and understand many languages but does not know the script of some of these languages. Transliteration plays a major role in such cases. Transliteration has been a supporting tool in machine translation and cross language information retrieval systems as most of the proper nouns are out of vocabulary words. In this paper, a sequence learning method for transliterating named entities from Tamil to Hindi is proposed. Through this approach, accuracy obtained is encouraging. This transliteration system can be embedded with Tamil to Hindi machine translation system in future.

Keywords: Named entities, Transliteration, Phonetic, Alphabet, Sequence Labeling, Support Vector Machines.

1   Introduction

Named entity transliteration is the process of producing an equivalent target name for a given source name. In any machine translation system, large bilingual lexicons provide major coverage of words encountered in the text, a significant portion of tokens which are not covered by such lexicons is proper nouns [1]. Though bilingual lexicons are updated time to time, new named entities are still appearing frequently. Automatic transliteration is helpful in such cases. The aim of cross lingual information retrieval (CLIR) system is to retrieve documents in one language while the query is given in another language. The out of vocabulary word problem can be effectively handled with transliteration [2]. Recently, several methodologies have been developed for machine transliteration. Pushpak Bhattacharya et al., developed compositional transliteration system [3].They proposed the idea of compositionality of transliteration functionality in two different methodologies: serial and parallel. By composing serially two transliteration systems namely, X $\rightarrow$Y and Y $\rightarrow$Z, practical

V.V. Das, E. Ariwa, and S.B. Rahayu (Eds.): SPIT 2011, LNICST 62, pp. 262–264, 2012.

transliteration functionality between two languages X & Z which has no direct parallel data between them are provided and improving the quality of an existing X → Z transliteration system through a parallel compositional methodology. In this paper, focus is on Tamil to Hindi transliteration. The recent work by Vijaya M S et al., [4] on Machine Transliteration based on Sequence Labeling Approach for English to Tamil using Memory-based Learning has been adopted.

2   Issues in Tamil to Hindi Transliteration

Hindi is phonetically strong compared to Tamil. There are several issues that have to be considered while transliteration. Single alphabet in Tamil corresponds to more than one alphabet in Hindi. For example, க (ka)is mapped to क, ख, ग, घ(ka, kha, ga, gha). There are certain names in Tamil whose pronunciation varies in Hindi. For example, equivalent name for லட்சுமி (ladsumi) is लक्ष्मी(lakshmi).

3   Transliteration Using Support Vector Machines

3.1   Transliteration Framework

Support vector machines belong to supervised learning methods that analyze data and recognize patterns, which are used for classification and regression analysis [5]. The aim of the supervised learning is to provide output label for the given input based on the learned model. The input is given as a sequence and corresponding label is obtained as a sequence. Therefore this can be formulated as a sequence labeling approach. Table 1 shows the algorithm followed.

Table 1. Algorithm of our framework

X ∈ {all possible transliterated units in Tamil}
Y ∈ {all possible transliterated units in Hindi}
x→ Tamil word segmented as $(x_1, x_2...x_n)$
y→ Hindi word segmented as $(y_1, y_2...y_n)$
For i=1 to n
$\quad\quad x_i \longrightarrow y_i$
$\quad\quad$ Each x_i is mapped with its phonetically equivalent y_i
end
y_i depends on,
{
$\quad\quad\quad$ Source language unit (x_i)
$\quad\quad\quad$ Adjacent units $(x_{i-2}, x_{i-1}, x_{i+1}, x_{i+2})$ surrounding x_i
$\quad\quad\quad$ Target language unit (y_i)
$\quad\quad\quad$ Adjacent units $(y_{i-2}, y_{i-1}, y_{i+1}, y_{i+2})$ surrounding y_i
$\quad\quad$ }

Corresponding to one unit, several output units are possible and hence, transliteration can be viewed as a multi-class classification problemWhile segmenting, twoapproaches have been carried out. In Approach I,Tamil alphabets are split along with its vowel. Approach II follows the same three steps as in the previous approach and also includes an additional step. One more level of splitting is done (i.e.) the splitting of consonants and vowels. In the previous approach, consonants and vowels are not split. More levels of splitting results in better accuracy. Accuracy obtained in Approach II is more compared to Approach I. After segmenting, corresponding Tamil and Hindi units are aligned. Alignment will be direct and easy if the number of units is same in Tamil and Hindi words. Problem will occur if there is mismatch in the number of units [4]. This mismatch is resolved either by inserting '$' symbol or by combining adjacent transliteration units of target side in such a way that phonetic structure is maintained. The other case will be to combine adjacent transliteration units when the number of units in Hindi word is more than that of the Tamil.

4   Experimental Results

Our model produces Hindi transliteration for Tamil words with an accuracy of 80-85% with Approach II and around 72% with Approach I. The character accuracy obtained in Approach II is 96.5% whereas for Approach I is 86.8%. The training data includes 30527 name and place names. The accuracy is affected because of the fact that, corresponding to a single character in Tamil, there are multiple transliterations possible in Hindi. Approach II gives better accuracy than Approach I. This methodology can be used for transliteration between any two languages.

References

1. Virga, P., Khudanpur, S.: Transliteration of Proper Names in Cross-Language Applications. In: 26th Annual International ACM SIGIR Conference on Research and Development in Information Retrieval (2003)
2. Kumaran, A., Kellner, T.: A Generic Framework for Machine Transliteration. In: The 30th Annual International ACM SIGIR Conference on Research and Development in Information Retrieval (2007)
3. Kumaran, A., Khapra, M.M., Bhattacharyya, P.: Compositional Machine Transliteration. ACM Transactions on Asian Language Information (2010)
4. Vijaya, M.S., Shivapratap, G., Dhanakshmi, V., Ajith, V.P., Soman, K.P.: Sequence labeling approach for English to Tamil Transliteration using Memory based Learning. In: International Conference on Natural Language Processing (2009)
5. Wikipedia, http://en.wikipedia.org/wiki/Support_vector_machine
6. Lin, W.-H., Chen, H.-H.: Backward Machine Transliteration by Learning Phonetic Similarity. In: The 6th Conference on Natural Language Learning, vol. 20 (2002)
7. TALP Research Center NLP group, http://www.lsi.upc.edu/~nlp/SVMTool/

Mobile Learning Concept and Its Effects on Student's Attitudes Case Study: Egyptian Faculties

Abeer A. Amer[1] and Hoda A. Abdelhafez[2]

[1] Department of Computer Science & Information System,
Sadat Academy for Management and Sciences, Alexandria, Egypt
abamer_2000@yahoo.com
[2] Information Systems & Decision Support Department,
Faculty of Computers & Informatics, Suez Canal University, Egypt
Hodaabdelhafez@gmail.com

Abstract. The spread of mobile devices and wireless networks help the learning process and offer opportunities for knowledge acquisition also brings hope to universities use technology to improve their services. The aim of this paper is to measure the Egyptian student's perception toward the concept and benefits of m-learning through a survey of two hundreds and eighteen students at different colleges in Egypt. Data was collected and analyzed using SPSS.

Keywords: Mobile Learning, Distance Learning, E-Learning Student Survey, Mobile Technology.

1 Introduction

The rapid growth of information and communication technologies (ICT) and rising computer knowledge of the students make possible appearance of new educational forms. Nowadays extremely actual and perspective is mobile learning (m-Learning) [1][2][3].

2 Related Work

Al Fahd (2009) investigates the students' attitudes and perceptions towards the effectiveness of mobile learning at King Saud University through analyzing the answers to the qualitative questions in the surveys which an attempt to gain an understanding of how current students view the use of mobile devices in learning environments.[4] Naji Shukri and Abdul Razak (2011) investigate students' awareness and requirements of mobile learning services among Malaysian students in the higher education environment the results of the study show that students have enough knowledge and well awareness to use such technology in their education environment.[5]

The Study Purpose: The aim of this study is to determine how students in Egypt will accept mobile learning as an instructional medium. The research objectives are:

V.V. Das, E. Ariwa, and S.B. Rahayu (Eds.): SPIT 2011, LNICST 62, pp. 265–268, 2012.
© Institute for Computer Sciences, Social Informatics and Telecommunications Engineering 2012

Ascertaining of students' acceptance level of mobile learning and Investigating possible factors which affecting mobile learning acceptance.

3   Methodology

To study the receptivity of students to the concept of mobile learning and its effectiveness a questionnaire was developed using ten closed questions to measure the acceptability of students to the perception of mobile learning and its effectiveness. The study was conducted in three educational institutions Sadat Academy for Management and Sciences (SAMS), computer and information systems department (CIS), Faculty of Commerce Transport College of International Transport and Logistics (CITL), Arab Academy for Sciences, Technology and Maritime at Alexandria, Egypt. (see Table.1) A sample of undergraduate male and female students (n=218), between the ages of 17 to -24 years they were asked to fill a questionnaire which measure the extent to accept students to the concept of mobile learning and its effectiveness The data collected was processed and statistically analyzed through SPSS Ver.17.

Table 1. Different Colleges Percentages

College	frequency	Percent
SAMS	74	%34
CITL	55	%25.2
CIS	89	%40.8
Total	218	%100.00

4   Results and Discussion

The data gathered from the respondents are presented in Table 2 which demonstrates the percentages of the descriptive statistics for the effectiveness and difficulties of mobile learning which measured by a Likert scale.

Data in Table 3 illustrates the mean and standard deviation. Mean scores of the sample indicate that the majority of the respondents preferred using the mobile technology in promotion of distance learning, also confirmed that mobile learning is a flexible method than traditional learning and can access easier to the sources of learning any time any where. Using Likert-type scales derive to calculate Cronbach's alpha. The generally agreed upon lower limit for Cronbach's alpha is 0.70 [6] which are regarded as acceptable reliability coefficients. The results of the reliability analysis presented that Effectiveness elements is 0.755 and the Difficulties of mobile learning is 0.703. Both are more than 0.7 so they are acceptable reliability coefficients.

Table 2. Descriptive Statistics for the Questionnaire Indicators

Item No.	Questionnaire Indicator	Strongly Agree	Agree	Undecided	Disagree	Strongly Disagree	Not Responded	Total
	Mobile Learning advantages							
1	Mobile Learning leads to easier access to sources	91 (41.8)	96 (44.0)	12 (5.5)	12 (5.5)	7 (3.2)	0 (0%)	218 100%
2	Mobile learning is an effective means of learning	54 (24.8%)	127 (58.3%)	21 (9.6%)	10 (4.6%)	6 (2.7%)	0 (0%)	218 100%
3	Mobile learning improves communication	51 (23.4%)	93 (42.7%)	21 (9.6%)	41 (18.8%)	12 (5.5%)	0 (0%)	218 100%
	Difficulties of the mobile learning							
4	Carrying laptops is an obstacle in the mobile learning	15 (6.9%)	59 (27.1%)	31 (14.2%)	89 (40.8%)	21 (9.6%)	3 (1.4%)	218 (100%)
5	Small screens phones and PDAs	23 (10.6%)	78 (35.5%)	43 (19.7%)	58 (26.6%)	13 (6.0%)	3 (1.4%)	218 (100%)

Table 3. Mean and Standard Deviation of the Questionnaire Indicators

Item No.	Questionnaire indicator	N Valid	Missing	Mean	Std. Deviation
1	Mobile learning leads to easier access to sources of learning	218	0	4.16	.981
2	Mobile learning is an effective means of learning	218	0	3.98	.882
3	Mobile learning improves communication between students and teachers.	218	0	3.60	1.192
Difficulties of the mobile learning					
4	do you think carrying laptops is an obstacle in the mobile learning	215	3	2.80	1.152
5	Small screens phones and PDA	215	3	3.19	1.129

5   Conclusion

This study investigates the students' attitudes and perceptions of 218 University Student's from different colleges towards effectiveness of mobile learning in their studies. Also shows that the students agreed that mobile phones had successfully enhanced the teaching and learning process. The analysis of the questionnaire leads to the fact that students is widely accepted the perception of mobile learning the students support the idea because it increases the flexibility of accessing to the resources and also can access information any time any where.

References

1. O'Malley, C., Vavoula, G., Glew, J.P., Taylor, J., Shaples, M., Lefrere, P.: Guidelines for learning/Teaching/Tutoring in a mobile environment (2003),
   http://www.mobilearn.org/download/results/guidelines.pdf
2. Dias, A., Carvalho, J., Keegan, D., Kismihok, G., Mileva, N., Nix, J., Rekkedal, T.: An Introduction To Mobile Learning (2008),
   http://www.ericsson.com/ericsson/corpinfo/programs/
   the_role_of_mobile_learning_in_european_education/products/
   wp/socrates_wp1_english.pdf
3. Norazah, N., Amin, E.M., Ruhizan, Y., Saemah, R., Melor, Y.: The Mobile Learning Readiness of the Post-Graduate Students (2010)
4. Alzaza, N.S., Yaakub, A.R.: Students' Awareness and Requirements of Mobile Learning Services in the Higher Education Environment. American Journal of Economics and Business Administration 3(1), 95–100 (2011)
5. Sultan, D.M.S., Saiful Islam, A.H.M., Mahmud, M.S.: M-Learning: A Prospective Learning Process of Bangladesh of Today (2010)
6. Binar, P.M.: The development of an instrument to measure student attitudes towards television course. The American Journal of Distance Education (1993)

Data Processing Consideration
and Model Validation
in Flight Vehicle System Identification

Sepehr Nesaei and Kamran Raissi

Amirkabir University of Technology (AUT) Tehran, Iran
sepehr_ne@yahoo.com
http://www.aut.ac.ir

Abstract. There are four steps in system identification. Data Processing constitutes the first and most essential step. In this paper an overview of the flight data processing for reaching a sound set of data is presented. It includes the analysis of the types of data available, the method of exclusion of outliers and noise, bias corrections, and filtering of disturbances. Filtering include time domain and frequency domain processing. On the other hand, model validation is considered the final step for aircraft identification. This was accomplished for an innovative model of elevator hinge moment (EHM) in a turboprop aircraft equipped with a mechanical control system. Here, optimization of the identification design has been achieved by iteratively estimating the unknown model parameters.

Keywords: Data Processing, Model Validation, Hinge Moment Parameters, Parameter Identification.

1 Introduction

It is a standard practice in industry and academic communities to use flight test data for system identification. The results are used for developmental purposes as well as design validation [1]. There are four steps to be followed for system identification: data gathering, model postulate, parameter identification and model validation. Data gathering is considered as the first and essential part in identification terminology, used as the input for the model which is prepared later. It consists of selecting an appropriate data set, pre-processing and processing them for the work [1], [2], [3], and [4]. It involves the implementation of the known algorithms together with the transcription of flight tapes, data storage and data management, calibration, processing, analysis and presentation. Moreover, Model validation is necessary to gain confidence in, or reject a particular model. In particular, the parameter estimation and the model validation are integral parts of the system identification. Validation refers to the process of confirming the conceptual model and demonstrating an adequate correspondence between the computational results of the model and the actual data. Identification for control is defined when modeling a dynamic system (e.g. EHM system) with identification techniques (like Maximum Likelihood (ML)

V.V. Das, E. Ariwa, and S.B. Rahayu (Eds.): SPIT 2011, LNICST 62, pp. 269–274, 2012.

Estimation Techniques based on an Optimization Cost Function). In doing so, a model of limited complexity (like Elevator surface control model) is used specially for feedback and feed forward control design (e.g. a control loader system) and evaluation purposes (e.g. by the use of raw flight recorded data and sensors' outputs) [5]. In what follows the special requirements and techniques for EHM identification will be discussed for each of the data processing and the model validation steps.

2   Choosing Appropriate Types of Data Sets

Flight data acquisition can be done by any of the two methods: first is through a preplanned flight test program during which attempts are made to perform the test in a proper and orderly manner as well as using adequate equipment for this purpose. Second is based on gathering normal flight data from their advance digital flight data recorders after each flight. Due to estimate the parameters, appropriate data sets are considered as flight test data, but availability of such a data from the second method requires a necessary pre-processing step in order to reach appropriate data sets for estimation process [4]. Dealing with normal flight data, *outliers* are series of points out of range by a wide margin and do not follow a normal trend. They may be produced by either sensor or related circuits installed for data acquisition. It may cause divergence problems when used for estimation purposes. However, selection of suitable criteria is of utmost importance since it could result in useful data losses. Fig. 1 shows the ψ angle data points taken by digital flight data recording devices from a normal flight. Points highlighted with circle seem to be outliers. Here, an innovative method has been coded in MATLAB software to omit them. The right side plot indicates a considerable improvement in the range of variations of the ψ angle [4].

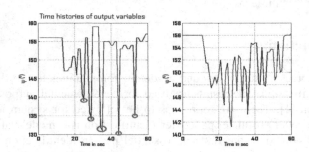

Fig. 1. Demonstration of the effect of outlier omission on a set of data [4]

2.1   Data Compatibility Check

There are techniques such as Flight Path Reconstructions (FPR) used when dealing with bias corrections. This is necessary when position and installation errors occur in aircraft construction, e.g. in accelerometers or rotational measuring instruments like rate gyros [1].Here, the instrument bias errors are the unknown parameters in pre-processing procedure; that is, Kinematic equations concerning measured quantities like linear accelerators, Euler angles and their angular rates can be corrected by considering their related bias parameters (such as Δa_x, Δa_y and Δa_z for accelerometers, and Δp, Δq and Δr for rate gyros) [1]. Fig. 2 shows convergence of bias parameter estimates with error bounds for a specified set of data by Output Error Method (OEM) [4], demonstrated for three accelerometers and angular rates. Order of magnitudes for angular rates is of small range about one thousandth or smaller, in comparison with those of accelerometers which is of about one tenth or a bit more [4].

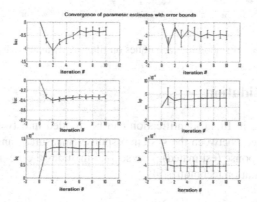

Fig. 2. Convergence of bias estimates with error bounds, ended in 10 iterations [4]

2.2   Disturbance and Noise

In general, there are two kinds of errors in parameter identification: measurement errors and the process noise. Some estimating algorithms like filter error method (FEM) based on ML Method consider both in their formulations. Others like OEM consider only measurement noise and are sensitive to the presence of process noise. However, preprocessing techniques can also help to eliminate it.Process noise, like the effect of Turbulence and gust loads, are unwanted inputs to the system and may enter the dynamic model via recorded flight data. However, dealing with normal FDR needs either sufficient knowledge about the allowable frequency domains of the sensors, called frequency bandwidth, or good understanding of the disturbance. Obviously, unavailability of both may cause the procedure useless. Experimental observations over several series of flight data points reveal that range of frequency domain for presence of process noise is usually less or equal than 0.5 Hz and for measurement noise is equal or larger than 10 Hz [6]. Hence, to decrease the turbulence effect with a lack of sufficient knowledge, implementation of such approximation may sounds good [4].Here, an innovative technique has been created in a MATLAB; it works based on weighted coefficients depending on the number of selected points to be smoothed over the whole data trend. Fig.3 shows the effect of filtering techniques for a normal FDR, in which red plots on the right are smoothed plots and the blue ones on the left are ordinary. Digital signatures are acceptable.

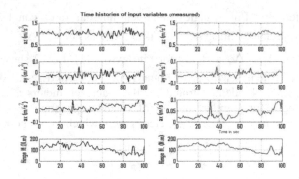

Fig. 3. Effect of smoothing techniques on filtering data points by FDR [4]

3   Model Validation

Validation procedure in flight identification can be divided into two parts. The first is the compatibility check between the system response (measured) and the mathematical model computed response (estimated). The second includes the numerical convergence of the specified estimation techniques [4].

3.1   Inverse Simulation in Identification of EHM

Here, an inverse simulation of elevator control surface has been designed for hinge moment identification. That is, the measured EHM can be supposed as system model response and the EHM coefficients may be defined as desired control inputs instead of elevator deflections themselves. The relationship between the known variables and the unknowns is formulated as [4]:

$$\begin{cases} C_{he} = \dfrac{HM_m}{qS_e \, \overline{C}_e} \\ C_{he} = C_{h\alpha}\alpha_t + C_{h\delta e}\delta_e \end{cases} \tag{4}$$

in which HM_m (the measured EHM), q (dynamic pressure), S_e (elevator control surface area), C_e (mean elevator chord), α_t (tail angle of attack), δ_e (measured elevator deflection) are the known variables and $C_{h\alpha}$ and $C_{h\delta e}$ are the unknowns. However, such equation can be written for any control surface. Figs.4.a and 4.b show the compatibility between the measured EHM and the estimated HM, in turn, done by the two estimation techniques of ML method. As it is observed, both plots admit the good tracking of the input hinge data points by the estimated ones during the off-line simulation [4].

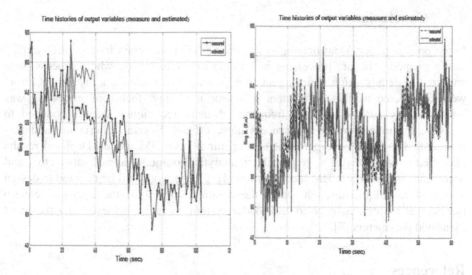

Fig. 4. Validation of HM: the measured (blue trend) and estimated (a) OEM, (b) FEM

3.2   Hinge Moment Validation via Cost Function Minimization

In an optimal based strategy algorithm like ML, a cost function (e.g. determinant of covariance matrix of the residuals) has been defined to be minimized. Better estimation results go with the lowest values obtained. Table 1 shows the feasibility of convergence procedure in the FEM applying for HM coefficients identification. Other values include the number of iterations, the numerical method of Levenberg-Marquardt algorithm, and the convergence tolerance magnitude. Numerical simulation confirms the identification process [4].

Table 1. FEM Convergence Procedure for Hinge Moment Identification [4]

Iter no	detR Correction of F (Updated R)	Iter no	detR Correction of F (Updated R)
0	5.1417e-021	7	4.4398e-029 Correction of F - 4.4243e-029
1	1.4533e-026		
2	2.4406e-027	8	4.4208e-029 Correction of F - 4.4096e-029
3	1.1412e-027 Correction of F - 8.3886e-029	9	4.4079e-029 Correction of F - 4.4002e-029
4	6.5701e-029 Correction of F - 4.8878e-029	10	4.3994e-029 Correction of F - 4.3942e-029
5	4.5131e-029 Correction of F - 4.4893e-029	11	4.3937e-029 Correction of F - 4.3902e-029
6	4.4624e-029 Correction of F - 4.451e-029	12	4.3899e-029

4   Conclusion

In the present paper, identification procedure of HM parameters for a control surface was presented. The pre-processing and validation steps of the whole process were analyzed in details. After choosing an appropriate set of flight data, instrument errors were considered as bias parameters in sensor modeling; then, pre-processing was introduced by FPR. Time and frequency domain techniques were introduced to decrease the measurement and process noise effects. Several criteria in validation procedure for EHM were performed on an innovative HM model. Depicted results classified in two categories, graphical and analytical outputs, showed satisfactory and acceptance of the whole HM identification [4]. Future work will be devoted to design a control technique, through which the position control of the hydro or electro mechanical system, namely control loader system, is to be achieved by the input identified parameters [7].

References

1. Jategaonkar, R.V.: Flight Vehicle System Identification: A Time Domain Methodology 216 (2006)
2. Nelles, O.: Nonlinear System Identification. NASA Report, ed. (2001)
3. Nesaei, S., Bahrami, B.: Data Processing Considerations in Flight Vehicle Identification. In: AEROTECH III 2009, Kuala Lumpur (2009)
4. Nesaei, S.: Estimation of Hinge Moment Characteristics of Horizontal Tail by Parameter Identification Methods from Raw Flight Data. M.S thesis, Iran (2009)
5. de Callafon, R.A., Van den Hof, P.M.J.: Identification for Control. In: Unbehauen, H (ed.) (2001)
6. Hoblit, F.M.: Gust Loads on Aircraft: Concepts and Applications. In: AIAA Education Series (1988)
7. Amirahmadi, S.: Design of Nonlinear Loading System for a Vertical Flight Motion Simulator. M.S thesis, Iran (2010)

Implementation of LFSR Counter
Using CMOS VLSI Technology

M. Mahaboob Basha[1], Towfeeq Fairooz[2], Nisar Hundewale[2],
K. Vasudeva Reddy[1], and B. Pradeep[1]

[1] AVR&SVRCET, JNTU, India
{mmehboobbasha,vasureddy}@gmail.com,
deepusummi@hotmail.com
[2] College of Computers and Information Technology, Taif University, Taif, K.S.A
towfeeq.fairooz@tu.edu.sa, nisar@computer.org

Abstract. CMOS stands for Complementary Metal Oxide Semiconductor. It is basically a class of integrated circuits, and is used in a range of applications with digital logic circuits, such as microprocessors, microcontrollers, static RAM, etc. It is also used in applications with analogue circuits, such as in data converters, image sensors, etc. There are quite a few advantages that the CMOS technology has to offer. One of the main advantage that CMOS technology, which makes it the most commonly-used technology for digital circuits today, is the fact that it enables chips that are small in size to have features like high operating speeds and efficient usage of energy. Besides, they have very low static power supply drain most of the time. Besides, devices using CMOS technology also have a high degree of noise immunity. This paper presents the implementation of a LFSR (Linear Feedback Shift Register) counter using the recent CMOS sub-micrometer layout tools. Adding to the advantage of CMOS technology, the LFSR counter can be used as a new trend setter in cryptography and can also be beneficial when compared to GRAY & BINARY counter while not forgetting the variety of other applications LFSR counter has.

Keywords: Chip technology, Layout level, LFSR, Pass Transistor.

1   Introduction

The main challenging areas in VLSI are performance, cost, testing, area, reliability and power. The demand for comparatively lesser price and portable computing devices and communications system are increasing rapidly. These applications require low power dissipation for VLSI circuits. There are main two sources of power dissipation in digital circuits; these are static (mainly due to leakage current and its contribution to total power dissipation is very small) and dynamic (due to switching i.e. the power consumed due to short circuit current flow and charging of load capacitances) power dissipation. Hence, it is important aspect to optimize power during testing. Power optimization is one of the main challenges.There has been various low power approaches proposed to solve the problem of power dissipation

V.V. Das, E. Ariwa, and S.B. Rahayu (Eds.): SPIT 2011, LNICST 62, pp. 275–281, 2012.
© Institute for Computer Sciences, Social Informatics and Telecommunications Engineering 2012

i.e. to decrease the power supply voltage, switching frequency and capacitance of transistor during the testing [1]. Here, this paper presents one such approach and that is LFSR counter which has low power architecture. The LFSR is used in variety of applications such as Built-in-self test (BIST) [2], cryptography, error correction code and in field of communication for generating pseudo-noise sequences. Nowadays LFSR's are present in nearly every coding scheme as they produce sequences with good statistical properties, and they can be easily analyzed. Moreover they have a low-cost realization in hardware. Counters like Binary, Gray suffer problem of power consumption, glitches, speed, and delay because they are implemented with techniques which have above drawbacks. They produce not only glitches, which increase power consumption but also complexity of design. The propagation delay of results of existing techniques is more which reduces speed & performance of system. LFSR counters overcome these problems which are implemented using different technologies of CMOS.

2   LFSR

LFSR i.e. Linear Feedback Shift Register is a shift register whose input bit is a linear function unlike most everyday devices whose inputs and operations are effectively predefined. LFSR when clocked moves the signal through the register from one flip flop to next. Some of the outputs are combined in exclusive-OR configuration to form a feedback mechanism. A LFSR can be formed by performing exclusive-OR on the outputs of two or more of the flip-flops together and feeding those outputs back into the input of one of the flip flops as shown in Fig.1.

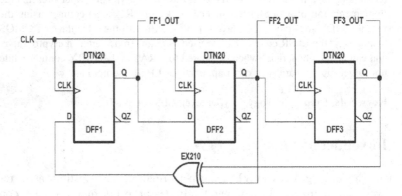

Fig. 1. Linear Feedback Shift Register

The initial value of the LFSR is called the seed, and because the operation of the register is deterministic, the sequence of values produced by the register is completely determined by its current (or previous) state. Likewise, because the register has a finite number of possible states, it must eventually enter a repeating cycle. However, a LFSR with a well-chosen feedback function can produce a sequence of bits which appears random in nature & which has a very long cycle.

2.1 Working

Pseudorandom Pattern Generation. Linear feedback shift registers make extremely good pseudorandom pattern generators. When the outputs of the flip-flops are loaded with a seed value (anything except all 0s, which would cause the LFSR to produce all 0 patterns) and when the LFSR is clocked, it will generate a pseudorandom pattern of 1s and 0s. Note that the only signal necessary to generate the test patterns is the clock. The list of bits position that affects the next state is called the tap sequence. The outputs that influence the input are called taps.The tap sequence of an LFSR can be represented as a polynomial mod 2. This means that the coefficients of the polynomial must be 1's or 0's. This is called the feedback polynomial or characteristic polynomial. For example: if the taps are at the 3rd, 4th, bits the resulting LFSR polynomial is $X4+x3+1$.The '1' in the polynomial does not correspond to a tap. The powers of the terms represent the tapped bits, counting from the left.

Table 1. Pattern Generation by LFSR Counter

Clock pulse	FF1OUT	FF2OUT	FF3OUT	FF4OUT
1	0	1	1	1
2	0	0	1	1
3	0	0	0	1
4	1	0	0	0
5	0	1	0	0
6	0	0	1	0
7	1	0	0	1
8	1	1	0	0
9	0	1	1	0
10	1	0	1	1
11	0	1	0	1
12	1	0	1	0
13	1	1	0	1
14	1	1	1	0
15	1	1	1	1
16	0	1	1	1

FF1OUT –Output of flip flop 1, FF2OUT-output of flip flop 2, FF3OUT-Output of flip flop 3, FF4OUT-Output of flip flop 4.

If (and only if) this polynomial is a primitive, then the LFSR is maximal. The LFSR will only be maximal if the number of taps is even. The tap values in a maximal LFSR will be relatively prime. There can be more than one maximal tap sequence for a given LFSR length. Its output for the various condition of input is expressed in Table 1.

2.2 Design Aspects

A CMOS layout of LFSR Counter is designed.The logic hardware contains a D FlipFlop, a 2-input OR gate, a 2 input XOR gate and inverters. The most important component of our LFSR Counter Design is D Flip Flop. The D-flip flop is designed using following different components: NAND Gates, Transmission gates, inverter and

Pass transistors. Firstly from among the three designs, comparison is done for the power consumption; then the most efficient D-flip flop is selected for the LFSR implementation.The design of D-flip flop and the implementation of LFSR counter are carried out in MICROWIND software.

2.3   Layout Aspects

Layout of D-FlipFlop. Before implementing the whole circuit, a gate-level schematic in DSCH3 is generated. DSCH3 program is a logic editor and simulator used to validate the architecture of logical circuit, before microelectronics started. It provides user friendly environment for hierarchical logic design and fast simulation with delay analysis, which allows design and validation of complex logic structures. After successful simulation the above designs of D Flip Flop are implemented with different components using MICROWIND 3.1 CMOS layout tool for its ease of use and availability. The result of the implementation is detailed below.

Design of D-FlipFlop Using NAND Gate. Layout of LFSR counter in which D Flip flop is implemented using NAND gates is as shown Fig.2.

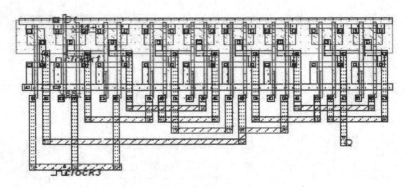

Fig. 2. Layout of D Flip Flop using NAND gate

Design of D-FlipFlop Using Transmission Gate. Layout of LFSR counter in which D Flip flop is implemented using transmission gates is as shown Fig.3.

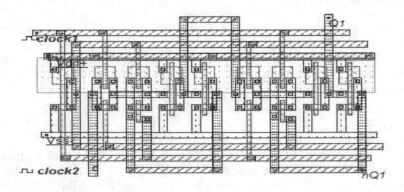

Fig. 3. Layout of D Flip Flop using Transmission gates

Design of D-FlipFlop using Transistor Pass. Layouts of LFSR counter in which D Flip Flop is implemented using transmission gates is as shown Fig.4.

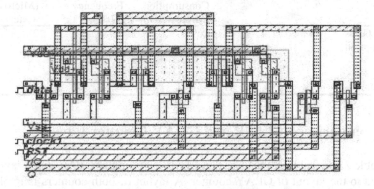

Fig. 4. Layout of D Flip Flop using Transistor Pass

Result of LFSR Layout Implementation. In Table 2 and Table 3the LFSR layouts are compared. The layouts are implemented in 120 nm and 90 nm technology respectively. The various parameters because of different technologies and D Flip Flop design is tabulated for further conclusion and CMOS layout using Pass transistors is as shown in Fig.5.

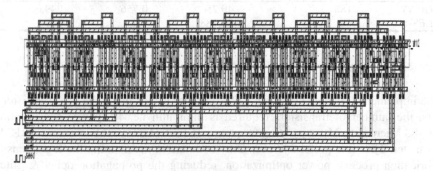

Fig. 5. Layout of LFSR in MICROWIND

Table 2. LFSR in 90 nm Technology

Component	No of Transistors	Power Consumption (Microwatt)	Max Frequency (GHz)	Layout Area (Micro Sq. Meter)
NAND Gates	148	106.0	1.96	295
Transmission Gates	86	99.6	1.7	270
Pass Transistors	68	28.188	1.4	321

Table 3. LFSR in 90 nm Technology

Component	No of Transistors	Power Consumption (Microwatt)	Max Frequency (GHz)	Layout Area (Micro Sq. Meter)
NAND Gates	148	169	1.78	224.8
Transmission Gates	86	155	1.8	390.1
Pass Transistors	68	50.471	1.814	460

3   Comparison of LFSR and GRAY Counter Layout

From Table 2 and Table 3 it is clear that LFSR is optimally implemented layout when compared to the layout of GRAY counter. A layout of both counters is implemented using 120 nm and 90 nm technology. From the layouts various critical parameters are tabulated in Table 4.

Table 4. LFSR in 90 nm Technology

Component	No of Transistors	Power Consumption (Microwatt)	Max Frequency (GHz)	Layout Area (Micro Sq. Meter)
GRAY	188	40.25	0.756	949.6
LFSR	68	28.188	1.4	321

4   Conclusion

The implementation concludes that LFSR counter is best using the pass transistors. In this, the number of transistors required is minimum i.e. 19, power consumption is 28.188 Microwatt, Max operating frequency is 1.4 GHz, layout Size area is 321 Micro Sq meter. Thus it is preferable over Gray counters in maintaining the logic density in fabrication process, power optimization, reducing the propagation delay & glitches. Thus LFSR implemented in CMOS chip technology, is the best illustration of VLSI.

References

1. Weste, N., Benerjee, H.: CMOS VLSI Design: A Circuits and Systems Perspective, 3/e (2006)
2. Sicard, E., Delmas Bendhia, S.: Basic CMOS Cell Design. McGraw Hill Publishers (2005)
3. Kang, S.-M., Leblebici, Y.: CMOS Digital Integrated Circuits-Analysis and Design (2003)
4. Wakerly, J.F.: Digital Design-Principles and practices. Prentice Hall Publishers (2005)
5. Weste, N., Kamran: Principles & Applications of CMOS Logic. Addison-Wesley Publishers (1993)
6. Massey, J.L.: On the Shift register Synthesis & BCH Decoding. IEEE Transactions. Information Theory IT-15(1), 122–127 (1969)

7. Singh, A., Servin, O., Lee, E.: LutfiBustami: 4017 CMOS LED Chaser Counter, A project (2004)
8. Brock, T.B.: Linear Feedback Shift Registers and Cyclic Codes in SAGE. Rose-Hulman Undergraduate Mathematics Journal 7(2) (2006)
9. Chakrabarty, K., Murray, B., Iyengar, V.: Deterministic Built-in Test Pattern Generation for High-Performance Circuits Using Twisted- Ring Counters. IEEE Journals on VLSI Sytems 8(5), 633–636 (2000)
10. Yano, K.: Top down pass-Transistor Logic Design. IEEE Journal of Solid-state Circuits 31(6) (1996)
11. Yano, K.: A 3.8 CMOS 16 * 16 –b multiplier using complementary pass-transistor Logic. IEEE Journal of Solid-state Circuits 25(2) (1990)
12. Yu, Z.: An Investigation into the Security of Self-timed Circuits: LFSR design and Implementation, Thesis, ch. 5 (2003)
13. Govindarajulu, S., et al.: Design of High Performance Dynamic CMOS Circuits in Deep Submicron Technology. International Journal of Engineering Science and Technology 2(7) (2010)

High Speed Data Loading
for Large Sized RDBMS Tables

Prabin R. Sahoo and Chetan Phalak

Tata Consultancy Services, Yantra Park, Thane,
Maharashtra, India
{prabin.sahoo,chetan1.phalak}@tcs.com

Abstract. Data loading into RDBMS is a common phenomenon over decades. Over the years RDBMS has dominated in the enterprise world. Conventional file systems are seen to be replaced with popular RDBMS such as Oracle ®, UDB ®, and Sybase ® etc. This has necessitated the need for data loading while migrating from file systems to RDBMS. In some cases data loading is an everyday activity, for example, dataware housing projects involving data gathering, mining and analysis. No matter what type of data loading it may be, the goal is common i.e. how to achieve high speed in data loading for large sized table to minimize the down time. In this paper we are demonstrating how we can achieve high speed data loading into large RDBMS tables.

Keywords: RDBMS, Loader, Partitions, Parallelism, Queries, Performance, sqlldr.

1 Introduction

High speed data loading is required to reduce the down time of business operations. While data loading involves a lot of preparation such as data gathering, transformations, mining which requires substantial time but in this paper we will be discussing on the data loading activity only. Our focus is to achieve high speed data loading for large sized tables. We assume that data is ready for our loading procedure to take off. We have used Oracle 10g ® as our target database and source is a comma separated data file. We are also using Oracle sqlldr utility [1, 2, 4] for our data loading activity. This utility provides several options as command line parameters for speed up of data loading. Parallel loading is one of the features for high speed data loading. In general when a table is loaded in parallel, DBMS may try to load the data from the loaders synchronizing with lock mechanism especially when the table is not partitioned. This can affect the performance of loading. We have demonstrated in this paper how we can achieve high speed data loading using parallelism.

2 Literature Review

High speed data loading into RDBMS using sqlldr [2] is not much being discussed directly. In [3] the authors have discussed about data load procedure for DB2 database

V.V. Das, E. Ariwa, and S.B. Rahayu (Eds.): SPIT 2011, LNICST 62, pp. 282–286, 2012.

and have cited the reason for using alternative methods for load and unload. In addition the authors have mentioned that the regular migration methods cannot be used *"when a large amount of data needs to be transferred from one system to the target system, when there is a big release differences between them and when time is limiting factor"* [3]. We have referred this article as we are also using standard load utility of Oracle and our aim is to load large database tables. However, our implementation approach is different and our focus is on the high speed data loading to reduce the down time. In [5] the author mentions various options for data loading. We have used the SQL* Loader with direct path option in our experiment. The author mentions *"For all of its awkwardness, SQL*Loader still seems to be about the fastest and most efficient way to get flat file data into Oracle. By default, SQL*Loader uses what it calls conventional path loading–bulk inserts, basically. The performance is not phenomenal, and there are faster alternatives. However, with a simple "direct=true" on the command line, you can invoke "direct path" loading. In a direct path load, SQL*Loader writes rows directly into new data blocks above the table's high water mark"* [5]. Though direct option is efficient way to go, but using this option is not pretty straight forward for large files specially while loading into a table for optimal loading. We have shown in our model how to use it effectively.

3   Model and Architecture

In our model we are assuming our input is having comma separated text file and each table in the target database has one text file. In Fig.1 "F" represents the file corresponding to a table in the target database. For parallel loading into a table we need the following conditions to be true in our high speed load model; a) Table structure should be such that loaders should be able to load concurrently these files. If tables are not large, there is no need to go for partitions. However, in this paper we are dealing with large file, so we are discussing about partitioning of tables [9]. Oracle provides partition option in the loader control file [8]. We assume that loading into partitioned table reduces the locking possibilities which can improve more parallelism in data loading. We are using range partition feature in our model. We do not claim on any other types of partitions. We further assume that as per reference [10] Oracle allows more than one partition loading at a time, and table size is large enough to qualify for partitions and direct option is applicable. b) Split files (F2, F3) which can be loaded in parallel. The table level file "F" can be split into multiple files. The split is not just straight forward. The split is based on a rule. For example if we are dealing with employee data, we can split the big file "F" into smaller files with a range of employees, employee staring with employee number 1 to 10000 in one file F1, 10001 to 20000 in F2, 20001 to 30000 in F3 and so on. It is based on the number of partitions [6] required for a table for optimal query performance with respect to the business need. However our focus in this paper is on data loading. So as a thumb rule we will split the file as per the number of partitions. If 5 partitions required for a table, then 5 split files are required. This we call the partition level of split, and for simplicity we would refer these as partitioned file. c) Addressing the Memory overflow Challenge for large files. If the database server does not have much memoryto hold large files while loading with direct option, the loader may run into memory overflow. In a typical data loading scenario if the loader is loading a large file and has taken substantial hours for loading the data into the table, and it ran out of memory, there is a waste of time as the loading process needs to be restarted from the beginning. In our experiment, we got "ORA-39776: fatal Direct Path API error loading table". We looked for this error, although there are alternatives like changing memory related parameters, moving to higher configuration server etc, we have used our chunk approach to resolve this error.As shown in fig 1, a split file F2 can be further split to smaller size which we call chunk file in our case. The chunk file is an internal split and is faster. Unix split command can be used for this. The chunk files can run be loaded in parallel from corresponding partitions. C1 from F2 and C1 from F3 can be loaded in parallel. d) Determining the optimum number of loaders to run in parallel [7] in a given environment. This step is a difficult one to deal with. As a thumb rule one may say number of partitions equals to the number of loaders since in our model we have number of partitions equals to the number of partitioned files. To determine the number of loaders we conducted an incremental experiment with 5GB data size as shown in fig. 2.

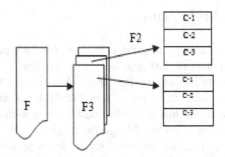

Fig. 1. Model and Architecture of high speed data loader

4   Case Study

Step 1. Split a large file (90GB) into 5 parts i.e F1, F2, F3, F4 and F5 with size 18GB which can be mapped into 5 partitions (We determined by using queries that 5 partitions are required for our test).
Step 2. Do chunk split into 3 each having 6 GB, invoke 5 loaders in parallel with direct option (We have determined by incremental experiment with 5 GB file that 5 loaders are optimal for 5 partitions as shown in fig.2).
Step 3. Each loader processes the partitioned file with direct option. Loop, till chunk files are loaded.
Step 4. Finish

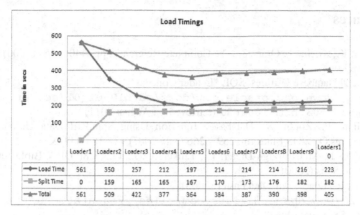

Fig. 2. Split and load time of simulation in secs

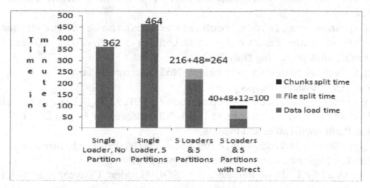

Fig. 3. Results of case study for high speed data loading time in **minutes** while loading 90GB data with various options

From fig. 3, it can be seen that having 5 loaders and 5 partitions with direct option, loading time has been decreased considerably. This is the optimum data loading performance for a given configuration in our experiment. The total time including file split, chunk split and loading takes 100 minutes with a speed up of about 3X compared to single loader without partition and a speed up of about 4X for single loader with partitions without direct option. The experiment was conducted in an Intel ® server with each processor having 2 cores.

5   Conclusions

We can see from our experiment with Oracle, using our model of splitting the files into partition files, chunk files and using the "direct" option in the SQL* Loader utility, and determining optimal number of parallel loaders, high speed data loading is achieved. Further, we have shown how to use chunk files in cases where the memory is less for loading with direct option. Though database partitions, parallel and direct options are well known to the database developers, however, determining the optimal numbers of loaders, numbers of partitions are few challenges which require deeper analysis.

References

1. Loney, K., Koch, G.: Oracle8i: The Complete Reference, pp. 440 – 452 (2000) ISBN 0-07-041167-0
2. Oracle 9i Database Utilities, SQL *Loader Concept,
   `http://download.oracle.com/docs/cd/B10501_01/server.920/`
   `a96652/ch03.htm#1004621` (retrieved on August 2011)
3. Branimir, P., Zoran, S.: Database Migration Using Standard Data Unload and Load Procedures On z/OS Platform, 259 – 266 (July 2007) 953-184-111-X
4. Gennick, J., McCullough-Dieter, C., Linker, G.-J.: Oracle8i DBA Bible, ch. 10. John Wiley & Sons (2000)
5. Schrag, R.: Load Your Data Faster (2005),
   `http://www.dbspecialists.com/files/presentations/`
   `load_faster.html`
6. Baer, H.: Partitioning with Oracle Database 11g Release 2 Oracle Corporation, USA (2010),
   `http://www.oracle.com/technetwork/database/focus-areas/`
   `bi-datawarehousing/twp-partitioning-11gr2-2010-10-189137.pdf`
7. Wikipedia, Multiprocessing (July 2011),
   `http://en.wikipedia.org/wiki/Multiprocessing`
8. Oracle, SQL*Loader Concepts,
   `http://download.oracle.com/docs/cd/B19306_01/server.102/`
   `b14215/ldr_concepts.htm#i1004652` (retrieved on August 2011)
9. Oracle, Partitioned Tables and Indexes,
   `http://download.oracle.com/docs/cd/B10500_01/server.920/`
   `a96524/c12parti.html` (retrieved August 2011)
10. Oracle, Oracle8i Utilities Release 8.1.5, SQL *Loader: Conventional and Direct Path Loads, Chapter 8,
    `http://www.cs.umbc.edu/portal/help/oracle8/server.815/`
    `a67792/ch08.htm#1665` (retrieved August 2011)
11. CentOS, CentOS 5.4 Release Notes,
    `http://wiki.centos.org/Manuals/ReleaseNotes/CentOS5.4` (retrieved August 2011)

Author Index

Printed in the United States
by Bookmasters

Printed in the United States
By Bookmasters